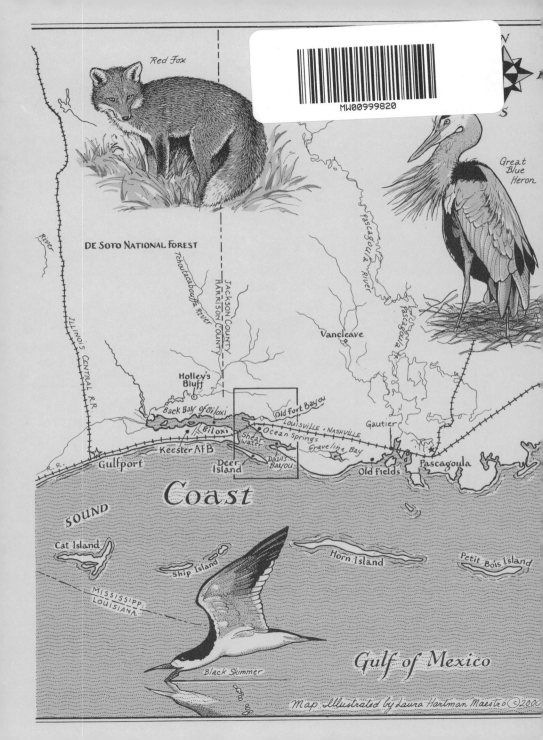

Red Fox

Great Blue Heron

DE SOTO NATIONAL FOREST

River

Tchoutacabouffa River

ILLINOIS CENTRAL R.R.

Pascagoula River

JACKSON COUNTY
HARRISON COUNTY

Pascagoula

Pascagoula River

Vancleave

Holley's Bluff

Old Fort Bayou

Back Bay of Biloxi

Louisville · NASHVILLE

Gautier

Biloxi

Ocean Springs

Keester AFB

Shear water

Graveline Bay

R.R.

Gulfport

Deer Island

Davis Bayou

Old fields

Pascagoula

Coast

SOUND

Cat Island

Ship Island

Horn Island

Petit Bois Island

MISSISSIPPI
LOUISIANA

Black Skimmer

Gulf of Mexico

DREAMING IN CLAY

on the Coast of Mississippi

Love and Art at

Shearwater

Doubleday

NEW YORK LONDON TORONTO SYDNEY AUCKLAND

DREAMING IN CLAY

on the Coast of Mississippi

By Christopher Maurer

WITH MARÍA ESTRELLA IGLESIAS

ILLUSTRATED BY WALTER I. ANDERSON

PUBLISHED BY DOUBLEDAY
a division of Random House, Inc.
1540 Broadway, New York, New York 10036

DOUBLEDAY and the portrayal of an anchor with a dolphin are
trademarks of Doubleday, a division of Random House, Inc.

Book design by Dana Leigh Treglia
Endpaper map and family tree by Laura Hartman Maestro
For more copyright information see page 357.

Library of Congress Cataloging-in-Publication Data

Maurer, Christopher.
Dreaming in clay on the coast of Mississippi: love and art at
Shearwater / by Christopher Maurer with María Estrella Iglesias.
p.   cm.
Includes bibliographical references and index.
1. Shearwater Pottery.   2. Potters—Mississippi—Ocean Springs—
Biography.   3. Artist colonies—Mississippi—Ocean Springs.
I. Iglesias, María Estrella.   II. Title.

NK 4210.S525 M38 2000
738'.092'276212—dc21
00-031448

ISBN 0-385-49063-1
Copyright © 2000 by Christopher Maurer

1   3   5   7   9   10   8   6   4   2

Contents

Acknowledgments

We are deeply grateful to the Anderson family for their trust in allowing us to draw, without restrictions, on Shearwater Pottery records and over one hundred years' of unpublished personal papers—letters, diaries, memoirs, essays, and poems. Special thanks to Marjorie Anderson Ashley, Mary Anderson Pickard, Leif Anderson, Sara Anderson, and to John Anderson and Linda Kerr for their unconditional support. Mary selected the drawings and linoleum blocks by her father, Walter Inglis Anderson, which adorn this book. Joan Gilley helped us in every way possible to find the materials we needed, and allowed us to use tapes and transcripts of her remarkable series of interviews with Agnes Grinstead Anderson. To Patricia Findeisen, we owe inspiration and insight. Ray L. Bellande of Ocean Springs—historian, photographer, newspaper columnist, and friend—attended to all of our requests with rare generosity and a peerless knowledge of Jackson County history, sending material from newspaper archives and from government records, often before we knew we needed it or realized it existed. Three members of the family—Mary, John, and Marjorie—read the manuscript and gave us excellent suggestions, as did Holly Maurer-Klein and our son Daniel, the best and most critical of editors. Norman Callis shared his knowledge of southern pottery, Diane Stevenson allowed us to quote from her essay on Shearwater, Leif Anderson from her unpublished memoirs, *Lifedance*, and Elizabeth Roberts permitted us to photograph her excellent collection of the works of James McConnell Anderson. Warm thanks to Debbie Fulcher and to Steve Robins for their connivance and support; also to Nancy McCall of the Alan Chesney Medical Archives at Johns Hopkins University, Pamela Arceneaux of the Historic New Orleans Collection, Guy and Honey Chatham, Laura Frederick, Jimmie L. Franklin, Elizabeth Gulacsy of the Scholes Library of Ceramics, Alfred University, the ornithologist Mark Harris, Eugene Hecht, Tom Jackson, Jeanne Lebow, Betty Rich, Else J. Martin of the Pascagoula Public Library, Susan Tucker and Shama Farooq of Newcomb College, Kip Peterson of the Brooks Museum of Art, Memphis, Marilyn Pilley, Jim Toplon, and Paula Covington of the Vanderbilt University Library, Joey Rice of the Walter Anderson Museum of Art, Betty Rodgers, Joseph Schwartz, M.D., of Johns Hopkins Hospital, Joseph Stephens, M.D., Wayne D. Stephens, Nancy Sweezy, Tommy Wixon, and staff members of Tulane University and the Virginia Museum of Fine Arts. All admirers of Walter I. Anderson are indebted to his widow, Agnes Grinstead Anderson, for her courageous memoir, *Approaching the Magic Hour*; to Patti Carr Black, who edited it; and to Mary Anderson Pickard and Redding S. Sugg, for their illuminating scholarship. We are deeply grateful to Siobhan Adcock of Random House, who read this book with patience, care, and imagination and made it better, and to Harriet Rubin, first to act upon our enthusiasm for Shearwater Pottery.

Christopher Maurer and María E. Iglesias
University of Illinois at Chicago

DREAMING IN CLAY

on the Coast of Mississippi

THE MAGIC UNION

María Estrella Iglesias

I spotted it a few years ago, in an antiques mall near Nashville: a small, bottle-shaped pottery vase, about eight inches high, glazed in an extraordinary blue. There was something mesmerizing about the color. Seeing it across the room, through the clutter, was like catching a glimpse of the ocean, and as I held it, I felt the relaxing, almost spiritual feeling that can come over us when we pick up an object and, through it, feel the hands of the artisan, a sort of magical union between maker and holder. My husband tells me I have a sort of "pottery radar." In the aisles of antiques malls, I seize on any color, shape, or texture that lures my senses. When a piece speaks to me, it is love at first sight. This vase wasn't old and did not look particularly valuable, but it had awakened something in me.

Without knowing that my life was about to change, I turned the vase over and read:

Over the next few months, I found three more pieces from the same pottery. Different shapes, different glazes, but with an unmistakable family resemblance. A coincidence? Perhaps, but I like to think that those pieces were looking for me. None of my other pottery-collecting friends had seen any, and we were looking in the same places. I was proud of myself. The third piece I found was unmarked, and I recognized it from twenty feet away and paid only $2 for it. It was old, but somehow timeless. Finally, wondering where and when and by whom those pieces were made, we went to a bookstore one night and looked at reference books. In one of them we read:

Shearwater Pottery. Ocean Springs, Mississippi, 1928 to present. G. W. Anderson ran the business and his son, Peter, was the potter when the business was founded in 1928. Peter's brothers, Walter I. and James McConnell Anderson (called Mac) worked with Peter after 1930. . . . Peter died in 1984, and [his youngest son] Jim became master potter. Mac, a brother of Peter, is still decorating and designing. . . .

"Lovely name, Ocean Springs!" my husband said, and I remember relishing the sound of "Shearwater," associating it with *sheer* water— cool, transparent water—and with the color of the glaze. Both names drew us irresistibly. As we looked at maps and guidebooks, neither of us had any idea that our curiosity about a small southern pottery would take us into the presence of an extraordinary family—one that had risked everything to make art a normal part of their daily lives. It was a complex, sophisticated family that had studied in art schools, traveled widely, and absorbed the art of the past, but had chosen to trade the comfort and safety of a bourgeois life for the love of art and nature. Our contact with them would change our outlook on a number of things: the healing power of art, the need to embrace the past as part of the present, and the spiritual treasures that are given to us—if we care to receive them—by the natural world. It taught us that our creativity can lie dormant and suddenly awaken at any moment, even in adverse situations and unexpected places. But we must sometimes awaken it ourselves, and not simply wait for this to happen.

It was in Spain, in grade school, that I first heard of the Mississippi River. *What* I learned, I don't know. What stuck in my mind forever was that it was the widest—or was it the longest?—river in the world. At the age of six or seven, during a family picnic, I almost drowned in a shallow, narrow brook that deepened unexpectedly into a pool. And the pool deepened in my imagination into the Mississippi. The Mississippi took on a wild, mysterious character. When I went to the movies, any American river became the Mississippi. It ran invisibly through *Gone With the Wind*. It *was* the South.

With a better sense of geography than I had as a girl, we left Nashville one weekend in May 1997, headed for Shearwater. I felt guilty and excited. Our two children were teenagers, and it was the first time we had ever left them alone. Route 65 seemed like any other U.S. highway, so monotonous that at times the blues and greens along the road faded out dreamily into a raging river. As we drew near the Coast, and headed toward my long-dreamed-of Mississippi, old river dreams seemed more and more possible. The air, the smells, the landscape started to change. Somewhere past Mobile and near Pascagoula, tall, slender pines on either side of the road seemed to lift us up ecstatically, making us think we were headed for the sky, not the sea. But not for long. Soon after leaving

Route 10, we crossed a wasteland of fast food and commerce almost identical to the one we had fled.

Just when our spirits were at their lowest, we spotted an odd home-made sign—TO SHEARWATER POTTERY—drove through shady residential streets, past a little harbor with shrimp boats and sailboats, and turned up a curving, sandy path into another world. Under a canopy of live oaks, pines, and towering magnolias were a number of silvery, weathered buildings of wood and corrugated tin. Both the buildings and their settings appeared suspended between the present and the past. Everything seemed homemade and eternal. It was like a clearing in a forest, a river bend of time, a place where the world fell silent, except for the rustle of a squirrel or a rabbit, this or that muted voice, and the distant hum of machinery. In the window of one of the first buildings was an unforgettable image: a potter working at his wheel. This can be a powerful image in *any* setting: there is something about throwing pottery that engages our most primitive emotions. As I watched Jimmy Anderson—the first potter I had ever seen at work—it crossed my mind that God might very well have been a potter on the first day of the creation. Shearwater's potter was standing at his window, absorbed in his work. His beautiful profile leaned now and then over clay in constant evolution, which rose magically into a surprisingly recognizable shape.

Across from his workshop stood another low, old building, the small, long decoration studio known as the Annex. A covered runway, a few feet long, connected it to a shed that housed a kiln. Two walls of the Annex were all windows. Through them you could see the pine forest, and beyond it, down a hill, the bayou. Here, too, everything had a well-worn, homemade look. Seated around a large table, covered with tools and art supplies, were three or four women, ranging from thirty to fifty, and a young girl. My attention was drawn to one of the women. She didn't seem to belong there. She looked like a Nordic goddess (not that I've ever seen one!), or a heroine from Wagner, but she was sitting on a molded plastic garden chair. While others were decorating figurines, she was painting a small vase with what looked like a forest or a jungle scene.

Her curly, abundant hair, parted in the center, covered most of her face as she bent over her work. Her body seemed ageless. Her slender arms showed signs of gentle exposure to the sun. None of the women looked up from what they were doing. It was obvious they were used to tourists and visitors, but I felt like an intruder. Trying to ease my discomfort, I began some small talk.

"Are you all family members?"

Playfully, the Scandinavian goddess lifted her head.

"No, not *all* of us."

Through the veil of her hair, I could see the brilliant blue-green of her eyes, and a wide smile.

"Oh, yes," I thought, and remembered reading somewhere that Shearwater had been used as an art colony. "She's probably visiting from Scandinavia."

Two walls of the room were—are—covered by wooden shelving filled with recently decorated but still-unglazed pieces. Feasting on the colors, my eyes stopped at a group of figurines that seemed to belong to a magic kingdom.

"These are like the colors in my dining room," I said.

The Nordic goddess raised her head again, brushing her hair timidly from her face, and revealing her strong, attractive features.

"Ah, well," she commented, in an almost singing voice. "I think that Uncle Walter had a bit of Aztec blood in him."

I realized later that I wasn't the only one with mistaken assumptions. My place of birth was as far from Mexico as hers was from Norway. And *who* was Uncle Walter?

Down the path from the Annex, nearly hidden behind some very tall azaleas, we found another building—the showroom—with the same weathered, sturdy, simple appearance. Inside, we were greeted by a petite, distinguished-looking woman to whom we didn't pay much attention: we were submerged in an unexpected variety of shapes, glazes, old and new decorated pieces, figurines, lamps, prints, and paintings. It was breathtaking. All our knowledge of Shearwater was based on four very beautifully shaped glazed pieces. Nothing compared to what we had in front of us, in three rooms that stepped down, one by one, toward the bayou. The walls were pickled pine—painted in white, but with the paint rubbed off, leaving the grain of the wood exposed. The floors were bare, worn boards, and the wide windows opened onto the woods. There was a comfortable old Arts and Crafts settle with leather cushions, and homemade shelves and stands covered with new pieces. Dusty show-cases on some of the walls were crowded with older treasures we could barely see: plain-glazed vases, and slip-decorated ones, exuberant plates and bowls and clay figures. They were kept under lock and key, but care-lessly arranged, as though they had been placed there to make room for new work. The decorated pieces, old and new, showed the sophistication of talented, worldly artists. As we walked dreamily around, gazing at those pots, hardly daring to touch them, the woman handed me a leaflet on the history of Shearwater. I thanked her and put it in my bag. Christopher was flipping the pages of an old scrapbook with yellowed newspaper clippings on a table beside a fireplace, where bricks glazed in turquoise made a striking pattern. A door led to an office no less re-markable than the showroom. Old plates, uniquely decorated, hung in a frieze around the walls. The packing table held a pile of newspapers rather than Styrofoam or bubble wrap. Instead of a computer or cash reg-ister, there was a little metal cashbox, screwed to the top of a dark, old Victorian desk. A calculator and ledger lay on the desk. We barely spoke. When we left, we sat in the car for a few seconds before putting the key in the ignition. Once again, we were overcome with a sense of timeless-ness, of a present imbued with past.

"Can you *believe* this place?"

We sat for a while in silence, with the feeling that we had come upon a family and a place outside the normal rhythms of everyday life, a proud, quiet world of difference. It was a place so beautiful, so defiantly *itself,* that we sensed that only extraordinary people could have brought it into existence and kept it that way. Although we knew hardly anything about these people—the ones we had spoken to or their ancestors—we were somehow certain that their lives were about to touch ours, and that we wanted to tell their story.

Later that night in the Holiday Inn, while Christopher telephoned the kids, I remembered the leaflet. There were photographs. The first was beautiful and old. Three handsome young men, in their twenties, on the front step of the showroom. One leans languidly against the doorpost, the others are seated on the steps. They look refined and melancholy. A caption identifies them as Peter, Walter ("Bob"), and Mac. This must be "Uncle Walter."★ Next picture. A more recent one. The Nordic goddess is here. Patricia Findeisen. And there *she* is too, the nice woman who handed me the leaflet: Marjorie Anderson Ashley, business manager. Peter, one of the three young men in the picture, was founder of Shearwater and the father of Marjorie, Patricia, and Jimmy, the potter we had seen in the window.

For days after that first visit, we struggled with the idea of writing a book, but two thoughts came to mind: Why was there so little information about Shearwater in pottery books? And, if more information became available, would the place ever be the same?

On our second trip South, we rehearsed what to say, how and when to say it. As we drove up the path to the showroom, I felt sure the family would be as excited as we were at the possibility of a book.

"Let's not scare them," we told each other as we entered, nervously looking about for Marjorie. There was an introductory bit of conversation. Christopher was taking forever to get to the point, and I burst out with what probably sounded to Marjorie—especially in my foreign accent—like a very foolish proposition: "We want to write a book about Shearwater!" Even before she replied, I could read the not-so-nice-anymore woman's face: "If anyone is going to write a book about Shearwater, it ought to be me. I owe it to my father. I've been trying for years to find the time."

I guess we tried to hide our disappointment and went on chatting for

★Throughout this book, Walter Inglis Anderson is referred to by his family name, Bob. His father is Walter, and his brother James McConnell Anderson, is Mac.

a few minutes. She told us about "the museum" in town where we could see more pottery. It was late, and we wanted to get there before it closed. Before we left, I asked who was the artist that had decorated the vases signed "D/P." I don't think I said "decorated": the images were more than "decorative." In many, you could sense something unusual and enigmatic.

"My sister Patricia," Marjorie answered. " 'D' for decorated and 'P' for Patricia." The puzzle of her identity now gave way to the enigma of her work. Who was Patricia, besides Marjorie's sister and Peter's daughter?

On the way to the museum, we felt confused and disappointed. We got there ten minutes before closing. They didn't want to charge us admission, since we wouldn't even have time to browse. And there our confusion deepened. We had been expecting to find pottery, but there were only a few pieces, all decorated by the same brother, the second one, Bob. What we found were paintings, huge wood carvings, prints and murals by a major artist with a profound love of the natural world. Here was a vibrant world of plants, animals, and insects—occasionally people—in bold lines and unexpected colors. Where was the work of his brothers, Peter and Mac? Time was passing quickly, and we dashed about, blinding ourselves to the paintings, trying to find the rest of Shearwater Pottery. Wasn't this the Shearwater museum?

"No," said a woman near the door. "This is the Walter Anderson Museum of Art. The *second* brother, the artist, the crazy one. They do have some Shearwater pieces. But the museum is dedicated to Walter's work."

Our ignorance was becoming comical. In a state of panic, minutes before closing, we dove into the museum's little bookstore and charged to a credit card more than $500 in books. There were many books about Walter Inglis Anderson (1903–1965), but nothing about Shearwater.

It was the reading of one of those books, *Approaching the Magic Hour,* by Walter's widow, Agnes Grinstead Anderson (Sissy), that deepened our resolve to tell the story of the family. It was an unforgettable book—the story of their courtship and tumultuous marriage. There were glimpses of other family members, and as we read it, we realized that, beneath the tranquillity of present-day Shearwater, lay a stormy past. Almost a century ago, a strong-willed woman had determined that her three children would become artists. Her dreams were realized, but in circumstances most people would find unbearable. Through times of poverty, illness, and excruciating tension within the family, the Andersons were held together by a proud faith in the work of their own hands: pottery, painting, and the written word. Neither of us could imagine a family that had lived art so deeply and had left a more beautiful, bountiful legacy.

It was the reading of that book of memoirs that propelled us, for a third time, down U.S. 65, knowing by then what we were getting into, and wanting more than anything to persuade Marjorie and the rest of the family that there was space in the world for more than one book about Shearwater, the people that made it possible, and the ones who continue to do so.

But what were we *doing,* we wondered on the way down. Two teachers of language and literature, writing a book about a southern family of artists? To the Andersons, we must have seemed an odd couple, with our different accents (Spanish/Yankee), appearance (short Mediterranean/tall Anglo-Saxon), and personalities, but with a common sense of humor. "Why *you two,*" we could hear them thinking, "and why *us?*" My answer must have disconcerted them. I had been drawn by chance to that first vase, and from the vase to them. Even my half-facetious supernatural explanation seemed more believable. It was as though the spirits of Peter and Bob, and perhaps their mother, Annette, had guided us there. Of course, during our first visits, it would never have occurred to me to kid around like that with the Andersons. The members of the third generation held themselves pretty aloof and skeptical. And who could blame them for their polite caution before two enthusiastic but ignorant strangers?

One of our biggest challenges was meeting Patricia. We knew that, as Shearwater's principal source of original decoration, she was crucially important to the Pottery. When we asked for her in the showroom, the answer was always the same: "She isn't here right now. . . . She didn't say where she was going. . . . Sometimes she works on the pier. . . ." Her telephone was unlisted, and someone in town described her as a "recluse." We had bought a couple of her pieces, and hoped we would meet her on our third visit, in November 1997, for the Peter Anderson Festival, an annual celebration in honor of Shearwater's founder that draws together more than two hundred artists and craftsmen. "Best time to meet the whole family," someone had told us.

When we got to Ocean Springs that day, it was already noon. Wandering the tree-lined streets, we found Shearwater's booth, in front of the railway depot, hoping to see lots of pieces and the entire family behind them. But only a few pieces were left, and Jimmy and Marjorie were the only Andersons available. When we asked for Patricia, the answer was "She doesn't take part in this sort of thing." Briefly, dryly, Marjorie answered our questions about the Pottery and the family. Jimmy fell silent, drinking a beer, absorbed in a football game on his portable TV. It was the first time I had seen him away from his potter's wheel, and he looked very much like an ordinary mortal.

We had thought of staying over until Sunday, but Shearwater had no more to sell, and neither Marjorie nor Jimmy planned to return to the festival the next day. We could, at least, try to meet Patricia. Marjorie offered to give her a note. We wrote one, telling her of our admiration for Shearwater, and our interest in telling as many people as possible about this "unique place." And shortly after our return to Nashville, we received a letter, on a sheet of paper torn from a spiral notebook. She found the book "an interesting idea" and would try to do her best to help us. Her phone number was included at the end.

As I dial, I'm not nervous, only expectant. I mustn't scare her with my enthusiasm. Must be careful not to seem overeager, intimidating. A remote, somewhat timid voice answers, intoning the *hello* like a big, soft question mark. Standing before me, Christopher is watching my face as he follows the conversation. As it progresses, he looks more and more relaxed. At one point he smiles, leaves the room, and returns to his work. He can tell from listening to me that Patricia will help us with the book.

Before hanging up, Patricia asks me if I am a potter myself. "I *wish,*" I answer. "I'm too old now to learn new tricks. I could only be a mediocre one, and there are too many of those already. I get what I need from the beauty created by others."

She offers names of artists who started late, in their forties and fifties. She omits to tell me that she is one of them herself. It was only a decade ago that she got serious about "decorating."

Weeks later, we are waiting for her in the showroom. She is not a young woman—I could tell from the scrapbook by the fireplace—but she looks like one. She has a slim, graceful body, and she is dressed in a pair of loose white linen pants. Her cappuccino-colored T-shirt, clinging gently to her straight, youthful torso, ends about an inch above her waist, leaving exposed, in a very casual way, a firm, tanned skin that would be the envy of many adolescents. You can see, from the timid way she approaches, that this must be an awkward situation for her. When I greet her in my European way with a gentle hug, and a kiss on each cheek, she retreats, confused, as though from a mild electric shock.

Patricia is hard to capture in dates, age, chronology. "You'll have to ask someone *else* about that." She refuses to dwell in the past—her own or anyone else's. Whenever she talked of a painful moment from years before, she would wake up with a phrase that became all too familiar to us: "But this is not for the book!"

She married very young to a military man, "was married for years"—she won't tell or doesn't remember how many—and had three sons, Richard, Michael, and Adam, whom she still refers to as her "babies." She divorced, and is still a friend of her ex-husband, though when they were living together, he never showed much interest in her work.

After her divorce, she was able to fully focus—through reading, writing, and painting—on some of the things that mattered to her: understanding human behavior, creativity, and the little miracles of nature. Her art has given her an escape from the deadening events of everyday life.

She has thought for years about the relation of creativity to what most people call "madness." A doctor once said there was an indefinable streak of it in the family, and for want of a better term, called it "Andersonitis." Often, when Patricia asked us not to quote her, we pressed her to write down her thoughts and send them to us. Even then, she apologized for "generalizing" and scribbled, "Not to be used as is!" across the top of the paper. "In creative people," she wrote on one occasion, "there is a sort of everyman, but with a bit of an added dimension. But it often happens that 'creatives' are downgraded by 'civilians' who appreciate the product but not the extra dimension within the producer. And the 'creatives,' without realizing it, accept demotion and come to fear and throttle and thereby distort, rather than rejoice and freely develop, that unavoidable bit of added dimension." Madness, craziness, was the convenient label people found for "disturbing behavior," which might be, "in the beginning, only a matter of ideas, unusual amounts of solitude, dress."

Patricia divides her pieces into two types: "pretty" and "not pretty." On different occasions, in the showroom, she would point timidly to a plate or a vase and say, "This is not a pretty one." We bought a lot of those "unpretty" pieces, the ones that best show her talent and personality. The "pretty" ones most people like and buy are fantastic pieces with exuberant colors where people mingle with all kinds of animals and flowers, and the elements of nature come harmoniously together. Few of her present pieces have anything to do with the decorative tradition of Shearwater. They cry loudly and brightly the sensitivity and skills of a real artist, with something to say. It is not surprising that she is still modestly signing "D/P" (decorated by Patricia) and I doubt that she will ever change. She herself "thoroughly dislikes" the word "artist," and rejects it when used to describe her. This she has in common with her father and uncles, the original Shearwater artists. On his passport, her uncle Bob called himself a "decorator," and Marjorie told us that she had seldom heard her father, or anyone else in the family, use the word "artist."

Patricia doesn't like to explain her work, but many of her pieces tell a story with unmistakable social overtones. The figures depicted on her vases—her "pot people"—take us into a world of moral contrasts. Trapped in her glazes are those who create and those who consume creation; those who conform and those who dream and rebel and suffer the consequences. A woman with an enormous head and a tiny body curving around the rim peers sadly from the bottom of a bowl. "There are times when I do nothing but think, times when I'm nothing but a head," Patricia tells us. A naked man and a woman whose voluptuous figure spreads over the form of the vase sit talking at a candlelit table. This is the way she imagines Saint Francis of Assisi and his companion, Saint Clare. On a tall, urn-shaped vase is a stylized frieze of mournful women, their heads bent forward. Some have their eyes wide open, and others have them closed. Beneath them, in another panel, in a parallel world, a woman is being beheaded. People—knowingly or blindly—have condemned her to death. A tanned, naked figure who looks like a primitive Indian squats on the side of a vase. His feet are planted firmly on the ground. A well-dressed woman comes floating toward him around the vase, extending her hand, offering him a coin or a nugget of gold. "There are those who create, and those who put a price on their creations," Patricia says.

She lives a very modest and frugal life. Does not have a checking account or a credit card. Drives an aging Nissan and rents from her cousin a one-room house where Bob's widow, Sissy, spent the last years of her life. She is passionate in whatever she does, and cares about others. She dresses plainly with her own peculiar elegance. Walks, rides her bike, swims, and protects the hours of solitude she spends painting, reading, writing poetry, and watching TV. Occasionally, but only when coaxed, she will open her spiral binder and share a recent poem or an old one, like these lines, written many years ago:

> God gave me
> the earth,
> the sea, the sky,
> things that grow

and cheep and run,
and things that
swim and fly,
to illuminate one day;
on another just
to keep humanity at bay.

Patricia isn't the only person living frugally at Shearwater. As a matter of fact, most of the family have a way of life that many of us would envy, but would find difficult to live. Nature, in its most naked way—for whose enjoyment people spend much money—has enriched three generations of Andersons. They may have worried, from time to time, about walls that needed painting, or leaky roofs, or when and how to replace an old truck or pay their medical bills. But they have awakened each day surrounded by beauty and by the miracle of how nature renews itself and takes care of them in every possible way. And nature they embrace, trust, and respect.

The first time we visited Jimmy and Margaret Anderson in their house in town, a mile or so from the Pottery, I was surprised that he did not live on the grounds at Shearwater. They were renting a rather small, old house. I had assumed that the Pottery—which appeared to be a thriving business—was prosperous enough to allow its members a comfortable living. Later, I realized that most of its income came from the sale of tableware, figurines, and hand-thrown art pottery done by Jimmy. Three years ago, when we first visited Shearwater, the prices seemed remarkably low. The decorative pieces were in the high range, especially the original ones, and they moved more slowly. Prices have gone up since then, but they are still a bargain for anyone who gets there the day they unload the kiln and can grab what is left after orders are filled.

The way they filled orders seemed particularly revealing. Both in the showroom and under the shelves in the office space where Marjorie works, I had seen a dozen mysterious cardboard boxes. While taking pictures of groups of new and old pieces for possible use in the book, I was finding it difficult to include a variety of forms and colors without repeating the same piece. So I peeked into one of those boxes and saw a beautiful glaze I hadn't seen before: wisteria. Other boxes held other unusual glazes, with shapes that were different from those in the showroom. I realized that the plates and vases in my photographs—the ones on the shelves—were the leftovers. The best were in the boxes. Why?

I went to the office and asked my friend Laura—who works in the showroom—if I could photograph the pieces in the boxes. She gave me a worried look, and her usual beautiful smile.

"Better not. Those are orders, and it would be very easy to get them mixed up. We'll ask Marjorie what to do."

Some of the orders, I learned, were from brides-to-be all over town; in fact, from all over the Gulf Coast. It is a tradition to come to the Pottery and select a set of dinnerware in a certain glaze and the decorative accessories that go with it. Couples paid as they could, and were given six months to a year after the wedding to pay for the completed order. So not only were the best pieces in the boxes, some of them would probably sit there for a year without being paid for.

At the time, I resented these "spoiled" local brides who prevented so many beautiful glazes and forms from ever reaching the shelves, leaving out-of-town buyers frustrated and disappointed, picking over scattered pieces in common glazes, after a long trip. Once in a while, of course, visitors are rewarded with a feast of colors and forms that feel still warm from the kiln.

Many of these recent pieces had been thrown and glazed by Peter Wade, the son of Jimmy and Margaret, who for many years had been business manager at the Pottery, a job that people say she did excellently and that she still misses. Peter Wade is a clear-eyed critic of his own work. As I examined one of his vases, he told me it was "too heavy." Another was "too square at the bottom."

A young woman was standing beside us, gazing fondly at Peter Wade, and when I agreed with his judgment, she gave me a painful look. Her annoyance grew when I reminded Peter Wade that in the twenties, his grandfather Peter broke a couple of thousand pieces before he opened the Pottery to the public. I tell him not to be afraid to break some himself.

"Don't you break anything!" the young woman said. "I'll keep them."

But there is no point in flattering Peter Wade about his work. He knows, better than anyone else, what a well-made pot should feel and look like. All his life, he has been eating and drinking from Shearwater tableware. He has, I think, the best and worst going for him. The best because he won't be starting from scratch, as his grandfather did as a young man. Peter Wade was born to an established family of potters and decorators, and the first thing he played with was probably clay. There are pictures of him at all stages of life, from toddler to adolescent, observing his cousin Adele (Mac and Sara's daughter) as she decorates her pieces; playing at his grandfather's wheel, loading and unloading the kiln. Over the past several years, he has been throwing and glazing with remarkable success. He has had everything one needs to become an excellent potter, including, his Aunt Patricia tells us, a temperament sensitive to beauty. But he also has the legacy left by his grandfather Peter and his own father, Jimmy, and at times this must seem a heavy burden. In that sense, it was easier for Peter, who did not have to follow in anyone's footsteps. It is hard to imagine that young Peter Wade will have the luxury of smashing as many pots as his grandfather did until he was ready to open for business, at least not without upsetting the entire family.

But to get back to those bridal orders. When I asked Jimmy why so many pieces were sitting in boxes without producing income for a year, his answer was simple: "What is the problem? If we don't get the money now, we get it later. Money is money, now or a year later."

You might think these people had never heard the words "interest," "inflation," or "depreciation." But you'd be wrong. It is just that once you enter Shearwater, the value of money seems to change. It matters. But it isn't what matters most.

Diane Stevenson, a friend of the family, noticed that attitude thirty years ago when she worked in the showroom as a teenager. This was in the sixties, when Bob's watercolors had already received some national attention. Peter's wife, Pat, was business manager, and her sister Agnes—Sissy—had chosen some of her late husband's work for a show at the Brooks Museum in Memphis.

The pottery was Peter's place, of course, the place of his art. It filled the shelves that lined the walls. Mac's paintings hung there too. What I knew of Bob's work were the designs he put on cups and bowls for Peter and his block prints, cut from linoleum and printed on wallpaper. That was all. But one day when I walked into the room where the desk with its money box and ledger sat (the ledger always looked moldy, however new, because of the high humidity), I discovered something new. A box of water colors had been returned from a show in Memphis. I began to shuffle through, and a whole new world opened up, a world of transforming beauty. Until then I had never seen pine trees for what they were, for their true shapes or true color. I was overwhelmed. I knew the importance of what I was seeing—and what I was feeling—and I could not let it go uncommemorated. I knew I had to have one. Of that I was certain. One painting in particular struck me, not for its art alone, for sentimental reasons too. It was a dead baby bird on a beach, a water color sketch with lines as eloquent as Chinese calligraphy. It was a combination of the subject and the pathos of those extraordinary sure and subtle lines—as palpable as sand or water. I was told one hundred and twenty-five dollars (though it might have been as low as seventy-five; I don't remember). It was a lot of money to me. In fact, it would mean all the money I was making for a very long time.

I asked if I could buy it on layaway. I was negotiating with Pat, and she said yes. I made a down payment of $25. Later that evening, Sissy called me. Didn't I want a different painting, one more complete, one with the background filled in? No, I said. I wanted that one. She told me the painting was mine and that I had paid enough. I was astonished, and shy. I could not have conveyed to her the magic that had come, at such a bargain, into my life. I still have that painting, and it still speaks its singular eloquence—of life and death and art.

I believe what some today consider to be old fashioned, that art is recuperative and transformative. I inherited something of the romantic bias of the An-

dersons' own art. It was a brave art in [Ocean Springs,] the small town where I grew up and where they lived, as far as possible from the commercial bustle of New York City, for example, where we've come to see art with a certain cynicism since what we see here is the commerce of art, its buying and selling, its display and the various motives for that display. But in Ocean Springs, Mississippi what I saw was not the consumption of art—the mirror of a consumer society—but the making of art. Art was work. Art was craft. Art was a way of life, a way of living, and it was a brave way of living. It was the opposite of complacency and alienation, and it appealed to my youth and continues to appeal. I believe in beauty. And so the pottery gave me not only beauty but politics, the sense that the world could be generously given and generously received, that life could be better. Those two integrates, the integrity of beauty and the integrity of truth, have seen me through.

Jimmy's philosophy of deferred income must have paid off. In the two years we have spent working on the book, he, Margaret, and Peter Wade have spent their weekends working on the new house where they now live, on the grounds of Shearwater, overlooking the bayou, steps from the kiln building and the workshop. It is built with the same simplicity and elegance as the older buildings at Shearwater: small, but spacious enough to welcome their daughter and grandchildren in times of family gatherings without Peter having to give up his own room.

Jimmy is a quiet, shy, very handsome man. Good looks run in the Anderson family, even in the fourth generation. Last year, during the Peter Anderson Festival, I took a picture of Peter Wade throwing at the wheel, with his father in the background. What the camera didn't capture was the group of teenage girls who were gazing at him, fastening their young eyes not on the work of his hands but on his beautiful face.

Every one of our trips to Shearwater began with a visit to Jimmy in the workshop. Without interrupting his throwing or lifting his head, he would say, "Hi! You just get here?" and for the next ten to fifteen minutes we would hope he would stop his throwing for a moment and engage in a normal conversation. It never happened. His answers to our questions were friendly, polite, laconic. When we asked him to tell us about something—himself, for example—he would reply, "What do you want to *know?* Ask me questions."

When we did, we always got the same little one-sentence responses, while his hands played magically at the wheel, and tumbler after tumbler emerged, to be placed behind him with dozens of others.

Sometimes, while Christopher asked Jimmy about some technicality—the name of a tool or his method of wedging clay—I would browse around the dusty shelves, filled with new and old, glazed and unglazed, defective and perfect pots. Some were there for Jimmy's own use: for storing his tools, drinking water, or holding small junk. One day, I discovered an unusually shaped pot, totally covered by clay dust. I grabbed it and rinsed it under the spigot of the little basin they use to wash their hands. Jimmy was throwing and answering Christopher's questions, but looked up, keeping an eye on me, as though to ask, "What the heck is *she* doing?" The water brought to light a great, deep double glaze of turquoise and gunmetal.

I asked him if I could take it to the showroom for Marjorie to price it.

"No. It's not for sale."

"But it's abandoned and covered with dust!"

"It's not for sale and it's not abandoned."

"Well, why don't you take it home for Margaret?"

"Oh, Margaret has all kinds of pots. It's fine where it is."

On subsequent visits, I would see the double-glazed vase standing out among the others, shiny and clean, on the shelf across from his wheel. It wasn't there on our last trip. I like to think Margaret spotted it, too, and that it now has a special place in their new house.

One of the few times I was able to pull Jimmy away from his wheel was by asking about glazes. I knew he would pause for a moment, for my question was based on one of the many myths that we had heard in town about the Andersons. We had heard that quite a few of the original Shearwater glazes are not used anymore because Peter Anderson died without revealing the secret of their composition, not wanting to pass the information on to his son. This seemed unlikely to us, but Peter wouldn't have been the first potter to take his secrets to the grave. So I asked.

"Let me show you something," said Jimmy, as he rinsed his hands. Turning around, he pointed to the frame around the big door at the back of the workroom, a door opening onto the marsh and the bayou. To the left, all over the frame, were letters and numbers written long ago in pencil.

"These are glaze formulas."

He moved to another part of the shop. On walls and counters were still more of the scribbled, almost illegible formulas.

He led us down an aisle, past shelves of unglazed pottery through wide double doors into the glazing room, with its ball mills for grinding glazes, its tubs and containers, and a little pot-bellied stove. Jimmy climbed up on a counter and took a ten-gallon bucket from the very top shelf. He opened the twelve-inch lid, and I assumed he would pull out all of his father's old notebooks. The bucket was full of some sort of powdery stuff.

Jimmy flipped over the round cover.

"These are more formulas."

The lid was covered with more of these hurried, nearly illegible notes.

"This is how my father worked. And this is what I've done with all of this," he said, showing me a small notebook where he has neatly transcribed all of the formulas he found here and there throughout the workshop. It was clear to me that Jimmy did not think his father had taken anything from him. Perhaps it never occurred to Peter that his son would need his formulas. By the end of his life, they had been working together for eighteen years, and Jimmy was already throwing beautiful pots. Peter would have appreciated his talent and artistic independence, although he probably didn't express this to Jimmy as often as he felt it.

Jimmy's quiet temperament doesn't lack a sense of humor, and those who know him well probably enjoy it often. I have seen it a couple of times over the past two years. The first time was early on, when I was still trying to get him to take a little break from the wheel to talk to us. I was snapping pictures around the workshop, and needed one of him looking directly into the camera. I wanted to capture those blue eyes of his.

"Jimmy, look at me," I said suddenly. "I want to show the readers how much you look like Paul Newman."

He looked at the camera with a slightly amused smile, and I snapped the picture. A few minutes later, he walked by Michelle Wickstrom, who was trimming figurines, and whispered, with a chuckle, "Did you hear that? I look like Paul Newman!"

Nearby, jiggering plates, was a young potter, Matt Steadman, who was working as an apprentice to Jimmy. He smiled when I told him of trying to rescue the dust-covered pot.

"It probably bothered him a bit," he said. "They don't let anything go out of here that he hasn't looked at and considered okay. There are pieces that are stacked up back there that I would have said 'That looks fine' or 'What's the matter with this one?' He has a sort of extrasensory perception, and he knows when anything's out of place. There'll be seven or eight plaster molds, and one hits the floor, and he notices it's missing. He's very particular about everything going back into the same spot. He's always telling me that 'time is the most important thing in a production pottery.' That's what things boil down to.

"When you come here to work, you change the way you learn to do things. Tools, for instance. In school, we were learning with modern tools, machine-made things you buy somewhere. Here, they're all home-made. Just about everything we use is made right here. Like the sponge stick. It's just a dowel you buy at a hardware store, and a sponge cut in half, with some little rubber washers. You use it to take the moisture from the inside of pots. Works ten times better than any you can buy. They sell the ones that have a whole sponge, attached with a screw. Well, they spin around and fly off. But these things cost us probably a quarter of the price to make, and they're so much better. Look at the modeling tools he uses over there. Just a splinter of wood from a tree that fell in the yard. And his 'calipers' are just a piece of wire.

"It's something I wasn't accustomed to, you know. Just figured if you can buy one it's probably better than what you could make. That's definitely not true. Because the person that made the store-bought tool didn't know exactly what you were using it for, what kinds of shapes, that sort of thing."

The elder Peter, they say, could make just about anything he needed at home or in the Pottery. Beside Jimmy was a sort of homemade table, a slab of pine, on legs, that he and his father used for years for wedging clay; they made it from a tree that had been cut down on the edge of the marsh. They put a lump of clay on it and beat the air out of it with a mallet made of live oak. Otherwise—if there were air pockets in the clay—the pots would explode in the kiln.

Jimmy's brother, Michael—Peter's oldest son—admires his father's versatility and is proud of that quality in himself. We would often find him in the Annex, or a few feet away in the little shed that houses the electric kiln, where he supervises the casting, decoration, and glazing of figurines, and the firing of the castware. Sometimes he would be feeding the squirrels peanut butter and crackers or working in the yard of his house, down the path. His father, Peter, he told us, could do anything he put his mind to, from boat-building to beekeeping to hunting to arranging flowers. Over the years, Michael himself had worked at a variety of jobs. He was a taxidermist in the Field Museum in Chicago, and after returning to Ocean Springs, he worked for two optical companies in town. At the Pottery, there seems to be almost nothing he hasn't done, except for throwing. He has always liked to read and write, and lately he had tried his hand at an essay or two. In a recent offering, he reflected on his role as "caretaker" at Shearwater. He felt himself a "shareholder" not only in a pottery business, but also in an "ecological environment" that was hard to capture in words.

The house that I share now with memories—for my mate is no longer here and my daughters have flown the nest—is in a small clearing. It is surrounded and shielded by large, virtually indestructible Live Oaks, Southern magnolia, and other magnolia, such as sweetbay, cucumber tree, umbrella magnolia and big-leaf magnolia. There are towering longleaf pine, sweetgum, hickory, cedar, dogwood, redbud, post oak, black oak and water oak.

Big blue herons, white egrets, rails, little blue and green herons and bitterns find food and refuge in the marshes or on the beach and in shallow waters. White egrets make a picturesque scene roosting in live oaks bordering the nearby boat harbor.

Urban sprawl, superhighways, concrete and asphalt surround us. In spite of this, or perhaps, in part, because of man's encroachment, rare visitors or transients, including white-tail deer, wild turkey, grey fox, bobcat and the eastern fox squirrel can still be seen here.

In my role as caretaker, I cut the grass quietly with my gasless push mower, pruning and watering when necessary. In return I am rewarded with a never-ending scenario of activity and drama. Territorial rights are disputed and a variety of predators keep other residents and visitors constantly on the alert.

In the early spring, buck rabbits, disputing territory, with mating in mind, leap at each other like kick boxers, fur flying. A minute later they may be running and dodging for their lives from a hunting dog or fox. Hawks swoop, and ground predators are always on the prowl. The cat stalks day and night, knowing when and where is the best time to catch its prey off guard. The raccoon and opossum are omnivorous hunters of the night, listening, sniffing and looking for young rabbits, fledgling birds, frogs, and of course ripe persimmons, grapes, figs from what I call my fig tree, or even an accessible garbage can. In the warmer months, turtles have learned where the kitchen is, and look up for leftovers. The king snake may catch a vole off guard, or dine on a small copperhead or moccasin that was itself searching for a toad for dinner. The toad, in turn, could have been looking for a cricket to nail with its sticky tongue, which it flicks out like a dart.

During each of our short but frequent trips, we met some new member of the family. Patricia was usually our ambassador. She would connect us to someone new and quickly slip away, back to her work. This is how we met her cousins, Bob's sons Billy and Johnny, and his daughters,

Mary and Leif. By the time we met Johnny, we were already on friendly terms with Leif and Mary. Johnny's companion, Linda Kerr, worked at Realizations, the company managed by Adele Lawton, Mac's daughter, which promotes and sells reproductions of Bob's works. The salesroom is in Ocean Springs's old L&N railway depot, and every so often a freight train goes rumbling by.

Linda is a sweet, serene woman, young-looking with long hair and playful blue eyes. She calls Johnny at home and tells him we are writing a book about Shearwater and want to talk to him. She listens for a while and pauses, holding the receiver away from her. "He wants to know what you want to know?"

"Oh, my," I think. "Nothing in particular. We just wanted to meet him and talk." We were hoping the questions would arise from the conversation. That was our technique at the beginning, until we learned enough about the family to ask for specific information. We must have looked very confused.

Linda returns to the phone and asks, "Do you want to talk to them?" She hands the receiver to us, and Christopher quickly steps aside, looking at me as if to say, "Are you crazy? *You* get it!" We probably look like a couple of dummies. I react quickly and grab the phone.

"Hello?"

"Hi. What do you want to know?"

How should I know! We were so ignorant, and so aware of it, that any question would have sounded stupid. Out of who-knows-where I hear myself say, "Oh, well, the truth is that we have met your two sisters, but we still haven't met any of Bob's boys. I'm just curious to see if you are as handsome as your father was."

I can see surprise on the faces of Christopher, Linda, and Adele. There is a brief silence on the other end of the line. Finally, I hear what sounds like an ironic, amused voice.

"If you put it like that, I'll be right there."

At a restaurant, over lunch, he seems the pure image of his father. Lucky me! And the questions *do* take care of themselves. He speaks slowly, eloquently, with infinite affection, about his family and his unconventional upbringing. He can understand our interest in the Pottery, and our growing desire to learn about its past. Shearwater "just happened," he says. "I think that Shearwater is something that happened, for whatever reason. It is like a flower in bloom. Those who have lived there have had certain insights. And those insights are meant to be shared with other people. They are not meant to be wasted, not disappear, but to be shared. I've been fortunate to experience some of that. And in my family, good fortune creates the responsibility to share it with others.

"When I was very young, about ten years old, one of my favorite things to do—though I wouldn't have admitted it—was go to the showroom. On Sunday mornings, the pottery was closed until one o'clock: everyone was in church. And people would occasionally come on those Sunday mornings, and these people were very special. They would come from all over. They might show up on Sunday morning because that was the only time they could get. And I really enjoyed letting them in and being with them for a little while. Because they brought something with them. The people that came to Shearwater tended to be looking for something *better,* not the least common denominator. They tended to be looking for something good in humanity, and so they brought with them this aura. And I *believed* that, at least I did as a young child. I could feel it. And I wanted to feel it. People created the place, and then the place created itself, and people come there and still bring something special."

It was a family of "strong women," he told us. Two brothers—Bob and Peter—married two sisters—Agnes ("Sissy") and Patricia Grinstead. And one of the strongest—one of those who had created Shearwater—was Peter's wife, Johnny's Aunt Pat.

"Her influence was irresistible. It wasn't a question of dominance or ego. It wasn't a matter of asserting her will. She *never* asserted her will. Her will was indomitable. The sun doesn't assert its will, the elements don't assert their will. She was the strongest human being you could imagine. The room would just adapt to her. Anything she did would move outward in waves. Any movement she made would just pass through people like a wave of force. My mother, Sissy, had a bit of difficulty becoming independent from Pat. I think that, up until the age of seventeen or eighteen, Pat determined everything they ever did. When my mother went off to Radcliffe, Pat didn't want her to. But my mother prevailed. That was the first time, I think, that she actually prevailed over the ocean. She stamped her foot and insisted. The hole that she left is still there. Oh yes, strong women! And the women in our lives today are strong also. They grew up under the influence of these strong people. Take Mary, for example. . . ."

When we first met Mary, Johnny's amazing older sister, she was going through a difficult time in her life. Her thirty-three-year-old daughter, Amelia, had just died after a battle with AIDS, and her second marriage was coming to an end. In her late fifties, she seemed to welcome the challenge of giving her life a new direction.

Mary is petite and lively, with the appearance of a pretty, ageless doll. She has bright eyes and a restless mind. At our first meeting, she sits in front of us in the sitting room of the Barn, an ancient building once used as a carriage house, where almost every member of the family has lived at one time or another. As she speaks, her expression ranges from melancholy to happiness. Sometimes she pauses with a lost look on her face, and comes back with a new thought. She moves her legs in a happy, rocking motion when she tells us about her experiments with watercolors or the book she is writing or answers our questions about her children or grandchildren. She seems full of vitality and love for life, every inch a writer and a thinker, passionately devoted to the work of her father: not simply caring for the works he left on clay and paper and canvas, but trying hard to understand them and allow others to do so, and using his work as a window onto all that she most loves—poetry and nature, painting and theater, special people and places she has known.

Her sophistication, her intellectual restlessness, go back to her grandmother, Annette McConnell, and to the seigneurial New Orleans of the early 1900s. Annette was the most interesting, though probably not the first, of the "strong women" referred to by Johnny. Born to a prominent, well-to-do family, the daughter of a lawyer and judge, she studied painting in her youth and married an export grain dealer. With an overwhelming faith in art, she awakened the creativity in her three children, Peter, Bob, and Mac. When her husband, Walter, was about to retire, and had given up hope that his three sons would follow him into the business, Annette asserted her independence and indomitable will, went to Ocean Springs, and bought a twenty-four-acre tract of woodland—the site of modern Shearwater—where art could become both a way of life and a means of making a living.

Driving through Ocean Springs with Mary is an unforgettable experience. Today, there is an art festival downtown—nothing unusual; there is always something connected with art going on. Mary and I are driving, well, cruising would be more accurate. There are quite a few people on the streets, and Mary stops every now and then to say hello to someone who has just purchased her son Jason's CD, or a couple that tells her how much they like her son Christopher's new watercolors and decorated pottery. Friends wave to her from both sides of the street. As she progresses slowly down Washington Avenue, she smiles and returns their greetings, left and right. It occurs to me that this must be like driving with the pope. And in her theatrical way, she does look a little pontifical in this situation.

It is probably Mary in whom most of the qualities and artistic talents of the Andersons and Grinsteads come together. Her sister Leif, who has many of those qualities but seems more soft-spoken and reserved, lives down the path in an unusual modern house built by Mary's "dear estranged" husband, the architect Ed Pickard. She, too, has been bitten by the need to write. She was working, when we first met her, on poems illustrated with pen-and-ink drawings, and on a book of memoirs, hoping to share with others the essence of a life passionately devoted to dance. Over the years, she has developed a concept called Airth, a dance technique "based on the balancing forces of air and earth, breath and body, a way of experiencing oneness in nature through dance." Like her brothers and sister—Johnny and Billy and Mary—she had a privileged, and sometimes painful, childhood. In her writing, she speaks of "the strange, compelling influence of a mostly absent father." When she was very young, Bob Anderson left his wife and four children to devote himself fully to his art. After years of trying to reconcile pottery, painting, and family life, he removed himself to a cottage at Shearwater and made it clear he didn't want visitors. He stayed for weeks at a time on a barrier island—Horn Island—where, through painting and loving observation, he yearned to become one with nature. He wasn't *there,* wasn't available to her, during most of her childhood and youth, but over the years, faced with the same dilemma her father had—reconciling art with family responsibilities—she has forgiven him. "Who says that one who heeds the call to be an artist is somehow guilty of depriving others of his love?" she wonders in her memoirs. "Why is it that one person's freedom to create is someone else's lack?"

Like Johnny and Mary, Leif is aware of Shearwater's special qualities. Her house, with its dance studio, is hidden away in the woods where she played as a child in a clearing she always called "Fairy Land." She remembers the freedom of summertime, "going swimming in the marshy Sound, with blue sky and tall pines and seabirds everywhere you look." She read *Green Mansions* in the back room at the showroom, the windows open to the woods outside, and imagined herself as a girl as Rima, a character beautifully captured in a ceramic figure by her father. Her world today is one of feeling and the quest for self-expression. Her writing is as luxuriant, untamed, and vivid as the green things that surround her house.

There was writing, there were "papers" everywhere at Shearwater, drawing us into the past. There were notebooks and memoirs, diaries and letters, old bills and blueprints. Papers in the Barn and in trunks at the Front House (the main residence); papers in old oak filing cabinets and in the attic of the showroom. The leaf drift of four generations. These were people for whom writing was an ordinary form of daily meditation and self-knowledge, of prayer and forgiveness, a means of capturing the beauty of each day and bringing the past more fully into the present. Marjorie, and then Mary, and Mary's unfailingly helpful assistant, Joan Gilley, brought out those papers little by little, and Christopher would sit for hours at the back of the showroom, or in the Front House, or at night in our motel room, copying them on a portable Canon, dreaming of weaving the family's voices into a narrative, and letting them tell their own story. The process seemed especially hard on Marjorie, for whom those old papers—particularly the letters of her parents—awakened both good memories and painful ones. In the letters Peter wrote as a young potter, she read of his aspirations, in pottery and in love, and wondered whether he had fulfilled them.

"So many things have been going on in my head since I read Daddy's letters," she told us. "And to me some of it is just heartbreaking. It may be presumptuous of me to say so, but, for different reasons, I don't think he ever had a chance to develop to his full desire."

Some of our most moving visits at Shearwater were those to Mac and Sara and their daughter Adele. Mac was the youngest of the three brothers and, in his late eighties when we met him, the only living one. He would receive us on the porch of the rammed-earth house he had built with his own hands sixty years earlier. Inside, Sara would offer us cold water in Shearwater tumblers that looked as though they had been used for generations. In this family, plates and tumblers and pitchers, old and new, decorated or plain, are not stored away for special occasions, but used every day by all of its members. Art—the graceful work of somebody's hands—is part of their daily lives. Over the years, Mac had covered doors, cabinets, a fire screen, even the kitchen stove with oil paintings of coastal animals, people, and landscapes. His own wood sculptures stood on the porch. Others had stood in the yard, until they were devoured by wind and rain. Block-printed curtains made by him and Sara hung by the entrance to the living room. Brushes and pencils lay on a table, and the smell of turpentine and pigment reminded us that he continued to paint. Like his brothers, Mac could have personified the artist envisioned long ago by English thinker William Morris. For Morris had wanted to show "how art entered into the life of every man, and entered in no merely passive or receptive way. The best joy," he thought, "was the joy of making things and knowing that you made them well. In this spirit . . . a man should be able to make all that he needs: not only his house and his furniture, his tools and utensils, his tapestries and pictures, but even his music and song." Annette McConnell Anderson had taught her children, when they were young, that the capacity for art existed in everyone. "Real artists are just people who are on the right track," she used to say. "The track is there for anyone to use."

Like his nephew and namesake Jimmy, Mac was not an easy conversationalist. He didn't like to dwell on the past. He had an inner peace that you could feel in his murals, oils, and prints. You could sense that tranquillity in the answer he gave to one of my questions. Had Annette given more attention to his older brothers, Peter and Bob, when they were growing up? He didn't give it much thought. "Yes, she did. So what the heck?" We laughed, and that was the end of talk about family history. It would have seemed churlish to ask him how he had dealt with the hard times when Bob was out of control and had to be hospitalized for long periods, or Peter's moments of deep depression, or his brothers' combative relationship. Both Bob and Peter had strong tempers, and it seemed that at times Mac was the only stable male figure for all those children growing up at Shearwater. "When I was a child," Mary told us, "I used to want to live inside one of his paintings."

We spent most of our visits taking pictures of the pieces in his and Sara's collection, and that of Sara's sister, Liz Roberts, who is fiercely devoted to his work and has built up a marvelous collection. Mac would sit on the corner of his screened porch, amused at our delight as we discovered "new" pieces, each of them masterfully executed. Many of them revealed his sense of humor. My favorite was a vase with a New Orleans street scene. A confused, middle-aged black man, pushing a barrow, is confronted by his angry wife, who points him in the opposite direction.

But turn the vase around, and you see a second woman, angrier than the first, telling him to go back where he came from.

I asked Mac for advice as I tried to arrange his work for the photographs, but he never wanted anything to do with it. He smiled at my struggle to get the perfect group, and my frustrations as an amateur photographer. None of my photos did justice to the beauty in front of me. I do feel proud of a family picture, taken a little before his death in 1998. It shows him the way I will always remember him, a kind, tender gentleman.

The fourth generation of Andersons, both inside and outside Shearwater, shows the creative energy and love of nature that flowered with Peter, Bob, and Mac. Many of them have worked at the Pottery at one point or another, some with special talent and passion, hoping to make it part of their daily lives. The Pottery is a small one—the way its founders envisioned it—and has not been able to provide work for all of them, nor could the family give them all of the encouragement they needed. Marjorie "had ideas," she said, on possible ways of working things out, "but I always get outvoted by the 'artists.'" She remembered a letter she had given us from her grandfather, George Walter Anderson—Walter—the Pottery's first business manager, who had once been "accused" of "commercializing the pottery."

"I wish I *could,*" he wrote in 1929, "but with four Artists in the family [his wife and three sons], I believe such a thing is impossible. Odds are 4 to 1 in favor of Art."

Marjorie has a thankless, complicated job. By keeping orders in check, and suspending them altogether on certain pieces, it is up to her to prevent her brother Jimmy from overextending himself. Besides handling the "business" side of Shearwater—running the showroom, doing the books, ordering supplies, doing much of the pricing and handling the payroll—it is she who arranges exhibits, deals with reporters and "book people," corresponds with the customers, and answers questions from visitors, many of whom have heard of Bob but not of her father or Mac. "Now which brother was the *artist,*" some of them ask, as though the other two were drones. Or "How does the Pottery survive without Bob?"

"Oh, Bob," she answered once. "He comes down from heaven on weekends to lend us a hand."

"She is a glorious person in a fundamental but unappreciated position," Johnny says of his cousin. "It's Margie who holds everything together. Over the years, this family—a family of artists—has always needed someone who could serve as an interface with the community. Before, Pat and Walter—Marjorie's mother and grandfather—had that role. Now, it is up to Margie to represent the Pottery and communicate with people."

One member of Peter Wade's generation who does participate in the Pottery is Mary's son—Bob's grandson—Christopher Stebly. But only "from time to time," he told us two years ago. He was trying, back then, to "paint more than once a week, maybe two or three or four days a week."

"What do you do the rest of the week?"

"I like to fish and sail and surf when the wind blows. Discipline is my weak point. I love to party, to socialize. I love people, I love women, and I love my family."

We have met for lunch in Catch of the Day, a local seafood restaurant. The waitress who is taking our order—oyster po'boys, Killian Reds, oyster and artichoke soup—cannot be older than twenty. Christopher is twenty-nine, but they seem to be friends.

"Do you want pickles in your sandwich?" she asks.

"Only if you put them on," he answers.

"Wow, it's hot in here!" the girl says, turning redder by the second.

"If I were your age," I tell her, "and a handsome guy told me that, I'd turn up the air-conditioning, too." And she leaves the table, fanning herself with our order slip.

It isn't easy to get Christopher Stebly to talk seriously about himself. It isn't in his nature. But he is making an effort to tell us something "substantial." I ask him how he got interested in decorating pottery.

"I first started on my brother Mark's houseboat as a fishing guide. A girlfriend gave me a pack of crayons, and I took them to the houseboat and discovered I had no paper to record my ideas on. I did have a stack of paper plates, so naturally I started to do circular designs on the plates. When I showed them to my mother, she told me I should really try to put them on pottery. So I checked with my cousin Jimmy, over at the Pottery, and he said, 'By all means. Give it a go.' I tried, and they started coming out okay, and I sold a couple." One thing led to another, and art became his main way of making a living. The few decorated pieces that he does for the pottery do not stay long on the shelves, though most of his income comes from work, on his own, as a painter of watercolors and oils. On one of our last visits, he was working on a big mural, on the side of a building in Ocean Springs: a commission he had won in a competition. Naturally, his work was being compared to that of his grandfather, whose murals at the nearby Community Center, done in 1951, are admired by thousands of visitors each year. The family resemblance may be there, but Christopher's style stands on its own.

In its seventy years of history, Shearwater Pottery has never made two pieces that are exactly alike. Even molded pieces are hand-painted and glazed, and even in the most routine sort of decorating, the decorator's personality comes into play. A vase thrown by Peter fifty years ago has a very different feel from one thrown—in a similar shape—by Jimmy. It is a world where difference, not sameness, is the norm. One of the greatest art potters of all time, George Ohr, who worked in nearby Biloxi, called his pots his "babies," and described himself once as an "apostle of individuality." He was "the brother of the human race," he said, "but I must be myself and want every pot to be itself." In his thinking, the potter is God, and part of God's glory is never to repeat himself. The Anderson family does not use that metaphor, but it comes to mind when one generation—that of Peter Wade and Christopher, say—struggles with the legacy of the preceding one. It seems wrong to say that Peter Wade will "replace" his father, or that Christopher "replaces" his grandfather. When a pot disappears, no master potter—not Jimmy, not Peter—can replace it with an identical one.

"There's a strong influence from my grandfather," Christopher has admitted. "How could there not be? I don't think there's anything wrong with using his sorts of techniques to jump off from. But I will be judged by my own work, I *am* judged that way. I can't help but emulate, and I don't hesitate to borrow. There's a difference between borrowing and copying."

I ask him about how "Andersonitis" affected his life, growing up in Ocean Springs. He laughs.

"I'd hate to be normal, wouldn't you? Tar and feather me. I was often teased as strange-looking in school. I had a hard time getting dates, wasn't one of the flock. My great-grandmother, who knew how to separate the sheep from the goats, preferred the goats. As for me, I'll eat just about anything. I guess that early on you have fewer friends, but they seem to be tighter friends. And they tend to be goats as well. And we can convert a few sheep here and there!"

Joyfully, sometimes sadly—when he tells us about his sister Amelia—he pours out his love for his family. His face brightens when he tells us about his brothers Mark—who organizes trips in the Chandeleur Islands—and Jason, who is developing a career as a songwriter and singer. His admiration for his cousin Jimmy deepened when he tried to turn pots. "Mine are grossly out of proportion and wobbly." He feels "like royalty" when he is able to choose one of Jimmy's pieces to decorate. "When I see an extravagant piece, one Jimmy doesn't make very often, I'll go and ask him politely if he minds if I take it to decorate. And he'll either say yes, or 'These are on order.' But it's very laid back, very easy for me to do what I do. Any hour of the night or day I can go in. . . . There's a bin, you know, where it says 'Do not decorate.' And usually the orders are on that side. But he does so much! The bin overfloweth! You can't hide 'em all from me! I love him. It's such a treat. He's a living master, and I get to scribble all over his pots. It's wonderful."

I am wondering, as I listen to him, how many of those pieces are really "on order." There must have been some of them that Jimmy had in mind for his fantastic glazes. A certain tension—between potter and decorator—has always been present at Shearwater. "My father didn't like it when his brothers walked in and took his pots," Marjorie tells us. "Like Jimmy says, sometimes when he finishes throwing a pot, he sees a particular glaze on it. And here come the decorators, and their eyes go straight to the purest, most beautiful form." For a while, Christopher was decorating commercially made pottery, mainly plates. The designs were extraordinary, but the feel of Shearwater was missing.

There has always been tension at Shearwater, not only that between the potter and decorators, but within the family. The Andersons, too, are "apostles of individuality," and to us, those family clashes seemed inevitable. In most families, children grow up and move away, and make occasional visits. Seldom do parents and children, brothers and sisters and cousins, live together for so long, in the same rather secluded place, their houses only steps away from one another, brought into contact by business decisions and by the need to deal, in a sensible and sensitive way, with the artistic legacy of their parents. These are people who grew up in each other's houses—the doors were never locked—and who have known each other since earliest childhood. You can feel that tension in their daily relations, and more than one member of the family reminded us not to "idealize" them and paint a falsely harmonious picture.

"We have been able to live together for so long," Marjorie told us, "because we've learned to give each other some space."

In a page of her memoirs, Leif, too, has acknowledged that tension: "You know that bible verse that says to turn the other cheek? I bear a lot. I think there are angry people in our family. . . . It is strange, because the surface looks so smooth and beautiful to strangers, and even friends. But actually there is a tension that can snap at any moment, and the bitterness leaps out and knocks you over. . . . I have cultivated tears and also creativity. When tension builds, and I feel tempted to lash out at someone, I turn it on myself, or sometimes, when I'm lucky, I can turn it into art. I can distract myself with dance."

Despite that tension, Patricia speaks of Shearwater as having given her an almost seductive feeling of security that pervaded her growing-up years and has stayed with her ever since.

"We were not an emotion-expressing nor a physically touching family, but there was a pervasive feeling of security and of each person's importance: the importance of our place and being in our world, which it has often been difficult to move beyond. . . . This despite omissions and commissions past and present. Our blessings, have, I believe, outnumbered our crosses, hugely.

"Mama [Pat] I remember as the caretaker, even when she was dying, expressing concern for the welfare and safety of others, though she spoke seldom in those last weeks. She who had been voluble and in motion as the family mover now only wanted to be quiet.

"Sometimes Mama overdirected. In her it seemed instinctive—the need to keep us all together and on the felt, more than thought-out, 'right track,' and I include all the families and people and world beyond family. But every one of us was of extraordinary importance to her. She was an inclusive person, inviting all family—and always extras—to wonderful holiday celebrations, and for years to every-Sunday dinners. . . .

"Daddy and Walter—I haven't seen or heard as much about Mac— were both volatile storms and distress under the sort of pressures that had probably been lacking as they grew up. Strong and deeply caring parents and a comfortable financial circumstance hadn't prepared them for the difficulties of providing, in much reduced circumstance, for family demands of every kind. . . . This together with their naturally passionate, expressive natures. Daddy was a constant in our lives, always working and providing play-routine, mixed with a teasing nature, and outbursts against fate, not against Mama or us."

After Mac died, we visited Sara a couple more times. She brought out old clippings, photographs, and letters, and cheerfully answered our questions. It had not been an easy year for her. Her marriage to Mac had been a good one. There was happiness and energy in the lives of the young people around her. And yet it seemed to her that not everyone was aware what hard work, what sacrifice, what trying moments the family had gone through, to create Shearwater and to keep it alive. The story of that past was waiting to be told.

BLUEPRINTS

From an old wooden trunk, Marjorie pulls a roll of blueprints and specifications for the ample "frame slate-roof dwelling" her grandparents constructed almost a century ago in New Orleans, at 553 Broadway, in the Garden District a few blocks from Audubon Park. The Anderson family moved here in 1905, five years after Annette McConnell married a prosperous grain dealer, George Walter Anderson.

The handsome sturdiness of that house—its "good hard burnt brick," its well-built chimney with two pottery thimbles, its four-by-nine-inch ceiling beams of heart pine—was more than a matter of comfort or social status. These were years when popular magazines, Arts and Crafts societies, and universities were spreading the gospel of English thinker John Ruskin: that our surroundings shape our character, and that "architecture and morality mutually reinforce each other." You *were* what you looked at every day. Annette would probably have subscribed to William Morris's advice: "Have nothing in your houses that you do not know to be useful or believe to be beautiful."

It was a spacious house, well suited for raising children. Annette was thirty-three when she married Walter (in January 1900); too old to have girls, she said, fearing they would be more trouble than boys. "For all her enlightenment," her granddaughter Mary writes, "she continued into old age believing that her husband knew the secret of having only boy babies." He had told her so during their long, twelve-year courtship, and he was as good as his word. Peter was born in 1901, Walter Inglis (Bobby) in 1903, and James McConnell ("Little Mac") in 1907.

Annette, who thought of herself as delicate in health, was less strict with the children, more inclined to indulge them, than Walter, who had graduated from boarding schools in England and Switzerland, and tempered his affection with talk of discipline and backbone. With a smile, he would sometimes remember his own Scottish father, who had a razor strap and "the vision necessary to apply it where it would do most good." But Walter worked long hours on Canal Street, where he worried over an unpredictable business partner and the price of wheat, corn, and cottonseed oil. It was Annette who stayed at home with her "darlings," and the succession of nannies who gave them most of their meals, watched them in the backyard, and took them for daily walks down quiet, tree-lined streets to Audubon Park, gathering green things for the house and finding real treasure on the way: locust shells and acorns and twigs of bamboo trimmed from the neighbor's hedge. Nearby, at the end of Broadway, were the levee and the mysterious objects left there by the river.

For Annette, writing was part of living, and to fully savor the time she spent with the children, she started a journal of "the boys' sayings and doings." In a series of vignettes scribbled in ink or pencil, we see them fill "pails and jars and bags with the green pecans that drop about the grass," or pick strawberries, or make tracks in the morning dew. They take joyful notice of rosebushes and their father's prized chrysanthemums (over a thousand of them), count the figs on a tree in the backyard, relax in front of the fire with their pet roosters and hens and kittens, or play with a lamb shipped in from the country, and wonder whether to put the animals "into the God blesses" in their prayers. The Andersons' backyard was a spacious one with camphor trees and a palm or two, wisteria, and an old pecan that sometimes blocked the breeze. There were poppies and sweet peas and snapdragons. From Walter's desk on the second floor, he could see nothing but greenery and shade. Next door was a grassy open lot. The Dominican convent across the street (where part of Loyola University now stands) kept its cows there, and the boys, especially Peter, became great friends of the cows and the cow man. Annette liked to read poetry to the two oldest as they ate their supper.

"I will read you 'The Sands of Dee,' " she said one evening as they had their bread and milk. *"Oh, Mary go and call the cattle home, /and call the cattle home, /across the Sands of Dee . . .* It's too sad. I'll read you something else."

"Is it sad about Mary or sad about the cows?" Peter asked.

"About Mary. It is terrible. She never comes home."

"Oh, then that's alright, Mother. Go ahead."

When Walter, Sr., gave up smoking for a while, "Peter, walking in the garden, picked up a little stick and put the end in his mouth like a cigar, as he often does. This time he took it out again and laid it down on the step, saying slowly, 'No, not today.' Then, after a pause, picking it up, 'Well, just this one.' "

She saw Peter at age five, picking up a foot rule like one he had been spanked with: "This is the sorry measure."

"What?"

He grinned and patted himself "appropriately, to show what he meant."

Seven-year-old Mac saved her from many a giant. "Every night when I put him to bed we play a game. Mac asks shyly, 'May we play *that* again?' *That* is the game of saving me from the giant. I crouch beside his little iron bed post and call for help, and he flies to the rescue from the washstand, with his wooden sword, made by Bobby. He smites the giant, the bed post, cuts off his head. I cry 'Oh, my preserver, my champion!' He says, 'Oh you mustn't say that. What's done is done. I needn't be boasted about.' Every night, the same words."

Mac was the sweetest and easiest of the three, Peter the steadiest worker, stacking wood or helping to fix supper. But it was rebellious Bobby who got most of Annette's affection, awakening jealousy in his brothers. At age six, he was a disobedient, "adorable, comical little ruffian." He "kicks, he even spits, he punches, he throws whatever happens to be handy at the offender, but he is level-headed, he is quick to see when he must be good, and he is sweeter than anything in the world when he *is* good. He plays by the house with blocks. Annie [the children's nanny] says he is going to be an 'arkle-atect.' Houses and yards of all shapes and sizes." Lying in bed one morning, "he called Peter a damned rascal. When Annie bathes Bobby and she loses her temper, Bobby with composure like an old person says, 'Now, Annie, you know I don't like hot water,' or 'Now, Annie, you wouldn't hurt your little boy, would you?' "

Like all children, Annette's boys dreamed of the future. Peter would be a carpenter, and Bobby would help dig the sewerage ditches. Or, maybe, he told his mother, he would "study to be an angel. . . . Then I can fly all about the sky and climb the trees and see the eggs in the birds' nests." He had been born in September, on the feast of Saint Michael and All Angels. "My little Saint Michael," Annette used to call him, singling him out from her other two.

As she imagined the future, Annette took special care to record her boys' first contacts with art. In her journals, she watches Peter modeling in wax or drawing on the blackboard, searches the house for tubes of oil paints for Mac, or follows a trail of ink upstairs to where Bobby, "at his own desk with the ink bottle on the slanting edge at his right elbow," is writing a book of short stories. She takes seven-year-old Bobby to an exhibition at Newcomb, but finds him curiously bored. He liked pictures of animals, he said, but there were none there. "When we were coming away, he said *'Mother,'* holding me back by the hand, 'Mother, what are those?,' pointing to the sphinxes at each side of the Art Building. 'Those,' I said, 'are sphinxes, half woman and half beast.' I began to realize how little I knew. 'Oh, yes,' said Bobby. 'I remember. Hercules told the maiden he had killed a sphinx.' "

The boys drew at home and at the park, and Annette copied the most amusing of their drawings into her journal, and put others carefully away. One, by Bobby, is a duck whose body and head are ovals. "If you want to draw a bird, start with an egg," Annette told the children. She believed in drawing as a daily discipline, gave them sketchbooks, and encouraged them to draw a flower, a leaf, or a bird each day. She believed that writing skills could be developed in the same way, and many of her own journal entries begin with the reminder: "750 words a day." When he was older, Bob took one of her notebooks, replaced "words" with "birds," and filled the pages with sketches of egrets, osprey, and sandpipers.

Through her children, especially Bobby, Annette hoped to realize her own aspirations as an artist and teacher and make art a normal part of family life. For over three decades, both before and after her marriage, she studied art and dabbled in painting both at Newcomb College (the women's college at Tulane University) and at local art associations. She entered Newcomb in 1889, two years after it opened, and her instructors knew immediately who she was. Her father, James McConnell, a prominent lawyer, had little interest in art, but he had played an important role in the founding of Tulane and would soon begin to wage a fierce battle against the family of Josephine Louise Newcomb to ensure that the money Miss Newcomb had given to found the college would be used as intended: to revolutionize the education of southern women.

A guiding idea at "the Newcomb"—one that Annette took to

heart—was to spread the study of the arts and crafts in the South. Annette's beloved teacher and mentor, Ellsworth Woodward, who had been
lured to Newcomb from the Rhode Island School of Design, used to
complain that the South had made only a "negligible" contribution to
American art. This was painful to acknowledge, Woodward said, but use-
less to deny:

> I sympathize profoundly with the bitter, inescapable fact that the
> South lost all in the outcome of the Civil War. . . . [This] does not
> touch your inner understanding until you have lived it. . . . *Of
> course* the South has no art. How *should* it have any when for fifty
> years, life was a struggle for bread and shelter? "From him who
> hath not, shall be taken even that which he hath." If you lose con-
> tact with the gracious influence of art for two generations, you
> will certainly lose desire for such contact and become unconscious
> of loss. To my way of thinking, a realization of this startling truth
> should be at the foundation upon which helpful art instruction
> must be based.

To a southerner at the turn of the century, art was always *elsewhere,*
and Woodward wanted his students to develop a sense of the beauty of
their surroundings. Annette lived within an easy walk of the college,
down oak-bowered Saint Charles Avenue in the Garden District, one of
the loveliest urban neighborhoods in the country. Woodward trained his
students to "see as much beauty in the old backyards of New Orleans as
in the canals of Venice," and to capture it in their painting, pottery, and
prints. When he first came to New Orleans, he had been appalled to find
his students producing Christmas cards "representing village churches
sending out a ruddy glow of cheer upon snowy landscapes. The apple
blossom was a favorite subject for imaginary compositions. Needless to
say, apple trees do not grow in the state, and snow falls only once in a
generation."

Woodward was an excellent painter, but he knew that teaching the fine arts (a term he disliked) would do less to change the public sensibility and "melt the hard crust of materialism" than teaching his students how to make beautiful things: pottery and jewelry, embroidery and wood carving. No matter that 70 percent of his students married and drifted away from the crafts they had learned: they would transmit their enthusiasm to their children and lead society "towards beauty of home and civic surroundings." They would create "common things of use, which our friends, the public, will be likely to desire and willing to buy." Art was not something to be searched for in a museum or picture gallery in the North, it was simply "truth made visible," and it ought to form part of daily routine.

All this provided the rationale for the founding of Newcomb Pottery and the college's crafts shops. And Newcomb quickly won international renown and helped spread Woodward's guiding ideal—which Annette made her own—that art is not a commodity or a material thing; "rather, it is a process of thought and expression, a means by which we symbolize our reactions to life and our intelligent emotions, our conception of beauty."

Annette followed her classes rather unsystematically. She was a "special art" student, exempt from the requirements of the normal degree, and she took eleven years, from 1889 to 1900, to gather enough credits to graduate. For much of that time—the years of her courtship with Walter—she was away from New Orleans, traveling with her parents in the North. Some time in the late 1890s—perhaps in 1897 or 1898—she seems to have studied at the Art Students League in New York, and visited the hills of Branchville, Connecticut, for two months' study with the American Impressionist Julian Alden Weir. Her daughter-in-law Sissy remembers, rather vaguely, that she also spent a summer at Shinnecock Hills, on Long Island, with William Merritt Chase. She graduated from Newcomb at the age of thirty-three, offering a stirring slogan in the yearbook: "The will to do; the soul to dare."

Annette was a natural teacher, who shared her enthusiasms easily and memorably. Pedagogy was among the courses she took, along with painting, modeling and casting in clay and in plaster, harmony and chemistry of color, decorative design, and drawing from life. Marriage and children swept away her plans for teaching, if she ever had any: Peter was born only a year after she graduated. But for years—both at Newcomb and later—she showed her works at the "unpretending little gallery" of the New Orleans Art Association. Old programs and the few works still extant suggest that she did most of her drawing at home. She seems to have worked slowly and produced—or saved—little. There were pastel or charcoal portraits and the occasional oil of her children "in white" or "in blue," asleep or reading or eating an orange. Walter smoking a pipe *(The Smoker),* a sketch of his sister Daisy, or Impressionistic studies like *Sunlight* or *Against the Light* or *At the Mouth of the Bayou,* showing Walter and the boys in a boat fishing. By the time the family left New Orleans, she had held a "one-man" show of pastel paintings at the Isaac Delgado Museum of Art. She also served on the board of directors of the art association founded by Woodward, and helped it organize art classes for children. She had acquired something more valuable than polite recognition as an artist. Thanks to her own enthusiasm for art, and to the friendships she formed at Newcomb, in the years ahead the family could draw for expert help and advice, should they ever need it, on a wide, talented, and knowledgeable circle of painters and craftsmen. These included the Woodwards, Newcomb's master potter, Joseph Fortune Meyer, and a handful of decorators who had helped bring Newcomb Pottery international fame: Mary Given Sheerer, Catherine Labouisse, Mazie Teresa Ryan, Gertrude Roberts Smith, Mary Williams Butler—all discerning makers of exquisite objects.

Annette must have given much thought to the boys' schooling. For generations, since well before the Civil War, education had been a passion in her family. Among their most treasured heirlooms was a service of silver plate presented in 1846 to Annette's great-grandfather, Samuel Jarvis Peters—Granpa Peters, she called him—merchant, banker, and civic leader. When he came to New Orleans from Toronto early in the nineteenth century, he helped found New Orleans's public school system, and worked tirelessly to improve the city, helping to turn it from an uninhabitable marsh into a great commercial emporium. It was Peters who arranged for the purchase of the lands now covered by the Garden District, where Annette grew up, and who laid out its orderly system of streets. He was known as New Orleans's "Father of Education," and once a year, when Annette's boys were growing up, all the public schools in the city commemorated him.

Annette's father, too, an admiralty lawyer, president of the Louisiana Bar Association, had worked tirelessly on behalf of education. Judge McConnell's obituary in the *Times-Picayune* in November 1914 recalls the years of patient labor on behalf of Newcomb, and his friendship with Paul Tulane, "founder of the great university which perpetuates his name. It was through [McConnell's] instrumentality that the Tulane fortune was left to the people of this State." Judge McConnell formed part of the university's first board of administrators. Before the Civil War, as a director in the public schools, he had dreamed that education could bring the moral world into consonance with the natural one. If the "material universe around us" exists in perfect harmony, could not education—and religious faith—redeem the moral universe, a "confused scene of inexplicable disorder, whose history presents no page unstained with blood, no era exempt from political oppression, spiritual intolerance and desolating wars"? Like Annette, he was an avid reader. In his will, he left her his personal library, and $500 to enlarge it, "especially for the benefit of my grandchildren." He was an intensely practical person. Late in life, when his savings were dwindling, he wrote to his son Jimmy that his greatest ambition was "to see my grandchildren all well-educated, especially the boys. But they must have their mental development in the direction of *industrial* pursuits, so as to enable them to become independent."

The education of three of his grandchildren—Peter, Bobby, and Little Mac—began at home and continued at Miss Maggie Finney's School, run by two sisters, friends of the family, where they learned to read and soaked up fable and myth—Hercules and the sphinx—at Friday storytelling hour. Discipline there was simple: if you misbehaved, you sat by yourself and didn't hear the end of the story. Mac was given private art lessons by one of the Newcomb decorators, Emma Urquhart, and by the time he was ten, he was "working away" at a lion, a little cat, and a tile with a four-leafed design. All three boys were good with their hands, and their patient parents allowed them to perform "weird feats of carpentership" like the pigeon house that Peter "belarded" with red paint and asked his father to install in the backyard. One of Walter's letters to Annette, when she was away, tells of "monstrous objects that [render] the sitting room a cross between a second-hand furniture depot and a drunken carpenter's workshop." Walter didn't mind. In fact, a few days after the pigeon house went up, *The Practical Pigeon-Keeper* appeared in the family library, alongside the books—which all three boys read avidly—of artist and naturalist Ernest Thompson Seton.

Peter and Bob were sent away at an early age (Peter was fourteen; Bobby, twelve) to St. John's School, a military academy in Manlius, New York, no doubt to develop their "discipline" and expose them to northern habits of thought (not only Granpa Peters, but also Annette and her father had studied in the North). They might meet "the right sort of people" there—it was one of Annette's constant concerns, when the boys were small. Perhaps she also felt she needed more time to herself. Years before, Walter had built her a studio with a skylight on the top floor of the house. Always she longed for time to use it. Not that Walter was entirely convinced that Manlius was a good idea. The "whole proposition," he thought, "was a good deal of a shot in the dark." It was "for the boys' good," Annette told him. The friendships they formed there would be of lasting benefit, and there were family friends and relatives in New York, in case anything went wrong. When Peter came down with scarlet fever, feeling "homesick, schoolsick and horsebacksick," Annette was there in a day or two to nurse him back to health and bring him home. What worried *her* was what they should study there. Walter had an inkling: "About lessons, I think we had better leave them for a bit and see how they develop before we decide on their courses of study. . . . Peter had better take the business course, with some Spanish and French thrown in. He will make a first-class businessman, and I don't think he will shine in any other direction. Bob is too young to know much about. I think he is cut out for a lawyer, but he doesn't know it yet, nor do you."

"We have only Little Mac," Annette wrote sadly in her journal at the beginning of 1916, and her husband vowed "to hold on to [him] now that the other two birds have flown." After a nearly fatal struggle with scarlet fever, and another with bronchitis, he was less robust than his brothers, and a bit more timid. For years, Annette would worry over his health, sending him to camp in New Hampshire or the mountains of North Carolina to harden him up. At the age of fourteen, he, too, would be sent away, to the McCallie School, in Chattanooga.

Peter adapted to Manlius far better than Bob: by the time he left, on the eve of World War I, he had become a good horseman, had risen to the rank of second lieutenant, and had to be discouraged by his parents from enlisting in the U.S. Cavalry. Bob was often in trouble, tangled in demerits, and in a rebellious mood. "Fraternal feelings," Sissy writes, "were often stretched to the breaking point." Once "both were invited home with a schoolmate. They slept in a large double bed and the host's mother [was] surprised to find her sheet neatly slit in the middle and each boy wrapped in his half, neatly balanced on opposite edges of the bed." Not that the boys didn't defend one another. "Just to think," Bob wrote, a little after his arrival, "I've been in a fight already and gotten a black eye and a bludy-nose, but it was not any shame to me because he was four years older than me, and then Peter fived him. Your loveing son." In other letters—confidentials to "Little Mac," aka "Mr. Mick"—Bob tells gleefully of his plans for stealing apples from the orchards around Manlius, joining a secret society and dropping "black-hand notes all over the place." He wrote those words in August, during vacation: his parents sometimes kept him there over the summer. At times, he must have enjoyed the place—his mother had threatened to bring him home if he didn't study hard, and he assured her he *was*. But looking back on those years, considering the experience as a whole, he sometimes felt a little bitter. The school's motto was "Manners Maketh Man." But much later he told his mother that Manlius was like prison, and that it had "nearly destroyed him." In a letter of 1930 to Sissy, before they were married, he wrote:

I know what [discipline] is, having had four years of it, and look at the result, although the Pennsylvania Academy of the Fine Arts undid a good deal of it. I still suffer from it. The one great virtue [at Manlius] was conformity. You can imagine what a good thing that would be for a young boy who is just beginning to show individuality. Dad is a victim of that system. He went to an English Public school when he was very young, and he still believes in the good taste and virtue of the majority, just because it is the majority, and if so many people believe a thing, it must be true, it's got to be.

In her father's letters from Manlius, Mary Anderson notices a positive note: "a sustaining and comforting awareness of nature," and the interest in birds and animals that he would feel for the rest of his life. There were surprises in the woods around Manlius—"special places where I go and read and draw," "a partridge's nest with twelve large cream-colored eggs," the nests of pheasants and robins and catbirds.

"Like many naturalists," Mary writes, her father "learned to recognize water fowl over the sights of a shotgun." On weekends before they went away and during school vacations, the boys made trips to Lake Catherine, east of New Orleans, where their father kept the *Wanda,* a forty-foot launch he had bought after a couple of "gorgeous" years in business. Bob remembered those trips for the rest of his life: the ride at sunup in the Coast train, "with the tracks shining like molten metal" and the lake shining like a looking glass; creatures emerging from the marsh, a flight of terns or a bunch of egrets. Turtles sunning on a log, the over-whelming love the boys felt for their father.

Walter . . . G.W.A. . . . also known affectionately as Wattie and Fabée. "The English-public-school-businessman with his Scotch severity," Annette called him, years after his death. From his letters, he seems anything but severe. He was a tender, ironic, fun-loving person, with a streak of melancholy and a dry, loving humor, and his visions of child-rearing came not from some "military" sense of rank and order but from confidence in his own domain: business. He had as much faith in its principles as Annette had in Art. If only the boys and their parents could be transformed into "Anderson Incorporated"! Once, when Annette was away and he was left in charge, he made a stab at it. A letter to "Dear A," written with a touch of humor in 1921, when the boys were twenty, eighteen, and fourteen, captures his hopes for the family:

I feel distinctly encouraged over "A. INCORPORATED", but it is very evident that in one or two directions, the Concern is going to have a hard road to travel. All on time for breakfast yesterday, also today. All three of the Junior Members in the machine [i.e., the family Ford], when I was ready to start. This is a small thing, but it is a great relief. All three Junior Directors pleading for a day of license tomorrow, it being Saturday. The plea has been sternly rejected and punctuality and tidiness will be required on holidays, as well as on work days. In a way it is amusing. You know I give credits for unsolicited service, and at breakfast this morning I told the gang that I was glad to say that Bob and Mac had each attained a service credit yesterday without knowing it, and Peter immediately jumped up from the table, went and swept the hearth and claimed a credit. I explained that motive entered into the matter and rejected the claim. I am going to attack table manners next, but am going to wait to do this until I have made the Saturday payment covering this week, so that they might have tangible proof of the benefits of the Association before I impose any fines. Bob started an ash tray and I found all his matches and cigarettes this morning in the ash tray. Yesterday morning, I found a lighted cigarette hidden under the washstand, its position betrayed by a column of smoke. Yesterday, burnt matches all over the floor; this morning, none. There is an awful lot to do, but it can be done by degrees. Although these two days may not have taught the boys very much, they have taught me a good deal.

Much love,
Yours,
GWA

MIDLIFE JOURNEY

Annette was known for her habit of just taking off for someplace, surprising others with her sudden "flights" and her escapes into the realm of ideas. Often she felt an urge to get away from husband and children and friends, and would disappear for a day or a week. For, as she put it, "a stream that does not flow becomes a swamp."

Walter encouraged those getaways. There were things he wanted to do without her. But once his wandering wife was gone, he would find himself "tired and lonesome and a bit blue" as he cared for the children "undiluted." She was the "presiding Genius" of the house, and he missed her, despite "the gentle ministrations of a pessimistic sister and the ruder consolations" of his closest friends. When she was away, he wrote her almost daily—

> *Dear Old Lady,*
> > *Gentle and Most Fair Lady,*
> > > *Dear Old Lady Mine . . .*

—and gave her news of home and work and Sunday trips with friends on the *Wanda* up the Tickfaw River or the Natalbany or the Blood. When she tarried, he would threaten jokingly to send a policeman after her. "I am beginning to find out that I am really fond of you. . . . It is long since you have been wandering about without my guiding hand, and, though you don't think much of it when you have it, possibly you miss it a bit when you haven't got it. How little we value what we have, and how much some people ought to."

When they were together, they rarely agreed on anything, but a certain tenderness came over him whenever she was away, either by herself or with the two oldest children—Bob and Petey—"the Bobby Boy and the Pepter Boy"—to the mountains of North Carolina, or New York, or to her family's place in Bay Saint Louis. "How I would like a peep at you and the children, bless all of your hearts, big one and little one. I have been thinking over things since you left and I am inclined to think that you have made a very good wife for me. What do you think? Perhaps better than I deserve, though this is unlikely."

Poking fun at her "artistic" temperament, he sometimes parodied the sort of talk he heard from *her.* Along with tidings of "the humdrum world" from which she seemed to be in perpetual flight, he sent her news of the Aesthetic:

The wisteria on our back porch is beyond reproach and is very decorative. A few years ago I should have ignorantly and prosaically said very pretty. *Now I say* decorative. *We have also a wild purple Iris in the back lot which has bloomed quite effectively against the weathered gray surface of the rotten fence behind it. It is true, the color is a little crude in that precise locality, [but] it forms a refreshing discord of inharmonies alongside the red of the Louis Philippes.*

Some of Annette's flights were short and sudden. Others showed a sense of mission. One day in June 1918, when the children were away at school, she went to the Louisville & Nashville depot in New Orleans and boarded the eastbound train "over the lake" to the Coast of Mississippi. She was fifty-one or fifty-two years old. Walter was fifty-seven, close to retirement. For the past few years, his business had been thriving, and the death of Annette's father in 1914 had left her with $40,000 or $50,000 of her own. Today, that would be about $825,000. It was time to start looking for a place where the family could begin the next phase of its existence. Walter had suggested that they rent a house in Biloxi for the summer.

When Annette traveled alone, she thought often about freedom. Freedom from housework, cooking, cleaning, and feminine fashion. Her granddaughter Mary remembers gleefully that she cooked hardly at all.

A soft-boiled egg and burned toast were all I remember of her culinary accomplishments, though I've been told she also burned oatmeal. A nurse cared for her children. [Her] role was to draw them as babies. . . . Clothes, fashion, and shopping bored her, so she chose a classic dress and jacket pattern with simple, elegant lines that, she said, "suited her style of beauty." She had it made in many fabrics for different seasons: serge, corduroy, light cotton, linen, dotted Swiss; altered slightly by changeable collars, a pin, or a flower on her lapel. It was her costume, a part of her recognizable self. Her hats, always the same— felt in winter, straw in summer—were purchased in the men's department and blocked to her order in a becoming shape. She used no cosmetics beyond Eau de Cologne for her migraine headaches, took cold baths, and washed her long thick grey-white hair in Packer's Pine Tar Soap.

She wasn't much on dusting, either, and longed at times for the bareness and beauty of the Japanese house. She hated not dust but the bric-a-brac it settled on. She asked herself, in an essay, whether marriage meant resignation to a life of material things. Must a woman, like "many American men," consider nonmaterial things as "inessential luxuries"? Can a wife and mother risk a chilly hearth and unwashed dishes? Two lines from Milton seemed to her to capture the balance she wanted:

> Thy soul was like a star and dwelt apart
> And yet thy heart the lowliest duties on itself did lay.

Train rides were good times to cherish her freedom, think about her boys, read, meditate, silently observe others. Leaving New Orleans, chugging past the old French market and the U.S. Mint, the L&N Coast train snaked through the outskirts of the city into the lakes and marshes where Walter hunted and fished with the boys. The Rigolets, Chef Menteur, Lake Catherine, the pinewoods, and, a little after Gulf View, the blue waters of the Mississippi Sound, dotted with "the white sails of pleasure craft and the larger and usually dingier sails of the ships of commerce." Breezes from the Gulf and from the barrier islands came through the windows. Annette sat among city people on their way to coastal boardinghouses or summer retreats, or tired shipworkers on their way to Pascagoula. With the war going on, International Shipbuilding was contributing its wooden ships to the war effort. Fern and bracken, "shining herons," a black squall over the marshes, the rain pelting the windows, the Gulf air, "fresh as Eden," all this conjured up freedom and what Annette called renewal. In a ballad, she tried to capture that feeling on the train, when the salt air quickens the senses, and the traveler rises up "like Lazarus," alive to wonder and beauty.

> Before you're halfway over, they meet you on the train,
> The winds from the islands that blow and come again.

They toss your hair and tease you; they blow your plans away,
They whisper to your drooping soul in dulcet tones and gay.

They bring you sounds of beaches with scent of burning pine,
And surf that pounds and hisses along a crescent line.
They give you news of skimmers wheeling about the land,
Above the white convolvulus that blossoms in the sand.

The hot sands off to leeward behind the dunes and tide,
Where, through the pink ropes of the vine, the ghost crabs
    race and hide;
The funny little ghost crabs that stop and watch and stare,
With eyes on stems like periscopes and buskins edged with hair.

They tell you how the pelicans that crowd the sandy keys,
Like solemn, sitting senators, in water to their knees,
Still rise with foolish, flapping feet, still do their matchless glide,
In solid companies above the shadow on the tide.

Oh lovely Island Beaches, oh winds of many tunes,
Sing me again the sedge songs and the surf songs of the dunes!

Bay Saint Louis awakened memories of childhood and adolescence.
Her father, "tall and cordial and kind," had bought a summer house there
"with all the modern conveniences of a nineteenth-century home." Its
large windows and doors, its octagon-shaped dining hall overlooking the
Bay, let in air from all sides, "so that when there is no breeze from the
Gulf the odors of the pines and the sweet flowers which grow in abundance all around the house" were swept through its rooms. When she
was a little girl, in days of stagecoaches and steamboats, and the arrival of
the packet boat from New Orleans was the event of the week, she liked
to visit the Bay house of her maternal grandparents, Jules Arnaud and

Harriet Blanc: "To pass from the heat and glare of a summer day through the shallow house into the dense shade at the back seemed a miracle of cool peace." Annette loved the family bustle. Seven cousins lived there, along with gardeners and grooms, house servants and cooks. "Each of the older children had a little colored child that they called their own 'fellow.' But it was a happy company." They were awakened at seven each morning by Mr. Perez, selling bread and croakers. She remembered the two goats the family kept as pets. Before anyone was up in the morning, the goats would climb into the two big rocking chairs on the front gallery. The noise was a nuisance, and it became a regular chore at night to see that the gallery chairs were turned up against the walls.

Often, she had taken the boys to the Bay for days or weeks at a time, leading them to ditches where they could hunt for crawfish and through the shallow coastal waters in search of minnows or shells. In August, in hurricane season, they would listen for a strange sort of croaking in the trees outside. "Those are the birds from the Islands," her father liked to say. "They come in before a storm." But she and the boys knew they were frogs enjoying the dampness that came with the rain before hurricanes reached the Coast.

When she thought of that house and of her father, she would often remember *his* attitude toward material things, and the melancholy of collecting objects—any objects. After the Civil War in New Orleans, Annette remembered, "there were women who had lost everything, except perhaps some precious personal possession. I remember my father's face when he passed windows on Royal Street, filled with trays of old lovely jewels. I would want to linger and be thrilled, but he would hurry me on and he looked as if he could not bear it. That enameled watch with the little shepherdess and the pink roses, that topaz bracelet with engraved links. . . . I saw only the enchanting beauty of amethyst and garnet and pearl. He saw past scenes of tenderness and heartbreak and [thought of the woman who had loved those things]."

He had suffered during the war; served in the trenches, commanded light artillery at Vicksburg, was a provost marshal in Mobile, and was imprisoned by Yankees in Biloxi. His first wife—Annette's mother, Delphine Angelique Blanc—was pregnant when he went away. The child, a little girl, died of yellow fever during his absence. When Delphine heard of his imprisonment, she pulled a pair of men's boots over her shoes and hid a Confederate uniform under her maternity clothes. She crossed Union lines and reached Biloxi, got her husband out of prison, had a new uniform made for him, and sent him back to his regiment. Mary remembers her grandmother—who had heard her parents tell of the humiliation of the Confederates by "Beast Butler"—saying she could not bear hearing the "Battle Hymn of the Republic." Yes, the music was beautiful, "but the words are so damned self-righteous."

Farther east down the Coast—past the stately homes and bobbing yachts of Pass Christian, past the oceangoing ships of Gulfport and just across the bay from busy Biloxi—lay the town of Ocean Springs, the oldest on the Coast, for a few brief years the capital of the entire Louisiana Colony. To Annette, it seemed a vision of loveliness. Decades earlier, the architect Louis Sullivan recorded his own first view of the place. He had come, exhausted, from Chicago, had choked on filthy New Orleans, and, like Annette, boarded a train eastward.

He was delighted and soothed by the novel journey through cypress swamp, wide placid marsh with the sails of ships mysteriously moving through the green, and the piney woods. Bay Saint Louis, so brilliant; more piney woods, then Biloxi Bay's wide crossing; then, as dusk neared, the little frame depot with its motley platform crowd; the crippled hacks, the drive to the old hotel . . . all passing into silhouette, for night comes fast. Ah, what delight, what luxury of peace within the velvety caressing air, the odor of the waters and the pines!

With daylight there revealed itself an undulating village all in bloom in softest sunshine, the gentle sparkle of the waters of a bay land-locked by Deer Island; a village sleeping as it had for generations with untroubled surface; a people soft-voiced, unconcerned, easy going, indolent; the general store, the post office, the barber shop, the meat market on Main Street, sheltered by ancient live oaks; the saloon near the depot, the one-man jail in the middle of the street back of the depot; shell roads in the village, wagon trails leading away into the hummock land; no "enterprise," no "progress," no booming for a "Greater Ocean Springs," no factories, no anxious faces, no glare of the dollar hunter, no land agents, no hustlers, no drummers, no white-staked lonely subdivisions.

Little had changed in Ocean Springs years later when Annette got off the train and made her way to the corner of Washington Avenue and Bowen Street to the offices of a real estate agent, Hiram F. Russell, who was less known for his realty business than as the originator and proprietor of a certain "toothsome nut." This was the Russell paper-shell pecan, the thinnest-shelled pecan known, so *very* thin that some of the nuts cracked in falling from the tree; a nut "broken as easily as a peanut between the forefingers." Did he have anything they could rent for the summer? Out came a long list of town and country properties, from small lots to "fine pear and pecan orchards under successful cultivation."

One property in particular caught Annette's attention. Not far from the beach cottage Louis Sullivan had built for himself was a twenty-four-acre tract of land jutting into the mouth of Back Bay. To the northwest was a sleepy bayou where a corn mill had once stood; in 1918, it was still known as Mill Dam Bayou. On rolling terrain, in the fragrant shade of magnolias, live oaks, and long-leaf pines, stood a large house overlooking the Bay (now the Front House occupied by Annette's granddaughter Marjorie and her husband "Pete" Ashley); a carriage house—known today as the Barn (which provides office and studio space for the Walter Anderson estate); and a little cottage (where one of Annette's great-grandchildren lives). All were built in the 1840s. The price of the land and buildings was $2,500 (about $32,000 today), and Annette told Russell she was interested.

In 1918, Ocean Springs's 2,000 inhabitants felt somewhat isolated from the culture and industry of New Orleans and Mobile. There were no factories (except for a seafood cannery that angered the affluent), no mills, no manufacturing, and—Annette noticed—not the slightest evidence of Art. The roads were poor, and ferries crossed the marshes and rivers. Land and labor were inexpensive, and for three decades citrus fruit—satsumas, grapefruit, and oranges—had thrived in its moderate climate. The pecan business had gotten its start here, and had created much wealth: in fall 1918, one of the larger growers had sold his entire crop—15,000 pounds—for 50 cents a pound (about $82,000 today). Not far from Annette's new property were several important nurseries. Off to the east, along the Pascagoula River, stands of one-hundred-foot longleaf pine rose to fifty or sixty feet without a branch and fed sawmills and shipyards. A single acre yielded from eight hundred to one thousand board feet a year. The seafood industry, especially in neighboring Biloxi, had grown to national importance: like its pecans, Ocean Springs's oysters were shipped all over the country and the L&N had chosen them to serve in its dining cars.

The beauty of the spot—the three-mile-long beachfront with its graceful gazebos and piers and bobbing catboats; the streets paved with crushed shells and lined with live oaks decked in Spanish moss; the sturdy, white wooden frame houses and mansions—all this attracted summer residents from New Orleans and visitors from the North. Some came from Chicago, down the Illinois Central, during tourist season, from mid-December to March 1; others, from the city to stay at any of the town's numerous boardinghouses and hotels, or on Sunday excursion trains. There was a buoyancy and quiet optimism about the place, the proud feeling that it had been uniquely blessed by nature, the collective will to make it "the Garden Spot of the South."

Sullivan saw "pigs and cows wandering familiarly in the streets," but Ocean Springs was no stranger to civic progress. The very month that Annette purchased her twenty-four acres of beachfront property, the mayor of Ocean Springs, on the front page of the *Jackson County Times,* implored women to persuade their husbands to vote for a new stock ordinance that would banish horses and cows, mules and pigs, from public thoroughfares and make for "better cattle, better milk, and a far more attractive city." The fences that kept animals away from people's property were to be taken down and used as kindling.

"Did you have any luck?" Walter asked her that night, after she had returned from Ocean Springs.

"I *bought* a place," she answered.

ART AND INDUSTRY

Annette, Walter, and the boys took at once to life on the Coast. Even before Walter retired, and the family moved there permanently in spring 1923, Bobby and Peter often went over to fish and hunt, and Annette sometimes stayed there by herself. By age seventeen, Bobby had acquired a catboat, sailing charts, and a taste for adventure. One Sunday afternoon in August 1920, when his mother was at the new place—then known as Fairhaven—and his father was at 553 Broadway, he ventured eastward down the Coast. Around four o'clock, L. B. Charlton, keeper of the Lake Borgne Lighthouse, peered through his spyglass and noticed a young man in a catboat sailing toward Biloxi. As it came abreast of Pearl River, the boat struck a heavy squall. It turned around and passed the lighthouse again, an hour and a half later. The storm had abated, and the keeper went in to eat supper with his family. When he returned to his spyglass, Charlton swept the waters for sign of the boat. It was over a mile from the lighthouse and it was empty.

Charlton took his sons out to investigate and found only the drifting boat (the tiller was missing), an oar, and a khaki shirt with $6.35 in the pocket. He towed the boat to the lighthouse, and sent in a report.

TIDE SWEEPS BOY IN SMALL BOAT TO DEATH read a headline in the morning newspaper. When Walter went to question the lightkeeper, he saw to his horror that the boat was Bobby's, and offered a reward of $100 for his son's body. A day later, his bedraggled son walked into the sitting room at Fairhaven and told his mother and a reporter that his adventure had been "thriller enough" to last him a lifetime. When his boat capsized, the tiller came loose, and he plunged into the choppy water to retrieve it. The boat drifted away, beyond his reach, and he swam two miles to a channel beacon. Lashed by wind and waves, clad in his bathing suit, he clung to it for twenty-eight hours. His voice was too weak to be heard by passing boats—one came within three hundred feet of him—and he grew so thirsty and so hungry that he "would have cheerfully given [his] front teeth for a drink of water," and "could have eaten the shadow of a bean." Finally, nearly unconscious, he was spotted by a passing fisherman, who gave him dry clothes and returned him to safety. He couldn't understand, a reporter says, why his parents should think he had drowned.

"You knew I could swim," he reminded his mother.

It was a sign of things to come and a signal to Walter that his adventurous sons would never follow him into the grain business. After their studies in private schools, Annette had enrolled Peter and Bob in Isidore Newman, a manual training school most of whose graduates went on to college but where, as at Newcomb, the crafts, from gardening to pottery to wood carving, held a privileged place in the curriculum. Mac had studied there briefly before departing for school in Chattanooga. "Learn by doing," was an oft-repeated phrase, both at the school and at its camp in Saluda, North Carolina. "Please try to get me a job where I won't be kept cooped up in an office," Bob wrote his father from camp one summer. In his last year at Newman, he carved a little wooden chest, decorated with elephants, in an effort to persuade his father to let him study art. Walter bowed to the inevitable, and in September 1922, his son entered the New York School of Fine and Applied Art (now known as Parsons). It was a compromise: not a full-fledged art school but a place where Bob could learn something "practical," like design. One of the first projects he worked on was an advertisement for duck decoys. It was September, he was homesick, and even in Manhattan, far from the Louisiana marshes, it felt like duck weather.

He decided, not long after his arrival, that "the usual art student may be divided into two classes. First the feminist, the one with affected ideals of art, and second, the commercialist, with no ideals, just frankly out to make money." Smiling at his own "supercilious cynicism," he told his mother he was a "snob, after all." His letters to her were, Walter said, part of the air she breathed. She missed him greatly, and to her husband she sometimes seemed "down in the mouth. . . . Goes about like a mournful ghost, seeing troubles everywhere." She asked a friend to call on him and drop her a note. He was living on the Upper West Side, a block from Morningside. Annette's friend, Alice Perkins, found him doing well, "a very civilized youth, charming to talk to." He reminded her of Annette, especially in his smile. His "tiny little room on the fifth floor" had something "rather sweet and peaceful about it, like a hermit's cell." She must have seen wood-carving tools lying about, and blocks of white pine, and cigarette butts, and paints and a very large pile of books, for he "made a beeline for Brentano's" whenever Annette sent him money, and a branch of the public library was just across the street. He liked to write his mother about the authors they both read.

At Christmas 1922, he was feeling lonely and joked to his parents that he was planning a private one-man show: an "exhibition," in his room, "by the artist, for the artist, and to the artist." It was to include "woodcarving—figures and bas-reliefs—and enormous compositions both in transparent and opaque water color." ("We do not use oils at all at school, just tempera and water color.") Instead, he opened his Christmas boxes from home, went to service at St. John the Divine, made his "usual pilgrimage to the Metropolitan" Opera, and wrote to his father, mother, and fifteen-year-old Mac, who was in New Orleans, ill with pinkeye, on vacation from McCallie. Shame on Mr. Mick! Why hadn't he written? Didn't he care about his older brother, "alone in the great city of New York, destitute of friends, family, money and social position? And you don't write! Hurry up before I hop a side-door Pullman and come down there and beat you up. Your most bitter enemy, Bob."

Not so. Mac's bitterest enemies were algebra and Latin. It was a bumpy time for him, and his report card showed it: he was demoted to first-year Latin after a 50 on the reexam, and had acquired eight demerits. "General deportment, unsatisfactory." There was amusing but unsettling news in his letters home. When Baylor beat McCallie that fall in football, "We went downtown with the gang and tried to get in a fight, but nothing stirring! While we were in town the Bellhops—so we call Baylorites—came out to school and heaved rocks and paint all over school. Most of them were drunk." No doubt he, too, was homesick, and was claiming his share of parental attention.

In New York, Bob was dazzled by the collection of Zuloagas and Sorollas in the Hispanic Society of America and by the Winslow Homers in the Metropolitan. He took a stab at Jay Hambidge's book on the "dynamic symmetry" of classical Greek art, and looked at the paintings of Adolfo Best Maugard, a young Mexican artist and pedagogue whose theory of drawing would permeate Bob's later work. A handful of those paintings were exhibited at the 1923 Independents Show, which he found, for the most part, "very depressing. If they simply want to be designers, let them say so, and stop pretending to be artists." Whom did he mean? Diego Rivera, John Sloan, Morris Kanter, and George Bellows were on display, along with Best Maugard. Ernst Barlach won his admiration as a wood-carver, and the murals of Boris Artzybasheff, who evoked the Russia of the icon painters, seemed well done when he saw them at the newly completed Russian Inn. Little survives of the work Bob did at Parsons: a carved totem pole, an "old mammy" and pirates, drawings and watercolors of birds he observed in the parks, in the Bronx Zoo, or, stuffed, in the Museum of Natural History. After a year of design, he was impatient to study painting. He entered the Pennsylvania Academy of Fine Arts and undertook the five-year course of study, which ranged from drawing and painting to costume design, decoration, illustration, and mural painting. He worked hard there, and won several prizes for studies made from living animals, a scholarship covering tuition in 1927–1928, and a Cresson Traveling Scholarship of $1,000. He used the money for a trip to France, where Chartres, Mont Saint Michel and the cave paintings at Les Eyzies, in the Dordogne, impressed him more than anything he saw in museums. At Fontainebleau, he visited the Institute for the Harmonious Development of Man, founded by George Ivanovitch Gurdjieff, a charismatic philosopher who preached the need to create the "Whole Man" by uniting body, mind, and emotions. A few years earlier, the novelist Katherine Mansfield had studied there.

With Bob on the right path—the path to Art—Annette turned her attention to her oldest son: Peter. From New York Bob advised her not to hurry him. "He hasn't found his groove yet, but he will. In the meantime give him rope." There would be no office job for Peter, either. For a while after leaving Newman, he worked in a shipyard. Walter took him to work with him at his grain-exporting firm, but quickly saw that his son would never do in an office. When the family moved to Fairhaven, Peter felt lost and a bit depressed, bewildered as to his vocation and isolated from the friends he had made in New Orleans and at Manlius. For a while, he worked hard, fixing up the dilapidated buildings at Fairhaven and trapping and sailing when he could find time. For $150 per thousand acres, Walter rented him a large tract of game land near Pearlington, Mississippi. In the dense, wild pine forests between the West Pearl and the East Pearl River he trapped for coon, mink, and muskrat.

As happened with Bob, the move to Fairhaven enlivened Peter's interest in sailing. Walter had sold the *Wanda* before the family left New Orleans, and in fall 1924 he and Peter made plans for a new boat. They ordered a "Callie Perfection detachable motor" from a yacht-supply place in New Orleans, and a couple of days after Christmas 1924, they went to the Poitevin Brothers Boat Yard in Pascagoula and signed the contract for the boat itself: the *Gypsy,* a twenty-five-foot, nine-foot-wide sloop. Years later, Bob had his own boat built, the *Pelican,* modeled on a New England dory: an ungainly little craft he constructed with the help of Alphonse Beaugez, an old carpenter from Ocean Springs. Neither the *Gypsy* nor the *Pelican* sailed very well, and they were quickly turned into "cruisers."

It must have been just about then—perhaps in 1924—that Peter discovered his vocation for pottery. No family papers capture that fatal moment: no diaries or allusions in letters or newspaper clippings, only family memory. Two great southern potters seem to have presided over that moment, although one of them, George Ohr, had died in Biloxi in 1918, the year Annette bought Fairhaven. Years after Ohr's death, when his widow and sons were trying to dispose of his unsold pottery and the equipment from his workshop, Annette—who considered his work "vulgar"—bought his kickwheel at an auction, thinking, perhaps, that she and her sons could learn to throw. She had dabbled in potting herself while at Newcomb. The other potter was Joseph Fortune Meyer, from Newcomb, who was once Ohr's associate. One day, Peter rowed to Deer Island, where Meyer had a summer home, to ask him for a lesson on the wheel. At sunset, when it was time to row back home, Peter asked when he could return for further instruction. Meyer smiled politely: "Go home and get to work!"

Soon after the move to Fairhaven, Peter, who was then twenty-two or twenty-three, built a rectangular, groundhog kiln three feet wide by nine feet deep, in the side of a hill. Pine knots were fed into one end, with the flue at the other. By the fall of 1925, Peter was peering into that kiln at all hours of the day and night. His enthusiasm began to draw the entire family, whether they liked it or not, toward pottery. Art and Industry were about to bear fruit. Walter's vision of "Anderson, Inc." and Annette's conviction that art should be useful and that useful things should be beautiful were about to be realized in a way no one had anticipated.

Before he knew it, Walter's golf and hunting, bridge and fishing, had given way to pots and dreams of better ones. "We are in trouble," he writes. "We used to be surrounded by pines and oaks and such. Now we are quite surrounded by pots, vases, bowls. . . . If you want a book off the bookshelves, you have to move 15 pots, and if you don't put 'em back, just as they were, there is a row of the largest dimensions. . . . We have had a successful firing—at least we think it was successful, knowing no better. Anyhow nothing exploded or blew up."

Months before, the first barrel of clay had arrived from Ohio. Number 2-C ball clay, from East Liverpool, to be mixed with the sandy stuff that Peter brought from four or five miles northwest of Biloxi, in a spot near Holley's Bluff, forty-five feet above the Tchoutacabouffa River. Years earlier, Ohr and Meyer had gotten some of their clay from the same spot, where today a housing subdivision has crowded out the yellow pine, magnolia, water oak, and palmetto. Months after the ball clay arrived, almost as an afterthought, Walter wrote to the company asking "at what temperature or rather at what cone the clay you sent . . . fires properly and at what cone the glaze should be fired."

The best source of guidance was one of Annette's friends, Mary Given Sheerer, professor of pottery and china decoration at Newcomb. She had taught there for over thirty years and was a member of the faculty jury that approved each piece for sale. What gave Peter the most trouble, probably, were glazes, and he must have looked admiringly at those developed at Newcomb. Under Sheerer's direction, Newcomb had widened its palette and won praise everywhere for its colors and tints, ranging from delicate greens and olives to old delft blue to rich terracotta and purple.

"Couldn't you send us a few different colors in glazes?" Walter wrote Sheerer. "We want the best, of course, and have every confidence in your taste. If you would send them by radio, we would appreciate it. Annette doesn't sleep well at night—she dreams of glazed pots."

Sheerer chuckled over his letter. "Your picture is a vivid one. There is no subject more fascinating [than pottery]. Its combination of art and science is hard to beat. Freedom and discipline together." She was much too busy to prepare a sampling of glazes, and told Walter that in Newcomb's earliest days, they had ordered their glazes ready-made. She could at least recommend some books—by Charles F. Binns and George Cox—and supply some helpful addresses: the Standard Pyrometric Cone company for pyrometers, and S. Reusche, on Union Square East, New York, for glazes. And with that she wished "Good luck to the budding chemists!!!"

Off the "chemists" wrote for a box of fifty pyrometric cones: the tooth-shaped little pyramids of specially prepared clay and glaze that allow potters to measure how evenly heat is distributed in the kiln and to predict at what temperature, and where in the kiln, each glazed piece will reach perfection. In oil-fired kilns, different glazes are used in the same firing, and some pots do best at the bottom of the kiln, where the temperature is lowest, and others at the top. Measuring the heat, placing the pots correctly, and firing the kiln is a difficult process: Peter once called it "the main test of a potter's capability. After he has made the ware, he has got to put it in the kiln and risk the whole sum of his efforts in one short period of about ten or twelve hours." So the purchase of those pyrometric cones in fall 1925 seems symbolic. After many months of potting by trial and error, he wanted to make the process more predictable.

It was clear, after his early experiments, that he needed some formal training. The best pottery school in the country was the New York State School of Clay-Working and Ceramics at Alfred University, but the regular four-year course of study was closed to him. Both he and Bob had left Manlius before graduating, when the Great War began. A summer at Alfred might be possible, but before that, someone at Newcomb recommended he spend a few months as an apprentice to Edmund deForest Curtis, who ran a small pottery in Wayne, Pennsylvania. Years later, Peter remembered that he "used to put bright-colors, *very* bright colors, on white enamel and fire them to a low temperature, just to get the bright color. . . . They weren't practical for dinnerware, just ornament." Curtis did not have a degree in ceramics, but could draw on "fifteen years of practical problems." He was a former director at Van Briggle Pottery, had managed Enfield Pottery, and taught a course at the Pennsylvania Museum and School of Industrial Art (now the Philadelphia Museum of Art). His own studio—the Conestoga Pottery—would provide a suitable model for the one Peter wanted to found.

The fastidious Mr. Curtis—Ned to his friends—kept one eye on art pottery and the other on the modern ceramic industry, and was passionate about the need to reconcile the two. By 1926, American manufacturers had taken an interest in color and design. It was enough, Curtis wrote, to look at magazine ads. Color was appearing everywhere. Corona was making a green typewriter, color was the vogue in fountain pens and cars, and Frigidaire was brightening up the kitchen. But in ceramics, art and industry seemed at odds. "The designers who work up through the industry lack [a] broad outlook and those who come from the schools lack technique."

The solution lay in education and in publicity. The ceramic engineer must be persuaded to "jar himself loose from the fascination of colloidal chemistry," and the art potter must get better technical training. Curtis was thinking hard about that training in fall 1925, when Walter asked him to take his son as an apprentice. What should a potter know? The craftsman potter "must have his art training in color, design, history of art, appreciation of beauty, development of taste." But he should also "have sufficient technical training to be able to build his own kilns and repair them, to form the clay, to make molds, to build, cast and throw pottery forms; to calculate, mix and apply his own glazes; to load and fire his kilns; and to be familiar with all the many decorative processes. He must know how to run his shop at a profit, and he must realize that he is undertaking work that calls for production."

Curtis's passion for education—for training the "practical potter"—struck a chord with Walter and Annette. Here was someone eager to try out his ideas on a talented disciple and who, much to Walter's delight, believed that in ceramics, there is no such thing as Art for Art's Sake. "I'm so glad that you think well of my proposition," Curtis wrote them. "I'm afraid you have too high an idea of my ability as a potter and teacher. I shall be particularly interested in this month with your son for I have an idea that our teaching methods might be revolutionized if any one really tried to do it, and he and I will have a good shot at it anyway."

Plans were made quickly. Curtis found Peter a boardinghouse on Bloomingdale Avenue, four or five blocks from the pottery and a short ride by train or trolley from Philadelphia, where Bob was studying. The brothers could visit with one another and see art and pottery together at the Pennsylvania Museum. Perhaps Peter could prod Bob into writing their parents; Annette was worried by his silence, and wondered whether he needed "help of some sort." She knew that he kept to himself at the academy, and had few close friends. Fellow students referred to him jokingly as "the Mystery Man."

With the two oldest boys in Philadelphia and Mac away at his boarding school in Chattanooga, Annette and Walter went back "over the lake," from Fairhaven into New Orleans, to the French Quarter—"a strange mixture of beautiful old things [and] unspeakable squalor"—and found a third-floor apartment, a block from Jackson Square, for three months. "Front gallery, large front room, smaller sitting room, bath, kitchenette, two open fires, and furnished, all for thirty a month." A "colored maid" was found, an amusing woman who "delights us with her funny expressions." Annette needed to be around interesting, artistic people, and soon found a studio where she could paint. She might, she said, do something with it.

There were frequent letters from Peter, in his familiar scrawl, and a couple from Curtis, who was delighted with his progress. From them, Walter gathered that Curtis's business practices were a little neglectful. His account books were probably a disaster. Without wanting to be a "butter-in," Walter couldn't resist giving some advice by letter, and, *en passant,* a few words of advice to his son:

> *Of course, it is impossible for a wholesale grain dealer to put down exactly the method of bookkeeping to be followed in selling pottery, but any business that is to make money, or make a living, or do anything but fizzle, must be on a systematic basis, and a clear record of what is coming to you, and what you are putting out, must be kept. Otherwise you don't know whether you are making or losing money. Even in Art production there must be a business basis, as the Art must, under present living conditions, be converted into money, or it cannot endure. Here endeth the lecture. You could think this out and with what you have seen might be able to make valuable suggestions to your boss.*

There it was again, that uneasy marriage of art and industry, business and beauty: how to turn Art into money. Through his work with the American Ceramic Society, his friendships with other potters, and his contacts at the Pennsylvania Museum, Curtis could easily find a job for Peter in the ceramic industry. There seemed to be an opening at an architectural firm in Coral Gables. But Peter hesitated. Did he want to work in business or try to survive as an art potter? He knew he had "tackled a big thing." Letters went back and forth, and his parents tried not to push him too enthusiastically in one direction or the other. "You are old enough to know your own mind," Walter wrote, "and I am beginning to entertain quite a respect for same." Discussing things by letter was almost a relief. "When you were here with me, you never talked nor am I much of a talker," he wrote, "so I don't know what is inside you." By letter it was easier to mull things over. Choices were more clearly delineated. More than pottery seemed to be at stake.

Dear old Peter:

If you can get my view of pottery as expressed in my last letter, without letting it submerge Curtis and the Artistic side—in fact, keeping the latter very prominently first, without losing sight of the former, I have little doubt but what you are, if not a made man, at least a very good man in the making.

I am so glad that you are taking Curtis's advice in matters outside pottery. I so very much want you to meet outsiders in a frank and friendly way. I am not sure that friends are not more important than anything else in this transitory life. You have to give liking in order to get it. Give liberally of kindness and thought to others. It is the pleasantest thing in life to do, and you will get it back many times. It is better than many muskrats. This of course refers to your going to the Bal Masque. And I am so pleased because you are going, without yourself wanting to go, but because he wants you [to]. Don't lose your independence. This you may lose by doing what you want to do, and thus becoming the slave of your own personal desires. But you will never lose it by making yourself do the thing you don't want to do. It is thus that man becomes man, and master of his fate.

I see what you say as to starting a shop of your own very soon. Don't be in too great a hurry. My advice would be to stay with Curtis as long as you can, at any rate until Summer School at Alfred opens, and then go there for the six-week course. Mother and I gave a lunch at the Green Shutter on Monday. We had as guests a Mrs. French and Mrs. [Leona Fischer] Nicholson, both potters of renown. The former, Mrs. French, is the nicest woman I have met for a long time. Both were nice. There must be something about pottery that makes people nice. Even I, who am only the father of a future potter, feel that I am becoming distinctly nicer. Mrs. French talked a lot about pottery, and also about Alfred. She strongly advises that you get the Alfred summer course, as does [Ellsworth] Woodward, and Mrs. Nicholson, before you start out. Of course you would be too busy afterwards. Ask Curtis what he thinks about it. . . .

My advice is to make haste slowly. I have no doubt you have learned a good deal in these two months, but there's lots to learn as you have said yourself in one of your letters to me. I am getting a bit ambitious for you, old man. Your letters to me and to mother have been something more than a pleasure. They have given me a picture of yourself, a side of you that I did not know, and I want to keep it as long as I live. By going on as you have begun, I won't lose it. If this letter is too serious, tell me, and I won't offend again. But before I stop, believe this: that your welfare and Bob's and Mac's come first for your mother and me. I would even go to Alfred, not to mention Timbuktu, if it helps along.

GWA

Annette added her own predictable advice. Buy a sketchbook at Wanamaker's. Copy the pottery in museums. Read Ruskin and Emerson—you "need to know what Art means." Conquer your "greatest fault . . . a certain impatience." "Think out quietly what would be the very best thing for Peter Anderson to do, not in reference to immediate financial returns, but for his development." And "stick to the artistic side of pottery. You will find the financial side will take care of itself. The greater includes the less." Walter agreed: "If you fail [on the artistic side], the most businesslike handling of a lot of trash would result in nothing." And yet, somehow, Peter ought to make up his mind "uninfluenced by me or by your mother."

By the end of Peter's stay in Wayne, shortly before he returned to Ocean Springs, Walter wrote him again at length, weighing possibilities for the future. By then, Peter had expressed a definite preference for art, and had all but decided to set up his own shop—something like Curtis's—rather than look for a job in industry. What no one knew, as yet, was *where* that shop would open. Florida, with its much-talked-about real-estate boom? Perhaps his Aunt Daisy—Walter's sister—could accompany him into "the wilds of Florida," and serve as his housekeeper? Or perhaps Biloxi, a few miles from Ocean Springs. Or New Orleans, where Walter owned a suitable lot on Broadway.

Dear Old Peter:

. . . As to Florida, my idea is that you should be free in the matter. . . . I would go and look over the ground first, if I were you. We both have heard something of a boom there. This would probably be a great thing for you if you were already established, but, as you are not, the initial cost of getting a site for your pottery might be prohibitive. I was talking to Watson [a business acquaintance] yesterday about Florida. He said he had gathered, from bankers and other sources, that the boom had been rather overdone, and though he did not anticipate anything like a collapse, he thought that a good deal of the attention now centered in Florida would be diverted to the Gulf Coast and elsewhere. Of course, to some extent, the wish may be father to the thought, but it sounds reasonable. I cannot say that either mother or I have any very definite alternative to suggest. Mr. Curtis told me in his last letter that he was going to write me shortly what he thought you had better do when you had decided between artistic and commercial pottery. From your letter to your mother, you are very definite in your preference for the former.

We have thought of a pottery on the key lot at Broadway, one in the French Quarter, one at Biloxi, and one at Fairhaven. I am opposed to the latter for many reasons. It is too out of the world, among other things such as the necessity I see of our having to sell the place sooner or later owing to increased value and owing to increased cost of keeping it: higher taxes, etc. I am rather in favor of Biloxi. Think you could find clay in the back country. Any site you bought for the pottery would not now be prohibitive in cost, and would almost certainly increase in value. On the other hand, New Orleans in time will do the same. It is spreading in all directions. A lot of new money and population is coming in. On the other hand, Biloxi is crowded as it never was before: a lot of rich people who have money to spend and might as well be given an opportunity to buy pottery as anything else. Life in the French Quarter would be rather confining; on the other hand, you would have good opportunities of selling. You would be meeting all sorts of people who are interested in your sort of work, and from whom you might get a lot of help. Broadway seems to be a little out of it. On the other hand, you have a site there waiting for you and could sell your pottery there after you became known, and in the meantime exhibit it somewhere on Royal Street, which is an established thoroughfare for Northern and Western visitors. Talk it over with Curtis. I am going to ask mother to write you her ideas. Of course, they differ from mine as our viewpoints are necessarily not the same. From the nature of my past occupations, mine are biased by the practical while hers are not. There is, no doubt, great merit in a combination of the two, and you can try to make them combine. One thing is quite certain, and that is, that we both want what is best for you.

In one of your letters, you ask me among other things about spelling. Paid should be paid, and not payed; *litterature, not literature; alcoholic, not alcholic; quantities, not quanties. Style and matter of your letters beyond any criticism of mine.

Tell me something about Bob in your next. Nothing from him for a long time. Have you any idea why he does not write? It must be something beyond mere dislike to writing.

Much love,
GWA

There is one thing to which I omitted to refer, more important than spelling. And that is Hampshire's red wine. I would strongly suggest that you leave it alone; also, all other matters alcoholic. This is equally important for pottery and for everything else that makes life worth living. I cannot put it strongly enough. Let the "rare occasions" be canceled. . . .

*Literature. You are right. Mother says I am wrong.

Days later, Peter caught the train for Ocean Springs. "He left here," Bob wrote, "wanting to go to Florida. For goodness sake, and my sake, and your sake, let Peter go to Florida or Maine or South Africa. The thing to do is to let him start in for himself with all of the responsibility on his own shoulders. He will have a hard time but will enjoy it. He's made that way, and thank God for it."

GROWING WEATHER

Fireing the
Kiln — Shearwater

Not Biloxi and not Coral Gables, far from parental prodding, but Ocean Springs. The decision to start the pottery there must have been made without delay. Within a month after Peter's return from Wayne, a writer from the local paper drove out East Beach Road and noticed some new buildings rising on a hill overlooking the Mill Dam bridge.

Here, we learn, is to be built a modern pottery. Peter Anderson, Mr. Anderson's eldest son, is head of the institution and will personally direct the work of designing and making unique and beautiful pottery, decorative tiles, etc. . . .

The metal building nearest the road will be used for the kiln house. In it will be installed four kilns, equipped with Hauck kerosene burners, capable of developing a heat, direct and reflected, of somewhat in excess of 2500 degrees Fahrenheit.

The second building, with a floor space of about 1000 square feet, is to be the workshop, holding the clay bins, potters wheel, emory wheel, clay and glaze mill, etc. The power will be furnished by an electric motor. Trucks running from the workshop to the kiln building will take the completed forms to the kiln building for firing, and return same after each unloading of the kiln.

We understand that Mr. Anderson contemplates producing quite a variety of pottery, such as vases, lamp bases, decorative tiles, bowls, etc. His pottery will depend upon well thought out shapes and on fine colored glazes for their attractiveness. Some will carry simple hand painted designs of things common to the Gulf Coast.

A slight test of some of the local clay has been made, we understand, with satisfactory results, and Mr. Anderson entertains no doubt but what he will be able to get all he requires locally for his basic clay. However, the necessary materials for mixing same will have to be brought here.

It was page-one news in a sleepy coastal town that had never had more than a nodding acquaintance with Art. Now, all of a sudden, the Andersons were to change all that: "Ocean Springs to Be Art Center of Coast"! Throughout the spring, as those buildings were rising in the pinewoods, and it rained steadily on the tin roof of Peter's workshop, Annette and one of her friends from the Arts and Crafts in New Orleans—Daniel G. Whitney, a teacher of portrait painting—were busy planning a "Summer Arts Colony" at Fairhaven. It was another exciting development for Ocean Springs. There were many such colonies in the North—Annette had been to a couple of them herself—but none at all in Mississippi. A reporter who came to see it predicted that the pottery, the colony, and the "nation-wide cycle of exhibitions" that was sure to follow would "do more toward making [this] carefree little town come into its own than all the real estate booms in creation."

The newspaper people who visited Fairhaven found Annette reticent about her painting: she shunned the glare of publicity, and said she dabbled in art just for the fun of it. What she and Whitney wanted to emphasize was "individuality," without insisting on methods and formulas. There were to be a variety of artistic activities, mostly plein-air painting, with no restrictions. Only serious workers were invited, "though one does not have to be an artist—if you're a serious writer, they will let you in, but you must be doing something—hangers-on are not desired." This was an experimental gathering of "working industrious artists," who could paint whatever they wanted, in whatever medium they desired. There were day students, and a handful of boarders who worked out-of-doors or on the wide screened porch at the Front House, overlooking the Sound. At sundown, "smocks or knickers are doffed, and playtime begins, under the direction of Catharine Whitney. There is bridge, if one is inclined; there are sailing parties; swimming, of course; floundering under flaming torches; even a treasure hunt was inaugurated one night. At the end of the pier, when the moon is shining down on the sparkling waters, one might hear singing, to the accompaniment of a Victrola or ukelele." Local children came to the Front House and demonstrated the Charleston. Journalists came, and vied with one another describing the charms of Ocean Springs and of Fairhaven.

> Fairhaven is an ideal spot for a summer art colony. Fronting the Mississippi Sound, extending back into the hills, one gets the tang of the sea and the lure of the woods. There are massive oaks, hundreds of years old, scattered over twenty-five acres of one of the

most beautiful spots on the coast. Wild flowers bloom luxuriantly almost to the water's edge; herons lazily dry their great white wings on the beach, while wild rabbits scurry through the wooded groves without fear of being molested.

Another praised Ocean Springs's charming "atmosphere of languor and inactivity" and its "rustic, old-fashioned Southern environment." Fresh from Philadelphia, Peter must have snickered at the *Jackson County Times:* "Down country roads, there are picturesque cabins, around which ripening corn fields rustle, and bare-foot pickaninnies play at mud-pies and ring-a-rosy—studies in ebony! This is the Negro quarter, where one may find the replica of 'Old Black Joe' smoking his corncob pipe on a honeysuckled verandah. Here simplicity exists in its lowest terms."

There is a photograph of Peter in his workshop that summer, surrounded by unfired pots, dreaming in clay, oblivious to reporters and ukulele players and "studies in ebony": the proud director of the Anderson Art Pottery. It was not until a little later that he spotted the word "Shearwater" in a book on birds, and made it the name of his business. To do so, he and Annette overruled Walter, who had his heart set on something more esoteric: "Roc Pottery." Rather than the legendary bird from the East, Peter wanted an ornithological emblem of life on the Coast: the black skimmer *(Rhynchops niger)* he could see in the bayou below his workshop—black above, white below, about the size of a crow, with a large red, black-tipped bill, the lower mandible longer than the upper. The skimmer tips its beak downward, "shearing" the surface of the water to scoop up small fish. No matter that a black skimmer is not exactly a shearwater. To Peter, the name had a "sort of poetry." Shearwater! It stayed in the mind.

While Annette tended to her visitors, Peter built a couple of small oil-burning kilns like the ones he had used in Curtis's workshop and dug clay from the Fairhaven beach. "What I always wanted to do," he said years later, "was to use the clay that underlies all of this region, about four to six feet down. Sedimentary clay, very fine grain." But the greasy beach clay didn't fire properly. "You put a piece of [that] clay in the kiln, and it all but fuses and it makes a gas. It bloats . . . it looks like a cinder when it comes out. It's all full of small holes. . . . I always wanted to fire it at a low temperature, just bisque to get rid of the plasticity, [and then] powder it up and add it to the body and find out what proportion was necessary to make it a good stoneware body." A few of those beach clay pieces were good enough to be sold. Peter gave them a colorless glaze, hoping to draw out the beauty of the brown clay itself. But he knew he would have to find something better.

A little after his return from Wayne, his father—who was now, legally, his business partner—had begun to keep an account of sales and expenses. On June 30, 1927, he tallied up his son's first year of work. The first two pottery buildings to rise on the grounds cost nearly $2,000. In them, Peter had produced "something like $600 worth of pottery" and had spent $673: almost $200 for potting supplies; $121 on kerosene, $37.25 in clay, and about $125 on the labor of his carpenter and handyman Herbert Beaugez (who was paid $12.50 a week) and his brother Mac, who was studying architecture at Tulane and worked, whenever he was in Ocean Springs, at the Pottery. On stock were eighty-nine large pieces of pottery and sixty-six small ones. A few of them, ranging from $2 to $9, were on consignment in retail shops in New Orleans. Walter's total investment came to $5,000 ($47,500 today), and the regular bills to about $50 a month. He had entered the business, he said, much against his inclination, and ignoring the warnings of his wife: "I am afraid Annette thinks I am commercializing Peter, and the artist will be lost in the businessman," he wrote Ellsworth Woodward. "I wouldn't like to do that, but would like the boy to make a living, and have a very clear plan outlined by which he can make a good one."

Part of that plan was a period of study at the prestigious School of Clay-Working and Ceramics at Alfred, New York, directed by Charles F. Binns, now known as the Father of American Studio Ceramics. Some of the country's finest potters had studied with him: Arthur Eugene Baggs (of Marblehead Pottery), R. Guy Cowan (of Cowan), Paul Ernest Cox, Elizabeth Gray Overbeck, Frederick Walrath, Mary Chase Perry Stratton (of Pewabic), and the legendary Adelaide Alsop Robineau, who once spent more than one thousand hours carving and glazing a vase. Alfred offered nondegree, six-week summer courses to eighteen or twenty students: teachers, sculptors, or potters who wanted to learn the basics of clay-working. Many were women who had worked as decorators and now wished to learn about the clay preparation, glazing, and high-fire work habitually done by men. Annette had seen the place—relatives and Newcomb friends lived nearby—and remembered there was "something about the atmosphere . . . that is very fine." Peter went in early July 1927, and took the course for beginners.

Like Peter's first teacher, Edmund deForest Curtis, with whom he kept up a correspondence, Binns was an idealist with a burning desire to form "artist-craftsmen." "The qualifications of a craftsman must be saturated and dominated by idealism," he wrote. "In the best, and in nothing but the best, can satisfaction be found, and no effort is too costly, no labor too severe to attain this end." He began each day with a wide-ranging lecture on the ceramics of different countries, and he opened Peter's eyes not only to ways of throwing, glazing, firing, and producing inexpensive tableware, but to the ideal of the "artist-potter." He was a master at high-fired stoneware, a wizard at glazes, a lover of simple, undecorated forms that did not stray too far from the practical. "A piece of pottery," he wrote, "is essentially a vessel, and as such should lend itself to some useful service. On the other hand, such a piece should be complete in itself. A vase should not need a bouquet or a spray of flowers to make it complete, but it should always be capable of such use. The same is true of a plate, and indeed of every example of the potter's art." Binns's classical simplicity left a deep mark on Peter.

From Ocean Springs, where they felt "as if we had lost a right arm," his parents sent news of the Pottery, the family, and Peter's beloved *Gypsy*. Mac was home for the summer from Tulane, working steadily on some figurines of Mexican "peons" and on a series of tiles, "with mother assisting." He had developed "a new motif of pine cone and needles that is very nice indeed," only one of which cracked in the firing. Bob was somewhere in France, walking toward Spain, on his traveling fellowship. Annette was thinking constantly about her children's artistic future. "Learn the fundamental ideas underlying design," she advised twenty-six-year-old Peter. "It will help you immensely. . . . The more you work at the artistic end, the better in every way. Don't go in for quantity, but quality. You cannot compete with the big factories if you wanted to, and I hope you don't want to. Individual distinguished work that is unique is what will . . . bring you the greatest happiness. . . . Don't forget that next summer you go to Copenhagen. I don't want you to be provincial." Those who had bought her son's first pieces—a lamp base, an "openwork lavender jar"—seemed delighted with them. In his absence, his little "fifty-cent pieces" had quickly disappeared. The owner of a New Orleans lunchroom and souvenir shop, the Green Shutter, wanted about two or three dozen little cream pitchers, cheap. "How about it?" Annette asked. "If you make the shapes, large mouths, small, I will put on the spouts and handles, and we will sell them cheap. It would be a good advertisement. Will you sell them for fifty cents apiece? I will not need pay." She was already busy making lamp shades for Peter's bases, hoping, as always, to get away by herself for a while—perhaps to New Orleans, where she could concentrate on writing and painting.

As had happened when he returned from Wayne, Peter's return from Alfred in August 1927 inspired a burst of activity. That fall, Walter wrote jokingly to a friend that Shearwater was building an Exhibition Hall more or less on the order of the Crystal Palace, and was going to stock it for the winter and spring Gulf Coast trade. Down the road from the workshop, carpenters hammered away at a showroom, with a packing room and office space. It was finished in time for Shearwater's opening to the public on January 19, 1928. Peter was in bed with the flu, but no

fewer than two hundred visitors came that day and the next to admire—
so the newspapers tell us—about two hundred pieces, ranging from small
jugs to large jardinieres. Business was brisk. By February 2, his father said,
he had sold about 10 percent of the cost of the showroom.

A month later, spring began on schedule, in all its fragrant splendor.
"It is so lovely down here that I wish you could see the place," Walter
wrote cruelly to a friend in Chicago. "Camellias are in full swing in the
open air and my rose bushes are sprouting to beat the band." The Pottery, too, seemed to be blossoming. It was what Bob called growing
weather. Shearwater was poised between two periods: the initial days of
trial and error, with local sales to family, friends, and occasional visitors,
and the not-so-distant time when it would receive its first modicum of
national recognition.

A stream of northern visitors came South between mid-December
and early March, and Walter was pleased to think that the pots were now
in homes from Massachusetts to California and as far north as Manitoba.
Wealthy buyers came also from nearby Gulf Hills, where Chicago devel-
opers were putting up "Spanish-style" homes around a magnificent golf
course. The local landscape had begun to change. As one newspaper put
it, "faith and confidence have been translated into stone and steel, concrete and creosote." A cement seawall was crawling down the coast toward Ocean Springs—it had already reached Biloxi—and a bridge now
spanned Back Bay. Bridges over Chef Menteur, the Rigolets, and the
West Pearl River began to replace the old ferries and make New Orleans
more accessible by car (it took the Andersons a good four hours to get
there in their Ford touring car: more than double what it takes today). A
smooth automobile road, the Old Spanish Trail, now passed Ocean
Springs on its way from San Diego, California, to Saint Augustine,
Florida. Sleek, punctual Pullmans like the *Panama Limited* and *Mississip-
pian* made the trip from Chicago to Gulfport in twenty-one hours (as
compared to forty-two hours by car along the "Magnolia Route"). New
hotels rose along the Coast, bringing tourists and conventioneers (one
arrived in a fur coat and wired his wife in Iowa: S.O.S. B.V.D. P.D.Q.).

To Walter, the future had become very clear: "The men who come fish, shoot and mainly play golf. Their wives sit in the hotels, play bridge, etc., and drive along the coast. Women like to shop, and like to have an object for their drives." It was time, he said, to put samples of Shearwater in every one of those new hotels; to "make Shearwater as well known as the Biloxi lighthouse"; to give northern travelers a taste of something other than "the regulation art shop." Something more charming and rustic. Like those who ran Jugtown Pottery, in North Carolina, Walter hoped to exploit that rusticity in a sensible way. "At first I thought of a showroom in Gulfport or Biloxi," he wrote to a friend. "But we have good concrete roads to within a quarter mile of the place coming from Bay St. Louis on one side and from Mobile on the other. It is on the main highway—New Orleans via Mobile North—known as the Old Spanish Trail, and I thought that the effect of finding such a place as I have built in the middle of the pine woods, would be more interesting to Northern visitors than the regulation art shop right in the middle of a town. So far our limited experience has proved me right. The Gulf Hills people put in my road up to the show room. Our place is almost the only place on the whole coast where the original pine trees are standing. It has never been cut over. My building is right in the thick of those woods with an outlook over Biloxi Bay. It couldn't have a prettier location."

The influx of northern visitors, and the competition with other vacation spots—California, and especially Florida—raised troubling questions of authenticity and identity. For both the town and the Pottery, this was a pivotal moment of self-definition. By 1928, all fifty-five miles of the Gulf Coast had been "built up almost like one big city." Given its natural beauty, the Coast hoped to "drain the Mississippi Valley of pleasure-seekers and tourists." The danger was that, in the rush of development, it would lose its own charm and character. Walter was aware of those issues: he heard them discussed at the Rotary Club and the Mississippi Coast Association. And Annette, always an avid reader, must have known of their national resonance. Southern writers like the Fugitives held forth in literary journals and popular magazines about saving the South from the industrial encroachments of the North. One distinguished visitor, George Horace Lorimer, editor of the *Saturday Evening Post,* posed the matter of individuality in botanical terms. "Why imitate Florida and California?" he asked a business group in February 1927. And why call the Gulf Coast "America's Riviera"? Little Pascagoula was touted in a brochure as the Los Angeles of Mississippi. Why not "cut out all the imitation stuff"? The greatest tourist spots were made "by sticking to native trees and shrubbery," and, presumably, to native clay. "The palms transplanted here are not native, look out of place, and are not nearly as attractive as the beautiful oaks, dogwood and other native growth. Anyway, the tourist prefers naturally to visit the original and not the imitation."

From its very earliest days, Shearwater was—quite consciously—a sort of oasis. Not an imitative oasis of fake pools and potted palms, stucco and "Colonial" roof tiles, alluding to a "Spanish Mission" past lifted from southern California. And not the organized earthly paradise of bungalows and tennis courts and golf courses promoted so strenuously at Gulf Hills or Miramar or Beach Park or Pines on the Bay or Edgewater (names like these were multiplying). Within a short walk of the Pottery, land was selling for as much as $5,000 ($48,000) an acre. The area was already, in 1928, being carved into what the newspapers called "modern residential sub-divisions." But at Shearwater, the Coast was allowed simply to be itself, in a quiet, unassuming way that sparked the imaginations of visitors. "It is a place for poets," wrote a sentimental journalist who visited the Pottery, a place "to weave dreams, to look out over the water and see if one's ship is coming, [and] live in the very atmosphere of romanticism."

Slowly, Peter's "art" business began to grow. By spring 1928, he was able to produce from 150 to 200 pieces per month, mostly thrown ones. His brothers were still away. Mac was studying for exams, and his plans were "still in the air." He was about to leave Tulane, where he had been studying architecture and drawing with the artist and archaeologist

William Spratling. For two years, he had been living in New Orleans, close to the campus, at the home of his Aunt Adele. To his father, he seemed less strong physically than he should be: it would be better to have him at Fairhaven, and give him more outdoor life for a year or two. Walter and Annette made much less fuss about him as an artist than about Peter and Bob. They thought of him as a future architect. But his talent for drawing and for carving was unmistakable, and, no doubt, he could contribute to the "design" department. Bob was in Philadelphia, in his final days at the Pennsylvania Academy of Fine Arts, a little the worse for wear: recently, another student had made a life mask of his face, painfully removing his mustache and some of his hair. He was doing a large work—a painting or a wood carving—for a space over the mantel of the Front House. Some knights, apparently. Not in armor, but, to his mother's astonishment, naked: "don't you think they need clothes?" Often, sometimes twice a week, she wrote him news of Fairhaven. A recent visitor had admired the wood carvings—some chests and a couple of angels—he had done the summer before; signs of genius, he had said. She hoped Bob would return for the summer: "With your studio and the pottery, you could go ahead wonderfully. . . . I have always seen you in the pottery with your painting going on at the same time. It sounds ideal." After Philadelphia, Ocean Springs would seem confining, and Fairhaven rather insular. She could see that it needed to be enlivened socially, "with outside people, teas, etc." She vowed to "develop that way." But it seemed obvious to her that "no one can do his best work in a school, and Ocean Springs is a wonderful spot if we can keep in touch with a bigger place."

For the moment, that bigger place was still New Orleans. There had been steady sales in a couple of shops there. A few vases and bowls had been exhibited and sold at Newcomb College, and many more at the Arts and Crafts Club, on Royal Street, where the boys' work was exhibited and praised in the New Orleans papers. In a gift shop on Coliseum Street, Catherine Priestly Labouisse, a former Newcomb decorator and family friend, sold Shearwater vases, lamp bases, flowerpots, bright yellow sculptures of fish, and wood carvings, and kept Peter and his "secretarial" father busy with advice and special requests. "Have you any demand for tableware?" Walter asked her. "The northerners who were down here this winter spoke of an increasing demand for plates, cups, saucers, goblets of pottery for table use and we are debating the advisability of taking this up." Bowls seemed less useful than small vases or large pieces that could be turned into lamps, especially turquoise or bright yellow, which sold better than any other color. And why not some inexpensive items, downright "pot-boilers"? Paper matchboxes were much too ugly for discerning people, and Mac's "fish match-holders" had been a great success. He had done them as "a private venture" during his vacations. Why not produce "some very simple ones for the fancy colored matches that are now the style. . . ? I sell the small boxes of matches and have had requests for something to hold them, as people like to have them on their table with the various colored match heads standing up."

Peter would try his hand at producing those "in quantity," eight or ten at a time. Attentive to her customers, alert to bubbles and slight imperfections, Catherine Labouisse was not afraid to criticize inferior work or scold the potter and his brothers. In her shop, Shearwater had to hold its own against truly exquisite pieces by Newcomb: bowls, tiles, vases, and pitchers thrown by the renowned Meyer and decorated and glazed by women with decades of experience. She taught Peter the right way to pierce a lamp base, and when the Andersons sent her some of Bob's carved angels to sell at Christmastime, she suggested he take them back "and put a dull antique finish on the gold and remove the screws and twine from the sides to back, and disguise the tacks or nails which, in one at present, stick so far out that they are really dangerous to handle. . . . Anything selling as high as these should have a more finished appearance." She provided advice on pricing, too, suggesting that the Pottery raise prices on one particular consignment from 33$\frac{1}{3}$ to 50 percent. Walter demurred: "We want to try and furnish better and better pottery, and except in the case of special pieces, at reasonable prices. We believe this will pay in the long run."

He took his own advice and made haste slowly, keeping a critical eye on Peter's work, some of which seemed "perfect or as near perfect of its kind" as any pottery he had seen. But quality would have to improve before he pushed for a national market. Having an outlet in Chicago—which sent so many tourists to Ocean Springs—seemed important; he wanted to look into that. But he politely turned down a suggestion that Peter exhibit and sell his work in New York's prestigious Potters' Shop, on Madison Avenue, where his vases would have stood beside those of his own teacher—Charles F. Binns—and other masters. "Peter's modesty must be inherited, as I feel that we are not quite ready to tackle New York." Embarrassed over having broken a piece Shearwater had loaned for display, Mississippi's commissioner of agriculture offered to include one of Peter's vases in a permanent exhibit in the Old Capitol Building. Another polite refusal from Walter: "Some day when we have made a name for our pottery, we will be glad to donate a piece for that purpose."

Much depended upon the kiln. Peter's original little wood-fired groundhog kiln never produced a single good pot. Later, in Wayne and at Alfred, he had heard of the advantages of oil, a relatively new technique in American potteries: so new that the nearly omniscient Binns found himself writing to Curtis for detailed instructions on evenly heating the oil kiln he had built at Alfred. A technical paper by a "consulting combustion engineer" in a trade journal of 1926 lists its advantages over coal. Ceramic bodies are affected not only by temperature, but also by the rate of heating, and with oil, "a turn of the valves will give any rate desired." Oil was more economical, underwent more complete combustion before hitting the ware, and was more practical in a small space: "There are no coal or ash heaps around the kiln or coal and ash dust in the air." With coal, then favored by industry, the ware had to be carried over two hundred feet from the adjoining shop to protect it from dust.

Curtis was an oil enthusiast. But the two little oil-burning kilns Peter had built on returning from Wayne had proved inadequate. In 1927, while Peter was at Alfred, his father had pointed out that, had even 90 percent of his pieces fired correctly, "you would have produced, [not $600, but] several thousand dollars of stuff at very little increased cost. . . . You would have needed more glaze, as very little reached the glazing stage. No doubt part of the trouble was in the clay, but the kiln was mainly responsible. Try and make up your mind, after going into it thoroughly, what kiln to get and we will get it. Get the figures on the different kinds, not only as to first cost, but cost of running. Try them yourself if you can, while you are with Binns, if possible."

With his son back home, his father made some inquiries, and by summer 1928 Peter had sent sketches for kilns to an engineer at Newcomb, W. Harry Rogers, for his suggestions. None of Peter's own designs seemed feasible. For room and board and $10 per week salary, and "no work on weekends," Rogers agreed to spend a month at Shearwater, supervising construction of the new kiln and teaching Peter to fire it. The weather would be hot, Walter predicted, "but the workshop is a cool place and it will be a great help to Peter to have someone with him who understands his work." Paul E. Cox, a student of Binns's who had worked for years at Newcomb, went to Ocean Springs to approve the final designs. He left Peter with a handful of glaze formulas that he would use for years, and some advice for speeding up production. The kiln had a steel shell, to keep the walls from bulging. A team of oxen pulled it down the shell road to its place on Pottery Hill. After it was ready, it had to be lined with firebrick. "There was a retired bricklayer, Taylor, that had built a chimney for my mother," Peter remembered. "He gave us suggestions about the brick to use. . . . The dome was built on a clay form supported by wooden timbers. Bricks were locked in one course at a time. He had to cut every brick in the dome. . . . He had a helper or two."

The imposing new kiln was similar in design and appearance to the one at Newcomb College. It was used regularly at Shearwater for almost seventy years until 1997, when it needed extensive repairs, no one could find the time to repair it, and the ware began to be fired in an electric kiln. Its beautiful brick chimney delighted Walter, that spring of 1928, as he watched it rising "majestically" through the pine trees. "It is to be 30 feet, and Taylor is the steeplejack."

It would take Peter many months to accommodate himself to the new kiln, fired for the first time, in an experimental way, on December 14, 1928. A couple of the last items to emerge from the old one were two ruined pieces by "Bob the maker of cats." One was—in Walter's words—a "cubistical blue cat," which, "with the perversity of all cubistical things," exploded. A family friend had wanted the other as a gift for someone in New York. "I am awfully sorry to say that the Shearwater kiln, ably handled by Mr. Peter Anderson—our venerable president—has misbehaved itself lamentably and turned a white cat into a very disreputable grey alley cat. If it were a good grey cat, a decent-looking animal, there would be some hope for him. As it stands he is one of the most horrible examples of the cat tribe: splotched and blistered all over; one palpable black eye on one side and none at all on the other. He might at a pinch do for the Bowery, but he would be a terrible blemish to Fifth Avenue. As a door stop he would have to go behind the door in the kitchen, and might be tolerated there in the dark."

Peter tossed both of them out the back of the workshop into the marsh. After his return from Wayne, he had started what the Mississippi painter Marie Hull later named the "Glory Road." With rubbish from the workshop, shards from pots he had deliberately broken, and the connivance of his paternal partner, he was making a path through the soggy ground to the pier where he kept the *Gypsy*. It was his road to success as a potter, and a great help to him whenever he loaded his boat. Years later, Bob's wife, Sissy, marveled over that path, "made of old saggers, bits of broken pots, anything hard, to bolster the trembling marsh. It was wheelbarrow width and the bright colors shining through the grass were startling. It was a sort of archaeologist's paradise. Heads and other parts of little figures stared up; pieces of molds with intricate designs, bits of copper red experiments: a wealth of artifacts." Peter and his father estimated that he had broken over 2,500 pots—sometimes entire kiln loads—before Shearwater opened to the public. His business between 1925 and 1927, Walter said, was "making and breaking pottery. It seemed to me at the time that no one else could possibly ever have made before so many shapes only to see them crack, blister, craze, crackle, and leak. I suppose it was only the ordinary experience of a young potter learning his job. But I do think he was a very unusually persevering and determined one."

LOVE AND GLAZES

One night in July 1929, Walter dreamed that his head was stuck inside a pot, and that the only way to get it out was to break it. "And *that* of course Peter will not stand for." Walter was "potbound." In the office, his elegant Victorian desk was afloat in "a sea of pots." By now, it wasn't his son who had to be restrained from smashing them; it was Mr. Anderson, Sr., who was wondering "what the Deuce to do with this avalanche without resorting to breakage on a large scale."

What had started that avalanche was love. In fact, it was love, as much as Walter's business head and Annette's passion for art, that helped

Shearwater grow from its infancy into a "going concern." It was Cupid himself who goaded the Anderson boys into digging clay and throwing pots, and who guided to their door two sisters, Patricia and Agnes Grinstead—Pat and Sissy—who lived down the Coast in Gautier on a country estate called Oldfields. In 1929, Pat had returned there after attending a secretarial school in Boston and working as a fund-raiser for the University of Pittsburgh. Sissy, almost two years younger, was on vacation from Radcliffe, where she was a fine arts major.

One day that spring, Pat, her mother (Marjorie Hellmuth Grinstead), and a friend went to have a look at the showroom. When Mrs. Grinstead asked in Ocean Springs for directions to the Pottery, someone told her, "You don't want to go *there*. There's an artist colony in the woods. They probably run around *naked.*" But the three of them persisted and were rewarded. A kiln had been opened days earlier, and the shelves and tables were crowded with bowls, pitchers, and lamp bases glazed by Peter in "frosty blue" or purple or "mottled green" on gray, bronzes, and mahoganies and white enamel. There were cubist cats by Bob in turquoise blue or "dark grey luster," gaily colored pirates, pelicans, ducks, and bookends, and a tall vase with a scene from the Battle of New Orleans.

While her mother was buying Sissy one of Bob's pieces—a cream-colored bowl with a frieze of horses—Pat saw Peter on one of the paths.

[He] walked toward me down a quiet road. How handsome he was! He shone in splendid beauty before me. He walked with such strength and grace. There was a glory round him. That minute, I adored him. He spoke [and] no music matched his voice. I loved him. I was transported. . . . We touched hands and I trembled. . . . How forward I may have been I cannot tell. I only existed for Peter. Such sweetness had never been in any life, ever. I was projected into him. Divinity came down and dwelt shining all about us two together. When he said one July day, walking across a beach, holding my hand, "I'm afraid I'm going to love you," I died and was reborn. . . . I know he did not kiss me then. One night we drove out in his car. We stopped and he

took me in his arms. That was the first kiss I had ever had, or ever wanted, and I can feel it still on my lips.

It was true, she wrote later, "that I had had the habit of falling in love quite madly ever since I can remember. I can't have been over four or five when I first tried it, and the loved one was at least twenty-five, perhaps thirty. He played the piano. . . ." Over the years, there had been other infatuations. She loved giving her "whole soul and heart to people." But Peter was different. He had a sort of aura.

Walter had never been able to discern any such halo around his son. But he never forgot that day. "You had with you two very nice young persons," he wrote Mrs. Grinstead, and "when I saw one of them, I thought her quite the nicest girl I had seen for many long days. I told the boys that if they wanted to meet some nice girls that there were at least two living in Gautier." He supposed it did not become him to praise either pottery or "boy." But Peter, too, was a treasure. "[He] has one very important possession. That is lots of courage. He has stuck to his pottery under conditions that would have taken all the heart out of most boys. Met failure after failure and worked away until he won some degree of success. I think Miss Patricia can count upon him absolutely, through good conditions or bad, and that he is sure to win out. Further, she has given him something very important to work for."

The meeting on the path occurred on Thursday, May 16, 1929, and for the rest of the month and all of June they saw each other every evening. Barely two months later, Walter was writing to a friend in New York that his son was "engaged to marry one of the nicest girls (and prettiest) you ever saw and is grinding out pots as if his and her future happiness depended on quality and quantity of out-turn, which is, of course, to a certain extent the case." The wedding date was set for April 16, William Grinstead's birthday. "That'll be my present to you, Daddy," Pat told him. "You'll be rid of me at last!"

The romance created a certain urgency at the Pottery. "Peter's latest idea," wrote Walter, "is that I should have some circus posters printed—

large and bright and not more than 1,000 or 10,000—and me and Mac jump in the Ford and paste placards from one end of the Gulf Coast to the other, advertising his blooming pots. He says it would work, but I *won't*. Would you? Even if your son told you to? Have to draw a line somewhere."

To Peter, no measure, not even those circus posters, seemed too extreme. "I'm going to marry you as soon as you'll have me," he wrote Pat. "I'll take that old pottery between my hands and squeeze until money has to come from it!" An exhibition was planned for August and announcements were sent to every local newspaper on the Coast. *That* was it, Walter thought, emphasize the *local:* "This Pottery is a local enterprise. The work is being done by local men, the clay used is mostly local mud, and the money collected from our buyers is spent locally, trying to keep the local wolves from the local door." From local Gautier, Pat's father came calling, and found himself "deeply impressed by the quality and beauty of the work your boy—may I say 'our boy'—is turning out." The conversation turned to how to transcend "the local," and sell Shearwater in the North. Days later, Walter wrote to "My dear Mr. Grinstead" and asked him to help find agents in Pittsburgh, reminding him that Shearwater was never going to produce in quantity, and that its aim was "to make better and better individual pieces, mostly variously glazed, but a good proportion in the shape of decorated pieces and figurines."

"With such good things to offer, and with the right sort of connections," Mr. Grinstead answered, Shearwater would doubtless "realize all of Peter's and your hopes. And I can think of no occupation more conducive to the happiness of our young people."

As Pat and Peter drew closer that summer—played tennis with Sissy and Bob and Mac, had tea at Oldfields or Shearwater, sailed on the Grinsteads' aging *Marjorie* or on Peter's *Gypsy*—they thought often about how different they were. Raised in Gautier and in Sewickley, a well-to-do suburb of Pittsburgh, and schooled in Boston, Pat was extraordinarily outgoing and gregarious, and accustomed to a larger world than that of Ocean Springs. Would she fit in there? At times it seemed rather isolated, and her "divine" Peter, her radiant vision, thought of himself as a little strange, "stupidly introspective," an "unsocial person," barely able to play a successful game of bridge with his parents and their friends: it was Mac who was the "varsity" bridge player. And who needed bridge? Who could stand the suffocating radiators and cigar smoke? It was the "sort of thing one wants in bi-annual doses," Peter wrote. How could a "hermit" like him marry his "revelation," his "angel of light"?

Among the family heirlooms is a thick scrapbook meticulously put together by Pat in 1924–1925. This was several years before she met Peter, a memento of a long stay in Paris together with Pat's mother, Sissy, and their friend Ellen Wassall. The two Grinstead girls had already made several trips there, accompanying their father on business, when they were little. Postcards and menus, concert programs and tourist pamphlets, are pasted to the carefully numbered and indexed pages. In 1924, the Grinsteads had sailed on the *Suffren,* and the elegantly printed list of cabin passengers reminds us what a curious and sociable person Pat was. Beside more than a third of those names, she has jotted down her verdicts: "uninteresting," "divine voice," "very sweet and very flirtatious." She would probably have gotten farther had she not collided with "the best looking man that ever was created," a wealthy farmer from Cleveland, with whom she spent hours on board and later in Paris, where his wholesome, down-home manner stood out against (Sissy joked), "the simpering Paris lads/who must keep the style and know the fads." For the next nine months, Sissy, Ellen, and Pat worked on their French at a lycée at Versailles and attended an art course at the Louvre.

By the time of her engagement to Peter, Pat had already made plans for another trip to France: this one to study piano in a musical academy near Sceaux, outside Paris. There was no question of canceling the trip; her parents believed the year away from Peter would give her time to think. Mr. Grinstead had hopes of her becoming a pianist, but that year (1929–1930), as she sat practicing or listening to records in the little studio at Sceaux, she often found herself "too empty-headed to do anything but admire the lights in my diamond," "practicing with a broad smile on my face—probably looking rather foolish." On her trips to Paris, she found herself, more than once, hunting for pottery in private galleries or climbing the marble stairways to the home of "ceramiques asi bien de poterie" at the Louvre. The city was full of pottery, "and everyone is interested in it." In fact, before boarding the *Carmania* in September, she had stopped at the Boston Society of Arts and Crafts, in hopes that Peter might sell his work there. "No pottery like Shearwater," she wrote him proudly. "I wanted you to be with me because you like to see other work and some of it was awfully nice—none that looked cheap. . . . I saw a batch the jury had just passed on, and it was very thick with dense-looking glazes and unground looking 'bottoms,' good colors, I think, beloved. Are you laughing at me, beloved? You might be, but you don't mind my arts and crafting, do you?" Peter's Boston debut—two turquoise pieces of his own and one decorated by Bob—was only months away.

Neither Peter nor Pat was used to writing what they referred to as "fiancé letters," and that fall and winter he sometimes apologized for his "vaporings" and chuckled at the "beautiful light airy things that pass back and forth between Pat and her Peter." Write about the pottery, she told him. And news of Shearwater kept them going all autumn and winter; news from Peter and from his parents. Not only had he bought "an awful lot of five-cent stamps," he was urging *everyone* on the place to write. First to obey was his father, with a "steamer letter" delivered to the dock in Boston. From behind a wall of pottery in the showroom, he wondered:

How should a father-in-law to be address you? Dear Pat, Dearest Pat or. . . ? I want the one that expresses most but am still somewhat diffident, so it shall be

Dear Pat:
A man named Peter Anderson—you may remember him—small man, about my size, usually rather muddy in his attire, has instructed me to write

you a steamer letter. Says you like steamer letters and further indicated force-
fully that if you liked them you had to have them, so this is a steamer letter.
He also told me to order some silicate of soda. That is a simple matter, and has
been attended to, but the other isn't so simple.

I suppose the first thing is to wish you very sincerely a pleasant voyage,
which I do with all my heart. May you have the blue skies and sunshine that
have steadily prevailed since you left us. All nature seems to be rejoicing at your
departure. That don't sound right . . .

There is an exception: Peter. He wasn't what I need as a cheerful com-
panion, not by any means. Saturday night we spent tête à tête. Mrs. Anderson
was in New Orleans with Bob, Mac was off at Movies, and Saturday night,
alone with Peter, will linger long in my memory as a sort of Noche Triste. *I*
suppose he was thinking about something, and words between us were few and
far apart. Of course, I was anxious to make up to him for your absence, but you
will readily understand that I failed miserably. Sunday he took the Gypsy *up*
to Lamey's Bridge for a fresh-water bath to last two weeks, and today is Mon-
day. I have mailed you three letters from him, and he has received one this
morning from you: I recognized your chirography. He fired the little kiln Sat-
urday morning, but it was a bust. Today he is glazing for a firing of the big kiln,
all wrapped up in a respirator arrangement; not the kiln, but Peter. . . .

Annette wrote, too, and, characteristically, asked her for samples of
her writing. "Some day, when you want to please your mother-in-law to
be, send me something you have written, like the little sketch Peter let
me see with your permission last summer. Poems, perhaps." Her son may
have looked lovelorn and grim as he did his glazing and fired his kilns,
but the whole family had noticed a change in him. He "never seems to
have had the understanding or home life that he wanted and needed,"
wrote Walter's sister, Peter's Aunt Daisy, who knew that Annette favored
Bob. "And now you have come into his life, he is already happier. I
wanted to help him, but did not know how. For he is not like anybody
but his own self, bless him. I loved him but could not reach him." "Dear
old Peter has not had an easy time," she added months later. "I am so

grateful that he has you. Bob and Mac will always get on, but Peter is different. He needs happiness, and you are giving it to him."

Pat, too, seemed transformed, "full of antics and excitements" as she made plans for the wedding and tried on her gown in a store in Paris, followed about the store by her friend and "almost-sister" Ellen Wassall and an exasperated *essayeuse*. Peter had never met Ellen, and Pat introduced her by letter. To Pat, her life seemed unbelievably tragic and eventful. She wanted Peter to know everything possible about his future almost-sister-in-law.

First, she is as much a part of the Grinstead family as any member of it bearing that name. And has been, since before I was born. She was there at Oldfields when I was born, so she knows me quite intimately as it were. Just at this moment I can't think of anyone who has had more unhappiness and sorrow than Ell, or who has come through it more beautifully. We all adore her as everyone who knows her does. Since she's to be one of your second family I'll tell you everything you might, after knowing her, ask yourself.

Through some miserable doctor's fault there was an injury at birth which has made her a little lame and she hasn't always complete control of her hands. There is enough misfortune to make most people bitterly unhappy for life! Her father and mother were divorced. From what I know, her mother, a musician, was a selfish, horrid person. Ell hates to even speak of her. Her father was a fine Englishman. When the two were divorced the mother took Ellen's brother and her new husband—the now famous [lawyer] Thomas Chadbourne— adopted him so that he is LeRoi Chadbourne instead of Joseph Wassall! (That Mrs. Chadbourne died some years ago. I remember the day and Ell showing me the telegram with a white face. "My mother is dead. It doesn't mean a thing to me!") My grandmother went to be with Ellen then, and gave her the first happiness she'd ever had, aside from her adoration of her father. When she was fourteen or fifteen Dr. Wassall was drowned in Lake Michigan, swept from the deck of a yacht in an icy blizzard with a heavy overcoat on. They never found the least trace of him. Ell was broken-hearted and adores him still. There was a great fracas and disagreement with Mrs. Chadbourne, who insisted that she should have Ellen, who refused to go to her, insisting that she would never leave Granny whom she worshiped. All kinds of legal fuss and disgusting publicity for Ellen and Granny. But finally Ell was a member of our family and she has been ever since. The two of them were at Oldfields a lot, and traveled the rest of the time. Once in a while I, being an adorer of Granny's, went off with them for a month or two. I know Ell was happy with Granny who gave her a wonderful self-confidence. Remember, my dearest one, that she could never do the things other people do. My grandmother died in 1919, which was as hard for Ellen as it was for all of us. We were inseparable by then and to have suggested that she do anything but stay with us would have been ridiculous. She and Granny had been abroad, so she welcomed the idea of crossing with us in 1924 with joy. . . . We came home the summer of '25 and Ell came back with us in the fall. Since then she has been in Paris, with side trips, and usually comes home in the summer as Oldfields is her most adored place.

Then, Peter, I think the saddest, most unbelievable thing of all happened. The Duncans had a charming scientist brother-half-brother, Egerton Grey, and year before last he and Ellen met and fell in love with each other. He had been married to an English-Egyptian, an unbearable sounding person, and was getting a divorce from her when he met Ell. He didn't want to tell her he loved her, but he couldn't help it. I think you can understand that, my darling, because I can so well. They were terribly happy. So happy, Peter, they adored each other, just as we do. I know it because I've heard Ellen talk so much about the few months they had together. Ell came to be with us at Gautier for the summer of 1928, when the divorce would have been culminated, and they could have been married. On Ellen's birthday we gave a party for her and a letter came saying very calmly that Egerton Grey was dead. Peter, I hate to write it even. . . . In spite of everything, Ellen is always ready for anything, always amusing, more fun than anyone else I know and the cleverest person you can imagine. Also as pretty, almost beautiful. If souls made one beautiful, she surely would be. So of course, Ell will come home with me in March for our wedding.

As he wrote to Pat that fall and winter, Peter sometimes felt as though he were writing to the artist in himself. He was defining Shearwater, deciding what was "Shearwaterish" and what wasn't (how she liked that suffix!). Writing things down was a great help, as it had been a couple of years back, in Wayne. It made "vague ideas less vague and gives birth to new ones." He was laying plans, and educating her about pottery—he had already gotten her to read a book or two—and trying to imagine her in the showroom at Shearwater. "Lucky lucky customers! I'm going to enjoy watching you with them. . . . I enjoy watching you always no matter what you're doing. Pat fishing—Pat turning somersaults on the Isle of Caprice—Pat wildly pursuing crabs on Horn Island—Pat nibbling on crackers as Peter drinks milk. Aren't we going to be perfectly idiotically sublimely happy together?"

Walter added his encouragement, sending a "help-wanted" ad on the letterhead of

SHEARWATER POTTERY

East Beach Road

Ocean Springs, Miss

WANTED BY THE ABOVE

Amiable young woman with a sunny disposition and a cheerful smile to act as stenographer, saleswoman, bookkeeper, cashier, corresponding clerk, packer, entertainer. Must love pottery (more than I do) and know all about ART. Salary no object (to her) so there isn't any. Apply to the above any time of the day or night.

Peter suspected the job would take some adjusting on her part. "Poor Pat, next winter, instead of Gay Paree, you'll have the Biloxi movie. But there will be other things, too, to reconcile you to the quiet life." Couldn't she slow down a bit, stop rushing around Paris, so that "the Ocean Springs sort of living will not be in too great a contrast"? Not that she ought to feel bound to Ocean Springs for life. "We might move north for the summer to make pots on the New England Coast. It's nice to know that it's possible, anyway. But we'll try hard to like Ocean Springs first; we both do now. . . . I was only thinking of the future, and a little of your past wanderings."

He was wrong, she told him; the simplicity attracted her. "Everything we do and everything you say is beautiful to me and I couldn't *glorify* any of it by being away because it is so *true* and clearly perfect in the beginning. I feel very humble and so thankful that it is you and that it really is me and not just a gorgeous fantasy to be dissolved by some sudden reality. Of course there will be lots of realities, and perhaps sudden ones, but never the kind that could hurt Peter's and Pat's love. I love you because you're Peter Anderson and because you're beautifully different, *not* strange, remember, and because I long to look at you and feel your hair and you have the finest eyes on earth and you never had any but splendid-nice thoughts and because you love me and I've never had one single tiny doubt of anything you've said or done. . . . "

With his "shock of lovely hair" that always needed cutting, Peter would have been anyone's dream, after the "French, American and English expatriated dandies," the "degenerate, fine-mannered, hairwaved, lacrimose men" that gazed at her in Parisian cafés. "Peter, I can't *believe* you when I see these people." He shouldn't worry about Ocean Springs or about her love of travel. Having spent her childhood at Oldfields, miles from a real town, she wasn't afraid of the isolation, and she would be glad not to live "in a big city where everything is rush and bother and money. I wonder if you've ever realized just how happy I am to come to Ocean Springs to live—or just how much I love the water, the islands— in fact just the Mississippi Coast. . . . And do you know how proud I am of Shearwater and that being proud of it is just a little of my love for you in another form? How miserably explained, but it's the best I can do!"

The best she could do! Expressing their love for one another was as difficult as describing glazes in the days before they could be captured easily in color photographs. It was glazes that Shearwater's future seemed most to depend on—this was what might set it apart from other small potteries—and it isn't surprising that Peter's love letters speak so often of

104

color. "It is in glazes," he says, "that I hope to make our fortune." It was novelty in the showroom that sold pots, and novelty depended on new shapes and, above all, on new glazes. He had grown weary of his best-selling everyday turquoise. Today, no matter how often one looks at it, that distinctive Shearwater blue suggests the cloudless radiance of the Gulf. Clear sky, translucent water. It *is* Shearwater. Back then, to Peter, it was simply routine. It was money. It was something of an embarrass-ment. He had been "sadly overdoing turquoise," and had to banish it from some of his kilns. "It gives you away. Says very plainly 'I want to make money no matter if I make good pots or not.' "

Sometimes, at night, when his daily work was over, he walked out to the workshop, measured out ingredients for new glazes and ground them in his five-gallon ball mills. It was cold that fall and winter, a dan-ger to the unfired pots called greenware. He had to start a fire in the pot-bellied stove, and leave it going until morning to keep his pots and molds from cracking, and even then the filter press would need to be thawed out. But at night, in the silence of Pottery Hill, there were no distrac-tions from Bob or questions from his helper Clair Scharr or from cus-tomers or high school classes that wandered into the workshop. Other evenings, after supper, Annette or Bobby would read aloud before the fireplace at the Barn, with Bobby's two cats—the "gray old gentleman" Interference and a kitten, Stomach—interrupting the readings, and Peter would draw sustenance for his work. He needed those restful evenings. "I believe you can do better work if there is a reserve of energy in your body. You think better and enjoy what you're doing more. . . . I learned that from mother, who specializes in the whys and wherefores of being artistically fit."

All converged on pottery. Even Annette's beloved Thoreau seemed to offer advice on glazing. Life in the Concord woods wasn't all that dif-ferent from life at Shearwater. "I hadn't read much of him before, and that long ago. Seems to have a good deal of sense, and peace with his sur-roundings. I'm going to read more of him in hopes of a permanent ef-fect on my own way of living. I am too impatient, and Henry is anything but. . . . An impatient potter is hopeless. He must be willing and anxious to find out new things. That is just as much his job as making pots, and a pleasant job to a good potter. A quiet, unostentatious sort of exploration, very satisfying when the object is achieved, and so much more useful than finding the north Pole."

A "quiet, unostentatious sort of exploration" was what he was doing with form and color. Setting out from turquoise, he wandered off pleasurably toward other parts of the spectrum. His canvas, his color chart, was the showroom. He and Annette composed it like a still life. She spent hours getting the pieces in just the right position. And Peter could tell, from a look in the door, what was missing. It "needs new, strong color," he wrote one day. "The color effect at present is horribly green, owing to turquoise and antique green." Something had to be done. Build a larger storeroom where overabundant colors could be hidden. Touch up the picture with wildflowers. Find new colors and combine them with textures. "The glazes I'm anxious to do now are not just colors but textures and effects. Almost emotion. Glazes you can't take your hands off." He wanted "a few really striking things," not only because they would sell, but because they would tone up the whole display and "give the average person who has no interest in pots something to remember."

Those glazes are caught forever, in black and white, in his letters that fall and winter. By spring, he had brought certain colors under control, to the point where his father was able to assign them numbers and abbreviations. Silver luster, which sparkled under lamplight; dark blue luster, silver blue and bronze. One day, a "lavender pink and a reddish pink" seemed "the best in texture and color." Pale blue with pink shoulders, or rather "capes." Rutile glazes with their streaked and runny effects did "nice things if coaxed properly." One firing was a "study in greens. Antique, crystalline and brownish green. All showing the effect of rutile on copper." There were greens with "small, paler green crystals" in "square or oblong" formations, a disappointing yellow, and numerous others that probably ended up in the marsh. Bob, Walter, and particularly Annette, with her critical eye, were there to judge his work and make suggestions.

"Mother and Dad went out to the kiln house to look at pots after supper, and the first time mother had seen this firing. She had been in New Orleans today. They were both so interested and appreciative. It's nice to have that sort of a family. No wonder I've been able to work. I've had plenty of backing financial and the other kind."

A number of new glazes were ready for inspection in the cool December air: "Pink enamel (not so good, with the exception of some large pieces decorated in a pinkish blueish brownish combination which were very nice), crystalline copper patina (too many crystals and too small to give the proper crystalline glaze) . . . Blue pinks (with blue ground pink haze around shoulders . . . I like it, though it's rather too sweet for a constant association). Lavender blue (a favorite of Mother's, who says it suggests a sort of plum unknown to me), with the blue over the lavender giving the bloom of the pristine plum with a darker tone under it. And two other glazes not worth mentioning. One a drab dark green, another watery blue with pink streaks (very negative). I believe I left out the antique green, of which you will receive a sample, so saving me the very great toil of describing it. I think the texture is fine, and want to get the same texture in other colors."

Another sort of chromatic fugue was being played out at the Front House. That fall of 1929, Annette and Walter had offered the house to Peter, who was living with them, Mac, and Bob at the Barn (Annette thought it blessed to have her three boys—twenty-eight, twenty-six, and twenty-two years old—under one roof). For years, only renters had lived at the Front House. Walter had always disliked it. The sound of the waves gave him a headache. As he lay awake at night, he could hear them lapping against a breakwater only feet from the front gallery and gnawing away at his property. The house was a bit run-down, Aunt Daisy told Pat, but it had great possibilities. "The rooms are very well proportioned, and the front gallery splendid. Also, the outlook from the dining room, which is unusually lovely . . . The garden has always been so untidy and neglected looking, but that's easily corrected if anyone cares." Peter moved into the place while he was renovating it. Unlike his father, he wanted to be as close to the water as possible, and liked to sleep on the gallery overlooking the Sound. Close to his cot lay a pen and paper:

It is early morning, the sun is just rising, and I am lying in bed on our front gallery finishing the letter begun last night to my darling Pat. This is a wonderful time of day, at this time of year particularly. . . . There is a nice little offshore breeze and the air is so fresh, almost alive, the light over the water is lovely and Deer Island looks unreal and far away. Oyster boats and crabbers are running about. . . . There is only one thing wrong—that is of men's doing of course and shouldn't be written, to spoil the picture I've made at such pains. . . . Them nasty low-down outboard motors destroy the beautiful morning quietness with their nerve-racking row. Blast em! Only at intervals. At the moment peace reigns once more.

There was much to do before Pat's arrival in the spring: a shower to install, with homemade tiles, and a new roof to put on, and, above all, the painting of walls and woodwork. In a gallant gesture, Peter decided to have them done in the colors of Pat's beloved Oldfields: black for the woodwork, and the walls in a white alabastrine, tinged with a strong orange. Annette objected. The woodwork wasn't very good, and black paint would only bring it out. Peter had to explain to Pat that his mother, as an "artist," was "terribly afraid of living with an inharmonious color scheme." After a few days, Annette acceded, and paid a visit to Oldfields, palette and oil paints in hand, to get the color exactly right. Peter spent a day in Biloxi hunting down the right paint stores and painters.

In February, when the ground had warmed up and the wind had blown away the last of the hickory leaves, and pear trees were in flower, Peter and Bob rowed to Eagle Point on Davis Bayou and drove to nearby Vancleave hunting for yellow azalea and snowbuds—there had been one at the house in New Orleans—to transplant to the Front House, "setting them out with much thought." Pink morning glories, the seeds brought from Horn Island, were to replace a wisteria Peter removed from the front steps, improving the view from the front gallery. He wanted no obstructions between the two of them and the water. He stood in the front yard at times, under the live oak trees, looking out over the Sound, savoring days so clear and cool that "you are not conscious of having a body."

That sort of weather reminded him of Pat: she was like the "gentle little offshore wind" he caught on the gallery in the early morning just before sunrise: "cool and deliciously fresh." The front yard, with its breakwater, was a wonderful place from which to observe a storm, and that, too, made him think of her.

A Northwester came out this morning just after breakfast. I was down at our house talking paint, standing on the edge of the bluff, and there suddenly appeared a great black bank of cloud almost like our summer squalls, only lower and with no lighter colored space over the horizon as they have. It led a strange dome-shaped band of greyer clouds above it, extending from southwest to northwest. First, little puffs of wind from the west with a fine drizzle, the wind rapidly strengthening and shifting northwest, and all the little oyster skiffs making for home just as fast as they could. The cloud bank dissolved in a second, and Back Bay became obscured in a white mist of rain with the railroad drawbridge showing vaguely through it. Whereupon, the raindrops descending with greater force and frequency upon my devoted head, I lost my taste for the beautiful spectacle before me and ran for the mud house. Next summer, my darling, we'll watch squalls come up in the same way, only we won't run away.

In the fall, those northwesters would sometimes blow all day, sweep the tides out, and promise to bring ducks. Peter would take off on Sundays and hunt with Mac and Bob, for "ducks need cold to make them circulate northward and duck hunters need it to disperse mosquitoes, flies, gnats and to preserve the kill." There were fishing trips on the *Gypsy* for redfish and speckled trout, croakers and channel mullet, and perch for "Father Abraham," Bob's pet pelican. But the *Gypsy* had other, more serious uses. Once or twice a year, Peter used her to haul clay from a spot up the Fish River in Alabama. He would dig it from a pit near a brickyard on the bank of the river, and load it into a little barge and into the *Gypsy* herself, leaving her much the worse for wear, smeared with wet, gooey clay and straining under the load. On the return trip, she was always "down in the front" and hard to steer. There are letters to Pat, written at the table "in the *Gypsy*'s odoriferous cabin" as Peter and a helper bounced around off Mobile "in an offshore chop." For years, he remembered how pleasant those trips were, despite the backbreaking work. After the clay was unloaded, he would mix it with flint, Tennessee ball clay, and soda spar from a spot in the Blue Ridge Mountains of North Carolina. Then, in liquid form, it was put through a homemade blunger (like a big mixing bowl), passed through a screen into a tub, and pressed into cakes in the filter press. Before he could use them on the wheel, the cakes had to be stacked and air-dried, sliced repeatedly on a wire, and "wedged" to drive out the air (air bubbles would make the pots explode in the kiln). Peter would continue to use that Fish River clay for decades—in fact, for a while he sold it to the Arts and Crafts Club in New Orleans—until it was replaced by clay brought from Lucedale, forty miles northeast of Ocean Springs, which is the clay now in use at Shearwater.

Sometimes, at night, he would go over his finances with his father, and his correspondence would turn more serious. In a good month, Shearwater was earning up to $350 in showroom sales. But could he depend on that income? Like his father, Peter wasn't one to spend his savings or "step casually into debt," and he pressed his paternal partner for an estimate on how much he could count on to begin life with Pat. "I've just spoken to Dad alone," he writes in January, "and he said about $200 a month, and I have $30,000 in bonds we could use in emergencies. . . . The 'about 200 a month' might mean a little more or a little less, as pottery sales fluctuate with the season, though their progress in general has been a steady advance with an increasing margin between expenses and sales . . . I should have warned you before that there won't be much of an income for us. . . . I want you to decide this for yourself, to think it over as calmly and coldbloodedly as you can, beloved, and I am going to be careful not to influence you."

She wasn't listening. How could she think *anything* over "coldbloodedly," when he was concerned?

Can't you know, beloved Peter, what a very splendid and wonderful person you are? By just being you, and by the way you love your adoring and thankful Patty, who sometimes wonders why she should be the one God allowed to have Peter's love. If I can deserve Peter's love then surely he more than deserves mine. I'm sorry for everyone who hasn't at least a little of the love I have, to make everything that's beautiful super-beautiful. Peter, if I had your arms around me now I couldn't believe that I was still on common everyday earth. As it is, life is pretty perfect, isn't it?

MUD AND PAINT

Unloading the Kiln

In August 1930, as Pat and Peter settled into their first months of married life, and Pat's sister Agnes (Sissy) was about to leave for her junior year at Radcliffe, Bob fell in love with her. It was the second summer they had spent together, sailing the Sound and roaming the countryside around Shearwater and Oldfields. But it wasn't until a couple of days before Sissy boarded the train north that he realized he loved her, "more than the world, the land, and sky and water." He remembered the very moment. The two of them were sitting in the car in the moonlight, waiting for Peter. The night was pulsing with crickets and frogs, and they heard a train go by. She said something about its taking her away, and Bob wanted to tell her how he hated the idea. But one of the frogs got into his throat, and "all I could do was croak. I had the feeling sitting beside you that something was going to happen, and it did, and I loved you, and I wanted to make our lives a fairy tale and live in a fairy tale house with a little black imp to wait on us, and all the water and islands to have adventures in, only I wasn't the King's third son at all, not at all, and I only had one key to the house where the Princess lived when I should have had three."

The night before she left, he took her in his arms and managed to tell her that he loved her. As in a medieval romance, he wanted to put one hand in the fire and hold her with the other, "to see whether I'd mind the heat." Her reaction was not the one he had hoped for. She could not really say that she loved him, not yet. The next morning—the day of her departure—he walked nervously in circles and cursed himself for his impulsive behavior: what a silly ass he must have seemed! When Pat and Peter were about to pick up Sissy at Oldfields and take her to the station, he scribbled a note and asked his brother to give it to her. He couldn't bring himself to see her off, but, once more, there was no hiding his passion.

Dearest Agnes,

I love you, and I'm going to miss you horribly. There is no reason for doing things without you here. You, my love, my darling. It's awfully hard to write it on paper when I want to tell it to you so badly, but Pete and Pat are leaving in five minutes, and I have to tell you somehow that I love you, and I think you're right not to love me. I'm not fit to be loved. I wanted you to go away liking me anyway, but after last night you can't even do that, can you, dear? That's why I'm afraid to come to you now. I love you. I'll always love you. And I can't help it.

They're going now.

My dearest, darling Agnes I can't say goodbye. I love you.

Bob

"Darling dearest, I love you," he added in a second note. "Won't you say it aloud as if I were there saying it to you? I've been saying it to you all day. I'm saying it now. Can't you hear me?"

On the train, somewhere past Mobile, Sissy looked out the window and remembered the flowers they had picked together that summer. Along the tracks were some of the tall, feathery bright scarlet bushes they had seen along the road from Ocean Springs to Vancleave. There were white lilies and ironwood and "adder's tongue galore." How to answer him? The night before, he had told her he was afraid his behavior would make her hate him.

Dear Bob:

You must know that no matter what happens you aren't capable of making me hate you. If I don't love you ever, I'll always like you tremendously, but I'll get very sad if you start calling yourself names. I think you can do anything you really want to, and I want you to want to make the most splendid plates and pots, and, if you want to, write and tell me about them. Pick flowers, too, and go on Pelican *trips when you aren't too busy. Don't live on air, and, when you start thinking I hate you, remember I like you. I'm only afraid you'll hate me some day, and we have such good times together. . . .*

It's hard to write what you feel but letters never mean to me just what's written in them. They mean that somewhere somebody sat down and wanted to talk to me, and of course they couldn't write what they would have said. . . .

Please, Bob, don't write me letters like the first one. Tell me the things you're doing as if you liked me the way I like you, and wanted me to know.

You've been very very extra nice to everybody this last week. I want you to know it.

I wish you could see the forest of goldenrod. It's all out, here.

Remember Horn Island and the nice walks we've had, and all the treasures we've found together.

Agnes

She was twenty-one, six years younger than he. Later in life she remembered how young she felt emotionally; she had always "liked romance vicariously." She had gone out with boys at Radcliffe, but those encounters had been "casual and rather intellectual." On dates, they went to Pops concerts and sat at tables, "drinking frosty lemonades, aloof and silent," or skated at night for miles, in a long string, over the bumpy ice of the Charles. Neither she nor her friends went to drinking parties, where "necking" might take place, and when her date showed up drunk to take her to the Harvard-Army game, she wrote Pat wistfully that she could find "no one to compare with *any* Anderson."

Like Pat and Peter, Bob and Sissy had a partly epistolary courtship, and tried to resign themselves to "one-sided conversation." But Bob's impulsive nature made him bad "at playing a waiting game." Writing letters was "like talking to a person with your eyes closed," he complained. You could only guess at the effect. It was a wonder she enjoyed his "inconceivably dull, stupid letters"! That fall and winter, he sometimes wrote two or three of them a day ("Any fire burns better for a little poking"), and did his best, after his initial outburst, not to be "maudlin" and "mushy," or turn his beloved into a "father confessor." He learned to read and speak between the lines. Sissy was such a cheerful, "sweet, steadying sort of person," the nicest he had ever known. Wouldn't his letters frighten her away? "If I *say* a fool thing to you there are ways of covering it up. But if it's written, it stays."

I have always been a great believer in the spoken word, more so now than ever. How can I write as if I were talking to you, putting words into your mouth when the words I want most to hear from you are words that you can't say? For your own good, be loved but never love. Take all you can without giving anything. I love you and I would have hurt you and at the same time I would gladly have given you anything. I loved you and because of that you felt that you had to go away. I wanted to do things for you, to make the world over so that you should be the happiest person in it, to work for you and live for you. I have known what it is to be happy through religion and through art and neither was enough, just ways of forgetting, of running away. Then I loved you and I thought that that was the answer to everything, and all that I wanted was a chance to make you love me. I had it, and failed miserably. I tried to show you how much I loved you but you couldn't see. So you went north and I stayed here. . . . Dearest, darling, my love, how could you leave me? I didn't ask much . . . just to see you now and then. Why should you rather be with other people who don't love you, rather than with me who do? And if you had rather be with me, why aren't you? Love, Bob.

He wished she would read only the beginning and the end of his letters, leaping from "Dearest Sissy" to "Love, Bob" or "I love you, blessed, darling Sissy." Hers began "Dear Bob," but ended "Affectionately, Agnes," in all possible variations. The more he wrote "love," the more playfully but firmly she held to "like." She *liked* being loved by him, she said, but she "might like somebody else's love better." She promised to tell him when her feelings changed. Why couldn't he treat her like a friend? She was sure he could be "a very great artist" if he wanted to. Couldn't he simply describe his daily work? With a friendly smile, his fairy tale "Princess" turned into a hockey player, a fine arts major, a "serious-minded senior" (so she described herself), and vanished. None of his "keys" seemed to open her heart, he said, and he wasn't really "the King's third son." In fact, he was "just the poor beast who loved the lady and when he found that the lady didn't love him . . . stayed at home and scratched pots."

"Scratching pots" was the sgraffito work he was doing to fire in Peter's kiln. A raw, leather-hard pot is given a layer of "slip" (clay in suspension), and the decorator carves into it, exposing the color of the body underneath. This can be done with any sharp instrument, but Bob had found, he wrote her, a "new way of scratching . . . with a razor blade. Sounds fun, doesn't it? But it's not as bad as it sounds. You take a pot covered with slip, and holding it in your lap with your left hand, and seizing the razor blade in your right, you proceed to scratch, with very surprising results. Birds, flowers grow like lightning and almost before you know it, lo and behold, the pot is done, and you're ready for another one, and so on, ad infinitum or ad nauseam. But seriously, I do think that I have found something that will help a lot in putting a decoration on a large piece quickly."

Two weeks after Sissy's departure, on August 30, 1930, he decided to put romance aside, and tell her of his first day "as a salaried employee of the Shearwater Pottery."

Peter has made some large deep bowls, painted them with red slip and given them a sort of feather polish on the wheel, which we hope they will keep in the firing. I spent most of today in decorating one of these, with large ducks flying and walking around it in a more or less Cretan manner, although I very much doubt whether any Cretan ghost would recognize the influence. It really is rather nice, and if I keep on liking it as I do now, I shall have a hard time to keep from sending it to you, and you would have an even harder time if I did, so I won't. My dear, there are going to be a terrible lot of atrocities committed in your name this winter, and speaking of atrocities, I will send your plates to you as soon as they come out of the kiln. Peter fired today. You must try to accept them in the spirit in which they are given, and not be too critical of them as works of art, because, to be quite frank with you, that they are not.

Love awakened his imagination as painter and decorator, and he worked fervidly, drawing on what his niece Patricia likes to call, undramatically, "the universal grab-bag." His imagination was teeming with ideas and styles: the cave paintings he had seen in France, Greek ceramics and sculpture from the museums of New York and Philadelphia, the Pennsylvania-Dutch sgraffito he had admired in Philadelphia, shards of Choctaw pottery he found on the beach at Graveline, the innumerable art and photography books that lay about the Barn and the Front House. Tulane's archaeologist Frans Blom visited Shearwater, accompanied by the writer Lyle Saxon, and chatted about pottery from the Southwest, Mexico, and Central America, and there were exhibitions of Aztec and

Maya things at Newcomb and at the Arts and Crafts. To ignore the art of the past, Bob once told his mother, was to "refuse one's heritage." In his letters to Sissy, he is always poking fun at himself for all those "mysterious influences."

Some of the plates and a big bowl have just come out of the kiln and look very well, even if the yellow did turn a dark grey in the firing, which makes them red and black and grey on a light ground. They are very startling. I'm still flitting from one influence to another. I've just finished a pair of bookends with a strong odor of Maya about them. They would have been quite good if I hadn't done them so carelessly, but I was down in the depths when I did them. I'm out now, and have started a bird, probably a seagull, which promises well.

Wood, clay, and paint suggested different styles and manners, and he wanted to try them all. Often he went off "half-cocked" over the joy of each medium. He had "too many ideas and not enough time," he wrote. "While I'm working on one idea, out pops another, and I'm off again on something else. If I could only be like an Indian god with one head to several pairs of arms!" A god who could work simultaneously in mud and paint and wood. "When I'm doing mudpies, I want to be doing slip. Now that I am doing slip, I have an overwhelming desire to use wood, and nothing is as it should be." At times, it seemed impossible "to shift from pots to painting and then back to pots, in the flash of an eyelid. . . . They both suffer, and as for me, it makes me hate them both."

Sometimes he set aside the bowls and bookends he was "mudding" for Shearwater and turned "violently" to wood, carving figurines or a big African god he called Mumbo Jumbo, polishing him up with wax until he felt like old leather. Peter had bought an infernal machine from Sears, Roebuck, an enormous buzz saw, and had "cut down half the trees on Pottery Hill to feed his monster." Bob liked to chop the blocks cut by the saw, stretching his limbs after sitting for hours in the Pottery. The wood set him dreaming of African sculpture. It may be "a bit revolting at first

George Walter Anderson
(1865–1937)

Annette McConnell Anderson
(1867–1964)

Peter Anderson,
Walter Inglis Anderson (Bob),
and James McConnell
Anderson (Mac),
on steps of the showroom

Peter and Patricia Grinstead Anderson
on their wedding day, Oldfields, 1930

Peter in uniform of Officers
Training School, *ca.* 1918

Peter working
at kickwheel,
March, 1928

Peter with his children, Patricia
and Michael, *ca.* 1934

Pat with her son Michael,
ca. 1932

Agnes Grinstead Anderson (Sissy),
in her days as a schoolteacher
in Ocean Springs

Bob and Agnes Grinstead Anderson (Sissy)
on their wedding day, 1933

Bob with carved vase,
ca. 1934

Oldfields, Gautier, Mississippi, 1925

Peter on the Gulf

George Walter Anderson with Patricia
and Michael, *ca.* 1936

Annette, 1940s

Pat painting figurines
at Shearwater Annex

Pat and Peter's daughter, Patricia,
decorating a plate, Shearwater Annex, 1980s

Mac in living room of his
rammed-earth house, surrounded
by his paintings, pottery, and
woodcarvings. Walter Anderson
Museum of Art

Jim's and Margaret's son, Peter Wade Anderson,
playing in workshop, *ca.* 1978

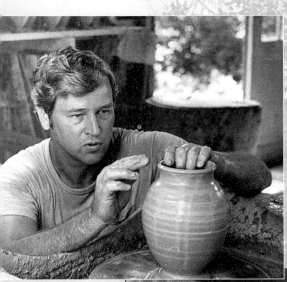

Peter Anderson, *ca.* 1978

Jim working at wheel,
ca. 1978

Hands of Peter Anderson. Photo Ed Sbardella

Shearwater
showroom,
ca. 1997

Front row, left to right: Patricia Findeisen, Peter Wade Anderson,
James McConnell Anderson, Sara Lemon Anderson. Back row,
left to right: James Anderson, Margaret Anderson, Michael Anderson,
Marjorie Anderson Ashley, and James E. Ashley, 1997.

sight," he told Sissy, but it possessed "an extraordinary amount of genuine feeling."

Peter really brought it on himself with his new buzz-saw by cutting up cedar logs and when I passed by and saw the pieces I couldn't resist them. It's wonderful stuff to cut into and you know what a nice polish it takes. There is only one drawback to it. It's very hard to keep from checking, that is, [it] cracks due to drying out too rapidly. It's fun carving in spite of that. I'm still subject to a strong African influence, you have probably noticed it in my letters.

"Scratching" and decorating with slip, modeling in clay, carving in lead or cedar, sketching designs for furniture, he "flitted" that fall and winter (1930–1931) from Greek to Arabian, Mayan to African. Working on his mudpies—his pots and vases—he remembered old Persian prints or paintings. What better style for a mural?

You've probably seen old Persian prints done in rich low tones with people in very bright colored cloth against them and divided by little carved fences and balconies. Well it struck me that this might be a very interesting way of doing the colored section of Ocean Springs, so I'm trying it out. It means a terrific lot of work, because it will have to be done very carefully. But I think it would be worth it. I'm sure I would learn a lot, and it might help the looks of the show room if it's ever finished. Unfortunately as a working man, I haven't much time.

Within days, that idea had given way to another, a mural of Horn Island.

I've had a hectic day. Spent most of it in painting a decoration on a large slab of beaverboard. What started by being the colored quarter of Ocean Springs has gradually evolved into a sort of map of Horn Island, of all places. The way I'm doing it was suggested by the slip decoration that I have been doing. You see, the slips were such awfully nice colors and went so well together before they were fired that I thought that I would do something where there would be no question of their losing their color. Hence the mural of Horn Island. It's three feet by six, so you see that I'm getting ambitious. Tomorrow being Labor Day I can go on with it. It's really the way that I've always wanted to paint: flat colors and forms playing one against another, letting one color influence another directly without actually painting the influence. The action takes place in the eye of the beholder rather than on the canvas, which sounds rather complicated, but is really very simple as far as the theory goes. It's in practice that it's difficult.

But even the second version would change. What started out as a "Persian" rendering of Ocean Springs's "colored section" became "Horn Island (a slip decoration), then Horn Island II (possibly Cretan), and finally ended as a Symphony in Color, or the Cat and the Flowers. So whoever buys it will be getting four for the price of one, which is not bad when you consider the amount of ground covered and paint used."

It is clear from Bob's letters that his duties as a decorator at the Pottery were beginning to place a strain on him, pulling him away from painting, and bringing him into conflict with his brother.

Why in the world when I had the choice didn't I paint—before I took this job of making mudpies for Peter? We had a sort of row this afternoon because I had done a rotten thing, a bookend, and I knew it, so I junked it without asking permission first. Peter doesn't understand that one good bookend or candlestick is worth a dozen mediocre ones, artistically and financially.

And, yet, his attitude toward painting was ambivalent. He wasn't sure of his own commitment to it, and was afraid that, if he found time to paint, he would quickly "burn out." That fall and winter, he thought of reserving it for moments when he had something "serious" to say, rather than give in sporadically to the joy of handling brushes and pigments. But often he felt himself "dragged by the hair," and went "up to the ears in paint, literally and figuratively." At those moments, you had to surrender, paint, and "get out . . . as well as you can, taking your wounded with you. The trouble is that each time it happens you leave something of yourself behind, until by and by you have nothing left to leave." He wished he could "stop fussing around" once he had begun a painting; follow a method, and save "wear and tear on the emotions," husband them carefully, "because feeling is the most valuable thing that we possess and we have only a certain amount of it which should be spent carefully." He had wonderful ideas for combining colors, if only there were time to work them out. He had always been an early riser, and he painted sometimes in the two hours before breakfast: "just long enough to get interested. Then I stop and eat and go back to the filthy clay." Often those sessions ended in failure. "Instead of reaching into the air and grabbing two big color notes and forcing them to work together," he was "pussyfooting around using sequences: that is, several friendly colors together, so that with any care there's not much chance of trouble."

As with Peter, love had sharpened his sense of color: in pottery, in painting, and in the world around them. He was a tangle of contradictions, but he wanted to live with Sissy in a "continuous sort of sunrise."

Just between you and me, Agnes, I think that if this fellow Bob had all the time he wanted, he would probably spend it either on Horn Island or making the despised mudpies or transplanting, or on almost anything except painting. This is just a guess, but I know him pretty well, and he is like everybody else in wanting the things he can't have. Dearest Dear, I want you and I want to paint, and I can't have or do either. I've wanted to paint ever since you left. It's possible that I wouldn't paint steadily if I had the time. It's very hard to paint nine hours a day for any length of time; it takes a lot out of you. But I really feel that I could now, and use color, gorgeous color. It's color for the first time. Before it was always people or flowers, and color was secondary. Since I've loved you, I want to live in a continuous sort of sunrise. . . . Why didn't I have the good sense to wait until you were through college and I was making a good living before I fell in love with you? Unfortunately I had no choice.

With each letter he invited her—directly or indirectly—to tell him that she loved him. But the entire school year went by without her doing so. In December, when he tried to persuade her to spend her vacation with him in Ocean Springs, rather than visit her family in Pittsburgh, she told him she couldn't desert the family.

You remember last summer, Bob. I tried to make you see how very much they enter into everything I do and feel. Time and distance don't make the slightest bit of difference in the way I feel about you. Your letters make me like you more, they're such nice ones, but Bob, I've told you that, just now, I cannot say I love you, because I don't feel it, and not feeling it I wouldn't say it for anything. If you want to stop writing and have me stop too, for heaven's sake say so. I don't want you to do anything you don't want to. But don't forget, I haven't changed my way of feeling. . . . Can't you just wait until all this college foolishness is off my mind—till next June when I won't have anything left to keep me preoccupied?

She knew there was much she could learn from his daily struggle. At Radcliffe, she was taking a studio course on painting, and she asked his advice whenever she felt discouraged. He was sure, after his many years in art school, that "what takes place in the mind of the student is of a great deal more importance than the mere material result on canvas. For a man or a woman may be an artist without ever even smelling paint, but very few of the painters are artists." There were things she could do when she felt herself getting stale. "Sometimes it helps to deliberately paint out the thing that you like best in your painting, just by way of giving yourself a vote of confidence: anything to change the atmosphere." She could get the same result by flinging her paint at the wall. That's what *he* did when he couldn't bear the boredom of the Pottery: threw gobs of "sticky wet clay at knot holes in the wall of the workshop." As he worked, they dried and fell to the floor with a continual thump, making it "rather difficult to concentrate on the mudpie of the moment." Peter's irritation can be imagined. He did his best, so Bob said, to "humor" his temperamental brother, who was wasting "perfectly good clay at three cents a pound." The best advice Bob could give Sissy was to "follow your nose, and never take anybody's advice, not even mine." Not paint anything at all, unless she truly cared for it. What she really ought to do was to return to Ocean Springs, so that the two of them could paint together.

By then, when "the college foolishness" was over, he hoped to have started a house for them. Like the paintings and mudpies, it would be an experiment in color. Peter would mix the right tones for him and he would put them on big tiles and make a frieze to go around the walls. He would "do *Don Quijote* or Aesop's *Fables.*" Their house would suggest the nicest things she had ever "felt or done. Horn Island and flowers and birds and boats, all jammed into one small house." Homemade furniture, with a carpenter doing the rough work, and Bob finishing it off with carving. And a pair of large red and black and white cats for the front steps.

During months of lonely labor, with only an occasional holiday from the Pottery, where everyone followed a strict schedule, he dreamed of taking her into a realm of their own, where, far from others, they could gaze up at the stars. Horn Island—"quite a nice place if you are there with the right person"—or the Great Barrier Reef; a shanty boat on the Mississippi, or "points East": Florida, for example. He heard that the Indians there had made better arrowheads than the local ones, and that there were mounds all over the place just waiting to be opened up. They would sail together, swim, dance in the water. Choose two or three tall pines, build a treehouse, forget about the Pottery and "bridge and movies and radios and everything else. Live as the birds live, taking no thought for the morrow."

I've been thinking of the things we would do if you were here. It's a painful sort of pleasure. First we would go to the valley of the flowers—that's the place on the Vancleave Road that I told you about—and we would pick all the flowers we could carry . . . adder's tongue, ironweed, possum berries, asters, deer-tongue, blazing star, everything. Then we would go out to Horn Island, just us together, no one else, and never come back. Stay there and live on palmetto, cab-

bage and ghost crabs, with an occasional salad of morning glory leaves. On moonlit nights we would stay up all night and catch turtles and we would see all the shades of people who had come to Horn Island but were afraid to stay and now would never come there again. . . . On dark nights we would swim in the surf and be able to see each other clearly because of the phosphorus and we would swim out a long way and then float and lie there together looking up at the stars and listen to the musical crying of the skimmers and the surf all down the Island for as far as you could hear. And we would dance. Have you ever tried that? Dancing to music on land can't compare with it. On land, it is one move to the music and then one to keep from falling over. But in the water every movement of your body is part of the rhythm. Then we would go ashore and sleep on the beach or, if you preferred it in the top of some nice tall pine tree. My love, I think I'm ten years older since I met you. It's at least ten years since you went away, and at that rate I'll be about a hundred and sixteen by the time you come back.

While he waited for her, he "chased wildflowers" around Shearwater. He found it extraordinary how much unsettled land there was nearby. You could walk two miles and see only a house or two. He returned by himself to the spots they had visited that summer. "I went out driving this evening and looked for the masses of cardinal flowers that we saw last fall. Do you remember? But there's not a sign of them. Either they are late this year or they have had too much salt water or the alligator has eaten their roots. Anyway, they aren't there, which is very sad . . . I told you that Peter and I had transplanted about sixty of them and put them down in our marsh, which is of course nothing but salt. No sign of *them,* either."

There were wood lilies up the road from Ocean Springs in Vancleave, "the most perfect wild flower we have down here . . . one of the most surprising things" that nature ever produced. Some day in the spring, when the azaleas and mountain laurel were in bloom, they would make a long trip up the Pascagoula, "tow a skiff and collect strange plants as we go along, and wrap their roots in wet moss to keep them moist.

And the nights we will spend on sand bars, build a fire and sit listening to the bull frogs." In one of his letters he sent her a stalk of yaupon that was growing outside the workshop. He had his eye on it for days, "heard a car drive in and then stop."

I looked out the window to see what the trouble was, and there was the car and there, near it, was a woman with hand outstretched in the act of breaking off that choice piece of yaupon. I yelled, and the only thing I could think of to say—all this happened in a second—was "Ah! Ah! Mustn't touch!" It was really very funny. I had no time to think, it had to be done at once and working all day in silence it's very hard to be tactful on the spur of the moment. She stood it well, though, even to the point of buying some pottery, which is the acid test.

Sissy put the yaupon in the bowl she most liked. It was the cream-colored one Pat and her mother had bought from Walter a year earlier, with black horses that evoked cave painting and that seemed to move like the wind.

With Peter and Mac, Bob listened for geese and waited for a north-wester. Then it was time for duck hunting in the Louisiana marshes where their father had taken them as children. There was a lot more to those trips, he told her, than just shooting ducks "or rather shooting at ducks." It was like traveling back in time, beyond their childhood, into landscapes wilder than anything they could see around Ocean Springs. There were marvelous places to the west, down the Coast, around Saint Malo; landscapes they had read about in Lafcadio Hearn. A decade earlier, Hearn had found villages of sullen Malay fishermen—speakers of Spanish—tormented by mosquitoes that rose "like a thick fog over the lowland" and sounded in the darkness "like the boiling of innumerable caldrons." They found no ducks there, only the damnable mosquitoes and "miles of new lagoons with thousands of little marshy islands in them." It reminded Bob of a prehistoric landscape.

Always, the quest for the unspoiled and "primitive." There were arrowheads at Old Fort Bayou, with its oaks and cedars, miles from the nearest house, and more of them at Graveline Bayou, where the waves had eaten away at the bluff and the Indian burial mounds, and washed ancient treasure onto the beach. For Pat and Sissy, it was a magical place. When the two of them were very young, bands of Choctaws would come down to Graveline in the fall, leaving their homes in northern Mississippi. Mrs. Grinstead warned the girls to avoid them, but they went anyway, creeping through the undergrowth to spy on the Indians. "There have been a lot of them around there," Sissy said, years later. "They came down in the season of mullet and of oysters and would live there while they were getting their supplies . . . I don't know what they did with the oysters, but they smoked the fish. . . . They [fished with] buckeyes. They collected the seeds and sprinkled them into the bayou in quantity when the mullet were up in the bayou, and the fish were poisoned by the buckeyes and floated to the top of the water. Then, they could just pick them up . . . I've never been to a mound or an encampment anywhere that there weren't lots of horse chestnuts all over the place—trees and bushes and buckeyes all over the floor of the woods."

Bob went there in the family car, sometimes with Peter, occasionally with his mother, who was no good at finding arrowheads, but relished the chance to be with her beloved Bobby, even when it meant a frightening ride: unlike Peter, he disliked motors of any kind, and expressed it in his reckless driving. She picked at bits of seaweed and empty oyster shells and found a buckeye or two.

Have you ever picked up arrowheads at Graveline?
Graveline is a bayou where bootleggers live
In little shanties like matchboxes.
I saw two on Sunday—bootleggers, not shanties—
I was there with Bob, who is making a collection of arrowheads.
Bob had said, "Mother, don't you want to go to Graveline?"
And something inside said, "No, you'd better not."
Aloud I said "Yes," and we went.

We went like the wind in the old Ford, forty miles an hour.
And I shut my eyes and wished I had stayed home.
While we raced, my soul was ruffled and disturbed,
Like a bird hanging to the top of a cage,
But we got there at last, and Bob ran ahead
To find arrowheads before the tide came in.
I followed after. I walked through grass
And I walked through sand, and I stepped over little streams
Full of water the color of tea.
The beach was full of logs and it turned a dozen corners.
And almost all the way the shanties were in sight.
I know because I watched them.
I watched them because a man watched me.
He had rowed across the water when we first drove up,
And I saw him for an hour when I looked that way.
He was a bootlegger.
I wondered whether it bothered him to know that we were there.
I couldn't find one arrowhead
So I sat on a log, at last,
And I saw the seagulls sitting crowded in a line
On a long bar a hundred feet away.
I did find a crabshell with a pattern
On the top of lavender and scarlet.
I did find a pod from a horse chestnut tree,
A wonderful pod made of grey and green network
That had split and showed the shining brown buckeyes within.

That fall, in weather just cool enough for fires in the evening—
weather that gave Bob a "conquer the world feeling"—he wrote of the
colors of Shearwater. His words are tinged with longing and frustration.
So many things would have been "really worth painting" had he been
able to take time from the hateful "mudpies"! Some enormous cabbages
he found growing on the Pointe aux Chenes Road. A possum eating

grapes at night, outlined against a moonlit cloud, "rat-tail and all." The huge leaves of the tung oil trees in the woods: leaves "trying to turn into flowers," with "yellow and pale green on top and a wonderful warm pink underneath." The burning of the fields on the road to Graveline: "a fog of drifting blue smoke with spots of fire all through it where pine stumps had caught, and beyond everything, the afterglow from the sunset." In September, the Shearwater woods themselves were ravishing: "The pine trees were blood red and purple and the ones next to the white walls of the mud house were silver in the shadow with reflected light, and the pine needles were emerald green and red gold. It was magnificent. And yet idiots try to copy nature! It's blasphemy. Art can be just as wonderful, more wonderful, but it must never try to do the same."

He knew she understood. She loved to write, and to tell him about her own special moments, those she could not capture as a painter: "Don't you love the sky in winter just after sunset when there's a green line of light along the horizon and everything else in the world is gray, except two twinkling lights and the black arms of trees against the sky?"

The colors he saw he held in his memory, or daubed onto his pots and hoped they wouldn't change too much in the firing: "I'm going to do some decorations in underglaze colors to go under an alkaline clear glaze. We tried some the last firing, but Peter didn't put enough glaze on them. There was just enough to show what they might be like under proper conditions. Very intense, high-keyed colors. Persian blue and lilac and green. If the results are what I hope, there will be something almost worthy of you. That is the way things always are before being done and then, afterwards, comes a slump. . . . Too much of a hurry, I suppose."

In Cambridge, she, too, was always in a hurry, and sometimes in a creative slump. But like him, she found moments of tranquillity and journeyed out into the countryside.

Sundays I usually do the things I like most. In the morning, quite early, three or four of us go out to Medford. We ride in the loveliest woods up over the little hills all over squat fir trees and patches of bright red maple or around two nice blue little lakes. It's wonderful now, except for the dryness, and a big woods fire is burning out some of the nicest timber. It creeps underground, even, and there's no stopping it. All afternoon we lay on our backs in the uncut hay of the slope of the paddock and watched the horses being schooled over the jumps. They were beautiful. No saddles or bridles, just horses, and they seemed to be having such a good time. You see I had a very lazy day. Today made up for it. I went to classes from 9 to 11, mixed colors and enjoyed myself from 11–1, at 2 classes again till 4. Then hockey. I just got back from the Fogg Museum, where I spent the evening reading about Baroque art. Now I have to read a long medieval Italian poem by a monk. It's all about his conversion: the visions he had and the voices he heard.

He wanted her in Ocean Springs with him. He felt a bit envious of the happiness his brother had found with her sister, and, although he told Sissy he never wanted to have children, he was discovering in himself "a surprising domestic streak" he didn't know he possessed. Peter and Pat loved being together, despite the daily grind. It was a peaceful life. Peter "nailing up bee frames or singing aloud" to baby Michael at the Front House. The bees working diligently. A frog chorus in the darkness outside. The staccato of the squirrels on the screened porch. The gyrations of their little Scottie when he was stung by a bee.

When Sissy graduated cum laude and returned home for the summer of 1931, something changed in their relationship. Bob told her he could not go on living unless she married him. She hesitated at first. She liked "quietness and tenderness," she told him, and "you make for violence and storms." But, somehow, as they became more intimate, her resistance gave way. There were times when they drifted away by themselves: arrowheading excursions, moments at night on the Oldfields pier, and "heavenly trips up the river" in the *Pelican*. They danced together, at last, in the phosphorescent water of the Sound. "Like" turned finally into "love."

Toward the end of the summer, Bob drove to Oldfields to ask her father for her hand. Mr. Grinstead responded "with considerable force and scorn," and asked for a statement of his assets. Although Bob had a plan, there seemed to be no way he could support his daughter on his decorator's salary. What would they live on—palmetto, cabbage, and ghost crabs? Mr. Grinstead asked Sissy to accompany him and his wife to Sewickley, where he went back to work for the bank. In Pittsburgh, she felt homesick for Mississippi, and desperate for Bob: "I want to muss your hair and rub your head and feel your arms around me." She bought a bicycle and rode into the countryside for flowers. She searched construction sites for arrowheads and "dug fossil oysters out of a sandstone cliff."

"What could I do?" she wondered, years later. Separation "seemed to be my parents' stock solution to their daughters' entanglements of the heart."

MAKING WIDGETS

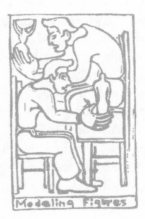

To marry Sissy, Bob needed more income than what he was making as one of Peter's salaried employees. Mr. Grinstead had reminded him of that before taking his wife and daughter from Oldfields back to Sewickley, and Bob assured him that he had given the matter more than a little thought.

For the past two years, he and Mac had talked about having their own kiln and doing their own firings. The plan had arisen one October night in 1929, at a long and animated family meeting, "where everybody seemed to have different ideas." They were to depend for pots and glazes and general information on Peter, who promised to work with "a max-imum amount of cooperation. . . . Everything made will be for the honor and glory of Shearwater." Fateful meeting, fateful month! The stock market had crashed on October 29 in New York, but in Ocean Springs, Peter and Bob were in the best of spirits. Peter told Pat, who was still away in Paris at the time, that he was living in the most perfect world imaginable. There wasn't a single thing to find fault with. Shear-water grossed about $350 for the month. The day panic struck Wall Street, the kiln was being loaded with about 280 pieces of small ware: mostly vases and bowls, but also goblets and pitchers, candlesticks in three different designs ("squat," "bowl," and "lighthouse"), and sixteen eggcups—special ones proudly designed by Peter: "not too large and with a rim that grips the egg, making them inseparable, come wind or high seas." Yellows and blues predominated, including a hard-to-produce Chinese blue. Bob had been working on his painting, and had nothing ready for the firing. Mac had contributed a couple of nice vases. A northwester was blowing, and the three brothers were about to take off for four days of duck hunting on the *Gypsy*. They would fire the kiln before leaving, allow it to cool in their absence, and unload it on their return.

Walter, too, had every reason to be pleased. Sales had grown steadily, and he had learned to share his desk space with "couchant cats that look like the sea serpent" and "artistic bean pots for Boston baked beans," pots "no self-respecting bean would ever enter." A display window the fam-ily rented in a store in Biloxi brought Shearwater into wider view and attracted new visitors to the showroom. There were sometimes as many as a dozen in the morning and a half dozen in the afternoon. Walter had decided to get his pottery into the two best department stores in Chicago: Marshall Field and Carson Pirie Scott. To each, he had sent seven or eight pieces of Shearwater's finest work. Lush glazes by Peter and a couple of pieces by Bob. He knew he was aiming high. It felt "a little presumptuous" for Shearwater to be offering its pots to stores like those, and he expected "to have them pots thrown back at my devoted head." But who could tell? Perhaps the "demnition Art Critics" there would treat him "with more leniency than the local crowd: Mrs. Anderson, Mr. PA, Mr. WIA and last but by no means least, little Mr. JMcCA, who kicked harder than the rest as he had to pack them and wanted to play tennis or golf or some other tootling game instead. . . . I think he thinks this Pot Business is another game, and could be done just the same tomorrow or next day if the weather was too wet to play tennis, etc. Strike while the iron is hot, is my motto."

In fact, since returning from Tulane, "little Mr. JMcCA"—Mac—had become much more than Shearwater's part-time packing force. In 1929, he had made over 130 vases and bowls of all sizes, mostly slip–decorated with fish and birds; a variety of lamp bases; a very popular molded perch; bookends and candlesticks, ashtrays with fish or turtles, and a couple of paperweights—more pieces, in fact, than Bob.

The pots did come back from Chicago, and Walter wondered whether it was a matter of price or of quality. "As an ex-European Grain Exporter," he didn't quite trust himself. "The writer is free to confess that he is very ignorant on the subject of pottery values. He is also very anxious to get a check on the prices his sons, who make up the working forces at the pottery, put upon their product." To Marshall Field, he would send more samples "when our pottery has reached another state of development."

The department store experience was a reminder how hard it was going to be to reconcile the Pottery's "individuality" with the world of modern retailing. The problem wasn't producing enough pots: it was finding the right price and the right way to get them into good stores in the North. Less than a year before, Shearwater had been an "infant industry," and "all we could make was meeting with a ready sale in the South," Walter wrote. But Peter had grown impatient with his local customers, who balked at anything expensive. There was no use worrying about the town. Perhaps fewer than a dozen people in Ocean

Springs came to the showroom. They were "not the people we want to sell to ultimately." He could produce cheaper things for the local trade, but "time taken from making first-class ware (or as near as I can come to it) delays the arrival of the day when Shearwater Pottery will be synonymous with perfect pots." By 1929, Shearwater was producing two thousand to three thousand pieces per year. And yet they never seemed to be making what the "big people" needed. Shearwater's aim, according to Walter, was "to make more and more beautiful pottery without increasing our prices very materially on the bulk of it, and without duplication to any great extent." On hand were plenty of "unique," expensive hand-decorated pieces, running up to $50 or $75 each ($480 to $725 today). But how could these be marketed in New York? Foreign currencies had been devalued, foreign pottery, earthen-ware, and dinnerware cost only a little more than American, and people had been trained to believe that it was better. The label "imported" seemed to mean "direct from heaven."

It must have been hard, once the Depression had begun, for Walter to decline a retailer's invitation to send "two or three dozen" of this or that vase. But, after all, that meant "commercialization" and "standardi-zation." Shearwater wasn't something you could order out of a catalogue; no such thing existed. Part of its charm lay in its variety, and no two pieces were the same when they came from the kiln. Even with molded, undecorated pieces, they spoke not of "pairs" or "duplicates" but of pieces that could be *considered* pairs: the notion of sameness was relative, and a lot depended on the benevolence of the buyer. When two pieces did look identical in color and form, there were blistering and bubbling and leaking to worry about, and perhaps those nearly identical pieces weren't the ones that had interested the buyer in the first place. Peter was young in the pottery business, too proud to send out work he considered outmoded. When the Lincoln Chair Company ordered "nearly $500 worth" of pottery—135 pieces—it seemed to him "a distinct step back-ward" to try to fill the order. In the space of a few months, he had "dis-carded many of the glazes—practically all of them except Turquoise

Blue" and had rejected the shapes as inferior. Here is Walter, patiently explaining the problem of "duplication" to the J. Strassel Company of Louisville:

[Item numbers] 1906 and 1936 [two medium red and blue vases] are a good pair, and 1967/68 [large yellow vases] a very good pair. The latter a color that you liked when here. They are not in the shapes you picked out, but the latter have repeatedly come out blistered and impossible. This is due to the fact that the kiln holds about 200 pieces, and Peter had to fire to the cone called for by the bulk of the loading, and not with special reference to the pieces ordered.

Shearwater was a world of irreducible difference, of quirky detail, at a time when American retailing was pushing for sameness. Everyone wanted pairs of lamps or pairs of vases, and Shearwater was simply "not willing to undertake the duplication of pieces." Walter would have liked to make up each order himself.

What I really want is a lot of buyers who are so impressed with the incalculable value of Shearwater Pottery, and who are A 1 in Bradstreet, that they will just write me letters from time to time ordering say 15–20 or 25 pieces of our pottery for say $100 cash, leaving me to give them their money's worth, ship the pottery, and receive the cash. This is the ideal I have formed for selling pottery. . . . Failing that sort of arrangement, I want some established and responsible firm, dealing in that sort of thing, to handle our pottery on commission. I would like one that was prepared to take a liberal supply, say 150 or 200 pieces in some big place like Chicago, and would push it as Shearwater Pottery. Commission 33¹/₃ on sales [on] pieces ranging from $25 each down to $1.00 each. I find a small stock does not work well, because it does not give a display large enough to show the variety of color and design.

That wasn't enough, of course. Those fifteen or twenty-five pieces would have to be reproducible, and those selling them had to talk them up. "An enthusiastic agent is worth a dozen who will put it on their shelves and leave it to talk for itself. Pottery is dumb. The man who handles it must not be."

That was especially true during the Depression. Walter found that Shearwater's pieces were "in steady demand all through the bad business" of 1930–1931. But it had hit the pottery industry hard. By 1932, over a third of America's 17,500 pottery workers had lost their jobs. About 11,000 were working less than two and a half days per week. Unionized pottery workers had accepted a 10 percent wage cut. All over the country, the largest companies—the ones that had thrived on mass production—were canceling lines and closing plants or going under. J. B. Owens and Teco closed their doors only months after the stock market crash. In Trenton, Fulper was unable to rebuild after its plant burned to the ground. California Faience stopped making art pottery in 1930, Cowan shut down in 1931, Marblehead in 1936. Weller closed two plants in 1936 and greatly simplified its lines. As construction projects fell off and architects turned to cement, steel, and glass instead of bricks and terra-cotta, many of the tile companies succumbed. Beaver Falls Art Tiles went under in 1930; Batchelder, two years later; and the American Encaustic Tiling Company and Wheatley closed their Ohio plants in 1936. Both Rookwood and the Mosaic Tile Company of Zanesville, which had helped decorate the New York subway system, ceased to make architectural tiles. Rookwood discontinued its more expensive artist-decorated lines, and Mosaic started making "hot plates, gadgets, boxes, bookends, souvenirs and wall panels." The American Ceramic Society lamented that reasonable wages were a thing of the past. The pottery industry was "gasping for breath," assailed "by competition of nonceramic and low-valued importation." At the society's annual meeting in Washington, D.C., in 1932, its president calmly predicted, "We shall never see the day again in commerce or in industry when the world in time of peace will be able to provide a full day's work for everybody."

The Depression hit especially hard in impoverished Mississippi. The state threatened to default on its bonds, and in Ocean Springs, schoolteachers were being paid in scrip. Annette organized a soup kitchen. Everywhere one looked, there were gangs of workers on PWA projects: resurfacing streets, seeding oyster beds, planting shrubbery, draining the places where mosquitoes bred. On Grant Street, in well-to-do Sewickley, Sissy marveled over the "number of poor out-of-workers who come to the door every day. It makes you shiver to think of what will happen to them this winter. I bet a lot of them hitch-hike to warmer climates." Ocean Springs was on the railroad, and hundreds of the jobless ended up there. As Bob tried to make enough money to marry her, Sissy couldn't help but ask, bewildered, why the world had gotten "so depressed when we needed it so inflated?" It seemed incredible to Bob that "a ridiculous thing like money or lack thereof" was allowed to keep them apart. It was too absurd. Something would have to be done about it.

By January 1931, Bob and Mac were ready to revive their old plan. They "have gone in together on a 50–50 basis," Peter wrote Pat, "and plan to go in strong for small figures." In preparation for that venture, a band of carpenters from the Beaugez family had descended on Shearwater in 1929, and put up the building known today as the Annex, as well as a smaller shed to house a new kerosene-burning muffle kiln: an 8,500-pound monster shipped by rail and truck from Colorado, which was soon looking "very much at home, in its own tin house, and resting in regal state on its concrete foundation." The showroom, too—which had always been mostly Peter's domain—was expanded. Bob drew the plans in consultation with Annette, dividing the old one into compartments and adding a wing at the back, with huge sliding windows letting in northern light from the pinewoods outside. Annette had been remembering Japanese architecture.

Figurines had become popular in the late 1920s and early 1930s. A writer for *The Gift and Art Gift Shop* remarked in November 1931 that "a host of funny little personages" had invaded American homes, covering mantels and book tables, smoking tables and window ledges. The best of those figurines had always been made in Europe, but American potters were now "expressing America in original arresting ceramic creations," made from native clays by artists who worked in "the locale of their birth and schooling." For a long time, both Bob and Mac had been carving and modeling figurines—of pirates and of blacks—for their own amusement. Pirates were part of Gulf Coast folklore: in the early nineteenth century, Jean Lafitte had prowled the Barataria Bay area, not far from where the boys hunted. Bob had carved pirates to make extra money as a student, and both Mac and he had always been interested in the artistic possibilities of "the American Negro."

The manufacturing of the figurines—a process overseen today by Michael—begins with a clay model (made back then by Bob and Mac), from which a plaster mold is made. Liquid clay—slip, made of white Kentucky ball clay—is poured into the mold and allowed to harden. When the mold is opened, the figure has to be trimmed, bisque-fired, decorated in a consistent manner, glazed and fired again. With repeated use, the plaster mold begins to lose its sharpness and must be remade, which means scraping the figurine used as a prototype. All this was to become a hateful daily routine for Bob and Mac, with only vase and plate decoration—which both continued to do—to offer any relief during the workday. Mind-numbing, bone-numbing work in mud and plaster, for up to eight hours at a stretch. Only the design and modeling of the figurines was any fun. After that, it was all the sort of duplication that Shearwater had always tried so hard to avoid.

A series of forty-nine figures of blacks began to emerge in 1930. A graceful horse and jockey was probably the first—Bob sent an early one to Sissy—followed by Charlestoners, cakewalkers, dancing women, and musicians. There were cotton pickers and field hands, a "Watermelon Woman" and "Washwoman," "Uncle Ned on Mule," a couple of mammies, "Chicken Thief," and "Possum Man." One of Bob's favorites was "Mr. Aspirin." Bob had awakened one morning with one of the terrible migraines he and his mother suffered from all their lives, had taken aspirin and gone off to the workshop, where he lost himself—and his headache—in modeling. "Mr. Aspirin . . . was a left-handed (he forgot the reversal of the molds) minstrel man playing his banjo and wearing his top hat and gaudy clothes." There were a log cabin and a chinaberry tree, and later a series of amusing black dockworkers designed by Mac, including a stevedore carrying a cotton bale or a box, and "Banana Man," designed in April of 1933.

No doubt some of these gaily colored figures—Mr. Aspirin among them—awaken racial stereotypes. And, yet, in their lighthearted humor and graceful, rhythmic lines, the Shearwater figurines stand apart, at least in their intention, from the world of what is now known as "black memorabilia" or "black Americana." It is a world of racist kitsch, of ceramic slavery, where black children are swallowed by porcelain alligators or molded into ridicule and servitude. From the 1890s through the 1950s, white America chuckled over those images. Black children are turned into holders for toothpicks or thermometers or pencils. They curl into handles on the sides of sugar bowls and creamers and climb the slippery white porcelain toward the sweet stuff within. Huge mammies offer syrup or pancake batter or split at the waist into cookie jars. On suburban lawns, blacks in livery or work clothes hold lawn hoses and lead imaginary horses. A red-capped figure called Jocko proffers his lantern or humbles himself into a cast-iron footscraper. An "Old Colored Mammy" dispenses cotton gauze from a basket on her head. Those images of subjugated "darkies" were everywhere in the early 1930s, when Bob and Mac started up the Annex. They were on food labels and postcards and cigar boxes, soap wrappers and powders. In 1928, Sears, Roebuck offered a trio of Charlestoners and a wind-up toy in which a "scared-looking negro shuffles along with a chicken dangling in his hand, a dog hanging in the seat of his pants." Kenneth Goings, an historian at the University of Memphis, estimates that over ten thousand different examples of black Americana were produced between 1890 and 1950.

Like everyone else, the Andersons were familiar with that sort of racist bric-a-brac. But neither they nor the Grinsteads felt anything but solicitude and affection for the blacks they had grown up with. The three Anderson boys had been raised by black nannies in New Orleans, and to help such women, who often had to leave their own children at home in order to serve in the homes of the wealthy, Annette had organized an informal day-care program, perhaps one of the first in the city. Pat and Sissy had been cared for by a married couple who, during their long lives, had been slaves and sharecroppers. Toward the end of her life, when she was selling the black figurines in the showroom, Pat thought about the "strained and misunderstood relationships" between whites and blacks and wistfully remembered the Grinsteads' nurse and housekeeper, Isabel Davis, her "joy and comfort" as a child at Oldfields. "In the early nineteen-hundreds," she wrote, "most 'colored Mammies' had been relegated to memory and storybook, but not in our lives." The black figurines made by Bob and Mac reminded her of the woman who had kept her company and watched over her in the isolation of Oldfields. And no doubt her description of the woman recalls the popular image of the southern "mammy."

> Her head was neatly bandanned in red and yellow checks. Her dresses were dark and neat, her aprons snowy white and voluminous. She wore very small gold earrings with tiny rubies in her pierced ears. She dipped snuff . . . and smoked [a pipe] when the day was over. She sat in her straw-seated rocker at the edge of the kitchen porch at dusk. Perfectly quiet she sat, and, just as quiet, I [used to lean] against her, seeing, feeling and hearing the beauty of the evening. We saw the . . . first stars come out. We felt the . . . gentle breeze from the bay and listened with wonder to the lonesome call of the chuck-wills-widow, or the quivering cry of a screech owl.

To Pat, Isabel seemed "beautiful," both inside and out. She had raised her and Sissy in the "ways of love, patience, and understanding." She had also helped bring up Pat and Sissy's mother—Miss Marjorie—and Pat had "never . . . decided whether Mamma ruled her with a rod of iron or whether it was the other way round." Late in her life, decades after Isabel was gone, Pat was still blessing her in her prayers.

It is hard to tell whether Bob and Mac ever gave much thought to the social import of the figurines they designed and produced. People, especially northerners, seemed to want comical depictions of blacks, and they made them the way they made the pirates and other figures: with verve and vibrant color and humor, avoiding the cruelty and racist ridicule of others they had seen. For the first time, what mattered more than anything were numbers. Peter could fret over individuality and artistic perfection, but at the Annex, it was brutally simple: the faster the figurines multiplied, the sooner Bob and Sissy could marry. There would have to be "hundreds and thousands and maybe millions" of those "miserable" little things. Bob could think "of all sorts of ridiculous ways of making money in a hurry, including buried treasure," even digging ditches, but who could say? Perhaps the figurines would succeed. While Bob's father worked on the department stores in Chicago and New York, Sissy searched for agents in Pittsburgh. And before very long came the breakthrough all of them had hoped for: an exhibition of Contemporary American Ceramics at W. & J. Sloane, a department store on Fifth Avenue, New York. A prestigious panel of judges, including Peter's discerning old teacher Charles F. Binns, the architect Alexander Archipenko, and William Sloane Coffin, curator of the Metropolitan, chose Shearwater to appear there alongside some of the best-known ceramists in the country: Henry Varnum Poor, Guy Cowan, Paul Bogatay, Victor Schrenkengost, Arthur Baggs, María Martínez, and potters from the Henry Street Settlement and Greenwich House. A friend of Sissy's spotted the figurines in Sloane's main Fifth Avenue window. "There they were: mule and rider in the middle, a progression of forward marchers to one side and dancers, etc. to the other." An energetic salesman named Wilson wanted to sell them in New York. "The trouble is," Bob wrote, "that he will probably want enormous quantities of each kind, and at the rate the molds are wearing out we would have a hard time keeping him supplied. Right now I am racking my brain to think of some way to increase production without increasing expenses, very much. It's quite a problem."

And then—at the beginning of November 1931—the exhibition garnered some enthusiastic reviews, Shearwater's first national publicity. The *New York Times* carried photographs of the brothers' work and praised the way "the black faces of these grotesquely modeled groups are artistically contrasted with the color of the costumes." There were reviews or photos in the *Christian Science Monitor,* the *Ceramic Age, Creative Art.* In Sewickley, Sissy was bursting with pride, almost ecstatic. Friends were calling, "wanting to know if we've seen this and that in the magazines and papers."

We're all so thrilled. We're jumping up and down with excitement, literally surrounded by portraits of various [figurines]. The New York Times *with its two pictures,* Home and Field *with a whole page, and* Arts and Decoration *and* Town and Country. *Aren't you proud of yourself? You've had a triumph, sure enough. Daddy is thrilled, because he thinks it's greatly due to your good business head! Isn't it really too superb? I can hardly stand thinking about all it means. Mamma is in a perfect fever . . .*

From New York, their new salesman, Wilson, wrote that business looked excellent, "and promises to be overwhelming in a few months. I hope that steps are being taken to increase production greatly." It was fun, Bob told Sissy, seeing his work in magazines, "and I can't help feeling a bit uplifted, even though it doesn't mean much. But I do feel that we have a little better ground for hoping."

Over the next few months, Bob and Mac cranked up production. There had been twenty-five worn-out molds in October 1931 when Sissy left for Sewickley. By the time of the exhibition, there were 125 nice new ones, and by the spring, about 260 of them divided into six lots, one for each day of the week. By Christmastime, Wilson, eager for his

15 percent commission, suggested that Shearwater produce one thousand little figures a week, and Bob had to remind him "that this is not a pretzel factory." It was beginning to feel like one. The Annex had grown to six people: three working full-time—Bob and Mac and (until he enlisted in the Navy) Clair Scharr, who made molds—and three "girls" from town, who painted and trimmed for about $7 a week, and were hard to train and to keep happy. The one who gave Bob the most trouble—a girl he called Anathema—had three strikes against her: a predilection for wearing bright pink beach pajamas to work, a very jealous husband, and the habit of using dirty brushes. "The three graces," Bob called the helpers, at one of his darker moments. "The dumbest, stupidest, clumsiest, most helpless idiots that it has ever been the misfortune of anyone to have to teach." Sometimes, when he surprised them at their work, he would find an alarming pile of clay arms, legs, and heads in the middle of the table. And yet their output was impressive. One person could paint 25 figurines in a day, the three graces, together, up to 79 or 80, and as many as 575 could be fired in the same kiln, although that could lead to disaster. In February 1932,

We opened the kiln and found five hundred [figurines] instead of being nice and shiny covered with a thin grey scum. And all because Mac had not seen fit to borrow five or ten gallons of oil from Peter and carry the firing on a little farther. It was sickening. Mac and I are not on speaking terms yet. We did close the kiln up without taking any of the stuff out and refired, but I'm afraid it was not much use. Tomorrow we can open it up and take a look. I thought that by this time I had all of the worst difficulties pretty well lined up, and then to have this kind of thing happen was rather discouraging. I've been leaving the firing entirely to Mac. But I think I shall have to do the next two or three firings by myself.

Angrily, but with a certain inner satisfaction, he dumped a wheelbarrow load of figurines into the marsh, and told himself not to complain about Mac, who was, after all, "a great help." Without him, the Annex could not have survived. Mac thought of himself, rather too modestly, as "a sort of handyman." He was "production manager, moldmaker, slip-pourer, kiln-firer and general factotum," and he had helped persuade Peter that his plain-glazed ware sold much better, in the showroom, when surrounded by decorated pieces. The Depression, he recalled years later, made it essential that Shearwater be as unlike other potteries as possible. It sharpened the family's wits and pushed them toward "variety." He worked "hard and steadily," Bob noted. "Never complains, and better still, never worries." And Bob, who could never fire the kiln properly without his brother's help, made plenty of mistakes of his own. When he fired some of his plates with the figurines, hundreds of pieces— all but two plates—were destroyed. "The Gods have turned against us again . . . I was abominably careless and let my interest in plates run away with me. It appears that I am unable to do two things well at the same time. They both suffer. And then I suffer."

Despite those setbacks, the Annex brought off feats that seem "astonishing" even to Michael, who oversees the operation today. Once, in just two and a half days, the three graces trimmed 614 figurines. At one point, Bob reported that Shearwater was able to produce four hundred figurines a week, sixteen hundred a month, twenty thousand a year. At first, demand far outstripped supply: there was simply no way the Annex could keep up with the orders, and, painfully, Bob had to tell Wilson to hold back. Later, when supply increased, demand fell off mysteriously: "people just weren't buying."

The whole business is working out beautifully with only one large fly in the ointment. We can produce a thousand [figurines] a month and have plenty of spare time for new things, and on half of that thousand you and I could get married if the fly, our friend Mr. Wilson, would only bestir himself. I could wring his neck when I think of the optimistic tone of his first letters at the time when we had no little figures with which to fill his orders.

The pressure of production and the ever-changing news from Wilson were nauseating. At times, Bob longed to be "tied to a log, face up" and "towed to the Horn Island Channel and turned loose with the tide running out strong." His own identity, his sense of self, seemed as uncertain as that of the grotesque, brightly clothed "little brutes" he was turning out by the barrelful. In *Beggar on Horseback,* a 1924 Broadway play by George S. Kaufman and Marc Connelly, a dreamy artistic young man is dragged by his bride and his father-in-law into the world of business, the "widget business."

"The widget business?"

"Yes, sir! I suppose I'm the biggest manufacturer in the world of overhead and underground Aerial widgets."

If Sissy had read the play, Bob told her, she would know what he felt like. A "manufacturer with a small factory for the production of widgets." Not a "potter," certainly, much as Sissy liked the sound of the word. He was "a great many things, most of them bad, but not a potter." Or maybe he *was* a potter. It was nothing to be proud of. "I'm an oaf, I'm a bum, I'm a potter." Not a painter, either, though he yearned for a day off, to put brush to canvas. Mostly, he was an "impatient addlepated ass," a widgetmaking "drudge."

I don't want to lead this sort of life after we are married. . . . After I leave the workshop I am dead. I can't take an interest in anything and I am disgustingly dull, as you may have noticed. I don't mind hard work, but I don't think it should kill you for anything else. This world is really a rather amusing place if you have time to look around a little bit, and by that I don't mean just arrowheads. The truth is that I would like to do a little painting, just enough to make me sick of it. But I can't take time out. I'm supposed to devote all of my time to the business of making money. It wouldn't be quite as bad if I were making it, but I'm not, not much, anyway. I suppose all this is the result of having been curled up in the kiln all afternoon. I'm just beginning to get the kinks out.

He was dead tired, depressed, but did his best not to complain. The Anderson emblem was a live oak, with the motto: "Stand sure."

Don't be bothered by any of this, just remember that discontent is one of the penalties of greatness. Continually driving and forcing us to greater heights of endeavor. Which simply means that I don't expect to spend the rest of my life making widgets. Also, and in parentheses, that I refuse to be thankful for the opportunity to make more and more widgets. That has no connection with our right to lead a happy life. We have no rights, except those we acquire by our own unaided efforts.

In a well-to-do family with parents who did everything possible to further his art, things had always come easily to him. This was his first job, the first time he had "caught the disease called work." He scolded himself for behaving "like a spoilt little boy with a craving for sympathy and a pat on the head."

Selling the figurines was no fun either. At Mardi Gras, Shearwater sent a truckload of pottery into New Orleans. A "constant stream of Andersons came and went" from a place on Royal Street. The unhappiest was Bob: "I have found one thing worse than making little figures and that is selling them. It seems the worst sort of hypocrisy trying to get money for something that you know is perfectly worthless." Peter, too, disliked them. Occasionally, he would pluck some of the brightly painted figurines from the shelves and dip them, with a chuckle, in Shearwater's characteristic turquoise, or in "brilliant blue, copper-splashed glaze." Those pieces sometimes reappear in antique stores and yard sales, the bright colors muted but still visible under turquoise or icy blue, perpetuating unresolved tensions between their makers. "Peter liked plain pottery," Sissy explained years later. "He liked shape . . . and he was always experimenting with different beautiful glazes, and it would have suited him, I think, to have had his showroom remain the one little room with special displays of special shapes and special glazes. But instead, he had to turn part of it over to his brothers. And soon the showroom was not what Peter had wanted it to be at all, but what his mother thought it should be, with everybody in together." No doubt Peter was tired of hearing Bob's complaints about the strain of working in the Pottery. If making "mudpies" was an inferior occupation for Bob, why was it good enough for him?

Bob would have dropped the widget business altogether if he could be sure of getting a steady job somewhere. Even office work had begun to seem appealing. It could hardly be more boring than the clay and plaster. But there was no chance of that, given the country's "beastly state of depression." He would be more likely to hop a freight train and show up in Sewickley. He saw himself "as an old man of ninety still trying to make enough little figures to make enough money to be married on." He felt abominably lonely, with aching bones and a "sort of caved-in feeling," a "buried-alive feeling: association of ideas, I suppose." Figurines . . . earth . . . dead and buried. He wished he could hibernate until Sissy returned, disappear, "commit suicide temporarily," though that would be "bad publicity for the Pottery." He dreamed of laying his head in her lap and having her stroke his forehead and help him forget about everything. Somehow the figurine business—casting and scraping and making molds—gave him an insatiable appetite for kisses, and he yearned for the day they would lie down with their "heads on the same pillow." And yet, for the moment, he thought, it was better to have her in Sewickley: "I'd give anything to have you here, and yet I think it may be a good thing in some ways that you aren't. It would be absolutely impossible to think nothing but molds and [figurines] all day if you were here, and that is what I have to do. But I wish I had you to come home to after it's all over . . . you are what I need more than anything else in the world."

There was no escape. If Sissy were there, he wouldn't be able to concentrate or do half as much work on the figurines, and their marriage would be delayed. On the other hand, "if it weren't for you, I probably wouldn't do any work at all." From Sewickley, she tried to cheer him up. Never mind about looking for work outside Shearwater, she told him.

[I don't think] there's a chance in a thousand of your getting a job, but if there was, I don't want you to. I like you as you are, and don't want you even to work the way job-people do. There's something freer about pottery, even

though you probably don't think so now when you're pretty much tied down. Oh, I wish you weren't, and it's my fault that you are, because before you could pick up and go off adventuring, and you must be tired, and I'd like to be there, because I can almost feel your head wanting my fingers to rub it and make it quickly well, and I will be, just as soon as I can, because that's what matters, now and always.

No, there was no time now for adventuring. He had hardly been out on the *Pelican,* and felt none of the creative joy of a few years earlier. In the midst of his deadly monotonous labor, he was afraid to look around him. A possum, a bird, some flowers, anything might reawaken the yearning to paint. He could not "get used to this business of living on what has happened and what will happen in the future." He had "never had to do it before," and hoped he would never have to do it again. Never wanted money so much ("filthy stuff, but rather useful at times"), and vowed never again to take an interest in it. "Spiritually, mentally, morally," he had changed, had become "a machine for the production of widgets." There was much he could do to prepare for her arrival. "All things are supposed to come to the man who can wait," he told himself. After work in the evening, in his little room upstairs in the Barn, he thought of the house he wanted to build for her, with an open fireplace and a cold wind whistling outside. It would be full of "strange and outlandish things," not the least of them her future husband. He carved a "very badly made chest, to hold our blankets, if we have any." In Sewickley, Sissy, too, was thinking of their house—"we'll have one of the 'ourest' houses in the world, won't we?" She didn't much care if it was a packing crate or a houseboat anchored in the Bay of Biloxi. She was knitting him a sweater and in Ocean Springs, in the evenings, when he wasn't too worn out from trimming and glazing figurines, he worked at a hooked rug, hoping to finish it before her arrival, mixing the colors, undoing his work when he was dissatisfied with it. Since they would probably be too poor to own even a bed, they could sleep *on* that rug in the summer and *under* it in the winter. "I hope you understand that it is symbolic of my desire to have you walk on me; also, as an outward and visible sign of my prostrate state whenever I think of you, which may or not sound like buncum, but is very near the truth." There would be an orange tree outside the house, so that they could pick their breakfast fresh every morning, and iris transplanted from the Louisiana swamps. And she ought to brush up on her cooking, consult her cookbook "and find out what can be done with catfish and purloined corn."

In spring 1932, in a state of exhaustion, entombed like a Chinese emperor, surrounded by his army of little earthen people, Bob told Sissy he could wait no longer to be married. In Sewickley, worn down by his own work in the trust department of a Pittsburgh bank, Mr. Grinstead had sunk into a severe depression. Alarmed by his condition, Sissy's mother moved him to a hospital in Baltimore—Sheppard and Enoch Pratt—and found a nearby apartment. Sissy moved to Shearwater, into the Front House with Pat and Peter, and then back to Baltimore to be with her parents. Eventually, they set a wedding date: April 29, 1933. Annette and Walter gave them the Cottage as a wedding gift.

Decades later, long after Bob's death, on a sunny spring day at Shearwater, with azaleas and dogwood in full bloom, Sissy remembered their wedding day. They had planned to drive together to the little church at Gautier where her parents had been married. She remembered putting on her finery—a pale blue dress, "on the green side, with gray flowers," and a hat to match, and strap slippers in beige with brown trim and fairly high heels. She remembered dressing in the second-floor bedroom at the Front House, donning a little capelet, coming downstairs, and waiting for Bob. When the groom did not appear, she said good-bye to Pat and the babies and walked down the path to the Barn, floating dreamily through the lush green foliage, past Annette's little flower bed, full of Saint-Joseph's-lilies and larkspur. But Bob was not at the Barn. He had gone to Biloxi for a ring, Mac told her. When he returned, they climbed into the little Chevrolet convertible her father had bought his daughters when

Sissy graduated from Radcliffe, and drove the twelve miles to Gautier. She looked over at him and longed "to be taken care of like a little child." But his look was not a "caring" one. Beside her, in the car, he was smiling, "but with a sort of diabolic ecstasy." There is a photograph of the wedding day. Annette and Walter, Pat and Peter, Mac and his girlfriend. The three brothers dressed smartly in white trousers with navy blue jackets. No one suspecting the trouble that lay ahead.

MOTHS AND BEES

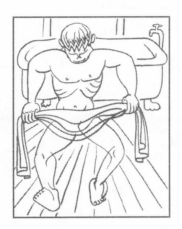

There were hours of grace in those days, moments when the family felt able to poke fun politely at the outside world, laugh at its own foibles, and defend itself against those unable to comprehend its creative energy. Sissy remembers such a moment on a fall morning in 1933 or 1934, early in her marriage. She and Bob were standing outside the showroom, summoned by Annette.

She was inside giving a highly colored tour to a national figure in the Church. His reputation was for spirituality and worldliness. His hair was white.

It was obvious that he had a great deal going for him, and Mère [Annette] was anxious for his opinion on this fledgling venture in which her sons were engaged. She knew, of course, how wonderful it was, but she wanted the world to know. And so we stood, a little off the path and under the sweet-gum tree. Bob was observing the pattern of five-pointed sweet-gum leaves and multi-colored fruit above his head. His head, of course, was thrown back but the smile on his lips was not the smile of one who gazes reverently upon beauty, rather it contained something of mischief. He must have relented because, as his mother and her guest, hand in hand, descended the steps, he leaned over and said to me:

"Move over into the clear, Sissy. One never knows when stars may fall, even in Mississippi."

His eye was upon the frail pink scalp with its fringe, nay halo, of silver hair. And now there were more introductions.

"Mr. Fosdick," Mère [asked], "don't you feel a tremendous sympathy and understanding? Besides the very real artistic achievement . . ."

His look was as cold as his halo.

"I cannot say that I do," he said. "Do you really want to know what I feel?"

"Of course," said Bob, looking suddenly intent. Mère did not answer.

The man of God fixed him with a gimlet eye.

"Only look about you," he said. "This is a land of overpowering physical beauty. The hand of the Creator is everywhere manifest. My heart is constantly bursting with praise and thanksgiving. What you offer me has no depth at all, young man."

He took the small negro figurine from Mère's hand. It was a small dancer in a gay print dress. Her hands were on her hips and a smile on her lips.

"Mundane," affirmed the man of God. "Almost a caricature!"

He reached out and took Bob by the hand.

"I would not say this," he told him very earnestly, "if I did not feel in your work and in your presence the promise of greatness. Your trouble is that you have no roots. Put them down, put them down deep. Without them, no growth is possible."

He had succeeded in touching Bob to the quick, though Bob did not show it.

"What about 'the watered shoot?' " he murmured gently as he detached his hand.

There was a ripple of laughter in the sunlight. A star did fall as the chauffeur opened the door of the limousine. Everyone waved. I was disentangling the points of the star from my hair, and when I looked up the car was gone. Bob had disappeared and Mère's back, rather stiff, was vanishing through the door of the Barn.

"I liked that about the watered shoot," Mr. Anderson remarked quietly. He was sinking a few well-placed putts in the roots of the hickory tree.

No, not all growth depended upon putting down "deep roots." Within sight, draped from the live oaks, the Spanish moss seemed to feed upon air, and like any gardener, Bob had propagated plants in water: the "watered shoot" with which he had mystified the pompous minister. The hickory tree is gone now, blown down in a storm, and underbrush and car tracks have covered Walter's old putting green: a stretch of sand in front of the Barn, with a red oak at one end and the hickory tree at the other. There were lounge chairs and benches, and the family gathered there sometimes for its meetings. Year round, golf clubs were leaning against the oak tree: a putter, a midiron, and a mashie for lofting balls toward the Front House. Michael stood on that spot one spring day and remembered that, as he watched his grandfather work on his putting, he tried to catch doodlebugs, pushing a sticky straw down into their burrows.

There were moments of hardship, too, but the family coped with them. The yearning that both Peter and Bob had described in their letters—to create simple, beautiful homes for their wives—was being realized. It was Mac who talked about it least and who went farthest: a few years later, he would build himself an entire house and much of its furniture. Ironically, the Arts and Crafts ideal of sturdy, homemade essential objects, became a necessity during the Depression. The family had no *choice* but to live simply. With three mouths to feed—Michael, Patsy, and Marjorie—Peter and Pat speared flounder, netted mullet, grew vegetables, hunted for ducks and geese, and started an oyster bed. As a first-anniversary present, Peter gave Pat a swarm of black bees. A one-eyed friend, Emil Beaugez, one of the carpenters who had worked on the Pottery buildings, had spotted them on a bush down the road, swept them into a box, and sold them for $1.50. Pat made a veil from window screening and blue-striped canvas, and Peter bought the *ABCs of Bee-keeping* and made his own hives from thin boards of cypress. Those bees were his "pride and joy," Pat said. He read about bees in all his spare moments. At six in the morning, he was tending the hives, and at five in the evening he was looking again.

He looked for everything. For queen cells, for eggs, for too many drones, for roaches, for honey, for sick bees, for weak queens. He decided two of the queens were old. Too many drones inhabited the hives. He wrote for new queens. They came in neat little cages surrounded by their small court. He gave one to the black bees. They balled her (a bee technicality) and killed her. Peter let them grow their own queen. He was so afraid she might swarm that he caught her to clip her wings, but cut off her leg. He almost wept when he cut it off. He spoke to her very endearingly and glared when I said she probably didn't feel it.

The Front House turned into a sticky mess, with bee frames and honey everywhere. Peter sold it at the Pottery, designed a new 50-cent honey pot, and made a little extra cash. Bob was different. Never one to budget or save, he spent his grocery money on W. J. Holland's magnificent book on moths. In it was a recipe for attracting them at night by smearing the trunks of trees with a mixture of stale beer and sugar. One day, Bob and Sissy painted pines and oaks with the gooey treacle and at nightfall went into the woods. Bob carried a kerosene-burning torch; Sissy, a net, a jar, and a flashlight. It was a moment she would remember forever.

*He swung the light here and there amongst the trees. . . . Small stuff,
[which had] more or less stuck to the bark, greeted us. . . . Suddenly a large
shadow flitted across his field of vision. He dropped the light.*

*"Net!" he cried, like a surgeon calling for a scalpel. . . . Into the flames
flew a magnificent creature. Now flames arose from the pine needles and dry
leaves upon which he had flung his flare. He raced to cut off the flow of
kerosene, lifted the light, stamped upon the flames.*

*"What the devil are you up to, you damned fool?" said a voice from the
shadows. "Put that thing out!"*

It was . . . Peter.

"It is out," was the quiet response.

*"Not to my way of thinking it's not. You'll douse that area with water or
you'll have the whole place up in smoke."*

*It was then that I made the mistake of shining my light against the drip-
ping trunk of the tree. At once, those small creatures showed up as bees, bees
heartily inebriated, bees staggering about, bees bumping each other and picking
fights.*

*Bob began to laugh . . . [but] these were Peter's most precious bees . . .
from whom he derived not only considerable income, but honey for the whole
family.*

*"If you think that's funny, you're a bigger damned fool than even I
thought," he said. . . .*

"What is that stuff, and how did it get on that tree?"

*"It's moth bait. I've as much right to bait moths as you have to keep
bees. . . ."*

*The fight took its course. You could hear the blows landing solidly, flesh
and bone against flesh and bone. Then both had had enough.*

*"Shake hands," said Peter, "and for God's sake get a bucket and wash that
stuff off that tree. You may have ruined my bee business already."*

*The whole incident seemed to pass off, leaving no memory. Only in my
heart the outrage and the terror remained, and the faint odor of poison in the
relationship.*

Moths and bees, butterfly hunters and beekeepers. How incompatible they seemed. Everyone was relieved, Sissy says, when Bob decided to hunt moths and butterflies in Florida rather than locally. They set off in an old truck, rigged up as a camper with canvas sides and a mattress, chased butterflies across the elegant lawns of Miami and Coral Gables, and made it all the way to Key Largo. They returned, Bob wrote, with six or seven moths with "wonderful, beautifully shaped wings, like the bark of a tree with lilac eyes." And "speaking of Sissy," he wrote to his mother, "this trip has added to my already great admiration for the young lady. If you could have seen her pursuing butterflies in the face of the Miami tribe, completely indifferent [to them], with her shirt-tails flying in the breeze!"

They made many such excursions in search of their favorite things: flowers and butterflies, arrowheads, ice cream and music. Bob had given her his wanderlust for places far and near. When their money problems worsened, they sold the beloved Chevy convertible, bought bikes, and made trips to Oldfields or Graveline, or through the countryside and across the Iberville bridge to the ice cream parlor in Biloxi. The highways were narrow and dangerous, and he laughed at her fear of passing cars. Sometimes they ventured farther afield. Before they were married, Sissy had told him she wanted to "float down the Mississippi with you and have just you and nobody else I know for days and days." Bob loved the idea. Some day, he promised, the two of them would do that on a shanty boat, or go out alone to the islands when the pelicans were nesting, he with pencil and paper, and she with her "unmentionable camera." She had consoled herself, during her lonely time in Sewickley, remembering their trips on the *Pelican* up the Pascagoula and their sailing trips from Oldfields to Horn Island. In the first year of their marriage, they made an excursion from one end to the other of the barrier islands, until the *Pelican* ran out of oil: Bob had forgotten to replenish it. A year later, they took a bus to Bethlehem, Pennsylvania, for the Bach festival, headed south to Louisville, and decided to return home in a canoe, down the Ohio and the Mississippi. Bob had done it before, the year he completed his course of study at the academy. Instead of wiring home for money for the trip, he had taken a construction job on the Pennsylvania Railroad, made $90, and bought a battered little boat. The front end leaked, but he sat in the back and tipped it out of the water, and began to paddle. Before reaching New Orleans, he ate some green corn and felt sick. An old black man on the riverbank offered him a bottle of Shane's liniment. He drank it down gratefully, and had to finish the trip overland. This time, in May 1934, Sissy's Grinstead relatives saw them off at the foot of Second Street, and they drifted for weeks, taking in the slow beauty of the river and the signs of the Depression along its banks—people living "in every conceivable shelter from cardboard cartons through wooden packing cases to tin-roof tents." Somewhere past Memphis, Bob contracted malaria and they had to complete their journey by train.

There were quiet times at home in the Cottage. In the evenings, she read aloud from Gibbon or Chesterton while he hooked rugs—her own work was tighter than he liked—or they listened to classical music on the phonograph. Like Peter and Pat, they kept a garden, made preserves and elderberry wine, and went shrimping with a little cast net when there was no money for food. At midday, they often ate dinner with Annette and Walter at the Barn. Bob was forever transforming their little house, making improbable but beautiful furniture from cypress planks they bought from a sawmill up the Pascagoula. He made a table, a bed, bookcases flush to the floor (no need to sweep under them). He made tall desks, too tall for chairs, so that they had to use them standing up and for years people in Ocean Springs gossiped that the Andersons were so strange they had no chairs in their houses. For all its oddity, she loved the Cottage and the little path behind it, which led down to the marsh. Years later, she remembered its enchantment.

Looking out the back door, the little path ran down the hill. I would stand there in the early morning wishing that my eyes might find some far horizon like the sweep from the bluff at Oldfields. Gradually I became intimate with

157

my little space and loved it for all its revealed intimacies. From the flight of four wooden steps painted heavily in gray deck enamel, "to hold them together," as he said, the path wiggled a little, shaking itself through the skinny chinaberry trees. These stood, spindly and shatterable, too close to the house. In the spring the clusters of purple flowers reminded me of lilacs. They attracted humming-birds and gnatcatchers. Through the warm months the berries matured. A violent summer squall might send showers of the fruit rattling against our shingles. The most mature would be as big as marbles and green as grass. All over Mississippi little boys would be having furious games. The best time, though, was the end of winter. The tattered clusters hung, pulpy and yellowed, plopping on our steps when the wind blew. Then came the robins on their way north. The flocks were perpetually hungry and stopped to strip the chinaberries. They never seemed to learn that fermentation had taken place and enough of the brew produced a ridiculous gang of inebriates strutting and squabbling among the fallen fruit. When one of the swashbucklers suddenly fell upon his side to his unutterable amazement it was so funny that we stood for hours just waiting for the event. It was a nervous time too, for the cats had to be reckoned with and rescue forays were frequent.

Beyond the space where the robins were beguiled, the wax myrtle bushes formed a year-round wall of greenery, glossy and dense. The path made a little jog as it entered their domain and vanished from sight. An occasional yaupon accented the wall with its light colored trunk or a flare of red berries at Christmas.

Through the late summer and fall the moonflowers spread the thick curtains of their vines across the myrtles. Oh, such ailanthus leaves, curled, pointy, deeply scalloped! Such tendrils! Such floating fuzzy puffs of seed pods! And at night, the miracle of the flowers! We would stand in the moonlight watching the pale lilac of the innumerable spirals trying to catch the very first movement of the unwinding spiral; trying to be the first to see the unfurled blossom; to catch the first whiff of the fragrance.

From 1933 until 1937, Bob continued to work at the Annex with Mac, who produced some of his most striking pieces. One of them, a tall green matte vase into which he had carved a spiraling fish, was selected to tour Europe with an exhibition of American ceramics selected by Syracuse University in memory of Adelaide Alsop Robineau. It stands today in the showroom, along with other creations from those years: a low bowl in the shape of a magnolia blossom, vases with patient, intricate carving; vases with brightly colored oyster tongers or scenes from New Orleans. Mac had sometimes joked, in his self-effacing way, that somehow art had "rubbed off" on him, that, in the family, he merely "rubbed elbows" with it. But no one in the family doubted now that he had become an artist in his own right.

In December 1933, Ellsworth Woodward, a family friend from Annette's days at Newcomb, was appointed head of the Gulf Coast division of the Public Works Administration. He thought of the Andersons, and commissioned Peter and Mac to create a tile mural for the entrance hall of the Ocean Springs Public School, and Bob to do a painted mural in the auditorium. Peter dug clay from the banks of the Tchoutacabouffa and bisque-fired a series of 228 6.5-square-inch tiles on which Mac painted—in black and royal blue—birds and fish native to the Coast. When Peter had glazed them and the two brothers had set them in place, they formed two seven-foot panels.

In his studio, Bob fell to work on a series of six paintings on the history of Ocean Springs. It was the most enjoyable work he had ever done. He leaped at the chance to paint on commission, and to set aside the "boilerplate" work he had been doing at the Pottery. Three of his paintings depicted the Biloxi Indians *(The Chase, Bringing the Deer Home,* and *Feast in Camp)* and three were scenes from modern life *(A Sea Cottage, Men Tonging for Oysters and Fishing with Nets,* and *A Sailing Scene).* Like some of his pottery pieces, the stylized figures reveal his passion for the cave painting he had seen on his travels in France and the ceramics of ancient Greece. To a visitor in 1934, they suggested "Egyptian friezes"; to Sissy, "Egyptian tomb painting or Minoan wall fragments." The commission was welcome in another way: like Woodward and his mother, Bob believed the artist had an important social role, and was grateful for the chance to share his painting with the town. He worked, Sissy writes, with the happiness of a child, but chafed against the strict specifications—on materials and their application—imposed by Woodward and the PWA. Sissy remembered Bob's irritation as he chased around New Orleans for supplies that were unavailable in Ocean Springs. "When you got finished paying for all these certain expensive paints and canvasses and all that, and the glue, and somebody to help you put them up, because you couldn't have done it by yourself, you didn't have very much money left."

Despite that frustration, the project brought publicity and public recognition to all three brothers. In June 1934, when the murals were about to be installed, Ann Craton, field coordinator of the PWA, spent a weekend at the Front House with Peter and Pat and spoke enthusiastically about the brothers' work in the Ocean Springs newspaper. Peter and Mac's tiles, she pointed out to local dignitaries, were "the only ones of the kind to be installed in any public building in the South, and perhaps in the U.S. under the PWA."

Before long, Bob was competing for another commission, a mural in the post office at Jackson, sponsored by the Treasury Relief Art Project. A memo to the TRAP commissioner from the local woman who was organizing the competition noted in September 1935 that he probably had "more training in Mural Art" than anyone else in the state, and that he had been to "art school in Philadelphia, Pa.," but that, unlike other artists, though he was "in need of work," he had failed to apply to the National Reemployment Service for relief, "hoping to avoid the embarrassment" of public assistance. Preference was given to those on the welfare rolls. Although his design was selected by a committee in Jackson, it was rejected—despite local protest and several revisions—in Washington. Once again, he was condemned to his work as a decorator at the Pottery.

There, he modeled figurines, decorated plates and vases, and turned over new ideas, not all of which found their way into production. Lampshades, for instance, made of brightly colored construction paper glued to parchment. He loved the idea of pottery lamps and dreamed of doing inexpensive shades that would have the effect of stained glass. Sissy remembered the problems: the glue that didn't stick or discolored the paper, the paper that peeled away at the warmth of the lightbulb. And Peter didn't always have time to help him with the right sort of lamp bases. "There was only so much time in a working day," Sissy wrote later, "and so much space in a kiln."

Peter's impatient brother could not take it. He wept and roared from weakness, and attacked his brother with his fists and his words. In spite of everything, there began to be lampshades. They were exciting and beautiful. People saw them in the showroom and bought them. He had been right. The stained glass effect was not quite what he had hoped for. Mostly the paper was too opaque. If he oiled it, which seemed a reasonable solution, the colors were not as good, the oil ran. I died a thousand deaths because it seemed to me that I should have been able to take over all those technical details and solve them for him, and I was no good, no good at all.

As always, Bob longed for more time to read, and to look at plants and animals. Painting seemed out of the question. When Sissy urged him to paint after work or on weekends, he said he couldn't: it absorbed him so completely he was unable to do it in his spare moments. Sissy struggled with the guilty feeling that his life would be simpler, less duty-bound, without her; that he would be more creative without a wife to support. There were times when she wondered to herself whether they should have married at all. Many years later, she remembered the enormous strain on both of them, and speculated that it had probably been harder for her than for Pat to adjust to married life. "It was a terrific step that I took," she said, "because I was not really very much like my sister. She was very domestic and she loved settling down into a little house with a husband and babies and whatnot, and seemed to give up the things that she had been used to fairly easily. But I didn't. I had a lot of stuff in me that still said, 'Now you don't want to do this.' I came to Ocean Springs after a fairly exciting life for a young girl." After graduating from Radcliffe, Sissy had been offered a teaching job at a boarding school in Virginia. Though she thought of herself as a born teacher, she had turned down that offer so that she could marry Bob. Her own aspirations seemed always to take second place to his needs, despite his own attempts to encourage her. In her journals, there are ideas for short stories and novels, and the continual resolution to develop them. Bob urged her to write poems, and sometimes she sat at a card table on the porch, composing an epic about the Spanish exploration of the Coast, taking it up like a patchwork quilt when there was nothing else to do: "By the faint light of one fast-dimming star . . ." There was a little theater group in Ocean Springs, and she and Pat sometimes did the costumes and stage sets, or acted in the plays, though they could never get their husbands to take an interest.

What Bob wanted, he told her a year before they married, was to have her depend on him, and to be alone with her. "Just you and I," was a recurrent phrase that began to annoy her. He wanted to help her conquer her fear of the dark, both literally and figuratively; to put her in touch with water and air and earth, enable her to go beyond her "silly ideas" about things, and help him search for whatever there was of paradise on the Coast of Mississippi. One gathers from her writing and reminiscences that she felt more alive in his presence, drawn to his sensuality, his energy, and his passion for life. He taught her to see beauty she would not have seen without him. She longed for him to "get something from me without having to put it in first." She marveled over the things he knew, "not only by observation but by a sort of intuition, a sort of basic and far-reaching knowledge that he himself was later to define as the ability to become one with any living thing."

Despite her devotion to him, or perhaps because of it, he often pushed her away or simply disappeared. She struggled with her temper, called him "selfish," accused him of having "no consideration," or, in more benevolent moods, tried to accustom herself "to being there when wanted and being a part of the general background when not." In her own family, she wrote, "the creative act was the giving of one-self to others in ordinary human intercourse." In his, what mattered was the artistic side of people, and what beauty they could produce from it. She wanted him to paint, but—so she said years later—"never really forgave him for constantly requiring periods of solitude." And yet she could see that the time he spent alone left him rejuvenated and trans-formed.

One fall day, without a word to anyone, he did not come home for lunch and vanished for the night, leaving her sick with worry. When he reappeared the following day, he told her that on his way to the work-shop in the morning, he had seen a flock of great white birds in the sky over the marsh. They looked so beautiful in the morning light that he followed them until he could go no farther on land, waded into the water and swam out into the Sound. He spent the rest of the day and most of the night watching them until they flew away into the moon-light. They were white pelicans, part of the paradise he was looking for. Years later, when he had made many such trips, he wrote of their fascination:

There comes a time when you realize that the pelican holds everything for you. It has the song of the thrush, the form and understanding of man, the tenderness and gentleness of the dove, the mystery and dynamic quality of the nightjar, and the potential qualities of all life.

In a word, you lose your heart to it. It becomes your child, and the hope and future of the world depend upon it. You share in all of its reactions and conditions of life, you awake with it, you feel the change from the cave of sleep to the beginning of consciousness and desire. You hear the cries of hunger with the need to cry to the first mover, the primum mobile.

Of all his birds, writes his daughter Mary, pelicans were the most im-portant to him. Before marrying Sissy, he had kept one as a pet, and late in his life, he lived with them during nesting season on the Chandeleur Islands, and even attempted to record a "Pelican Dictionary of Common Terms." "Beautiful and ugly, dignified and comical, graceful and awkward, fragile yet indomitable, the pelican is a union of opposites reflecting the ambivalence of my father's own nature and for that reason endlessly fascinating to him."

Although Sissy understood that fascination, his sudden disappearances troubled her. Years later, she remembered the uneasiness she felt every morning when he set out for the Annex, and the excuses she found for passing by during the day. As he went off to work in the morning, the door banging behind him, and walked the two hundred yards or so to the Annex, she told herself that she had little to worry about. She could have called to him across the marsh. And "when he reached work he would be in a lovely place" with Mac as a companion. "He would be working with nothing more dangerous than soft clay and a bamboo stick. What did I fear? How could he vanish? I don't know. I think it was because he could come back a completely different person even when he came back as scheduled at lunch time." Especially after the Mississippi River trip, there were things about him that made her uneasy: "little flare-ups, small explosions of unbearable intensity." Just a year after they were married, for example, she surprised him with a set of phonograph records—Beethoven's *Missa Solemnis*—for his birthday. He listened to them for a while and caught her up in a somber dance. And then, for no apparent reason, he threw the records to the floor, smashing them to pieces, and bolted out the door. At times like those she felt bewildered and consulted with Annette. Long ago, she had realized how dependent Bob was upon his mother.

It was not just the fact that he was [Annette's] favorite; circumstances had made the situation far more complicated. She was an artist; he was an artist. Similar interests, similar temperaments drew them together. Then there was their isolation from professionals of their calling. They needed each other for crit-

icism, for speaking the same language. He loved her very deeply and respected her even more. She had demonstrated over and over her faith in him. In my moments of doubting him during the early years of our marriage and right on through, it meant a great deal to me. I can hear her now: "Bobby is Bobby. You cannot set ordinary standards by which to judge him."

"TREMBLING, ON THE
EDGE OF LIGHT . . ."

Bob and Sissy liked to drive each spring to the Honey Island Swamp, in Louisiana, in search of irises to transplant to the marsh at the end of the path behind the Cottage. On their trip one year—it must have been 1936—they rambled over the countryside in the family car, and, miles from civilization, came upon a Cajun patriarch and his numerous progeny, who were celebrating his fiftieth birthday. A helping of homemade ice cream brought both of them low for months with an excruciating attack of undulant fever. At first, neither was able to get out of bed. Bob was stricken especially hard, with soaring fever and headache. He lay motionless, with glazed eyes.

That fall, Walter, too, fell ill. He was seventy-five, and for a long time he had been feeling tired and sad. Annette nursed him at the Barn, skeptical of conventional medicine and placing her hope in prayer and in Christian Science. During the last few years of his life, he thought incessantly about golf, about a book he had written that would revolutionize the art of putting, making it "almost as accurate as billiards." He was certain that, if he could get his book into the hands of Gene Sarazen or Bobby Jones, it would become a best-seller. He wrote to Quentin Reynolds and offered to share his royalties with him in return for publicity. During his illness, he appointed a literary executor. There would be hundreds of thousands of dollars of royalties, the fruit of his experiments at the Biloxi Country Club and under the hickory tree. He died of stomach cancer on February 23, 1937, and was buried in the family plot overlooking Fort Bayou, at Evergreen Cemetery. Among his papers were several drafts of the "book"—a thirty-page manuscript—and a pile of financial statements. The Depression had eaten away at his stocks and bonds, leaving the family almost entirely dependent on the Pottery.

His death provoked a crisis in Bob, who had not yet fully recovered from his own illness. Sissy remembers him consoling himself by listening to Bach—"Jesu, Joy of Man's Desiring"—and withdrawing into silence. Annette guessed that he was grieving for his father; Sissy, that he could no longer "face the routine of making a living. . . . His life was based on someone else's pattern and he could not conform." Probably both of them were right. Somber moods gave way to delirium and violence. He cut his wrists with a razor and told Sissy he wanted to throw himself under a passing car. He growled at her like a dog, and sank his teeth into her leg. He "gamboled about on all fours saying he was a child of six." He believed that Sissy was mocking him; that certain people around him were members of the Gurdjieff Institute—the spiritual center he had visited during his student travel in France—and that they were "trying to debase and hurt him." He said that he was impotent, stricken with venereal disease, and that God was speaking to him in allegorical suggestions over the radio. One thing especially tormented him. A decade earlier, at the Academy of Fine Arts, he and a friend had traveled from Philadelphia to New York to a spiritual retreat run by A. R. Orage, one of Gurdjieff's spokesmen in America. There, he said, he had had a "homosexual" experience: he had slept in the same bed with a male friend, and the friend had put his arm around him. No one was sure whether this had really happened, but he felt so deeply guilty about it that he could barely discuss it, even with Sissy.

Family papers reveal little in his past to explain the sudden and devastating breakdown of late March 1937. For years, the family had worried about his lack of close friends, his terrible temper, and the vehemence of his passions. His study of Gurdjieff had given him the idea that one can strengthen the spirit by punishing the body, and he had the habit, shown in different ways, of toughening himself through physical pain. More than once Sissy saw him put out a cigarette on the palm of his hand, and a little before his breakdown, he plunged his hand into the fireplace, burning it badly. The long struggle with undulant fever may also have been a factor, along with his failure to win the competition for the mural in Jackson.

As they tried to decide what to do, the family remembered relatives in Baltimore. Sissy and Pat's cousin Grinstead Vaughan lived there, and their "almost sister" Ellen had moved to Rodgers Forge and was living at the home of an important pediatrician at Johns Hopkins, Edwards A. Park. She had introduced Bob and Sissy to him a couple of years before when they were in Baltimore on their way to the Bach festival in Bethlehem, and he and Bob had gone birding together. It was probably at Park's suggestion that Bob was admitted, on April 4, 1937, to the Henry Phipps Psychiatric Clinic under the care of its founder and director, Adolf Meyer, the dominant figure in American psychiatry for over four decades. Around him—treating Bob—were some of the best psychiatrists in the country, including Norman Cameron (who later became a friend),

Maurice Partridge, Theodore Lidz, A. H. Leighton, and Wendell S. Muncie: all authors of important monographs on mental illness. Meyer's fame attracted interns and "externs" from all over the United States. One whom Bob seemed to trust, and who helped take down his history upon admission to the clinic, was a forty-six-year-old general practitioner, Henry Mead, who came to Meyer from Chicago for guidance and training. He had become aware, he said, of the "growing shadow of the psyche [even] in the plainest of medical etiologies."

The language of Meyer's diagnosis—on which other physicians collaborated—probably mystified both Mead and the Anderson family: "hypothymergasia with homosexual panic and paranoid trends, and parergasic features." Ergasia (from the Greek "work") meant behavior. Hypothymergasia was a specific kind of depression in which the patient exhibited feelings of guilt and the desire to harm himself. Parergasia was Meyer's peculiar name for schizophrenia. But Meyer spoke of parergasic *features* and paranoid *trends;* in his view, people did not simply *have* schizophrenia, they exhibited behaviors and fell into mistaken habits of thought that psychiatry could help them correct. Theodore Lidz, who was familiar with Bob's case, and who later became head of the Department of Psychiatry at Yale, writes that Meyer was "profoundly pragmatic." He "focused on what could be worked with—change the environment, alter habit patterns and ways of thinking, help the patient solve or resolve problems. See what works and what does not work; mobilize the patient's assets. . . . Meyer was a meliorist, interested in improvement when he could not cure." His was a holistic approach. He scorned approaches that were purely biological or hereditary, laughed at his own terminological "word palaces," and believed in the importance of crucial "life events" in triggering pathological behavior. Each of his patients was an "experiment in nature." This meant spending as much time as possible gathering information from his patients and their families. Bob's case was "exceedingly interesting," he told another doctor in 1939, "but I am afraid he has never given any real access to us with regard to the undercurrents." This was the most difficult, most inaccessible patient to enter Phipps in a year, Meyer told his colleagues, and no one disagreed.

In her memoirs, *Approaching the Magic Hour,* Sissy told of agonizing visits to the clinic during the first eight months of Bob's confinement. Neither interviews nor sedatives nor hydrotherapy nor attempts to rekindle his interest in art seemed to help. When a nurse gave him a pencil, hoping he would draw, he swallowed it and had to undergo an operation. According to Sissy, when she told him she was pregnant—despite their precautions—he repeated that he was impotent, and that the child, unquestionably his, must have been fathered by someone else. He flailed at his attendants, struck at Sissy, put his fist through the double glass on a door, and made repeated attempts on his own life. There were long, silent days when he shuffled about the clinic, muttering to himself or staring into space and hearing "religious voices." He told Sissy, much later, that he realized he was sick and wanted to "stop the workings of his mind."

Annette accompanied Sissy to Baltimore, and the two shared a little room near the clinic. Sissy did her best to fight off despair and to nurture the new life growing inside her. Would Bob ever be well enough to share it with her? Poetry ran through her head, and at times she jotted down some verse in her journal.

> Sweet as the morn
> as yet unfurled:
> my babe unborn
> within me curled.
> His little stirrings, like the night
> still trembling on the edge of light;
> his growing form, tucked safe away,
> is like the promise of the day. . . .

Those lines were written early one December morning, as she lay in the maternity ward at Hopkins, days before giving birth to a baby girl.

From her window, she could see Bob's corner of Phipps, a world away. She longed for him. Annette, who was keeping her company, told her of the sweltering September afternoon in 1903 when Bobby was born: "I felt as if my whole self, my dreams, my hopes, any gifts I possessed had flowed out of me into this child. He was not beautiful as the first baby had been. I remember thinking, 'He's scrawny, ugly,' and loving him with an absolutely devastating love."

After the baby was born, Bob's doctors noticed a change in him. He smiled on hearing the news, wanted to send some flowers, and told the attendant he had thought of a name: Mary Anne. Soon he was working on a basket for her. She was "a little dream of beauty," Sissy wrote in her journal, "an egg-shell pink and white, [with] Mongolian eyes and dark hair and the most heavenly hands and fingernails." During her pregnancy, she had often dreamed that the baby would come to term along with Bob's illness. Both had begun at the same time. By the time Mary arrived, her father had been at Phipps for eight months. "I suppose I've never really believed in his illness," she wrote. "It's been a sort of interlude, like waiting for the baby, and now, now it ought to be over too. I guess I had counted on that." Depression, she thought, "must be similar in release to a birth, not so much sudden wellness, but a sort of rupture that will permit cessation."

In January 1938, when no such release seemed likely, Bob's doctors requested her permission to use an experimental and frightening form of therapy. Several years earlier, two decades before the introduction of psychotropic drugs in 1953, medical researchers had discovered a helpful clue to treating schizophrenics: a biochemical antagonism between epilepsy and schizophrenia. A Hungarian physician, Ladislaus von Meduna, had already attempted to utilize this antagonism, "if not for curative purposes, at least to arrest or modify the course of schizophrenia." By 1934, he was experimenting with producing epileptiform seizures in his patients, and in 1939, the year Bob was admitted to Phipps, he reported that, in a study of 110 of them, about half achieved remission. No one believed that his treatment would cure schizophrenia, but it allowed doctors better access to the patient's troubles. At Phipps, it seemed to produce an "alert cooperative attitude in patients who [were] confused, 'stand-offish,' or lapsing into stupor."

Before the introduction of electroconvulsive therapy in 1938, the agent used to induce seizures, both in Meduna's experiments and at Phipps, was pentylenetetrazol (either Cardiazol or Metrazol), injected into the patient's muscles or temples. An alternative treatment, often used in combination with Metrazol injections, was the injection of insulin in graduated doses, three to five times weekly, to induce a hypoglycemic coma. Still other patients were drugged into a prolonged sleep, occasionally for as long as three weeks, allowing "sub-conscious mechanisms of self-healing or of amelioration by suggestion to do their work." The grand mal convulsions produced with Cardiazol and Metrazol could be so painful and harrowing that many patients refused subsequent treatments, and described the seizure, or "aura," as "an electrical sensation," "an infernal chill," "sinking slowly into a hole" or "well," or a "falling into non-existence." Before the seizures began, there were several seconds of "terror," and, when too little Metrazol was given, patients experienced "protracted panic with confusion and disorientation lasting an hour or more." "You can throw anybody into a convulsion," Meyer said, in a discussion of Bob's case, "but to get to where we may be able to do it so that it is not a terrifying experience when it does not go perfectly well, will be a great achievement in psychiatry." At a symposium on schizophrenia in May 1938—while Bob was in Phipps—Meduna reported that the seizure "lasts from 30 to 80 seconds."

Since the attack begins with the opening of the mouth, there is ample time to insert a gag between the patient's teeth and so prevent the tongue from being bitten. After the seizure the patient goes to sleep for several minutes but soon regains consciousness. The best evidence for the simplicity of the procedure is that 60–80 patients can be treated in one morning, with the aid of only one assisting physician and at most two or three nurses.

It was, he admitted, a brutal procedure, in part because so little was known about the neuropathology of schizophrenia. In some mysterious way, Metrazol simply altered the patient's chemical milieu.

[Schizophrenia] represents merely the logical result of a chain of chemical processes, concerning which we know nothing and can only make the academic assumption that they develop from a series of reactions conditioning one another . . . On this pathological but logically developed process we act with both methods [of induced seizures], to blow asunder the pathological sequences and restore the diseased organism to normal functioning.

Another researcher compared Metrazol treatment to "an explosive which makes a breach but at the same time may produce damage so far not well-defined."

It was Sissy alone, desperate and already bearing responsibility for newborn Mary, who faced the terrifying decision. "They want to use the shock treatment," she wrote in her diary, "not insulin, but the other . . . Of course my first reaction is *no,* but I've got to have all the facts and I've got to think it out. Oh, I feel as if I just plain couldn't have it done to him, couldn't. I can't believe it's necessary. . . . What should I do? No one's advice seems to be worth taking. Guidance seems to be beyond my reach or strength, but oh, my God, I pray that I may have it, and I have a sort of infinite trust that all will be well."

She did her research, asked her doctors to show her the relevant articles from medical journals, talked, "full of statistics," with Annette, and "wept like an idiot" as both of them signed the papers. The doctors warned her of the dangers: "minute hemorrhages leading to brain destruction," possible paralysis; in rare cases, death. But there were grounds for hope. Bob had sent word through his nurse that "he wished they would find something to help him," and took the first treatment "with the best possible spirit." On her best days, Sissy knew that he would be "just as energetic and quick about getting well as he is about everything."

She took some comfort in the happiness of her "almost-sister," Ellen. One day, Ellen visited her in the hospital, accompanied by Dr. Mead, and Sissy saw from the way that they looked at one another that they had fallen in love, drawn together, among other things, by their interest in Bob. Ellen had been to the clinic to give the doctors information about Bob and his family. It seemed that her long years of misfortune were coming to an end.

Shortly after the treatments began, in January 1938, Sissy and the baby left Baltimore and returned to Ocean Springs. The doctors had told her there was little she could do, and reminded her of her duty to stay strong for Bob and for the baby. Annette remained for a few more months in Baltimore while Bob underwent his treatments—twenty-five injections in January and February, with improvements and setbacks following rapidly upon one another.

Meyer wondered what precedents there were for Bob's illness, and asked Annette for a family history. On the train to Baltimore, as she accompanied Bob and Mac and Sissy to Phipps, she had remembered another journey, almost half a century before, in spring 1891, a couple of years after Walter had begun to court her. Her older sister, Delphine Margaret McConnell (Dellie), a lovely woman with big dark eyes—"big dark eyes like shoes," their mother used to say—had fallen in love with a French painter who was living in New Orleans. Although Dellie was in her mid-twenties, Judge McConnell opposed the relationship, and she began behaving strangely: "laughing and crying without reason." At dinner one day, she reached out to keep her father from picking up a silver napkin ring. It fell to the floor and before he could retrieve it, she threw it into the fire. Judge McConnell was alarmed, and took her to the doctor.

Dellie was diagnosed with dementia praecox (the term "schizophrenia" had yet to be introduced). The family doctor, John B. Elliott, was asked for his opinion and wrote discreetly to her father, "concerning the usual treatment of patients suffering from mental disorder." All specialists agreed, he wrote, "that it is decidedly best for the patient to be entirely separated from all family ties and associations. . . . If the patient is even conscious of being able to fall back upon the sympathies of near relatives, it has an evil influence. . . . This is especially true of the nervous disorders of young persons."

She was to be admitted at once to an asylum in Philadelphia. Perhaps, if she improved quickly, no one would notice her absence. In those days, Annette wrote, "someone got sick, the matter was not discussed, and she would be back before too long, with no one the wiser."

Annette remembered boarding the train for Philadelphia—she and Dellie, their parents and a cousin. "My father and I were more or less nervous or distracted. My mother, as always, was the calm, wise one. . . . [She] wanted time to see if the doctor in Philadelphia agreed with [Dellie's] New Orleans doctors. At the hotel in Philadelphia, we saw Dr. Sinkler, who was associated with Dr. Weir Mitchell. My sister was taken to the Philadelphia Hospital."

For the next three or four years, life in the McConnell family was topsy-turvy. Judge McConnell left his newly married son—Annette's hotheaded brother Jimmy—in charge of his law practice, and accompanied his wife and two daughters from one asylum and sanatorium to another until, in 1900, he signed the papers and paid out $10,000 committing Dellie—for life, if necessary—to Friends Hospital, said to be the best asylum in the country. Doctors there found her to have "a morbid sexual tendency, showing itself in undue fondness for men."

Annette's mother, too, was afflicted by weakness and "nervous spells," and died in 1896, a few years before the commitment of her daughter. There were family rumors that she had been mentally unbalanced. Annette did her best to dispel them. Her mother was her "dearest friend," she said, "and in her last illness I nursed her day and night for nearly six months. . . . Never, in all those months, was her mind clouded."

In New Orleans, while his parents were away, Jimmy McConnell saw much of George Walter Anderson and his family. There were dinners, trips to the theater with Walter's sister Daisy and with their mother—Bob's grandmother, Adele Briggs, a melancholy woman to whom Walter felt extraordinarily close and who suffered from severe depression. And then, suddenly, there was more bad news. Longing to be with Annette, under great stress at work, Walter had a nervous breakdown. He told Jimmy he intended to go North to bring Annette back to New Orleans. In Philadelphia, Judge McConnell shuddered at the idea. "Nothing could be worse for him until he gets well," he wrote his son.

He is improving rapidly where he is, and it will require some time to have him fully restored. And if he is kept away from work and remains at someplace on the lakeshore and has such diversions as fishing, hunting, riding and other out of door exercise (as Dr. Elliott recommends) I feel he will speedily recover. Tell him his marriage is a certainty, but merely put off until he gets well. To come North to see Annie in his present condition would increase his excitement and might lead to his permanent disability. By all means—all gentle and persuasive means—dissuade him from the thought of coming North. Recreation in the open air at the Pass [Pass Christian] or at the Bay [Bay Saint Louis] is best for him.

He went, instead, to Baltimore, where he lived for a year with friends, suffering from delusions and groundless fears of imminent death.

Given Walter's nervous troubles and the illness of her sister, Annette had thought hard before having children. She had written Dr. Sinkler in Philadelphia, and Dr. Elliott in New Orleans, asking if they considered it wise to marry Walter. Neither objected. "Dr. Sinkler . . . , knowing *about both families,* wrote that it was quite right. Dr. Elliott wrote that he did not know about the Andersons, but on my side it was entirely right." Decades later, before marrying Peter and Bob, Pat and Sissy had heard disturbing rumors about their future family. When Pat announced her engagement, members of the Blanc and Monroe families—relatives of Annette—had gone to one of Marjorie Grinstead's friends and asked her if the Grinsteads "knew of the peculiarities of *both* sides of the family their daughter was marrying into. . . . Everyone in New Orleans" knew about Dellie; about the "severe and often continued depression" of the Blancs—Annette's aunts and uncles—and of the instability of her brother Jimmy. Did she know that Walter's mother had died in a mental asylum in New Orleans? Annette made little of all this, dismissing it as malicious gossip about her admittedly "moody" family. Besides, Dellie had largely recovered. During her first five years in the hospital, she went through a "stormy time"—she was destructive, noisy, and occasionally aggressive—but by 1914, after her father died, she was able to visit New Orleans for the settlement of his estate, and seemed to enjoy being home again. Judge McConnell had asked Annette to care for her, "both as regards her person and her property," and in 1919, Annette went to Philadelphia to bring her sister home. Pat remembered Annette's pride in doing so. She thought it a "crusade against injustice, a protest against tyranny and a triumph over the mental hospital." Dellie was an occasional guest at Shearwater. Pat met her a little after she and Peter were engaged, and Sissy shortly after marrying Bob. Both of them found her undeniably queer. Dellie had made a trip to Europe, but Annette had to manage her money for her. "She was living in Bay St. Louis," Sissy wrote. "Strange little woman . . . She wrote short, fresh little pieces in the local paper, the *Sea Coast Echo.* They were about walks on the beach, sunsets, seabirds, flowers, gentle and poetic. . . . She told me that she wanted to go to California. 'It's new,' she said, 'and it suits my temperament. I've read everything in the library.' " She died there, and Annette took the train to California for her funeral, admiring the "democratic" tombstones and burial markers at Forest Lawn cemetery, a world away from the showy mausoleums of New Orleans.

After returning alone from Baltimore to Ocean Springs, Sissy could not bear to move back into the Cottage, and she and baby Mary moved in with Peter's family at the Front House. Even there, everything reminded her of Bob. While she cared for Patsy and Michael and Marjorie, and Pat and Peter were away mulleting or at the movies in Biloxi, or sailing on the *Gypsy,* she wrote to him: "Each night, when I come up the stairs, it's a haunted room with its misty crooked mirror, fallen plaster, flaking paint, furniture . . . and the spots on the wall where you tried your mural." It was the room in which she had dressed for her wedding. In March, when she went out to pick the pitcher plant flowers they had loved, she could "almost pretend that he was out in the wild cutover land somewhere with me, and that I just had to go back to the car and wait for him." The treatment, she was told, would last at least another year, possibly more. In the hospital, her husband's behavior had swung back and forth between "depressive panic and then an outburst into excitement with very much greater explosiveness and quite a good deal of activity and talkativeness." No one was willing to predict what would become of him—parergasic patients, the doctors told her, often remained "at home for long years with a modicum of useful living," provided the family made an effort to understand them. Sissy vowed to "count with joy the blessings of the moment. . . . The present can be pretty perfect if one can leave the past alone and count on the future with sure hope of happiness."

She put in long hours with Pat at the showroom and tried to interest herself in forms and glazes: a beautiful firing of turquoise, a new bright green, or a little nursery set made by Mac ("Not so hot. The glaze too painty"). Peter was still dreaming of luscious glazes and textures. A gift shop in New Orleans was delighted by one of his recent discoveries: a "method of glazing and re-firing which changes blue into a glorious red—something like the famous Chinese Oxblood. . . . Beneath a lamp or near a piece of copper or brass it glows like a jewel." That year, three of Mac's plates done in that glaze—copper red—toured the United States with the Robineau exhibition. Peter had thrown them, and Mac carved, glazed, and fired them. By now, the Pottery's account books—which Sissy and Pat were keeping—were a tangle of gift shops and department stores across the country, attended to by a couple of agents who sold on a 20 percent commission. Walter's hopes had been realized. There were

Shearwater pieces in Filene's and Gimbels, Lord & Taylor and Strawbridge. And the work of all three brothers was gaining renown. An August 1937 article in the *Christian Science Monitor*, with accompanying photographs, noted that Shearwater pottery had been exhibited at all the most prestigious places: the Society of Arts and Crafts in Boston, the Craftsman Studio and Rena Rosenthal, Inc., in New York City, the Arts and Crafts Guild in Philadelphia, and Marshall Field and Company, Chicago. There were exhibitions at Syracuse University and the Virginia Museum of Fine Arts, whose curator had happened upon the odd-looking Shearwater sign in Ocean Springs. "Somehow I couldn't pass [it,] so I drove into a by-road which led me to one of the most artistic workshops in America." A thoughtful review in the Richmond *Times-Dispatch* praised Peter's "simple, sturdy tea and beverage sets," and paused over "the most beautiful of the urns . . . in a deep, glowing rose-red with copper and opalescent lights" and "a heavy, dull-sheened urn in gleaming black like gun metal." Some of Bob's pieces were singled out, including "a bold, arresting presentation of the adoration of the Shepherds and Wise Men," and "a sleepy cat in the subtle, dull gun-metal shade . . . It all depends on how you look at him, whether he is friendly and sleepy, or alert and evil." People continued to enjoy the figurines: "all the once famed darkies of plantation days dancing, fishing or playing the banjo [and] made with a sense of humor." There were other exhibitions at the Toledo Museum of Art (March 1939) and the Number 10 Gallery in New York (November 1940).

Despite the increased recognition, money had become "a curse." Sissy worried not only about the Pottery—which was, all things considered, "pretty poor"—but about her father's finances. Annette had begun to sell her bonds to pay for the cost of Bob's hospitalization. "There is no money," Sissy wrote, "and yet we all seem to go on and on spending. How to get away from it all or how to make more?"

From Sissy's journals during spring and early summer 1938, when Bob was away at Phipps and she and the baby were in Ocean Springs, it is clear that she suffered intensely. Surrounded by her busy family, she felt utterly alone. She could see that others, too, were lonely and weary—she worried especially about Annette—but she felt powerless to help them. She saw them as in a dream, and felt herself growing "farther and farther away from people." It seemed incredible that, in the midst of such a "nice" family, she did not feel close to anyone, not even to her "wonderful old Pat. . . . She is too absorbed. The Pottery is a little sad, and everyone works so darned hard."

I feel lonely. Now why? With all the people who are around me. It's just that every time I walk down the Pottery Hill everything says "Bob." The whole place does, of course, but for some reason the pine trees there and the lay of the land seem to mean something special. If I can say to myself "be happy, let thy heart sing with the winds singing here . . . and with the light upon these shining trees . . ." But I can't even go into my house, where there is so much to be done, so much. I go through the door and stop and look around, and it's like an actual physical pain. I seem to have to stay half atrophied, and it makes me stupid, so I know I must try not to.

Perhaps, she thought, a path would open up, "like an old road found in the woods, and lost, and suddenly plain again." It would not do to be lonely. "So many people have followed [that path]. I think one must know and grasp the fact that 'I' am not alone in anything and make a glory of it, instead of wanting to be the only one." "I love you," she wrote to Bob in her journal.

Love me, and lift me up once more to those high places where you and I have been together, so much that it seems we must have been the most favored of mortals. Do you think of how infinitely happy we have been and know that we will be again? . . . Here I sit, under the barn tree, thinking of you and of your father. A sweetness that belonged to both . . .

The radiance of spring and summer, the sight of Peter's family coming back from a moonlight swim, or the caress of a little northwester made her sing for joy sometimes. But often she lapsed into her "half-atrophy," unable to take much pleasure in the baby because she could not share her with Bob. "Why can't I just enjoy her and stop having this dreadful weakness and feeling that if I give way to the least emotion I shall weep? It is such a hard sort of feeling, as if I were trying to turn into stone." She resisted the temptation to feel nothing. As she nursed Mary, she wanted to "feel placid like a cow," to "count no hours, hope no hopes, but be as faithful as the day is long"; to "try and possess my mind in peace and quietness and with enough depth—just enough—not to be a vegetable." She reproached herself for not taking more pleasure in Mary's development. "Something is sort of hibernating," she wrote.

In order to hide and quiet fears and sorrows it seems to be necessary to squash everything flat and this should not be so. It would almost be better to feel every moment than to lose one's whole self like this. Ordinary daily living is so easy unless one wants to make an effort. Oh God, how I wish sometimes that I were only a little, little child!

She had no one with whom to share those feelings; everyone seemed busy and preoccupied. Mac was engaged now and working hard at the Pottery on his carved pieces. By summer 1937, he was producing a new series of figurines: football players, glazed in white enamel, which Bob had designed before leaving for Phipps. He was also block-printing fabrics for use as drapes and curtains, and sent photos of his best work to a company in New York. The response was disappointing. Someone in the "Market Art Ability Dept." told him his designs lacked what the buyers called "sales appeal." Some were "a bit too elaborate for present trends, too brilliant for modern interior decoration." There were a couple of paragraphs of suggestions, "to aid you on what is a good start toward designing for industry." In June, when Bob had been at Phipps for a few months, Mac began building a house for his future wife, Jacqueline Hause, a lively dark-haired woman from Arkansas—"nobody's doormat"—whom he had met in New Orleans. No less than Peter, Mac was dreaming in clay, or rather earth. He had seen a magazine article about houses made of rammed earth, one of the oldest but rarest forms of domestic architecture. He read that they were amazingly sturdy, cool in summer—up to ten degrees cooler than outside—and could cost as little as $500 to build. So he wrote to the Department of Agriculture for Farmers Bulletin #1500, *Rammed Earth Walls for Buildings.* It took awhile in the mail, and meanwhile, drawing on his architectural training at Tulane, he fell to work, clearing the yaupon bushes from a parcel of land overlooking the marsh and Shearwater's little harbor, not far from the Front House. He wanted the northern end of the house, overlooking the water, to be all windows, from ceiling to floor, letting in the light he needed for his art.

Money was scarce and earth was much cheaper than pine. From a pit owned by the Highway Department, he got earth for 2 cents a yard. Enough for the entire house cost him only 88 cents. A bricklayer came from Biloxi, bringing a little boy to help—a different boy on each of four days—and built a fireplace and chimney. With two of the carpenters that had helped build the showroom, Mac laid a twenty-two-inch concrete foundation and an eighteen-inch footing on top, to which he clamped a series of wooden forms. Earth, strained clean of vegetable matter, was carried in a wheelbarrow, shoveled into the forms, and packed down tightly with an iron tamper in six-inch layers, until it rang like stone. After each layer, the forms were unbolted and moved upward. When the walls reached the right height, he let them dry for two weeks and gave them a coat of linseed oil and another one of white base paint. The process took most of the summer. He married Jackie in Little Rock on September 9, 1937, and by the time they returned from their honeymoon, the entire house—kitchen, bathroom, screened-in porch, and a thirty-five- by eighteen-foot living area—was ready for its tin roof. He built furniture: cabinets and chairs, a long window seat, and a desk. The Farmers Bulletin, with its detailed instructions, came in the mail when the job was almost over. The day it arrived, he was putting the finishing touches on the porch. The new house was cool, sturdy enough for hurricanes and high winds, and practically soundproof, and cost about half of what he would have paid for a wooden or brick one. In an article about the new house for *American Home,* Jackie tallied up expenses:

Foundation and chimney	$375
Tin roof	$108
Mud for walls	88 cents
Hauling mud	$44
Wooden forms	$30
Doors and windows	$95
Floor, ceiling, jambs, joists and scaffolding	$240
Wiring and fixtures	$35
Bathroom fixtures	$52.45
Pipe, nails, incidentals	$40
	$1,020.33

It was July 1938—Bob had been at Phipps for over a year—before Sissy and her baby Mary were able to move back to Baltimore to be closer to him. Ellen had found her a place to live: an apartment left vacant for the summer by one of Bob's doctors. That spring, Annette had sent encouraging letters from Baltimore. Bob's progress had been slow but steady. By February, after the long series of Metrazol injections, he was going out for walks and had begun to draw again: first a stylized horse and rider, and then "two excellent realistic black and white pictures of a daffodil and of other flowers" to give to the nurses. By March, he had done many drawings of his attendant, Mr. Hitchcock, of whom he was beginning to feel fond. He was also able to write to Sissy and ask for photographs, and in April he sent her a gift: a box of hankies, each one different, and a card. "I am an idiot," she wrote. "I cried. I love him. I put my face on them and cried!" He and the attendants had made a little cradle for Mary's dolls—to be saved for when she was older. He had woven a handbag and was hooking rugs he was proud of—a "yellow, green and black 'natural man' " and one with dogs. He was reading biography and travel books, taking piano lessons, and showing an interest in pottery. One of the attendants had given him a newspaper clipping about the Richmond exhibit, months earlier, in which his own work had been praised. "It mentioned the various pieces very favorably," he wrote Sissy, "and gave a photo of some of them. . . . I see that the works are still in motion. Would that I were participating! I have had several ideas lately, which might work out in the show room. There is a pottery connected with the Hospital, and Miss Rochmell, the nurse in charge, has suggested that I try some work in connection with it. I am particularly anxious to learn to throw on the wheel." Then, a little later, other discoveries: "I'm also glad to learn that the Pottery is being so much admired. I used to admire it myself. But yesterday I saw some at an art gallery here that would put even the Shearwater in the shade; at least that's the way I feel now. Some of the glazes and decorations and shapes were marvelous. I wish that Peter and Mac could have seen them. I didn't begin to see everything and expect to go back again soon."

By August, he learned that his mother and wife and daughter were close by, and thought that perhaps he would like to see Sissy. He had grown very close to his nurse, Miss Rochmell, who stayed with him after each Metrazol treatment, and reported on his progress. There were hopeful little signs. There had been a party at Phipps, "and he sang in a quartet, up on the stage, in the upstairs auditorium with an audience of 100! Then passed food and drinks on the gallery and dancing." Life seemed to be "straightening itself out." Sissy remembers the nurse as an extraordinary woman.

She was Russian, so she told me with a strange accent, a lilting blend with something of the orient in it, I was sure. She was very beautiful, delicate and dark, lit by some internal fire. The morning after his [Metrazol] treatments she would feed him his breakfast over and over until she succeeded in making one stay down. Then she would go with him to an upstairs hall or parlor of some kind where there was a grand piano. She was a truly accomplished pianist and she would play and play for him. "Music hath charms . . ." she told me. My goodness, but I was jealous. I knew in my heart that they were in love. I do not even know if they ever knew it themselves or what kind of love it was or how far it went. Only a few years ago I was still dreaming about her in an agony of resentment, an agony of gratitude.

"I love you," Sissy wrote Bob in her journal. "Don't bother about it, though, and if you feel you can't go it with me, it's all right. . . . I wish you could feel how all things are happy. Nothing could ever in the world take you from me." Emotion—he had told her once—must be spent very carefully. But lately she had been overwhelmed by "a desire to spend: not money, but whatever there is within me that is worth anything. Spend it in sympathy, in writing, in doing, just so it is not squandered eternally." During Bob's months at Phipps, she had found new strength and confidence, both as a woman and perhaps also as a writer. It consoled her to think that her fate, and Bob's, was not entirely within their own hands.

> I am the wand, the willow wand
> the man of magic bravely waves.
> I am the rabbit from the hat,
> the hat I am, as well.
> I am the whole, the act contained
> upon one stage, within one hall.
> Loudly I claim that I am all;
> all save the waver of the wand.

HOMECOMING

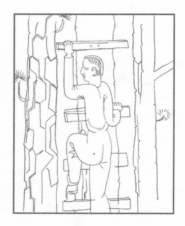

In September 1938, more than sixteen months after he entered Phipps, Bob told Meyer that it would mean a great deal to him to do some physical work, and that he wanted to go home with his wife and mother. He spoke with great ease, Meyer noted, "somewhat slowly, but with perfectly normal modulation of voice, and it was obvious that he had the conviction of his capacity." Toward the end of the month, Bob, Sissy, Mary, Annette, and an attendant from the clinic boarded a train to Ocean Springs. They went down not in a compartment of their own, as Annette had wanted, but in a more public drawing room with berths.

"We are to be Siamese twins," she told her son, determined not to let him out of her sight. Once she followed him to the platform between cars, where he seemed about to leap from the train, but for the most part, he was docile. While the train was shifted in Atlanta, he walked by himself on the platform. As they got closer to home, he seemed to want to talk, and he and his mother chatted uneasily about the family. Annette brought up the "new scientific theory that most physical illnesses have a mental cure," and Bob probably wondered whether mental illnesses have a physical one.

Peter and Mac were waiting at the station in Ocean Springs. Bob held the baby and picked up a suitcase. When Peter saw his brother, he was appalled by how little he had improved. They got to Shearwater after dark. All the lights were on at the Barn, and someone had brought flowers. Jackie and Mac, Pat, Peter, and the children crowded into the sitting room to welcome him home. Bob walked to the showroom, and then to his Cottage, and looked at Mac's new house. When he woke up the next day, he went to work cutting grass, clearing undergrowth, and cutting out tree roots with an ax. Over the next few days, the family watched him closely. He swept out his studio and spread his drawings on the floor, set up an easel and arranged his paints and dyes on a table. Soon he was painting again, pleased with his work.

Sissy marveled at the beauty of fall. "Yellow butterflies today float upon the wind. . . . Sometimes one thinks: 'Is that a leaf, fresh from some Autumn tree?' And then, veering in its course, the creature lights upon some last fall flower." It was "bliss and heaven" to have Bob nearby, and she stopped writing in her journal. "Blank pages that whisper of contentment when we riffle them." As her own depression lifted, she felt herself reawakening to poetic emotion. "It's funny how the world sometimes will be bathed in a sort of poem. Each sight, sound, taste, smell will lead to a sort of rhythmic line of expression, and the whole will be sort of continuous, running from one thing into another, so that we see connections we have never seen or contemplated before. Now I hear the sound of a train starting up in the distance, and see the waving of yellowed leaves on a redbud tree, and a sort of repeat pattern of shadows on the screen, and . . . it all goes together inarticulately to make the moment through which I am passing."

By October 17, 1938, she was ready to report to Meyer.

Dear Dr. Meyer:

We have been home two weeks now and I should like very much to give you my point of view on my husband's condition, and to ask your advice in certain things that bother me. Generally speaking, I think he has been, and is, perfectly wonderful. The first time I saw him after he left the hospital I felt that he was getting back to himself, and that it was necessary for him to do it alone, and that he was ready to do it. I think this is true, and I don't suppose you can advise me as to how far the "aloneness" should go.

That is what I would like to know. I will try to give you an idea of his usual day, most of which is an absolutely closed book to me.

He gets up very early in the morning. The time has varied from 12:30 to 3:30 or 4 o'clock [a.m.]. Sometimes he takes a cold bath, sometimes not. Then he eats a sandwich and has coffee. At first he let me come and get his breakfast ready, but now he won't, and he eats any scraps he finds in the ice box. At first he went out for walks or rows, but now he stays in the house, drawing or looking at art magazines or books until it gets light. Then he has a second pick-up meal and leaves about five o'clock. I think he goes right down to his studio by a back path which he fixed so that he passes no house and sees no one. I have gone to call him for dinner, and he is there. For the first few days he came in with paint on his fingers, and asked me to order paint, which I did and he has it. But lately there have been no signs of paint. He comes in for dinner about 11:30, eats quite well usually, clears up, and washes all the dishes for me. After each meal, he spends a long time in the bathroom. Then he goes back to his studio and I see him no more until 5:00 or 5:30.

He comes in, takes a cold bath, and washes out his clothes. Unless he is early, he has to wait for supper until I get the baby in bed. He pays very little attention to her. Sometimes shakes her hand and smiles back at her, but seems to get no pleasure from watching her. Sometimes he leaves when I bring him to her. *After supper he looks at magazines, and until last night has read aloud to me a chapter from Hudson's* Far Away and Long Ago. *He goes to bed about 7:30, and I usually go at the same time. He treats me, part of the time, as if I were not present, and the rest of the time as if I were a piece of furniture. It is very rare that he speaks without being spoken to, and his voice and manner have an unused quality. If I kiss him, or take hold of his hand in passing, or any natural little gesture, he allows it, but doesn't respond unless I make myself a nuisance.*

This seems a very strange existence, but I have had the feeling so strongly that he wanted nothing so much as to be left alone to find himself that I have tried to go along with him as far as possible. Sometimes I have asked him to come back to bed. Once I asked him if I disturbed him or worried him, and he answered, "Not much," with a little smile. I asked him if he took naps at his studio, and he said, "What do you think?" I have not questioned him about his work, as that seems to me something he will speak about when he is ready.

As I believe Mrs. Anderson wrote you, he was terribly anxious to get down to his own house. At first, I was a little afraid, and I arranged not to take the baby, but he insisted, so we all came down and are very much together, as the house has only one room. However, we are having a room added for the baby, and that has disturbed him very little. He chose the place for it himself, but has had nothing more to do with it. He avoids the carpenters, who are old friends, but speaks if he happens to meet them. A few days ago, he borrowed their ladder and fixed a broken pane of glass in the back window. Occasionally he goes into the show room when visitors come to show them the pottery. Only once since we came has he been upset, and that was one evening in the show room. He had gone over with his mother to do some arranging, and stayed over when she came back. She thought I had better go over, so that he would not be lonely, and I did. After a few minutes he picked up a pot (a very nice specially glazed decorated one of his), took it over to the hearth, and dropped it. Then he said, "That's too bad. I lost control of myself." He cleared it up himself.

He does not see any of the family except his mother. She comes down in the evening, and when I ask him if he wouldn't like to, he asks her to supper. We were going to have dinner with her every day, but he refused. I did not want him to feel that I didn't trust him with the baby, so I left her with him for a little while one evening, but he sat her up on the edge of the couch with her legs hanging and no support. Of course, she fell off on her head, and now I don't like to leave her with him.

This is a very long and mixed up account, but I hope it will give you the general idea of how things are going with him. Perhaps you can advise me about whether or not I should leave him less alone, and tell me if you can think of anything that might be good for him. I feel very stupid about it all. Sometimes he seems so much himself that one forgets he has been ill.

I hope you do not mind my consulting you. I shall always feel that you were the one person who helped him.

Sincerely yours,
Agnes Grinstead Anderson

October 22, 1938

Dear Mrs. Anderson:

I fully understand the real difficulty which you have to meet. I feel that you have chosen the course that gives the best possible opportunity to your husband to be free of a sense of pressure that might increase his tension. We have to realize that, even at the hospital, there was a great deal of this "aloneness," and that the best way to do is to offer opportunities, but without conveying a sense of one's forcing issues. With regard to the problem of meals, it may be a good thing to bear in mind that leaving something in the icebox will be a help without causing too much of a feeling that it is done on purpose. I am quite sure that it is somewhat difficult for your husband to plan and keep up his work, and one simply has got to be patient. Perhaps there are moments when one may give a remark of approval with the hint that he can feel sure that one does not want to over-reach.

The incident with your child shows of course the unpreparedness to meet perfectly plain responsibilities in this state of preoccupations. I do not know whether he is at all willing or able to share his thought either by letter or by conversation. *The incident with the glazed pot shows how easily he can get into a state of discouragement or tension. The situation is one of giving opportunities but without demands. I hope that you do not feel discouraged. Anyone else would have very much the same task and difficulty, but I am glad to hear of his chances of being very much himself, and expect that that will expand with patience. If he had stayed with us it also would have been a question of months to gain the ease which one would like to call normal.*

I appreciate your letter and only wish I could give more specific instructions. As I say, we would have exactly the same task here.

> *With best regards,*
> *Most sincerely yours,*
> *Adolf Meyer*

November 21, 1938

Dear Dr. Meyer:

Your confirmation of my own feeling, that the best thing we can do for my husband is to leave him alone, came as a great relief to me. I am trying in every way to curb my impatience, and to realize that it is probably my feeling that makes things seem to go so slowly. I suppose one always has the feeling that one must, and should, be able to do something to help. Thank you for your letter. I assure you it was a great help to me.

When I sit down to think over these past few weeks with the idea of making some sort of report to you, I am suddenly struck by the fact that there have, to my knowledge, been no upsets at all, and that, in every way, except seeing other people, there has been improvement. Perhaps the best thing has been his continued painting and drawing. He is consuming pencils, paper and paints at a great rate, and I have seen some of his sketches of the baby. She has begun to pose for him in the evenings, and the hasty things he has done look like his old sure work, that is, as far as I could see surreptitiously. He still never speaks to me, rarely answers, except for a nod. When the room for the baby was finished he did

191

all the painting, inside and out, at his own request, and made a very professional job of it. Every now and then he does other little jobs around the house that need doing—never saying anything. He gets large quantities of wood and sees that the fire is supplied on cold days. He still washes all the dishes, and all his own clothes for me. He sleeps very much better at night. Usually goes to bed about eight-thirty and gets up about four-thirty. He is eating well and even regulating his own diet. I was so afraid he wouldn't eat that I had cakes and pies in the icebox to tempt him, but he very sensibly eats sandwiches and cereals and apples. He reads aloud almost every evening, but spends most of his time drawing or paint-ing. Lately, I am sure he has been painting flowers. Sometimes he looks so happy as though his work were going well. I told him that the wife of our retired min-ister had been to see us, and had expressed a desire for a bracket to hang plants on the wall. He made ours and the next Sunday morning he brought me one for her, always without a word. You see, he is thinking of other people, but his not seeing anyone worries me. The only time he has been in the least upset was when his brothers came back from a duck hunt, and gave us a duck. He ate a little, but took the rest out, and threw it away. Duck hunts have meant a great deal to all of them since they were little boys, so I was a little worried about it. I have the feeling that each time I allow myself to worry it shows in him.

His mother was having a bad time with her teeth, and he has not been to see her, but one morning he left a very beautiful pumpkin flower on her doorstep.

Don't you think he is doing well? If you ever think of anything that we might do for him, or anything we might read to help, please tell me. He says grace now before every meal, and kneels for a minute before getting into bed, and has read one of the books his Mother has left for him. I will let you know something of what he does from time to time, and still feel free to consult you, if you don't mind.

Sincerely yours,
Agnes Grinstead Anderson

On All Saints' Day, November 1, 1938, Sissy stood on the steps of her Cottage and looked down the path into the marsh, covered with mist, and across the hill into the pines and flaming sweet gums. Wrapped in the morning stillness, she thought of the dead and of how things pass suddenly into another life. Death always seems final, and yet, after a few years, we suddenly think of the dead "with all continuity severed," and enter into a new relation with them. Perhaps that was most likely to happen after some important event. It seemed that something in her own life had come to an end; that life was "straightening out" for Bob, and the two of them were entering a new phase of their relationship. But the strain of the Pottery and of family problems were taking their toll on Peter.

Through the months of his father's illness and his brother's erratic behavior, Peter and Pat had struggled to keep the Pottery going with a minimum of disruption. With the death of his beloved Aunt Daisy in 1935, and that of his father in 1937, Peter had lost two of his principal sources of love and appreciation: it had always been apparent to him, and to the rest of the family, that Annette gave much more of her affection to Bob, even more so during his illness. During the summer of 1938, with Bob away at Phipps, Peter's problems began to seem insurmountable, and he had an extramarital affair, a dalliance with an attractive young woman who was an apprentice at the workshop and was living at the Front House. He began to come home in a sullen mood, was cross with Pat and the children, and began drinking heavily, though he had always had a strong intolerance of alcohol. Tortured by remorse, he cursed himself and his family. In September and October, after the young woman had left Shearwater, his behavior became more strange. He attempted to harm himself, and bitterly blamed his wife for having put him in a compromising situation. "Peter is down in the depths," Sissy wrote the day before Thanksgiving, 1938. "God bless and lift him up." And then, days later, these terrified words: "Yes, it has happened to Peter, too." And this strange couplet:

We must with love and knowledge dwell
whose hearts have plumbed the depths of hell.

As Bob recovered, painted fall flowers, and worked on a high chair for Mary's birthday, Mac found himself accompanying Peter, Pat, Peter's doctor, and a friend—but not Annette, who wanted to remain with Bobby—to Phipps. There, doctors were soon shaking their heads in bewilderment over what one referred to as "Andersonitis." They arrived in the early hours of December 1, and in the morning, Peter told his doctors that he was suffering "from a severe case of guilty conscience." On December 13, back in Ocean Springs, a little before Peter's thirty-seventh birthday, Mac fired the kiln in his absence.

Pat stayed with Peter in Baltimore through Christmas and the New Year, and there seemed to be some improvement, leaving Sissy "a little jealous." Why couldn't she have been like her sister, staying in Baltimore until Bob had completely recovered? "It's all my fault that Bob didn't come out the same way." When Pat returned to Ocean Springs on January 2, 1939, Sissy found her "as full of courage and strength as always" and felt suddenly "ashamed of my weakness, my failure to keep hold of faith and happiness."

But Peter was far from well, and stayed at Phipps another eight and a half months. Pat had no choice but to remain at Shearwater, caring for her children, minding the showroom, keeping the books and correspondence, tending to the bees and the garden, and "counting the minutes between Johns Hopkins envelopes." News of her husband was mixed. In December, a week after he entered the clinic, he was calm enough to type a letter to his mother with news of his activities: "You have always wanted letters from your sons, and I'll make up for lost time while the chance presents itself."

The room I have is very comfortable and is sunny all morning. I have been playing cards. . . . This morning . . . I was making little things out of modeling clay. . . . There is a pottery shop under the building I am in but I have not been down there yet. The lady in charge has brought me some plastina and just lately some more clay for modeling. The last is a New Jersey clay from Tren-

ton. *Aside from clay work, the occupational therapy consists of leather-work baskets, and there is also volleyball and a gym.*

Annette and Pat sent him news of the Pottery. Occasionally, when she could think of something that might cheer him, Sissy wrote him, too. By January, Peter's assistant, Henry Weyerstall, was learning to throw, and was going to Mac and Annette for criticism. "We all miss you terribly," Sissy wrote Peter.

Something is always coming up for which we need Peter. However, we're making out, temporarily, and the Assistant Secretary Treasurer is pleased to report that business has not been so good at this time for many a long year. You know when sales total over two hundred dollars before the tenth of the month it makes me feel fine! Our new agents seem to be up to their stuff, and we are able to fill orders on schedule. New firings are being planned right now. Henry is a wonder. Of course, he hasn't terribly many thrown things, but he has some nice shapes. He uses you for a model, as it were, and he couldn't find a better. I asked him today about finding a new boy to help cast, etc., and he thinks he knows a good one. . . . Yesterday we drove down the Coast and looked at the pottery shops. The stuff is awful. Even Patsy [Peter's daughter] said it was "pretty nice" in polite fashion, but she liked ours. They have dozens of wretchedly shaped plain, unglazed garden stuff at the old Jugtown Place: "to be painted whatever color you like," as the girl explained.

Neither Pat nor Sissy was sure how Peter would receive news from home. His behavior fluctuated from day to day and from hour to hour. One week, he told Annette of his work in clay and plastiline, and the next, he was swallowing the clay. A cat that he had modeled "suddenly developed the meaning 'Nine lives and I shall lose them all.' " Even after a series of Metrazol treatments in January, he was still showing "considerable impulsiveness in the direction of self-harm and self-punishment." The staff had diagnosed him with severe depression, though Meyer noted that "he speaks much more freely and in that respect presents an easier task than his brother." In his periods of agitation, between one treatment and another, he was overwhelmed by fears that he would be punished for his sins and never allowed to return home. Ten days of sleep treatment produced only a slight improvement. With a haunted look in his eyes, he asked whether he had the same "incurable" illness as Bob.

At Phipps and at Shearwater, Peter's doctors and the family were asking themselves the same question, and Pat devoted much thought to the differences between Bob (whom she considered a genius) and her husband. Both were selfish, but sensitive to the feelings of others. There was Bob's passion for birds, and Peter's interest in bees; Peter's skill with machinery, and Bob's hatred of it. Both were hard workers, and neither paused to rest or eat when they were absorbed in something, though Bob worked in spurts and Peter was more consistent. Peter was "such a tremendous *doer*," she wrote.

I can't look about the place without seeing his handiwork. Our short boat pier, made and kept up by him; Michael's rowboat, so beautifully made, just last spring; the dogs' kennels and their lots—not just lots, but beautifully made "enclosures"—one he called the Alcazar *for shutting up the females. Even the brick chimney and fireplace in his mother's room. The children's play table. His own tackle box and trolling rods, done from Calcutta bamboo. Our shower—cement with set-in tiles of frogs and toadstools he designed. Quantities of beehives. Everything about our boat done by Peter: painting her, putting her out on ways every two or three months. Even working on our dirt roads after heavy rains because no one else would. At the workshop it is all Peter. The brick test kiln, built and designed by him (of brick). The new "kick wheel" he made this summer. A good substitute ball mill for slip (liquid clay), made from a cypress barrel to save money. So many things. I think all day of Peter, and most of the night. He has been such an exceptionally fine person. . . . I can see his selfishness, but I think it is only the selfishness of a man who always had something*

196

to do and never had time for trivial things. In thinking back I can never re-member, in our lives together, Peter making a wrong decision. I do love him very much, but I am not altogether prejudiced. I am the one who has been triv-ial and often "nagging." I am, as told by too many people, dominating, but don't feel it. I have been selfish in that I adored Peter, so that I was in heaven with his love, and forgot to notice whether he was with mine, all of which he has had without swerving, ever since I knew him.

For a long time, absorbed by his own illness, Bob seemed unaware that his brother was gone from Shearwater. Meyer regretted that contact between the two of them had ceased; surely they could help one another. Sissy agreed: "I hope Peter will soon be able to help you with himself, and perhaps with Bob too. At least [Peter] talks." Meyer and his doctors had been struck by the same thing: while Bob was "exceedingly difficult to approach," Peter was "friendly, almost desperately asking for attention and help most of the time." In a way, the clinic had loosened him up. "He is never a talker," Pat told his doctor, "unless anything about which he knows—or about which he is particularly interested comes up." When he warmed to the subject, he was charming, intelligent, amusing.

Annette, too, felt strongly that Bob's cure was bound up with Peter's. But despite the hope he had given the family during his first few days at home, Bob seemed less and less able to cope with those around him. He was trying to resume his old life, but seldom said more than a word or two, leaving the family to guess at what he was thinking. Sissy was almost sick with worry.

He has picked out the tallest pine tree on the place and has nailed cross pieces up it to a height of a hundred feet or more. Up there, he is making a plat-form or treehouse. He has always, before his illness, wanted a treehouse, and been most interested in what he describes as "levitation." It has something to do with height, and he used to say that he attained it once when he was nearly drowned. He could get close to it by listening to Bach music, particularly the B

Minor Mass. Also, a slight degree of drunkenness. It's something like flying, as far as I can make out. Perhaps that is what he is after in the tree. I think he is after some sort of religious experience, even if he doesn't call it by that name. I suppose he has to find it for himself, but I wish someone could help.

"I'm going to heaven," he told Annette with a smile, as he nailed crosspieces to the tree. And then, to Sissy: "Don't worry, I won't go up again."

She sometimes wept at his kindness. At Christmas, he made a box for Mary and filled it with an amazing collection of carved animals. In one of his pots, decorated with waves, he planted a little Christmas tree, with a candle at the top. He carved a cedar pelican for his nephew Michael, and left it for him at the back door of the Front House. "He has also given him his precious set of Audubon books," Sissy wrote. "I try to tell him things that seem to make life seem worthwhile after all, and I happened to tell him how Michael, when he first went to school, came home without his coat. When questioned he said he had another, and a friend of his had none, so he had given it to him. Bob liked that, and I think that's why he gives him things."

Once in a while, he showed interest in the Pottery, as though remembering his parents' old ideal of the three brothers, working together in harmony. There was to be a big pageant on the Coast commemorating the landing of d'Iberville, Sissy wrote Meyer,

and we have been talking about a poster to advertise the pottery. His mother was trying to do one, which she brought to show him. He said, "Do you want me to do it?" "Of course," we said, "yes," and day before yesterday he came in with the most perfect one, which he had done in two days' steady work. He never even comes in to dinner when he is working hard. The poster is done in oils on a big piece of plywood painted a beautiful gray. The colors are beautiful. I [have made] a little sketch of it. . . . We are pretty sure it represents the three brothers at work in the pottery.

As she copied the poster for Meyer, Sissy thought it *"too* perfect. The three of them, the kiln, the wheel, heavenly color and letters. He is a marvel. . . . Oh God, help me to help him!"

Meyer, too, found it admirable. "There is no doubt a wonderful degree of talent in Mr. Anderson, and I hope it will come more and more into a setting of greater ease and contact with those who are so anxious to collaborate and to make a real success of rehabilitation."

Despite such successes, Bob's behavior was strange, unsettling, and sometimes terrifying. More than once, he burned himself, pushing his foot into the hot coals in the fireplace, searing his face or hands, or grabbing a carving knife and holding it against his throat. One day, he swallowed turpentine, explaining that "he could not paint without a medium." Music made him tense beyond control. Sissy called him for dinner one day as he was chopping firewood for Pat.

He came in in about ten minutes, went straight to the phonograph and played one of Bach's Brandenburg Concertos. *The slow movement of the third—to which he danced a perfectly beautiful dance—mostly movements of the arms—ended with a very decided death, falling to the floor, etc. He sat down to dinner and did not take any of the meat dish. About half way through dinner, he looked at the baby in a very strange manner, half rose from his chair toward her, and suddenly, picked up the dish of meat and crashed it to the floor, just missing her.*

Sissy could not help "bothering" Meyer again: "I do not know how much longer I can carry on under the present conditions, and I do not feel that the rest of the family, particularly my sister and her children, ought to be asked to share the strain." It was true, Pat added. "Bob is far from well. He looks very badly, stands in a peculiar way, and altogether is most strange." He seemed "unreachable," impossible to help. She worried about the "severe strain" on her sister, about her children, who were growing up in a "more or less unhealthy atmosphere"; and about Mac, "who is not of the same temperament but who *does* get depressed at times."

No doubt Mac's role as a designer in the Pottery was often over-shadowed by another more urgent one: to prevent his brothers from harming themselves and each other; to remain *sane,* to be *normal.* Someone had to be. He made a good job of it, carving his remarkable pots, keeping things in repair at Shearwater and running the work-shop and Annex in their absence, consulting Peter—through Pat—about glazes and clay and other matters when Peter was well enough to answer questions. Mac's wife, Jackie, was unable to carry on with the same sang froid. More than once she came close to a nervous breakdown herself, and she sometimes went away, leaving Mac won-dering when she would return. "Jackie has gone back to Philadelphia," Sissy wrote one day. "It seems she couldn't take it. I don't understand her. . . . Not that I ever did much to help her. Poor old Mac! God bless him and keep him!"

One can only guess at Mac's feelings as he accompanied first Bob and then Peter to Baltimore, wondering whether he would be spared from whatever it was that had affected *them.* To anyone in Ocean Springs, he must have seemed the most accessible of the three brothers, the one who mingled most easily with ordinary people. Often he had served as family peacemaker, keeping his brothers from fighting or pulling them apart when they did. And it was only Mac who had friends in town. Peter and especially Bob kept more to themselves, and, despite her charitable work with the church, Annette was too much of an intellectual to fit in there or make things easier for her sons. The whole family, except for Pat, who had friends everywhere, was regarded as "markedly queer" in Ocean Springs, for they were devoted to art and lived by themselves, if not on an island, on their own little peninsula, in a world apart. It had always been that way. Even Pat and Sissy had been made to feel self-conscious at times. In the early years of their marriages, the two of them had gone to town to the grocery store. They were dressed informally, as they al-ways were, more like the wives of "artists" than like the other denizens of Ocean Springs. From behind a little window where eggs were sold came the disappointed voice of someone who had known the Grinsteads for years:

"You should have seen your great grandmother, the prettiest, sweetest little woman I ever saw, and your grandmother, as lovely as a picture, and your mother, the most beautiful woman that ever grew up in Ocean Springs."

There was an audible sigh of disapproval. Pat and Sissy could almost hear her thinking: "Just *look* at you two!"

That winter, both sisters wondered whether it wouldn't be better for Bob and for everyone else if he were confined again: sent to another clinic, or perhaps to some sort of ranch where he could paint and do physical labor. He had spoken often of helping himself by working out-of-doors. Sissy wrote to one in Montana and another in Vermont, but both were too expensive, and Bob thought they sounded like penal colonies.

Meyer warned against the idea, and advised confinement in an asylum. Bob's "present obsessive behavior is difficult to endure and too dangerous." Phipps was unable to receive him, but he could be committed to the state hospital until the situation improved. Sissy couldn't bring herself to decide. Every day he seemed to "come out of his shell" a little more, bestowing his kind, silent little gifts on different members of the family. He made a pair of stilts for Michael and planted a garden for Mary.

One day he brought a carved bird to one of the children's playmates, presenting it and saying, "This is Helen (the child's name), isn't it?" One evening he went down to his mother and said, "I want to work, Mother, what shall I do?" She told him to rake leaves, chop wood. She said perhaps work in the pottery. He raked leaves violently for a while, and chopped wood too, but I think he really meant that he wanted to settle to something regular. He has made a garden and a special bed all on his own under the baby's window, planted it with wild violets and other plants. He brought in a beautiful bird which he nailed to her door. It is fitted together, done in plywood. Then yesterday morn-

ing I looked out and there was a wonderful carved cedar bird with a bird feeder on its head, carefully sprinkled with bread crumbs.

He finished his treehouse yesterday. It's just a platform. He sat up there all afternoon. When he came in in the evening he asked me if I would climb up with him. I said I would if I could, but I'm terribly afraid I won't be able to. It must be two hundred feet up, and the cross pieces nailed to the tree trunk are far apart. I do so want to go all the way with him in anything he asks. Unfortunately, high places make me shaky. To me it seems a tremendous accomplishment for one person alone. It is (or looks) beautifully done.

He continues to hurt himself. . . . Several times he has cut himself with a razor blade.

He was "definitely not normal," Pat told a doctor at Phipps, "or whatever we ever approach of that state." The strain was so appalling at times that Sissy and Pat wondered "whether there ought to be some sort of clinic for poor wives. Somebody ought to teach us something." Again, Pat added some observations of her own.

[Bob] has been on more or less of a fast, eating only very little at supper time. On Tuesday about noon I was in our showroom selling pottery to two women when Bob came in, looking very pale and distraught. I said, "Hello, Bob." He nodded to me abruptly, then knelt down and raising his head began, "Oh, my God . . . !" I held out my hand to him saying, "I think that is enough now, Bob." He took my hand, rose quickly, and went out. The ladies were very fine, and it was not mentioned. Agnes says he kneels frequently to the baby, but does not speak.

Toward the end of February 1939—almost two years after the onset of his illness—Bob was admitted to the Mississippi State Hospital in Whitfield. The diagnosis was "dementia praecox, catatonic type." When two doctors came for him, he "knelt down to them and asked, 'Which of you is God?' " Whitfield was a far cry from a top-flight clinic like Phipps, but the buildings were new and well kept and at least, Sissy told herself, it was "a very beautiful place, in the country with fields, orchards and gardens all about." When she returned to Ocean Springs the following day, she felt like a traitor for having taken him there—she had, after all, told Meyer that *she* would take care of him. She went to his studio and looked at all he had drawn in the five months since his return from Baltimore: "the evidence of his work and the life he was making for himself." She found, she told Meyer,

a stack of drawings, done on this [8¹/₂ x 11] paper, in every conceivable technique, about six inches high. Some of the most beautiful things I have ever seen. He isn't just gifted or talented, you know, he is really an artist—a genius. I hope I have not done wrong or spoiled things by shutting him up again. For the last three weeks he has more and more frequently gone into a sort of animal-like frenzy with me. . . . The other night for the first time since he was first ill I felt that he might have killed himself.

Pat added:

Bob went more or less willingly. Everything, as you suggested, was ready in advance and he made no struggle, changed his clothes and went without a murmur and without any sedative. We have had such a hard time. . . . It was a most difficult decision to make and seemed so unfair. Today we have been looking over a few of the tremendous pile of drawings he has done. They are arranged in sequence since his return here, and are very very fine. I would like to bring them to show you when I come up [to see Peter], as they are speech in drawing to a great extent, many self-portraits of his daily occupations. I can't help believing that there must be a place where he can find expression and give some of his genius to others. I feel very sure that place is not with a family. I would like to found a colony for him . . . ! It is a wonderful relief to have him not here, but in one way we feel lost, though why I should hardly know. Perhaps just from hearing him work in his studio all day. It is by my house.

More and more I have realized how different the natures of Bob and my husband are. There is, I think, much less of complication in Peter's makeup. I hope for him. I think he will get well, and I am willing to have patience for years, if necessary. He is a very fine person with a beautiful simplicity. If only he could know his own worth, and realize what a need there is for him here.

Weeks later, in March, Sissy realized that, once again, despite the precautions she had taken, she was pregnant. She agonized with Annette, Pat, and—by mail—with Meyer, over whether to have the baby. Would it be a normal child, or bear some hereditary defect? Meyer had little doubt that "abnormal" parents influenced their children's development. It had become an especially sensitive issue. The war had begun, and as they labored patiently to understand their patients' lives and thought processes, doctors at Phipps were aware that in Nazi Germany "parergasics"—schizophrenics—were required by law to be sterilized. Even if the child were healthy, Sissy wondered, would she be able to share it with Bob? He had been absent for Mary's birth and much of her infancy, but who could predict the future? She would have had a baby each year if that were possible; so she confessed in her journal one night while she watched little Mary and all four of Peter's children sleeping in the Front House, which had turned, in Peter's absence, into "a sort of zoo": dogs, a mother possum and babies, and a "strong alligator snapping-turtle." As for the children, each was a separate little world, with a distinct life. What dreams Mary could build "around one small dogwood flower or a rattle!" It was a shame that people lost that capacity. There was anxiety around her—"everyone seems to be full of some sort of worry and trouble"—and she realized "more and more that children should have the lightest touch . . . and calmness, too, a sort of peace." But they also required a certain detachment: the ability to draw back in reverence and simply let them be, and she sensed that, when he recovered, Bob would be good at granting that sort of independence. He had always told her that he did not want to have children, that he "would not want to bring a child into a world so filled with pain and terror." Sissy had agreed to practice birth control, but could not believe someone with such a passion for life could feel the world was hell and agony. Pat sensed that it was because Bob feared his children would be abnormal. Sometimes he seemed "violently opposed" to having children, but for a long time he had not been able to think clearly, and she prayed that the treatments would bring about a change in him. As she waited for the baby, she could not help resenting her circumstances, and her own feelings of guilt for not being a better nurturer, for "not doing well for Bob."

> I should have lived one hundred years ago
> Or more, at least, when women knew their duty,
> And in that simple walk of life
> Where knowledge equaled doing,
> I would have made so excellent a wife.

> A baby always at the breast,
> And all my soul wrapped up
> In feeding my beloved all the ways
> That woman can feed a man to his delight:
> With food, with love, with flattering . . .
> I would have made so excellent a wife!

Peter seemed easier to help than Bob. Pat felt that what he needed was reassurance and affection from those around him, both at home and at Phipps. It seemed to Sissy that Pat had probably "shown her affection too plainly" to him, and that at Peter's moments of depression and self-doubt, he found it hard to believe that her love was sincere. "He may have wanted to think he wasn't worthy" of it. Probably he had felt overwhelmed at times by her buoyant personality. But Pat adored him still, and their long ordeal had only deepened her love. She had no regrets, she told the doctors.

I believe Mrs. Anderson was right in not telling us the "moody" side of her ancestry. . . . A vague worry would certainly not have helped [Peter] in any of the wonderful times we have had. . . . I would have married him no matter what. His illness now has given me a steady kind of love that I don't think I had quite discovered before, and so I feel, most of the time, that no matter how long the time of his illness, all I have had and have now and expect to have will have been and will be wonderfully worthwhile.

At Whitfield, Bob underwent more of the Metrazol injections until, one day in March, after only a month, he slipped away and walked the 180 miles home, from Jackson to Ocean Springs. It was nothing more than an "insane asylum," he told Annette, imploring her not to take him back: "You can tie me up and take me there, but I'll never go willingly." She and Sissy found that the struggle to get home had been good for him. For a week he rested, ate, and slept. He looked beautiful, Annette said, and "was almost ready to go out and meet people." But in late April his behavior deteriorated again and, against the advice of Meyer and other doctors, who were afraid it would upset Peter, Annette decided to take Bob back to Baltimore, to the Sheppard and Enoch Pratt Hospital. Sissy agreed it was for the best. When Annette told her son that Pratt was a hospital somewhat like Phipps, rather than an asylum, he acquiesced. On the train to Baltimore, he told her that he "knew he was very sick, and couldn't think." At Pratt, where the staff quickly translated Meyer's diagnosis (hypothymergasia) as schizophrenia, he seemed to make some headway. He played ball and read all he could about myth and epic in the clinic's magnificent library. He did "a moderate amount of work at his drawing, limiting himself chiefly to wallpaper designs," for he had learned of the family's money problems, and thought the designs would help him "to earn money as soon as possible." For the most part, he kept to himself, tried to deafen himself to the noisy antics of other patients, and begged to be taken out-of-doors to the zoo or a park where he could draw. For a while, Annette stayed in Baltimore, with Bob at Sheppard Pratt, and Peter seven miles away at Phipps. A letter from Meyer brought her up-to-date in May 1939:

From something [your son Peter] said to a nurse I should infer that he feels that he does not rank in your affections with his brother. At any rate, it may be an important point to see that since visits on your part would at present be inadvisable, it would probably be wise for you to return home so that there would not be any appearance of partiality or difference that he might learn of.

Return home? She would hear nothing of it. "About Peter," she replied, "it is incredible that he should not know how much I love him. We have come to a crisis in the lives of the whole family but there must be a way out." Rarely was she allowed to see either of her sons—the staff at Phipps considered her an "exciting" influence on her sons and somewhat of a "pest," always hovering about the clinic—but she did get a look at the drawings Bob had done at Pratt, and found them beautiful. She asked Meyer whether that wasn't a hopeful sign. Wasn't there a new theory about mental troubles being cured by creative work? A young doctor at Sheppard Pratt had told her that it was not so; that Bob's "sickness was entirely apart from his art; that no matter what he did in drawing or painting, it would not be a sign of improvement."

By the beginning of July, Bob had decided that Sheppard Pratt had not done him any good, and that he would take things into his own hands. After a good deal of planning and weeks of posing as a model patient, he lured an attendant into the stacks of the library, pulled a shelf of books crashing down on him, and fled through a door onto the street. Both Pat and the doctors at Phipps sensed immediately that it would harm Peter to be told of his brother's escape. He had made steady progress in May and June, after insulin and sleep treatments and barbital to take the edge off his fears, and by now the clinic was talking about discharging him. But with Bob on the loose, and the entire family frightened of him and locking doors they had never locked before, Shearwater seemed to Pat "a wretched place for him to come home to." There was the continual "apprehension about [Bob] and a pretty continuous struggle for weekly wages." Paying Peter's medical bills had been an ordeal.

To "keep him in medication," Pat had to part with the silver tea service given in 1846 to Samuel Jarvis Peters. "I was hoping by some miracle that perhaps the Phipps would like my husband just as a guest," she joked to Lidz. "But I suppose it is too great a hope. The Shearwater Pottery has a bank account in one figure this week."

Peter's doctors, too, were troubled by all that he was facing.

It is evident that we are still very much in the dark concerning the workings of [Peter's] mind. The family set-up is remarkably complicated with loves, hates, jealousies, suppressed aggressions, ambivalent attitudes, and one can only guess as to the relationships. We do not really know if the patient loves his mother or hates her intensely; if he hates her because of her fondness for [Bob] or loves her and is merely jealous.

There was another worry on all of their minds: that Peter might try, in some way, to emulate his brother by making an escape of his own. In May, he had alarmed his doctors by telling them it would do him good to work his way back home, or paddle down the Mississippi, the way Bob had done after his studies in Philadelphia. In August, a day before Pat went up to get Peter, a doctor told him of his brother's escape. He listened quietly and said that, despite the family's problems, he knew it would help him to return to his old routine, and that he hoped to get the family over its economic difficulties. "They are very broke," a doctor noted. "Business has been poor, although they have plenty of pottery on hand to sell. The tourist season is poor in Mississippi."

No one at Phipps was sure what would become of him. Pat worried about his influence on the children. She was determined to raise them "to be normal persons." On the day of his discharge—August 18, 1939—he seemed "more alert and cheerful" than he had ever been. He helped Pat with the packing, and "carefully included all of [her] letters, as if he intended to keep on living."

The first few days back at Shearwater were difficult. The family seemed "subdued," and didn't quite know how to speak or act around him. The day after his return, Peter walked down the path to the work-shop, looked around, and told Pat that there wasn't much to do there. The comment worried her: orders, particularly on large pieces, had been piling up in his absence. A couple of days later, he began to work for three hours each morning. "Whatever his troubles and his depression, he is a wonder," Pat wrote to his doctors. "It is a joy to see his beautiful work again—and something a bit sizeable in the line of 'pots.' He has lost nothing of his craftsmanship." By September 4, two weeks after his discharge from Phipps, Pat was wishing happily that the staff there could make an "invisible call on Shearwater" to see his progress. Peter was depressed and apprehensive, but was working five or six hours a day in the workshop, and showing "real interest and concern." Before long, he was firing the kiln again and staying at his work for up to fifteen hours at a stretch. In a report to Meyer, Pat spoke of her delight in having "a practically well-seeming husband."

He is looking splendidly, sleeping perfectly, eating well, and the children are joyous. Peter says I have never looked happier, which should be a sort of barometer of him. He is very quiet, but the "slowness" has departed. He has doubts of our "wanting him on the place," he is still very reproachful, but has few "strange" ideas. He speaks readily on all subjects. His work is done beautifully. He plays tennis, is still a fine fisherman. He has, I feel, done a splendid job being himself and I am proud of him and proud of the Phipps Clinic. . . . Also, at odd moments, a little proud of myself. There has been enough of joy in this last week to carry us far, and I hope it can go on for all of Peter's life. Peter is such a fine person that I believe he may be able to hold onto the reassurance he has been able to find. I have much thankfulness in my heart for having had the privilege of having my husband at the Clinic under your supervision.

In July, when Pat and Sissy had first learned of Bob's escape from Sheppard Pratt, they had tried to calculate how long it would take him to reach Ocean Springs. They were sure, somehow, that he would come directly home. "After his 180 miles from Jackson, he was near exhaustion," Pat wrote Peter's doctor. "We have figured that at the same rate it would take him about seven months to get home, unless he rode a freight." Fall came—a warm, dry fall, with temperatures over 100 in September—and there was still no sign of him. The family looked for him in the woods on moonlit nights, and debated what to do when he arrived. Sissy was eight months pregnant, fearful for herself and for the baby, whom she could feel kicking inside her, and Annette assured her she would keep Bob safe and care for him. On the night of October 5, 1939, Sissy looked up from her reading and saw her husband standing silently before her. He had been traveling for more than three months, and had followed the railroad tracks from Maryland to Mississippi for over a thousand miles.

If Annette had any illusions about him returning to "normal" life, they were quickly dispelled. Her son was "completely mute," though Peter went to the Cottage and did his best to try to get him to talk. For a few days he prowled the grounds, and then, without a word to anyone, disappeared in his boat. When the Coast Guard found him on one of the barrier islands, they took him back not to Whitfield but, mistakenly, to Peter's little dock at Shearwater. He fled for the woods, but Peter went after him, spoke to him with affection and persuaded him to return at least "temporarily" to the asylum. He was grief-stricken to see Bob's condition, and "wanted to go along" to Whitfield to care for him. "But we really did need him here, and he stayed," Pat wrote. Peter had done enough: "Bob would have been lost without him."

The incident only deepened Peter's depression and anxiety. But, once again, work seemed to save him. "His greatest luck is a zest for doing; [it] has been one of his greatest assets always," Pat wrote Lidz on November 21, a year after Peter's breakdown. "I feel often that he *makes* himself work. He longs for energy. . . . With Bob you feel a boundless energy through all his illness, but it is sadly misdirected."

Much of that "boundless energy" went into Bob's escapes from confinement. He fled at least three more times from Whitfield, once by lowering himself from his window on a bedsheet and walking the 180 miles home to Ocean Springs in a little over two weeks. Police all over the state were on the lookout for him. On the walls under his window, as a taunt to his keepers, he had drawn some birds with a bar of soap. He was out again on December 9, dressed in his hospital whites, with no over-coat. "Bob escaped yesterday afternoon . . . and all is a turmoil as usual," Sissy wrote a couple of days later. "Billy yells—hunger and upset tummy. God damn it all to hell. . . . I've had all I can stand. That's that! It took him 17 days to get back last time. 17 + 11 = 28. He'll be late for Christ-mas unless he hurries." Days later, he was picked up and sent back again. Sissy went to visit him with their two-month-old child.

> *Poor old Bob only wants to get away. He says he can't get well there. He talks a great deal more, but it is a tremendous effort. In so many ways I can see that he is not well yet, not even well enough to go to [the ranch in Vermont] . . . He is so sad I cannot think about him without tears.*

Annette did her best to deal with Bob's hatred of hospitals—he had always been a person "who liked to get off by himself out of doors to work off any disturbed feeling." On Christmas Eve, 1939, she moved him into a rented house in Jackson, where a six-foot-two attendant—half a foot taller than Bob—helped her care for him. But that, too, proved confining, and on February 7, 1940, he slipped away during his daily walk. It was bitter cold—Mississippi had not had such a winter for the past fifty years. All of the greenware in the workshop froze, Peter's fam-ily caught the flu, and he climbed out of bed and took up his duties as wood getter, nurse, and "amateur plumber," repairing burst pipes.

After twenty-one days on the road, Bob returned to Shearwater, looking strangely restored, with a new zest for life. He had emerged from his silence and seemed "a different person," Sissy wrote. "Talks, works every day at the workshop. It is like a miracle." Everyone in the family was amazed by the change. "He came home a renewed person," Pat wrote to Lidz. "Something perfectly remarkable has happened." He kept odd hours and sometimes slept in the woods. He "saturated" himself with music, and the family heard him dancing by himself late at night. He seemed to Pat to be "more elated than depressed, full of ideas" and better able to share them. "I used to be an intellectual," he joked, emerging from his long silence, "but I'm now like Rousseau—both of us conked!" He was turning out a "mass" of "wonderful" decorated pottery; one day he did twenty-five vases. Soon he was working beside Sissy on printed dresses and block prints, decorating plates, and firing the kiln at the Annex. That fall or winter she had founded a sort of "decorating circle," making handbags and Christmas cards and prints—which were selling very well at the Pottery—and devising ways to develop Shearwater into an artistic "cooperative" of the sort she, and probably Annette, had been thinking about for years. Now that Bob was back, he could help her. "I've never known such a worker," she wrote. "He ought to be the leader of just such a center as I dream of: wood, weaving, etc."

As Pat and Peter worked on their garden, tended to the bees, or did jigsaw puzzles with the children, Bob and Sissy resumed their old walkabouts in search of flowers. In April, Sissy and the children moved from the Barn back into the Cottage with him. She and Bob went on picnics, started their own garden, or sat lazily watching a pair of thrashers build a nest in the Cherokee rose at their door. Unlike Peter, Bob spent little time with his children, though he would sometimes steal into their room at night to watch them sleeping. He took a special liking to his niece and nephew Marjorie and Michael. Marjorie, Pat explained, "is the only one who stands up to him, and when he roughly tells her to get out, she tells him in no uncertain terms where to go, and he likes it, and [she] likes him, and prays for him every night." His long ordeal had drawn him closer to his brother, and had made him want to help him with his depression. "Pete has complained to Bob of his troubles," Pat noted. "Bob gives him *fine* advice. Talks and can be delightful."

Through the spring and summer of 1940, life at Shearwater was busy, odd, and unpredictable. Business was picking up and the showroom had never looked better. All three brothers had been doing "wonderful things," including a series of vases that Bob slip-decorated in black and white. Peter took a two-week vacation, loafed around, gained a few pounds, and got some "un-pottery things done." Bob was unable to find the same peace of mind, and, despite their efforts and their moments of harmony, the two brothers were often on each other's nerves, with Mac playing his usual role as peacemaker. When Peter took Bob out on a fishing trip, he plunged overboard far from shore. It was one of many such incidents, Pat told Lidz; there was no way to avoid them. "All of Bob's queer and super-strange actions Pete takes as personal insults to himself and to the Shearwater Pottery. He says he hates Bob at times, but Bob says he loves just three people: his wife, mother, and Peter."

By July, it had become clear to Sissy that, despite her love for Bob, she simply couldn't go on living with him. Beyond the "normal" craziness of their married life, his sexual demands on her had become exhausting, sometimes frightening. She felt overwhelmed. She begged him to leave her alone, if only for a week. She consulted a lawyer about divorce, but remembered her marriage vows—"in sickness and in health"—every time she was tempted to "skitter." She had little doubt that she loved him, and felt uncertain even about separation. In July, she traveled to Winnetka, Illinois, with the children, to visit her Hellmuth relatives (Uncle Ted and Aunt Hulda), get some long-needed rest, and think calmly about the future. Her uncle, who had always been fond of her, did his best to persuade her to divorce Bob, and offered to help in any way he could. Perhaps, Sissy wrote Bob, they should separate for a while. The Andersons had sometimes spoken about creating another outlet for Shearwater. It was time to make it a reality.

We've always, even in the best days, felt the need of some other outlet there on the place. I don't mean just a pottery sales outlet but a place the family could take turns using for a vacation from too monotonous living. Well, I'm going to try to establish the outlet. As the winter season is approaching, my first idea is to start in Florida, but, with luck and care, the affair could be moveable, going to North Carolina or New England in summer. I have all sorts of flights of fancy

213

in connection with it, and see the various families rotating in the management of the shop and, mostly, having a wonderful time. Of course, it would be plenty of work, too. But couldn't you and I have fun if we got Maine some year? Anyway, while you are getting entirely well, I would at least feel that I was doing something useful, and would not be so terribly far away.

Bob wanted none of it. A month later, he came up for her on the train, appearing without warning, cutting a strange figure on the elegant, tree-lined street in suburban Chicago. Decades later, she remembered his coming into the house. He took her in his arms, carried her to the bathroom, and put her down in a tub of icy water. "Wake up!" he said. "For God's sake wake up before it's too late. . . . You and I belong together. We are one in a rare and special way. You have to wake up and see it. It's impossible to separate us. I am not sick any more. I promise to behave. Promise that you will come home. Promise!"

Back in Ocean Springs, she found herself dreaming once again of escape, longing for even an inkling of consideration or tenderness from her husband. For a while, she and the children lived in the Barn, under Annette's watchful eye, and then for a few weeks in Biloxi, with a painter friend, Dusti Bonge. It was there, perhaps, that she began to think of Oldfields. It pained her whenever she thought of the house, beautiful and empty. No one had lived there for years. Her mother had died in 1933, months after she and Bob married, and her father, who sometimes came to Shearwater to visit his daughter and grandchildren, was living in a rented house in Ocean Springs, cared for by an attendant. Perhaps she could open Oldfields as a "guest house" and take her father back to the place he had always loved.

OLDFIELDS

One morning in late January 1941, Bob and Sissy left three-year-old Mary and one-year-old Billy with Annette and sailed to Oldfields, to take a good look at the empty house and see if they could live there with Sissy's father. They spent the night on Deer Island and from there rowed for hours against the wind to the Oldfields pier. They set up camp in the office room, with a couple of lamps and a wood-burning stove. Leaving a pot of beans simmering on the stove, they walked the three miles to Graveline, where they searched for arrowheads and shards of pottery and spied a morning cloak butterfly and the freshly vacated cocoons of some

Prometheus moths—a sign, perhaps, of renewal. In Gautier, they chatted with old friends. In the barn, the following day at dusk, they watched Yocum, who had been the overseer at Oldfields, as he fed and milked the cows. Sissy listened to "the long sizz of the milk stream, and the contented munching, and looked out with momentary joy to the long line of Horn Island and over the closer open grassland to the great beauty of the house."

Sissy felt that she was about to recover part of her inmost self. Through the years of turmoil with Bob—years when the present seemed unbearable and the future uncertain—she had retained a vivid sense of the past, a "feeling of continuity," the comforting "sense of having come from a particular place." That place was not Shearwater—the Andersons' stormy domain—but Oldfields, the plantation house in nearby Gautier that her father had purchased decades earlier.

Born and raised in Louisville, William Wade Grinstead had graduated from Harvard Law School and practiced law in Louisville and Chicago, looking after the investments of wealthy clients. When health problems drove him from the fiendish climate of Chicago, he moved into a boardinghouse in Ocean Springs, where he met his future wife, Marjorie Hellmuth. In 1904, he bought a huge tract of land with a large, elegant antebellum house, and two years later he moved there with his bride. His new home, Oldfields, where Pat and Sissy spent their childhood, stood on a bluff overlooking the Mississippi Sound, with a magnificent gallery and a long pier jutting out into the water. It was an awe-inspiring house, built in 1840, and on its grounds the two little girls found marvelous places to play: the barn and carriage house, the four hundred acres of "woods and orchards, pine ridges and cutover land, streams, marshes and narrow beaches." With the help of servants, Billie Grinstead grew pecans and grapefruit, satsumas, peanuts and a prodigious vegetable garden. He made a modest living selling pecans and holiday boxes, persuaded that he would "find as satisfactory an income in farming as in any city occupation, and probably more contentment." In 1918, the year Annette bought Fairhaven, he was called away on assignment for the government.

The war had begun, and he was needed as a lawyer in Washington and later in Pittsburgh. Only in the summers was he able to return South. In Sewickley, the Pittsburgh suburb to which he had moved his wife and daughters, he cursed the northern cold and the city, "with all its sham," and worried about the pecans and fruit trees he had planted.

As they sailed to Oldfields that January day in 1941, Sissy and Bob were doing their best to put an end to the troubles of recent months. "We have a new method," Sissy wrote. "Bob says 'V.T.' (vile temper) to me, and I say 'L.N.' (lower nature) to him." In the morning, on the front gallery, they did deep-breathing exercises in the cool air of the Sound. Two months later, in mid-April, they returned with the children and Mr. Grinstead, made some repairs to the house, and moved in. Bob remained at first in Ocean Springs. He did his decorating for the Pottery during the week and sailed over to Oldfields on weekends on a new little boat, the *Dos*. Later, when he decided to rejoin his family, he would often pedal the fifteen miles to work on his bicycle, with the Oldfields dog, Enkado, running along behind him.

Henry Mead, who came with Ellen to visit the family in April 1941, noticed a change in Bob, and wrote to one of his former colleagues at Phipps. He had no illusions about Bob's total recovery—he was violent at times, both with Sissy and with Peter—but there had been a peculiar change in him.

I think you will be interested with respect to the situation in Mississippi. Bob (Walter I.) Anderson has definitely changed. There is no longer a shuffle in his gait, he seems assured in his manner, and looks like a person who seems to know what he is about. . . . A change has definitely come over him. He sailed around one day to the house where the Hamills live and, soaking wet from wading ashore in a heavy rain and covered with mud from climbing up a bluff which the cattle are not able to get up—ten or twelve feet high—, came in during dinnertime to present himself to Dr. Ralph Hamill, the psychiatrist who has known him and his case for some time, to see what a change there had been. . . . Dr. Hamill's comment was that he had rarely seen such a change in a man and that "something seems to have gone out of him." Whatever it was that made him shuffle and seem to slink about and to mumble for eighteen months at Phipps to avoid saying a word is not present now. There is a change in the motifs of his work. There is a new style of bird, which is to say, a new style of design. His work is, if anything, better than it has been.

As for Peter, Mead noted, he "mumbles [and appears] quite shy, but I was surprised that during the evening he came up and discussed a volume of photographs with me, put in his oar in a discussion of the war and aside from a mumbling enunciation seems like any quiet, normal person. He did not look awfully well to me. He works continuously putting out a large amount of pottery for his brother to decorate day by day."

Sissy, more than anyone, was aware of a change in Bob. She was always getting the impression that he "was a new creature coming from some far, strange place where he had been dipped in a river or had suffered a sea change." During his confinement, he had often spoken of finding peace by working on a ranch. He had never lived on a farm before or felt so close to the water, and each day brought something new. "I had never seen the sea before I stepped out on the front gallery," he wrote of his years at Oldfields. "I was this year's bird born in the mountains. I had never seen the sea." He was particularly fascinated by the barn. Years later, in her memoirs, Sissy reflected that "the alienated must seek forever the means of reentry into the world of man. Bob was seeking, for some reason, through the simpler world of animals. 'Dogs, cats, birds are holes in heaven through which man may pass,' he said." She rejoiced in his discoveries and in those of the children, and led the way to the special places she remembered from her childhood. Through the arched root of an oak tree, over a carpet of moss, was an entrance to Fairy Land. Near it, they found the two old bricks and the round top of an old nail keg that Pat and Sissy had used, decades before, to create a banquet table. There *must* be fairies, Sissy thought. How else would those objects have survived? "We found acorn saucers and [filled them with] crumbs of peanut butter and honey."

Bob was beginning one of his happiest, most productive periods as an artist. For him, the early 1940s were a time of renewal and healing, of playing with his children, watching birds and animals, observing plants and insects, and making another attempt at the married life he had once pined for. He had time to draw, paint, and make block prints; to illustrate some of his favorite books—*Don Quijote,* Pope's *Iliad, Paradise Lost, Faust;* to translate from Spanish part of a history of art; to build his own kiln and fire a new series of figurines. He kept the house stocked with firewood—no small job—and built a rental cottage with his own hands. He celebrated the passing of the seasons and daily hours in a series of watercolors and lyrical "calendar drawings" that capture the life around him: his children at play, fishing, gardening, bird-watching, sailing, sketches of animals. These were pen-and-ink drawings, with a bright watercolor wash. Sissy longed for time to write: a novel, children's stories, fables she could share with the children. Sometimes in the evening she wrote a poem, and Bob did an illustration. They had done so often, back in Ocean Springs.

He transformed the attic into a studio, bought rolls of surplus linoleum and wallpaper, and made huge prints, most of them nineteen inches wide and six feet long, but some over thirty feet. He hoped these prints—the horizontal ones that he called "overmantels" and the vertical ones he called "scrolls"—would provide inexpensive art to ordinary people, especially for children's rooms; better art than they could find, say, at the local five-and-ten.

Within weeks after they moved in, Sissy felt her nerves untangling. The days drifted by for her "in the fine dreamy fashion of old childhood years." Electricity had been installed at Oldfields in spring 1941, but wartime blackouts kept the family from using it at night. "We rather revel in candles and lamps," Sissy wrote. "It feels like yesterday." Mary remembers the never-ending stories her mother would tell by candlelight. " 'Tell,' we'd say, and she would go on and on, continuing the adventures of Alice and Sandy and Mr. Pym, who solved mysteries and adventured all over the world. Sometimes she made us believe those sto-

"Walter and Sissy at the Table," drawing by Walter Inglis Anderson,
poem by Agnes Grinstead Anderson, Ocean Springs, 1930s.
Reproduced courtesy of the family of Walter Anderson,
Joan Gilley, curator.

ries were more real than reality. It was her gift, since reality was frequently not pleasant."

Sissy worried continually over the condition of her father, who spent much of the day in a chair on the gallery, smoking cigars, saying little, looking out over the Sound. Bob had disliked him from the beginning, back when he had met Sissy; one of his delusions at Phipps was that, while courting her in 1929, he had caused his father-in-law to have a nervous breakdown. Sissy was appalled by their hostilities. By the time he moved back into Oldfields, her father "had reached a time in his life when all the accustomed parts of it had left him, and any small familiar bit seemed so precious that he could bear no change. . . . There could be no paint on walls that should be white. He was even loath to allow the performance of plays and spectacles in the wide hall or the huge attic. Something [bad], such as fire, was sure to happen if people came into the house. My children, as well as their father, chafed against what seemed utter foolishness, and they devised ways to get around Granpa's prohibitions. Singly and together, they put on dozens of performances at Oldfields." Forbidden to paint the walls with murals, Bob did them on huge sheets of charcoal paper, and taped or tacked them in place.

There were blissful times on the gallery, with Bob and Mary standing side by side, watching the seagulls along the shore. He asked her to compose poems about them, and as she recited, he carefully wrote down each word. At the age of six, Mary wrote a little play, and produced it, with crepe paper costumes she stitched together herself. She wrote many such things back then—"marvelous plays and all kinds of fairy tales and tales that she made up herself"—and performed them with her friends on an improvised stage: an abandoned oyster-shucking house beside the water. Mary's memories of Oldfields came back to life, years later, in a short story:

FAMILY CIRCLE

"Why can't we have breakfast together like a civilized family? Is that too much to ask?"

At the pain in my mother's voice I clutched my green crayon so tightly it broke. Under the dining room window on the front gallery floor I had just finished drawing the largest green circle in the world. And the ends had met! But the voice from the dining room reminded me that my circle, like many of the things I did, might add to my mother's unhappiness. I sighed and put my broken crayon down on the grey board beside me.

"Damn it, I was hungry!"

So, my father was the guilty one this time. He tried to explain.

"I've been up since before dawn. I need to draw while the light is right. Fall's coming and the morning glories will be over before you know it." He stopped. "Is it really so important to you, Sissy?"

He hadn't meant to hurt her feelings. I knew that, and I knew what had happened. Like me, he'd smelled pancakes and bacon and slipped in to grab a bite. Only my work on the circle had delivered me from temptation.

I stood up and peeped over the window sill. In the dining room my father moved toward my mother. His arm encircled her shoulders and his fingers touched the braided crown of her hair. The hand closest to me held two pancakes.

"I'm sorry. Really, I am. We can have breakfast. Why not? Go get the children."

He paused. "And your father. I'll wait right here."

Her head lifted.

"Really, Bob?"

"Confound it! Do I have to swear?"

She vanished quickly into the sitting room. Daddy looked after her and I could see his face. I sat down again on the floor.

"He wants to make things better, but he doesn't know how," I thought. "Like me."

The screen door squeaked open and he came out, catching the door so it wouldn't bang. He was trying. Usually he banged even louder than Billy and I did. He walked as though he carried something heavier than pancakes. He didn't notice me sitting still under the window but crossed directly to the gallery railing to look out over the water where the islands waited on the horizon. He stood very still, shoulders back, head balanced on his straight neck like a soldier. I could smell the familiar smell of him, a strong animal-like smell mixed with woods and cigarettes. At last he raised his hand and looked at the pancakes, broke off a piece of one and tasted it.

A flock of red-winged blackbirds exploded from the dark cedar at the west end of the gallery and dropped together to the grass. They were not alarmed when Daddy moved. He crumbled the pancakes and scattered them across the yard, chuckling to see the blackbirds rush to feast. Two birds, blue-black in the morning sun, epaulets flaming yellow-orange-red, collided in mid-air and I laughed too. My father turned quickly and I shrank back.

"I was just drawing," I began, but he wasn't angry.

"Good Lord!" He was looking at my circle on the floor. "How did you make it so big and keep it round?"

I scrambled to my feet.

"I figured it out before I started. See the spokes like a bicycle wheel? I drew them out from the center. I used that board to make them all the same length."

"It's the biggest green circle I think I've ever seen," he said. I felt older than five. He bent forward, looking carefully at my drawing. I looked too. There were a few jiggles where the crayon had bumped over the rough boards but my plan had worked. The great curve of the outer line connected all the spokes and met itself at the starting point.

"This is good work."

I flushed with pride. My father could draw anything and frequently did while I sat beside him and watched. His dip pen leapt from ink bottle to paper. Its flowing line swam, flew, dashed across the white page, leaving fish, birds, chickens in its wake. My circle was interesting to him.

"I made one with shells on the beach yesterday. I guess it's still there if the tide didn't get it."

He laughed.

"I saw it early this morning," he said. "The sandpipers had run right through the middle of it, and the waves were licking at the edge."

I longed to see my beach circle divided by the footprints of the little peeps but Daddy opened the screen door.

"Good work," he repeated, holding the door for me. "Ready for break-fast?"

I passed him as I entered the dining room and he bowed his head politely, as though I were a lady.

"Your mother's gone to find Billy. And your grandfather."

"My mother . . ." I looked at the carefully set table, the white table cloth, then, at my grubby hands. I still had on my nightgown, and I certainly hadn't brushed my hair.

"I'll be right back," I gasped.

I narrowly missed running into my brother Billy, who was trotting toward the dining room, combed and dressed, anticipating pancakes. Five minutes later, I found him gravely regarding our father from his perch atop the slippery cushion which made him tall enough to reach his plate. Daddy's narrow blue eyes studied his son with a look I knew from watching him draw, but Billy was not happy. My three-year-old brother's large long-lashed grey eyes were topped by dark thick eyebrows like our mother's, which spoke as clearly as a voice. Meals with our father were always exciting, especially when Granpa was there too. Billy's eyebrows wondered what this morning might bring. I climbed up on my chair beside his and reached for my napkin ring, silver, with flowers and vines. It had been my mother's when she was my age. Watching me, Billy picked up his. Our napkin rings were toys which we used as spy-glasses to peer at the spider who lived high in the corner of the room, at the flowers in the blue bowl in the middle of the table, or at each other. We liked to roll them about on the table cloth steering them with our forks. As I pulled out my napkin I saw that Daddy at the end of the table seemed to be doing something with his. I poked Billy with my elbow. Daddy looked at us. The corners of his mouth twitched as he held up his napkin. He had tied a knot in one end to make a head. As we watched he pulled out his pencil and drew two eyes. Holding two unknotted corners in his hands, he flipped the napkin repeatedly in the air, rolling its center into a body and legs. One of his hands held the tail of cloth above the head. The other clutched the "toes." Softly he chanted:

"Miss Nancy Spence, for fifty cents,
will dance the TA RA BOOM DE AYE!"

His fingers let go and the napkin flew whirling through the air in a wild dance. I slid down from my chair and ran to retrieve the napkin. He rolled it again, this time more tightly. Suzy, our cook, came in from the kitchen just as he let go. Miss Nancy Spence spun, legs flopping outlandishly, straight toward Suzy. In her dark face her eyes grew round and white behind her thick glasses, before she threw up her hands to protect her face. The milk pitcher crashed to the floor.

"What the debil was that?"

Suzy stood shaking and wet to the knees, her eyes darting to find the flying creature. Somehow Daddy was already on the floor picking up the pieces of the broken pitcher and sopping up the milk with a soggy knotted napkin. I joined him and by using the fireplace shovel and the ash bucket we made a fast job of the cleanup. Over our heads Suzy appealed to Billy.

"What kind of bird was that flying right up in my face? You seen it didn't you, Baby? Weren't no butterfly. Didn't you see it? Tried to peck my eyes out. Flew right at me! Look like a white bat."

Billy didn't answer.

"Oh, Lordy. How I gonna tell Miss Agnes 'bout her mother's milk pitcher? She set store by that pitcher. I ain't never seen such a thing . . ."

Daddy stood up.

"It's all right, Suzy. I'll tell her. It was my fault. I was playing with the children and I didn't mean to startle you. Please go and get more milk in another pitcher and bring in the rest of the breakfast. Miss Agnes is coming in with Mr. Grinstead."

He was right. Suzy had no sooner sputtered out into the kitchen when we heard the thump of Granpa's walking stick in the hall. Daddy and I were seated in our places when they appeared in the sitting-room doorway. Mama stopped there and just looked at all of us. Then she smiled. I smiled back thinking how tall and pretty she looked when she was happy and how glad I was she hadn't come sooner. Daddy stood up again very polite and handsome even though his thick brown hair was unbrushed and his clothes old and damp at the knees.

"Here we all are for breakfast." Mama led Granpa to his seat and helped him sit down. "Do you know I felt a little north wind on the breezeway, and Robert said Daddy refused to wear his seersucker suit this morning. He wanted his grey one. It was so warm yesterday, but perhaps summer is over."

She hung Granpa's cane on the back of his chair and leaned over to remove his napkin from its ring and tie it around his neck. Our father glanced impatiently toward the kitchen but Mama didn't notice. She patted Granpa's shoulder.

"We're having your favorite breakfast, Daddy. Pancakes."

"Pancakes?"

An unsteady smile sweetened his smooth pink face. Granpa was more than eighty years old but sometimes he seemed like a baby. Each morning Robert, who was our handyman, drove out from Ocean Springs to bathe him, shave him, and dress him in his lawyer clothes, business suits he insisted on wearing with his Harvard tie, his polished black shoes, his gold watch and chain and his hat. So dressed, Granpa would sit out in the yard in his favorite wicker chair all day looking out at the pecan trees he had planted and grafted, cared for and loved.

"Morning, Granpa." I spoke loudly, knowing he didn't hear very well, but though he turned his head toward my voice his vague watery eyes wandered over my face without recognition.

"Morning, Granpa," echoed Billy. "Pancakes is my favorite, too."

"Mine too," I agreed, "and bacon."

"I like them so much that once I wrote a poem about them," said Daddy, tapping on the table, impatiently. "I wonder where they are?"

Suzy appeared with a stoneware pitcher, placed it on the table, and withdrew almost quickly, before my mother could speak to her. Mama looked at the pitcher, started to speak, and stopped. Daddy had crossed the room and was holding her chair. She left Granpa with a final pat and sat gracefully in her chair.

As Daddy returned to his seat I could see that his eyes looked longingly toward the window.

"There were warblers in the scrub oaks at the top of the hill, and I see that the dogwood leaves are rusty. Maybe we could go out for firewood soon?"

"Yeah! I can drive old Jim!" I loved to go wooding.

"I can! I can! Let me, Daddy." I kicked Billy's chair. He was much too young to drive a horse.

"Now calm down, both of you," but Mama's eyes were on Daddy who was drawing on the tablecloth. He dropped his pencil into his pocket and twisted his hands together impatiently. Under the dining room table my feet found the ledge under which I could hook my toes and push and lift the front legs of my chair off the floor.

"I love this time of year," said Mama. "Before you know it there'll be sugar cane and pecans."

"Sugar and pecans?" Granpa touched his plate with fumbling fingers, then peered uncertainly toward the kitchen door. Daddy stared at him, about to speak, but just then Suzy came in with our breakfast. She placed the big covered serving dish before Mama.

"Suzy, please get two more napkins for Mary and Mr. Bob, and the cane syrup for Mr. Grinstead."

"Cane syrup," repeated Granpa, nodding.

Suzy looked at me sharply and then at my father's empty napkin ring. Then she shuffled from the room. Daddy jumped up angrily.

"Why can't that woman pick up her feet when she walks?"

"Oh, Bob, I suppose it's because she's so heavy." She smiled at him but her eyebrows were begging. "Please sit down. Here's everyone's favorite breakfast."

She lifted the silver lid and uncovered stacks of golden brown hot cakes surrounded by wavy stripes of bacon. To these distractions of sight and smell she added another as she quickly began to serve our plates. Her voice, gentle and ladylike, was richly expressive and enveloped the listener.

"Fall and pancakes always remind me of Granny and the deer who came to breakfast."

She put Billy's plate down in front of him, poured a little honey on his pancakes, and cut them up.

"Granny and Mamma and Daddy, your grandfather, were sitting at this very table, in this same dining room, in October, having breakfast forty years ago."

She put down my plate and handed me the honey.

"They were just beginning to eat their pancakes when they heard a gun-shot east of the house." She pointed toward the window behind me. "They knew that hunting season had begun but they had never heard the hunters so close before."

Suzy came in with the napkins and the syrup.

"Just in time," said Mama. She carried Granpa's plate to him and taking the carafe from Suzy, poured the thick syrup onto his pancakes and began to cut them up.

"Mama, Granpa's drooling," I observed.

"Never mind!" Daddy's voice was too loud.

"He is drooling, look," said Billy.

"Hunters have never been allowed on the Oldfields land." Mama spoke very quickly, wiping Granpa's mouth and feeding him a bite of pancake.

"I know," I said, "I've seen the posted signs."

Daddy sounded very angry. "Why do you fuss so with the food, Sissy? Do you want to eat it for them?" She had filled his plate and started toward him.

"But they could hear the hunting dogs coming closer and closer."

"They was barking," Billy added, spoon poised over his plate.

"Wait for grace," I whispered, rocking gently on the back legs of my chair.

"Don't tilt, Mary." My mother was back in her seat, putting pancakes on her own plate.

"Bob, will you please say Grace?"

We bowed our heads and waited.

"Bob. Please."

"For what we are about to receive, may the Lord make us truly thankful."

"Amen."

My mother lifted her fork and we began.

"There were no screens on the windows then," she continued, "and Granny could hear running hoofs. Suddenly a deer leapt in through the open window! He stopped right there staring at the family at breakfast."

"More syrup," said Granpa.

My mother pushed the carafe toward him, looking at my father. Granpa picked up the carafe and examined it, unsure of how it worked. Watching him I teetered on my chair.

"Granpa's pancakes are all gone," said Billy sadly. We loved Granpa. When he knew who we were he patted our heads and called us "Sweetie." Now the cane syrup had run down the corners of his mouth. He looked old and helpless. His thick eyebrows, like Mama's and Billy's but white, were drawn together like a white bird's wings.

"You are right, Billy." Our father was standing beside the table. "Granpa needs more pancakes and I'm going to see he gets them."

He picked up a pancake and threw it at the old man's face, knocking off his glasses.

"What's the matter? Not enough syrup on that one? Try this!" It landed on Granpa's chest and stuck like an ornament, dripping golden honey.

"Bob! Stop it! Stop it! What's the matter with you?"

Mama stood between the two men as Daddy lifted the third pancake. But before he could throw it my chair legs slipped and I felt myself falling. I grabbed at the table to catch myself and caught the tablecloth. I crashed to the floor pulling the whole breakfast—tablecloth, china, glasses, silverware, pancakes, bacon, syrup, everything—down on top of me! When Mama finally uncovered me and helped me to my feet, Daddy was gone. Robert was leading Granpa out of the room patting his back.

"It's all right, Mr. Grinstead. It's going to be just fine."

Billy was still sitting on top of his cushion, clutching his spoon. Mama stood up, holding the silver serving dish, and handed it to Suzy.

"Mama?" Billy's voice sounded far away.

"Yes, Billy."

"What happened?"

"What happened???"

"What happened to the deer?"

"Oh! The deer! Oh. Well, Granny said it just stood there for a minute looking at them. Then your Granpa stood up and just waved his napkin and the deer turned and leapt right back out that window."

Billy looked at his spoon.

"They should have given it a pancake."

"I don't think deer like pancakes, Billy." She stopped.

"Not in dining rooms, anyway," I added. "That deer just came in by mistake."

All this might have taken place in the fall of 1944, when Mary's creativity was blossoming and Sissy felt her own imagination growing rusty as the dogwood leaves under the strain of running the household. There were times when she couldn't bear her husband's selfishness. "Sometimes I wonder why he has never guessed what it is that I want," she wrote one day. "A little tenderness. Just a little. That's a wonderful word. Tenderness. Linger over it. It goes with caress and has much to do with love, less with passion. It connotes sympathy and understanding and thoughtfulness." A day later—November 6, 1944—she told of the incident that gave rise, half a century later, to Mary's story.

Is it fair to ask Daddy to go on living in the same house with Bob? Tonight at supper, suddenly, for no reason (all was quiet and peaceful) he picked up a pancake and threw it hard and hit him in the eye. Is it fair to let the children in for the fear and nervous tension that goes with that kind of craziness, lack of any right feeling, or control? No, it isn't. Mary is a darling. Billy, very sane and strong. Imagine relying on a five-year-old. That's how I feel about him, a sort of "put your trust." Mary needs protection and much love. They all need that, and so do I. Bob needs the constant protection of a wall of prayer. It is incredible that an artist—a person of supreme sensitivity—should be so impervious to others, so soaked in self . . .

And yet, for all his egotism, there were moments when her husband seemed the best father imaginable. In the attic where Bob had his workroom, he put on a marvelous puppet show for Mary and Billy. He made figures out of beaverboard and tied them to ropes and slung them over the rafters. It was a celebration of spring, Mary remembers, with huge turtles, frogs, moths, ducks, and stalks of corn. At Christmastime, their

1

2

3

4

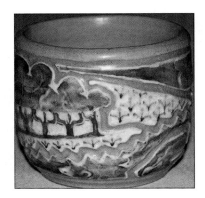

5

6

7

8

9

10

11

12

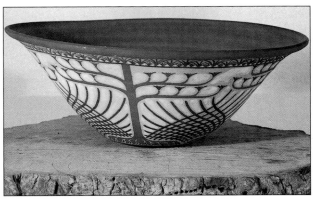

13

14

15

16

17

18

19

20

21

22

23

24

25

first year in Oldfields, he transformed the hall into a forest and made an Indian tepee for Mary and Billy, and he "illustrated" Homer's *Odyssey* with a three-foot model of Odysseus's ship, with oars that moved. His love of epic was overwhelming. When Sissy told him, dreading his reaction, that she was pregnant again, he was sure that the baby would be a boy and named it Leif, for Leif Ericsson. No matter that it was a girl; the name remained, though Sissy changed it silently to "Leaf" in her journals. There was "no feeling of disappointment" on Bob's part. Before the umbilical cord was healed, he took her swimming in the water off the end of the pier. "He aggravated me so," Sissy told Leif years later, but "now, when I look back, he was always doing the thing that was intrinsically right and perfect."

Over the years, the grounds of Oldfields had undergone a transformation. Long ago, Mr. Grinstead's pecan trees had been overtaken by undergrowth. A fire had damaged some of the pine forest, and even before the family moved back in, Mr. Grinstead, Pat, and Sissy walked the grounds with Yocum and decided reluctantly to sell part of the timber. It was, Mary recalled years later, "one of the last stands of virgin pine on the Mississippi Gulf Coast." She returned there one July day in the early nineties, and tried to recapture a lost world.

My father recorded the fall of the forest in drawings of confused disorder. Broken bushes and trees, discarded branches surrounded the great raw stumps like a lurid battlefield after the army of loggers with their oxen teams had gone away. My mother never dwelt on the tragedy when she told the story, but on the extraordinary transformation. She believed that the cutting of the trees somehow altered the surface drainage and caused a wetland. As the ravaged earth, newly open to the sun and to the drenching rain, began to heal, plants appeared that had not grown there before. Long golden grasses of the pine savannah waved across the cutover land, replacing the long-leaf pineneedled carpet of the lost forest.

Pale gold, the grass was a perfect foil for the jewel-like collection of life, both flora and fauna which miraculously appeared beside the road. The profuse wildflowers marked the seasons of the year. In July pitcher plants of March and April stand stiffly dry in the hot sunshine. Once pale yellow-green, they have darkened to gold, red and even maroon in vivid contrast to the jaunty flags of white-topped sedge and the repetitious white dots of the pipewort buttons. Here and there a yellow spear of colic root rises like a thin candle from the green and orange whorl that forms its base. Blue-violet stokesias star the ditch. Loose-petalled pink meadow beauty and the bushy St. John's wort in orange-yellow are only the most obvious of July's show. The earth itself is patterned by crawling mosses and insect-eating sundew.

Plants share this boggy world with assorted dragonflies, spiders, grasshoppers, beetles, wasps in wild red and blue, marvelously dressed frogs, crawfish and turtles. My father brought me here when I was very young. He had discovered it at a time in his life when his difficulties with other people seemed unsurmountable. When I look at his angry drawings of the destroyed forest and then at the joyful musical celebrations of the varied forms he found in the bog, I understand a verse I found among his writings:

> *But if thou canst not love thy friends,*
> *thou still mayst love thy foe.*
> *For he hath brought thee low*
> *and taught thy ear to know*
> *the voice of growing grass.*

Other drawings from Oldfields are designs for plates and vases and for a series of twenty-two figurines done around 1941 or 1942: animals, bathing beauties, fishermen, people rowing. He was doing the entire process by himself: carving and modeling, making the molds, casting, trimming, and painting. Pat thought him one of the world's worst mold-makers when Mac wasn't there to guide him, but he was working enjoyably, at a more leisurely pace than during the widget-making years. Often he had time to look up from what he was doing, and to record his impressions in a journal.

I spent the day painting little figures. 15 plowmen, 21 geese, 20 horses and watching the red leaves go by, blown by a Northwest wind, and hearing little myrtle warblers and white-throated sparrows. In the morning I worked indoors with a fire and with hundreds of little clay figures around me. Yesterday, when Sissy came, I looked at them and suddenly they turned a wonderful lilac on one side and green on the other. It was like a miracle, and I spent the rest of the day glaring at them and wondering why the color was gone. I thought my eyes had gone bad. But today I found out what caused it. The wind swung the blind open and the sun shone on it (it is painted green), and suddenly all the little figures turned the most wonderful green on one side and lilac on the other. It was still a miracle. But a miracle realized.

Before long, he was at work on a kiln in which to fire those figures. Peter must have been too busy to help, or was disinclined to do so, for Bob drew the kiln design from that of a great Renaissance Italian maker of majolica, Cipriano Piccolpasso, who had avoided firing his ware during the waning of the moon (the pieces, he thought, would lack brightness). Over Sissy's protests and those of her father, Bob chose the old carriage house at Oldfields—a former slave quarters—to house the kiln. They fired it for the first time at eleven o'clock one day in February 1942, when the earth seemed to be coming to life after their first winter at Oldfields. A sluggish, blind old water moccasin was basking in the sun, and sparrows twittered in the cypress trees at the end of the gallery. Little white asters, "whose petals blush behind and who close their eyes and sleep at night," dotted the meadow, and they could see violets in sheltered spots. Sissy felt that the first firing was "a happening of magnitude," and recorded it in her journal. All day they fed the kiln a "fairly slim diet of fat pine," and watched the smoke coming from its vents: black at first and then much paler. The sun sank into the Sound, and later, in the moonlight, flanked by two of their cats, Webb and One-Eye, they peeked through a watch hole in the kiln and saw a clear, "diamond-pure atmosphere." It was a joyful moment. They longed for the presence of the family, especially Peter, to observe and advise. They cut off the fuel after twelve hours, cooled the ware for a day, and removed the figurine of a woman in a flowered dress. She "stuck slightly to the tongue"—could be harder—and they wished they had pyrometric cones.

Their joy was short-lived. One day it rained, the fireclay washed out of the bricks, and the roof fell in. It was only a matter of time before the carriage house burned to the ground. "It was a horrible loss," Sissy wrote years later.

I do not know just how terrible a blow it was to him. I was more concerned with the loss of the old building, which . . . was a part of my childhood, one of those material things which we cleave to so foolishly. A few pieces from that unlucky kiln are still extant. Of course, they did not come out as they were planned. He had made them in slip without glaze, and the strange alchemy of the firing had turned the natural clay color a smoky gray and the red a rich chocolate, while the surface was hard, almost vitrified. Most of the figures belonged to the farm—cows, horses, ducks, guinea hens, a plowman, a corn harvester. A few figures belonged to the sea—a magnificent schooner, an oyster opener in his skiff, a fisherman, and a strange little standing lute-player. Most of them he dumped over the bluff. Future archaeologists may have quite a time figuring those out. All this he lost, and he said very little, but took the molds from the attic and [in 1944] hauled them over to Ocean Springs and received a fresh rebuff: "Those molds are too hard to cast."

But hope arose from the ashes. New molds were made, the figurines went into permanent production at Shearwater, and that spring Bob used bricks from the burned building to make a terrace with a place in the center for a fountain or a bird feeder. In February, he harnessed one of the horses—Jim—and plowed and disked the ground and applied manure and planted a vegetable garden. Onions flourished amongst the petunias, and at one end of the garden, Sissy remembers, there were zinnias, sunflowers, tithonias, and marigolds. The children were given a space for radishes and carrots and beets, raccoons shared the corn, and

Sissy put up shelves and shelves of canned beans and tomatoes. Despite war rationing, she noted with satisfaction that they were elegantly provided for, thanks to the garden her husband had made on a whim, with "never a coupon gone from the books." They could get by without help from anyone. In a single day, the farm and garden produced "more milk and cream than we know what to do with (about five quarts); twenty-one eggs . . . . ; a half bushel beans; a half pound butter; two quarts buttermilk; potatoes ad lib; crabs ad lib; blackberries, honey, squash. . . . I suppose there would be fish for the fishing. It is a joyful feeling."

Back in Ocean Springs, Peter and his family were having much the same experience. Peter grew more than enough food for the family, and they managed to survive. A reporter who visited the Pottery remarked that it seemed "a tonic in this war-torn world." In the early forties, the newspapers spoke of "arming the country at the expense of its luxuries," and at the Front House Pat wondered "if Shearwater Pottery isn't pretty much a luxury. Perhaps we shall be taxed out of existence." The Defense Department had cut off the supply of tin oxide, one of the glazing materials they needed most. The Army Air Corps had built a little "Crash-Boat Base" nearby, and the quiet of Mill Dam Bayou was shattered, day and night, by soldiers training for rescue operations in the Gulf. Pat and Peter stayed up late now, listening to war news on the BBC, and were awakened in the morning by Marjorie with the paper, "its tall black headlines all war." The children, too, thought often about the war. "Oh, God," said Michael. "I pray you to take care of the Europe soldiers. Keep them safe and help them to beat the ones trying to beat them. Amen!"

Gradually, the war drew to an end, and so did Bob and Sissy's years at Oldfields. As earlier in his marriage, Bob chafed at the distractions and interruptions of a life with small children. He was the deer that had "come in by mistake," the one who leaped through the window in Mary's story. He quarreled often with Sissy, who resented having to bear all of the responsibilities of running the place, raising the children, and caring for him and for her father. She was unspeakably tired most of the time and felt she "was bearing horrible burdens." "Why are you so cross? What have I done?" he asked her one day, without knowing the anxiety she was feeling. Everything seemed to devolve upon *her*. One spring night she realized what a "tremendous urge" she felt to write. She wanted to do so "in tapestry form," with a panoramic view of the Coast, weaving people into that background. She had the story—a novel— "half-planned, the characters, many, half-drawn. From life, and yet not." She wondered about the moments she must be wasting each day, and made a list of all she had to do, from the time she got up, at seven, to the time she crawled into bed, between nine-thirty and ten. "Each day," she thought, "should contain a measure of creative effort." The daily round included fixing meals, caring for the chickens, pigs, and cow, gathering things for dinner, mending clothes, housecleaning, taking the children swimming, and putting them to bed. But there was so much more; the chores seemed endless:

> *If dog, cat or what-not is sick or needs fleaing, bathing: me.*
> *If screens need attention: me. House.*
> *If trash needs burning, cans burying: me.*
> *You see, I have that dreadful feeling of being alone at the center.*

In December 1946, she told him she was pregnant with their fourth child (Johnny), and the news hit him hard. He told her he was going to move back into the Cottage at Shearwater and devote all of his time to drawing and painting. "I'm not coming back, ever! I can't take it. I'm an artist; I have to be."

Sometime after Christmas, she decided to clean the attic.

The puppets hung wearily from their fishing twine. The last bursts of linoleum chips lay at the head of the stairs. Clay scraps, plaster scraps, drawings . . .

I sat on the edge of the old workbench and began to gather up scraps of paper. Most of them had writing on them, bits of poetry, bits of wisdom. I did try to bundle things into old trunks. . . . Suddenly, in the closeness of the attic, a horrible depression descended upon me. I was utterly unable to go on. I could not even get down the attic steps. I sat on the top step and slowly bumped myself to the bottom. I went straight to bed and did not tackle the attic again for about ten years. There were many circumstances, but the real reason was of course reluctance—the holding back from final things that plagues so many lives.

TENDER MIRACLES

For a "matriarch"—and that was what people had begun to call her—Annette sometimes felt very lonely. By the 1940s, she wasn't Annette anymore. When her sons married, and her grandchildren were born, the family had begun to call her Mère. The purpose of life, she told herself, is "to grow into the person you were meant to be, like a tree. Then the birds will find shelter and the shade in summer will be a blessing." Had she done enough to provide shade to her family? She liked to read about the psychology of religion and the "conjunctive emotions": sympathy, modesty, joy. If only she could feel happy, she could lift up her sons. Over the fireplace in her bedroom, which Peter had built for her, she had painted some lines from an Irish poet:

> He whom a dream hath possessed
> knoweth no more of doubting.

And yet there were days when she felt herself in "an agony of depression" and doubt and feared that she had lost her faith. She worried constantly about her boys and her grandchildren. She rested, meditated, jotted down advice to herself in the copybooks that lay about her room. Through good times and bad, even in the 1950s, when her sight began to fail and she could barely see the words, she prodded herself to read the Bible and to write her 750 words a day. With a touch of humor, she put together a "Gospel According to Annette McConnell Anderson," and read it to her closest friends. Keep busy and block "negative critical thoughts." Stop giving advice to others ("Love does not try to reform, no more than does Art or Science"). Stop being critical, and try to like people, see them, "always with an enthusiasm for what they are, not *might* be." How silly they seemed at times, especially when they tried to be nice: "After church, Mrs. [X] said *how sweet it was of me to come!* (The disastrous habit of trying to be pleasant!)" Above all, she prayed for inner quiet. If she could only learn to be *still,* she would be better able to nurture her family. She wanted to be like the little dog at the Front House. He would twitch his ears when he heard a car coming, far away, at the entrance to the Pottery on East Beach Road. Perhaps the key to happiness and to getting along with others was simply to *listen.* "Eyes, perhaps, are not so important and it is only my *eyes* that have been trained." Now, with her sight beginning to deteriorate, it was time to develop her hearing, to become a little less domineering, and more tolerant of others. "Stop contradicting people," she told herself.

> I always take the other side
> when anything is said.

239

It may be art or politics
or the last book someone read.
I always know that everyone
is nearly always wrong.
Unless they use my yardstick,
there's no hope for them at all.

Only late in life had she begun to learn "the lesson I should have learned many years ago: the love of beauty leads you astray too often. You pride yourself on your taste. Joyously you care for design and color of a certain sort. It may be the wrong sort but to you it is absolute." It leads you, she said, into conflict with others, into putting taste over feelings. She had always demanded much of her sons, and perhaps she had always been too hard to please. Even as a little girl, she had been too picky. When her father had given her a gift she thought ugly, she had shown her indifference, rather than her appreciation for the care he had taken to select it.

Her aesthetic approach to life, her strong opinions on just about anything, her overwhelming faith in the work of her favorite child, her criticism of all three boys—the cavils of a perfectionist—sometimes led to confrontations with Pat. It wasn't that they didn't admire or feel grateful for one another. For years after Walter's death, Pat cared for her mother-in-law and gave her lunch every day at the Front House. But at times Pat and Sissy felt that Annette simply wanted to stir up trouble. Both Pat and Annette were strong-willed, determined people. They tried, said Sissy, "but they could not get on together. Never." When Annette helped Pat in the showroom, she often drew a deep breath and said a little prayer. There were sharp words at the Front House over the best way to bring up children. Annette sometimes found her daughter-in-law too strict with Patsy, Michael, Marjorie, and Jimmy: much stricter, in an eat-your-broccoli kind of way, than Sissy was with Mary, Billy, Leif, and Johnny. They seldom agreed, either, on pricing the pottery, especially Bob's. After Walter's death, when Pat became business manager, she had the unenviable task of determining the market value of the three brothers' work. Annette liked to price things according to their "intrinsic value." But to Pat, Annette's aesthetic appraisals seemed a bit too arbitrary. She didn't, after all, need her mother-in-law to help her recognize a good pot, and her family didn't make its modest living from "intrinsic" values. After those quarrels, Pat felt "as guilty as a goat," and Annette used to feel empty and helpless: "I spoke at the wrong time," Annette would complain in her journal. "Silence, silence is what I must practice. Silence and love."

To cultivate those virtues, she prayed a lot. It was a terrible effort at times but occasionally the rewards were impressive. Through prayer and "inner quiet," she could cure a cold or get rid of a fever. Once, in New Orleans, she used prayer to lower her temperature from 102 to 98 degrees: four degrees in two hours. She had never worked harder in her life. "Plowing would be nothing to it!" Prayer, even reading the Bible, changed your breathing.

"Who needs me? Who can I help?" she would ask herself on waking each day. Most often it was Bob. Often, he seemed wholly himself, healed of whatever it was that had kept him in hospitals. There were happy moments when he came by on his "wheel"—his bike—and paused at the Barn on his way to the Pottery. He would read aloud to her, or pop into her room unexpectedly to kiss her goodnight. In 1946, after leaving Oldfields, he lived by himself at the Cottage. Often Peter took his lunch to him, and sometimes he would go to the Front House at midday to get a book and grab a sandwich, removing the meat and feeding it, as he left, to his nephew Jimmy's beagle. "It isn't that he doesn't like meat," Michael said one day to Annette, "but he can't bear to eat a fellow mammal."

After Johnny's birth, in March 1947, and the death of her father in 1948, Sissy began teaching school in Ocean Springs. She had wanted to teach since graduating from Radcliffe, and, in middle age, she was entering a period of bittersweet independence. She was a teacher now, but was unable to live with the man she had loved and cared for. For a while, she and the four children rented a little house in town. They would see Bob riding through Ocean Springs on his bicycle, in a world of his own, wearing his work clothes and—year round—his battered old gray felt hat, as recognizable from a distance as the barber's basin of his beloved Don Quixote. He would tip it courteously when he recognized someone. The old-fashioned gesture reminded his daughter Leif of "a gentleman on a horse . . . or in a carriage." Absorbed by his art, he had little time for his family. Annette saw as much of him as Sissy did. But once in a while, she and Bob, Sissy, and the children gathered together at the Barn:

Last night Billy and then Mary burst into the Barn where I was sitting with Bob. They were fresh and sunburned and happy. They had been to Horn Island for the first time. They had shells to show. Then Jimmy came. They had one piece of a broken shell. Bob told them it was rare. I brought out the box of shells and showed them the treasures from the island. There were some wonderful halves of cockle shells that Bob had brought back from France. How they loved them! Mary was ecstatic and Jimmy . . . so sweet, so wonderful the children were. The beauty and sweetness stayed for hours.

In her memoirs, Leif evokes the tension and strangeness of those family gatherings and the way she saw them when she was growing up:

Sometimes my grandmother, Mère, has supper specially to get our family together. Her Bobby is invited; sometimes I'm the one to go and tell him when to come. I am so nervous, but I knock and knock. I think that he is nervous too; or shy like me. Sometimes he never comes. Sometimes he does and he is nice. One time, finally, he comes and blood is dripping through a rag wrapped round his hand. I am afraid and he seems sort of angry . . . or embarrassed. I run home quickly and tell Mama, and she goes to fix his hand. Mama says his hand is cut from carving linoleum blocks.

I guess my father's kind of like a character in a book; he is dramatic. But it is difficult to live real close to someone in a book. It is unreal. You go through

motions and you wish that you were somewhere else; perhaps in another book.
Mère's supper parties are like that. They are so weird. Mère doesn't know how
to cook, though she is very old. So we have tuna fish out of a can. I try to help,
because my mama says to. But Mère's the boss. So we put lettuce on a platter
and in the middle goes the tuna fish. We fluff this out and put some mayon-
naise on top. Then pieces of tomato go around, and slices of hard boiled egg.
But sometimes these are not so hard. Then we have rolls that Mama warms,
out of a package.

Daddy comes, and we all sit around the table in Mère's living room. It's
sort of elegant, with pretty china painted blue and white, and shiny glasses, but
maybe not too clean. It's also not so very comfortable. We children try to be po-
lite which means we're pretty quiet. And Mère works hard to keep the conver-
sation going, talking about art and books. Daddy answers when he has to; you
can tell he has read lots of books. My Mama too. But you can tell that every-
one is glad when supper's over. I think it's sad that we're not sad when Daddy
goes away. But then we do not have to try; we do not have to go through mo-
tions just to get to where we'd rather be.

Annette often had the sense that her son was happy, pleased with the
work he was doing. When he was away on a bicycle trip or a visit to the
Islands she would go to the Cottage and straighten things up and look at
his paintings and sketchbooks. As she herself had done so often, he was
trying to teach art to others. He would cycle to Gulfport, for example,
and teach pottery to patients at the Veterans Administration Hospital.
One summer day, she found him giving lessons to a troop of Brownie
Scouts at the Front House. On the wall, going up the stairs, where Peter
and Pat had once worried over the color of the paint, they were doing a
collective mural. There are also times, in the journals, when two sorts of
solitude—the mother's and her son's—come together. Times when the
talk went beyond "art and books."

Last night went down to Bob's. I went intending to listen. I told him that
I remembered what he had said: that I was different this year. "How?" I asked.

He said "You have gone into your cave. . . ." I wondered what he meant. "How?" I asked again. "Is this your cave?" "Oh, no," he said, "this is a palace. I do not go into my cave. In my cave is a monster." I did not know what to say. At home again, I thought I should have said, "Turn on the light and you will see there is no monster."

Peter, too, often seemed preoccupied and worried. There were lapses in his self-confidence, and times when Pat thought him "the most suspicious of humans," too much given to self-pity and complaining. Annette noticed a certain indefinable unhappiness, and thought he needed more laughter in his life. At times he was rude to her, and at others behaved "like a saint." He would come by the Barn to play checkers with her, or bring her vegetables from the garden, or repair things around the house and tell her about his work. Throughout the forties and fifties, he longed for more freedom to experiment. His brothers were conscientious workers, but it wasn't *them* who had to carry the weight of the Pottery and keep up with orders. "[Peter] said that if he did not have to spend so much time throwing on the wheel he could make new experiments in glazes," Annette wrote. "I had asked for alkaline glazes. He said you had to keep at it, making a new batch in the experimental kiln every day. He sounded as if he would like to try it. I think it might be well to have for a time Welber [Beaugez] make whatever ware can be made without the wheel, and have Peter experiment."

As for Mac, he had drifted away. In 1941, weary of his work at the Annex and of the years of helping care for his brothers and keep peace between them, he had struck out on his own, apprenticing himself in a shipyard in Pascagoula. He moved a few years later to New Orleans, where he did the same sort of work. He welcomed the steady pay, and his job as a "straightener" was hazardous but challenging. Once he was hit between the eyes with a maul, and he fell forty feet from his scaffold into the canal. The metal plates used in shipbuilding buckled when they were welded together, and, as a "straightener," it was his job to flatten them with heat and water. It was an awe-inspiring job, he joked. "When you've got a blow torch in one hand and a stream of water in the other, people tend to get along with you." In his spare time, he sketched and painted. The Arts and Crafts Club where Annette and her boys had often exhibited their work was buzzing with servicemen. For two years, from 1943 to 1945, Mac took classes a couple of nights a week with the consul of Uruguay, an amateur painter with the euphonious name of Juan José Calandria. Mac's wife, Jackie, who had suffered from depression, liked city life and was grateful to be rid of the strain and tension of Shearwater. One day in the early forties—no one in the family remembers when—she took off with another man and left him forever. They divorced in 1945.

That year, though, on weekend trips to Ocean Springs, Mac was falling in love with Sara Lemon, the sister of his best friend, George Lemon. She had worked at Shearwater for the past eleven years, trimming figurines and helping out in the showroom. Since the death of her mother, she had cared for her eight brothers and sisters. The Andersons had developed quite an affection for her; in fact, it was she who took care of Patsy, Michael, and Marjorie during Pat's visits to Peter in Baltimore, and Sissy often asked her to mind her own children. One day, Annette sat down to tea with her at the Barn and jotted down her thoughts. Sara seemed as lovely as a Pre-Raphaelite painting.

Always she is pleasant, always she puts aside whatever trouble may be bothering her and smiles and gives a helping hand to any task. She never sits and waits for someone to attend to her. She is well disciplined by many tasks and love for the large family that needs her care. She always will go with you in your talk and almost never disagrees and she would be a perfect wife. I wonder how she'd change? She is too timid in her thought. She does not read, perhaps, enough. She's tall and slender as a reed with masses of curly copper-colored hair about her neck that curves up just as does Rossetti's picture of the Beatrice of Dante's poem. The Beatrice with poppies in her lap with eyes closed and her head thrown back. The dress, I think, is green with sleeves of red. Sara is almost beautiful. The nose too thin, the mouth too small, but just a trifle. The outline of her chin and throat is lovely and [so is] her brow.

Sara and Mac married in Ocean Springs on April 8, 1946, and set out for their honeymoon on Avery Island, stopping between Gulfport and Pass Christian "to clear as much rice as we could out of the car." Sara's brother J. K. had lent it to them and told them not to drive over thirty-five miles per hour. "We had time," Mac said, "to enjoy the scenery." They found Avery Island somewhat rundown, perhaps because of the war, but snowy egrets and anhingas were nesting, and primrose, verbena, and iris were in bloom. When they returned to Shearwater and moved into the rammed-earth house he had built nine years earlier, Mac fell to work, as he had years earlier when he and Bob had opened the Annex. Together with Sara, he had decided to make a fresh start at the Pottery. Through the window beside his potter's wheel, Peter watched his brother rebuild the huge muffle kiln: he put in new pipes to improve the draft, and changed it from kerosene to gasoline. He made new frames for the molds, replacing linoleum with wood. He designed a couple of new ashtrays (dogwood and flower) and some new figurines: a Rip Van Winkle, hunters, a series of nine comical baseball players, New Orleans street scenes of black men, women, children, and dancers. He devised a number of "gadgets": miniature pieces—shells, birds, crabs, etc.—that could be placed between the larger pieces in the Annex kiln, utilizing space that would have been wasted.

Annette told a reporter that there was nothing the family feared more than large orders. But, with the three brothers united again at Shearwater, there was talk of expanding it into a huge company with a nationwide market. Sara's brother J. K. was in on some of the discussions and helped advance the idea, which was front-page news on September 24, 1948, in the *Jackson County Times*. A group of local businessmen laid out plans for a new corporation, Shearwater Crafts. Peter, Bob, and Mac were to retain "a substantial interest," and there would be a public offering of stock. The payroll was to be expanded to 60 persons the first year and 120 the second. Ocean Springs had been talking about obtaining some industry for a long time, but this was "the first real proposal that had been made." Shearwater Crafts "would be chartered for the manufacture and sale of art and functional pottery, decorative tile, block printed textiles, wall paper and several other craft products." Raw materials were close to hand and the Andersons, someone remarked, had "accumulated enough designs to last them for years." Annette's old idea of the arts colony would be expanded and systematized. There would be "studio-cabins to house visiting craftsmen . . . 'paying guests' seeking to improve their techniques through observation of the work of the Andersons." To purchase two acres of land and build a suitable factory, showroom, and "park"—to turn Shearwater into "the Art Center of the South" and "a Mecca for art lovers"—a $40,000 bond issue was proposed. Over the next several months, the Chamber of Commerce and Rotary Club climbed aboard. Polls were taken, and the town seemed to be in favor. But eventually the proposal disappeared into a bureaucratic labyrinth at the state capital. Once again, the Pottery was preserved from large-scale production, and Pat and Peter went on as always, eking out their modest living.

Back when he was courting Pat, Peter had joked to her about marrying such an "unsociable person" as he. Over the years, she had drawn him out, filling the Front House with interesting people. She was "a sort of magnet," Sissy said. She "shed her love about her with that wonderful smile and it was as if she belonged to anyone who needed her." Her love of life, her ebullient personality, made her the center of any group. She "could make anybody feel better, just by taking them in." One of her favorite people during the war years was the singer Pete Seeger, who had dropped out of Harvard and gone into the service. More than once, while he was stationed at Keesler Air Force Base and for years afterward, Seeger and his wife, Toshi, ate dinner with the Andersons. "I was twenty-four years old, just drafted into the army,"

Seeger recalls. "A fellow soldier who had been at Keesler Field longer than I—I've forgotten his name—introduced me to the Anderson family. I was intrigued by old Mrs. Anderson, who wanted her children to be artists and saw that they went to art school. I only knew them for a few months, but never forgot them. . . . [We] were deeply impressed that they were finding a way to stay rooted in their house, and produce beautiful things which one did not need to be a millionaire to buy. Our two daughters are potters now."

"A fine boy," Annette called him in her journal. She found other unusual people in the showroom. When she heard the bell, she would cross the path, avid for conversation. She had "a great appetite for ideas, for words, for design, for beauty." Marjorie remembers the questions she asked of visitors.

> *And what do you do?*
> *Are you a painter?*
> *Do you draw?*
> *Do you write?*
> *Then you must be a musician.*

Those questions and others "separated the sheep from the goats," Mary writes. "Mère preferred the goats." And yet her intellectual snobbery, her endless search for people who thought about the larger questions in life—art and religion, nature and science—was tempered with kindness and sympathy. When business was slow, she enjoyed getting to know her visitors' "beliefs and likes and tastes in books, etc." Many of those encounters found their way into her journals.

On Sunday I was alone with the Showroom. The Front House family was off in the boat for a picnic and Horn Island. To the showroom a man came, a young man disheveled and a little bit drunk. He was tall and lean. He lived in Pascagoula, he said, and worked at Ingalls [Shipbuilding]. For a long time he had been hearing of the Pottery, he wanted to see it, and now he had come. His wife was dead, he had a baby four months old. He wouldn't take a million for that baby. He had not been friendly with her brother, but now they lived to-gether and it was all right. The brother and his wife were taking care of the child—helping him. . . . He wanted to talk. He said if you studied too much you lost your personality and had to stop and get it back. He said that over and over in different ways. It was so true, I agreed with him. When he left he said he wouldn't take a million for our talk. When other people came he lingered about outside looking at the leaflet, and later came back and wanted the four football players that were on the back of the folder. He gave me a check for them and his address, but asked that they should not be sent to him until the check was cashed.

Yesterday a young couple came to the show room. The young woman was sweet and sensitive and pretty in a worn way. She said they were from Cali-fornia. They were camped in New Orleans with a trailer on the way to Florida, but perhaps this was as far as they would get. The climate was not bracing as it was in California. "What is your husband's business," I asked. "He was in the restaurant business," she said. "Strange for her," I thought, and I turned to look at him. He looked big and coarse, I thought, for her. "He is having trouble with his eyes," she said. "There is a tumor at the back pressing on the nerves. The doctors say there is no help, there is nothing to be done." Going blind! I could see him now with different eyes. I told them that there was always help when the doctors gave up if you tried it. I told them about Dr. Banks clinic in San Diego. She thanked me, too much moved to say much. They had planned to spend the summer in one of the national parks. I cannot forget them. I thought him coarse!

In the quiet of the Barn, she spent the days reading, sketching, modeling in clay, or designing plates or fans for her own amusement. Her grandchildren and great-grandchildren recall the art classes she gave them. Mary has written about the "long summer mornings working with clay, making designs . . . , drawing leaves or flowers in daily note-books, cutting linoleum to make prints, or other adventures under the old ceiling fan amid the shadows of ivy and grape leaves on the Barn porch." Annette organized a "plate group" for the girls who worked at painting and trimming figurines in the Shearwater Annex. They made round designs—on flat cardboard disks—using indigenous plants and animals, and the best of them were transferred to Shearwater plates, glazed and fired.

Sometimes a poem would come to her, and she jotted it down and worked on it for days, until she put it aside or gave it to Marjorie to be typed. There were times when she rejoiced in her solitude, listening in winter to the creaking stovepipe, the clock on the mantel, with its "rasping metallic note"; the fire shaking the pots on the stove; the crackle of her little radio; or the wind coming in through the window. She would sit outside under the hickory tree, getting up to thwack the fallen hickory nuts with her walking stick. Her cat kept her company when the children and grandchildren weren't around; she sat up with it all night when it was sick, and kept it away from creatures large and small. A tiny frog, for example, spread like a blown leaf on the screen door, "green and black and gold," its small skeleton, hands and feet "finished with little watery knobs," or the creature she found fluttering in the cream:

This morning after precautions taken last night to keep the doors tight, I went out to the kitchen porch. I was late for Church at 8:30. There was a large moth in the half-bottle of sour milk, fluttering and swimming around, its wings wet, its antennae full of sour milk curds. I must fish it out, I thought, even if it makes me late. So I lifted the bottle, stepped out to empty it onto the ground. Strangely the creature moved. It was larger. It was a rat, a little rat that had been swimming around all night in sour milk. Pathetic little creature. All my shuddering dislike for rats was gone. I emptied it out onto the pine needles and I sat there dazed. I hurried to secure the cat in the house, and to give it a chance to escape. How strange, I thought, to see some abhorred animal in trouble. Gives our minds a jolt to normality. Why do we train ourselves to callousness, to hardness of heart?

She was not really—even after decades of life at Shearwater—completely happy to be living in a small town. The scent of sweet olive in the Shearwater woods brought back the streets of her youth in New Orleans. "Damp flag stones in the early morning and violets and the cool air filled with the odor of the tiny white flowers of sweet olive." She had grown up in a two-story house at the corner of Saint Charles and Saint Mary. Mule-drawn trolleys ran down the center of the boulevard. Back then, there was no drainage system, and when it rained hard, water would collect in the roadbed on both sides of the tracks. "The sounds and sights belonged to another world," she wrote. "It was a scene to be enjoyed and remembered. . . . Wooden boxes were placed at intervals like stepping stones to cross the watery way. Small barelegged boys would help the long-skirted ladies step from one box to the next." After those rainstorms, neighbors would come out onto their galleries to take in the sight.

"As you get older," she wrote, "your life seems all in the past." She fought against that nostalgia, but often it overwhelmed her. In her journals, she returned, again and again, to her grandparents' house at Bouligny. The grounds covered four city blocks, with "curving, brick-edged paths that led through blossoming shrubs and bright flowers, in a sort of maze, to the shade of live oaks and magnolias. The flower beds were bordered with violets and besides roses and camellias there were rose geraniums and lemon verbenas, sweet olive and the magnolia fascata." There was a vegetable garden where Jules Arnaud Blanc was "said to have cut down a long row of cauliflowers, thinking them degenerate cabbages." There were so many roses that they had made rosewater from the petals. It was gone now, all of it. The house had become a convent. A used-car lot covered the lawn where she had played croquet. There was talk of doing away with the trolleys. She longed for that lawn and those gardens, and the ones at the Blanc mansion on the levee. She longed, still more, for the chance to get away, to be alone in the city.

> My mind is just a path
> trodden hard,

251

from the kitchen to the gate
    in the yard.
But let me get away
    even for a day,
and green things sprout and grow.
The hard earth softens,
    even in a day.

My mind is full of little tender shoots,
    and roots
of lovely things crushed,
waiting in the dark
    to bloom.
    A room
is all I need,
a city room, Y.W.C.A.
You know the sort,
a Gideon bible and a cushioned chair,
a glimpse above the roofs
    of sky
    and there
my mind begins to blossom like a flower,
    a poppy,
    not a rose.
A sheath bursts
and, the crumpled petals
    free,
my mind begins to open
    as the wings
of locusts crowded in the shell
    long years
    far underground,

and now
at last
released,
unfold
in tender miracles of green and gold.

FORTUNE'S FAVORITE

CHILD

The years at Oldfields were Bob's last—in fact, his only—attempt to live with Sissy and the children. For the last nineteen years of his life, from 1946 until his death in 1965, he would live by himself in the Cottage at Shearwater, pursuing his art and earning a meager living—usually $10 per week; about $65 today—by decorating pottery for Peter. Eventually, Sissy and the children moved into the Barn with Annette. But they saw little of him. When Bob first met Sissy, he had dreamed of carrying her off to an island so that they could rejoice together in the natural world. But over the years, it became clear that he could better realize that quest alone. From the Cottage, where he painted and sketched, carved and decorated pots, he sallied out on many an adventure. He rode his old bike to Atlanta, New Orleans, Memphis, western Texas, and to Florida, to see Frank Baisden, a friend from his days at the Pennsylvania Academy of Fine Arts. When he heard that the Academy was about to put on an exhibition of paintings by his old instructor the American Impressionist Henry McCarter, he pedaled a thousand miles to Washington, D.C., and caught the train to Philadelphia. He traveled on to New York and returned to his beloved Metropolitan, where he lingered over the Egyptian ceramics: "small figures, both in red and black slip on a white body and wonderful copper blue, and a magnificent relief of boats with sails and rowers." When he traveled, he cut across the countryside and slept in fields or under bridges. He delighted in things unnoticed by ordinary travelers, and felt himself growing strong. In a journal from those years, he evokes "the horizontal line of the horizon and the vertical figure of a man. The horizontal longing for death and the vertical, passionate will to live." He dawdled over anything beautiful, and sometimes paused to draw. Plants, animals, a beetle more radiant than any jewel; any queer feature of the landscape, especially water. He lay down to rest and to heal in the little pools he called "nullahs": the backwaters of streams, ditches beside the road, places in fields—shared with cows—where rainwater had collected. No two nullahs were alike, he said. "The elements may be the same, but in their composition, they are always different. They are always magical: the magic of water, above all of running water, has never been explained." Of a trip through Alabama and Tennessee, he wrote: "I have just traveled over a thousand miles, and all my joys were associated with water. Watercolors, watermelons, water from clouds in the form of rain: all contributed to my happiness. As far as I knew, it was all fresh water. I left the sea behind me, and as far as I know I caused no tears to flow." In Chattanooga, he had gone through a tunnel under a mountain, and "couldn't resist tasting the seepage that was coming through the wall. I found it very good. But the climax, half past ten on a hot June night, was a five-pound bag of crushed ice which I placed open on the basket in front of me and rode on into the night, melting ice as I rode."

There were longer trips *across* water. He traveled to Costa Rica, and one day in 1949 Sissy found a reminder on the Cottage door: "Gone to China." He had always longed to travel across China to Tibet. Using the inheritance left to him by an aunt, he pedaled off to New Orleans where he caught a flight to Hong Kong. In China, where the civil war was going on, his passport and wallet were stolen, and he had to trade his drawings for food. Sissy wired him money, and he returned home, cycling from New Orleans back to Ocean Springs. "It was late evening when he appeared at the Barn," she wrote. "My god, how worn he looked. How terribly thin he was. What would he say, back from the ends of the earth? 'Had a flat tire,' he said casually."

While he was gone, the Brooklyn Museum put on an exhibition of his "scroll prints": twenty of the fairy tale scenes he had done at Old-fields. Cinderella, Old King Cole, Jack the Giant Killer, Three Billy Goats Gruff, Noah's Ark . . . He showed no interest in attending the opening, and was unmoved by the prospect of making a little money. Asked about prices, he wrote the curator: "I hope that you will be able to reach the people who cannot afford to pay a great deal for works of art but still have an appetite for beauty and the imaginative world of fairy tales."

A little later, the American Association of University Women put on a traveling exhibit of his prints and watercolors. The reviews were enthusiastic. "A genius is amongst us," wrote Guy Northrop in the Memphis *Commercial Appeal*. Annette cut out the article, which was reprinted in the Ocean Springs newspaper, and Sissy showed it to the children. "The watercolors are from the brush of an individual giant," Northrop continued. "Like a Japanese poem, they are brief, lyrical, but so all-encompassing of the nature of life and death it frightens you. Their glittering colors are like raindrops on a window when the sun follows a storm." Again, Bob missed the opening and seemed indifferent to the sale of his work. Lura Beam, who helped organize the show, reported to a friend that there was no need to take any special pains with orders. She had heard that "Walter Anderson couldn't find half of the blocks to reprint the Noah's Ark when the orders came in from Memphis. . . . The story was, he guessed he had thrown it away!!!!"

His overwhelming love, from the late 1940s until the end of his life, was Horn Island, an uninhabited little world blessed with hundreds of species of plants and animals about twelve miles southeast of Ocean Springs and nine miles south of Oldfields. Sissy felt it drawing him from her like some beautiful, "infinitely seductive" woman. The largest of the barrier islands, it had been occupied only occasionally since 1699 when it was first "discovered"—or mentioned—by a French explorer. It was over seventeen miles long in Bob's day, but narrow enough for him to imagine himself walking the back of a huge white whale. His living conditions, during the one- to three-week periods he spent there, were primitive. He had neither a sailboat nor a motor—he had sold the *Pelican* long ago—and he would cross to the island in a skiff with a blanket or, at times, an umbrella for a sail. He calculated that he had "at least five methods of propulsion: getting overboard and towing (in shallow water); getting overboard and shoving in deep water (this method requires a fair wind and if possible a fair tide); sailing—with the sail, or sailing with an umbrella; then the ordinary propulsion of oars, either rowing or pushing." When, late in his life, his family bought him a motor, he used it for a while as an anchor and hoped they wouldn't notice. Redding Sugg, editor of the logbooks he kept on Horn Island and the Chandeleurs, explains that "he wished to approach nature by oar and sail, by foot, and if necessary by hands and knees and belly in order not to disrupt the scene. Providence, though often clumsy, was, he felt, on his side; it was a form of courtesy to accept what was provided." His daughter Mary writes: "The band of his old felt hat or a rare pocket without holes held his paint tubes. He sometimes carried dabs of paint on a paper palette when traveling far on foot. Pencils and brushes were apt to ride behind his ears. En route to and from the island, supplies were secured in a tightly closed metal garbage can, but accidents happened. Once, a kind beachcomber returned a clipboard full of watercolors to the Shearwater showroom."

He seemed, in the simplicity of his island life, to have inherited treasures no one else had time for. His senses awakened, and he marveled that other people made so little use of theirs: man "can smell and touch and hear and taste and even see; but his relation to life, to being, to existence is so incredibly vague that, to his intelligence, he can barely seem alive."

He was, he wrote one morning, Fortune's favorite child.

A bleak dawn, but the sun has come out. I took a walk and found a much-needed pair of shoes that fit me. Fortune's favorite child. Indeed, if man refuses to allow himself to be distracted—driven wild, mad, sick, raving—he would often realize that he was Fortune's favorite child, and not simply an idle ass with an empty saddle, begging to be ridden—and driven. God knows there are plenty willing to ride him—professionals and the virgin youths full of confidence in their own skill.

On his Fortunate Isle—his paradise of coons and wild pigs, snakes and alligators, rats and gnats and mosquitoes—he led his life almost entirely in the present. He combed the beach and smiled at Providence. One day it gave him a pair of shoes, and the next a few cans of Puss n' Boots cat food. Was Providence more interested in feeding his pet raccoon than in feeding him? He studied animals, both in the wild and in captivity in his camp, listened to birds, and caught the colors of the sea and clouds. He grew familiar enough with certain animals to give them names: an octopus called Barrel-of-Monkeys that he transported to Ocean Springs to show the children, Bill the Lizard, Reddy the Duck, Slimy the Frog, an injured scaup he called Simy. In blinding sunlight, he sketched and painted thousands of watercolors of the life around him. Over the years, he became more and more a part of that life, "no longer a spectator, given a role in the drama of nature." That role was a romantic, though unsentimental, one: to allow nature to "realize" itself in the human psyche. The word occurs sometimes in his journals:

I saw a wonderful thick flock of [terns], a pattern of terns, almost a tone, changing from white to dark in flight, so that the spiral form is brought out by the values of the bodies against the sky. A mosaic of sky, of birds, of feathers. The celestial inverted cone of heaven, always there but needing to be realized.

Without man and without the artist, without being "observed and appreciated," the natural world seemed incapable of attaining the highest unity of which it is capable. It was up to man to pull together all of her sprawling sensorial beauty into a "magic hour" in which all things were one, and to share that "realization" whenever possible with others. He wanted not poetry, but the moment spoken of, long before, by Sissy: that moment of unity, in which all things are caught in an unforgettable prepoetic "image."

I looked up into a dead pine [and] saw a young heron climb up, using feet, wings, and the point of its bill. Then it reached a branch and stood, and stretched and stretched, silhouetted against an enormous white cloud. It seemed that with very little effort it would climb the cloud and take the kingdom of heaven by force. God knows it needs taking. I drew it in ecstasy. It was a concentrated image that nothing could take from me. If it was not poetry it was the image asked for by Yeats from which poetry is made. I am a painter, so this morning I did two watercolors of it before I got out of bed. This does not mean that I am going to be content with that one image for the rest of my life. It will generate power in me for a while, then I need another. One image succeeds another with surprising regularity on Horn Island. Whether they could be shared is another matter. People need different things.

One image followed another, in fabulous abundance, and yet, to anyone who knew how to look, each was infinite. "One single beautiful image is practically inexhaustible," he wrote. "Man is a wasteful fool."

Much depended upon bodily strength, patience, cunning: Bob had to deal with the sting of gnats or the bite of water moccasins, with contrary tides and the rats that burrowed into his lair, a foot from his head, hungry for his food. Once, absorbed in his painting, he began to feel pain in his foot. He had cut it on something, and when he looked down the wound was swarming with red ants. They were having their dinner, he said. Often he would fall to his hands and knees and use the paths that alligators and wild pigs had made through the undergrowth. At the end of those tunnels, and everywhere around him, lay "the miracle of Form." To the intellectual, he wrote, "life is an incidental thing generating from form. To the islander, form itself is a miracle." Nature loves to surprise us, he said, and seems to "justify itself to man in that way, restoring his youth." In one of the logbooks, Bob wrote:

Man begins by saying, "of course," before any of his senses have a chance to come to his aid with wonder and surprise. The result is that he dies, and his neighbors and friends murmur with the wind, "of course!" The love of bird or shell which might have restored his life flies away, carried by the same wind which has destroyed him. The bird flies, and in that fraction of a fraction of a second, man and the bird are real. He is not only king, he is man. He is not only man, he is the only man, and that is the only bird and every feather, every mark, every part of the pattern of its feathers is real and he, man, exists, and he is almost as wonderful as the thing he sees.

As with Sissy and Annette, writing was now a normal part of his life, like "the repetitive rhythms" of the wind. His editor, Redding Sugg, estimates that he must have written over ninety journals of his trips to the islands, though only about forty survived. "Why do I write this?" he asks in one of them. "I think writing has a cleansing effect, and altho' it is easy enough to keep the body clean, the mind seems to grow clogged." He would have agreed with Emerson: "The man is only half himself; the other half is his expression." And to him, expression was more than a literary event. The logbooks are only notes: mere kindling for what he called the "third poetry." "The first poetry is always written by sailors and farmers who sing with the wind in their teeth. The second poetry is written by scholars and students, wine drinkers who have learned to know a good thing. The third poetry is sometimes never written; but when it is, it is written by those who have brought nature and art into one thing."

Like the drawings and watercolors, writing was a way of sharing his adventures on the island with the rest of his family. At times, on returning to Shearwater, he read the logs to his children, who listened to him ranged on the stairs in the Barn. Sissy remembers her husband sitting under the lightbulb that hung from the ceiling, a coating of soot—from the fat-pine fires he lit on the island—covering both him and the logbook. Their daughter Leif sometimes listened to his tales. She had felt abandoned when he left Oldfields—he had taken more of an interest in her as a baby than in any of his other children—and she felt uneasy around him when he lived by himself in the Cottage. As she grew older, she began to feel compassion and to reflect on what had driven him from society and from his family. He lived on an island *within* him, she wrote. And there can be no doubt that, during his years as an "islander," he thought often about togetherness and aloneness; about his relation not only to nature but also to other people. "The world of man is far away, and so is man. How pleasant without him," Bob wrote one day. He was grateful, on Horn Island, to be far from "the sordid thing most people call reality" the "dominant mode on shore." But every so often, that reality would respond. On the island, he slept under his overturned boat, banking up the sand to keep out animals and mosquitoes and the elements. Often, he shooed away sunbathers and children. People who had come over for the day, or those who speared flounder at night, would sometimes bang on this battered wooden carapace, like children poking at a turtle or a horseshoe crab. The overturned shell made a fine sound box, and the noise was frightening and unbearable.

More than once, he emerged angrily, ready to defend himself. To his tormentors, he was a "crazy old hermit." To his animal friends, he was more hospitable.

I had something like a house warming last night—with birds and animals. I fed the birds rice and the coon prunes, peanut butter, and rice; but the rat may have gotten them. There were about twenty red-winged blackbirds, four grackles, two or three rabbits, one poldeau which wandered in due to the high water within a few feet of the fire, then turned and wandered out again: an absent-minded guest. The coon, which also ignored the host, ate some rice, looked around for something better and left. The white-throated sparrow, almost invisible until it moved, and a white grain of rice would disappear.

When he returned to Ocean Springs after weeks spent this way, it was as though he were stepping into a glaring light. There was his decorating for the Pottery to worry about, and the need to meet his monthly quota. "He tried. He really tried," Pat remembered. "Sometimes he would work three days straight, right thru the nights, to get his forty [monthly] pieces done. But sometimes he didn't finish anyway, and then we'd find a note in the Pottery cashbox: 'I O U, $20, Bob.' " Those around him, especially Annette, worried about a recurrence of his mental problems, and urged him—unsuccessfully—to see a psychiatrist every few months. Like Peter, he was unusually sensitive to alcohol. Alone in the Cottage, he sometimes drank beer or cheap wine and occasionally he lost control of himself, attacking members of the family. Sometimes he would wobble on his bike, fall off, and be picked up by the police. More than once, the family persuaded him to get treatment for alcoholism in New Orleans or Mobile. On the island, he drank almost no alcohol; he trapped groundwater and rainwater or trekked for miles to an island spring.

When his son Johnny was older, and had lived on Horn Island as a ranger, he was able to understand what it must have felt like to return from the island to life at Shearwater and in Ocean Springs, and why his father found it so difficult to adjust to life with others. On the island, he says, his father had grown accustomed to a sort of "celestial music" and had written:

All movement is invisible music, although few people hear it. It comes from the sun and the wind and the movement of water and a running rabbit and a crowing cock, and together it is part of a great symphony. The longer we listen, and the quieter we are, the more we hear, and when we do hear, we are part of the music instead of an unwelcome interruption.

"You can imagine what it was like when he came in to shore," Johnny said. "I lived on Horn Island by myself for long periods during the winter. And I found that when I came in, even to a little town like Ocean Springs, it was difficult. People develop a sort of shield, a social shield to protect themselves from the insensitive acts of others. You live alone in nature like that, and the shield gradually dissolves. And so you come in, and you're totally vulnerable, totally sensitive. You meet somebody who has just had a bad day—somebody stepped on their toe—and they step on *your* toe. And a minor blow feels like you've been hit like a sledge hammer. And I think that Daddy experienced that. I think that he felt it more dramatically than I did, and that he responded at times with depression and anxiety. I really believe that he loved people, more than most people do. He was trying to share with people something that he had discovered. I believe that, on the Island, he felt he was in heaven, and he wanted other people to be in heaven too, and was eager to share that with them, and tried desperately. He felt he had discovered riches beyond the reach of any king. And his frustration at not being able to share them caused a lot of emotional trouble and pain. Mother was aware of that pain. We know she was aware of what he was trying to give her. He wanted her to experience her oneness with everything else. He wanted to give her the most precious thing that he had: freedom from fear. He wanted to free her from fear."

He lived like a hermit, but was anything but antisocial. Over the years, he had thought much about the mutual obligations of the artist and society. The Oldfields figurines and block prints, the murals at the high school, his decoration at the Pottery were all attempts to provide art to the community. In 1951, when Ocean Springs was building a new Community Center, he offered to adorn its cinder-block walls with a mural. For the fee of $1 plus expenses, he covered the center's more than 250 feet of running wall space with two oil paintings so glorious and beautiful that they turn the humble cinder-block building into a Renaissance palace. Down one ninety-foot wall, he portrayed the landing of French adventurer Pierre Le Moyne d'Iberville, who claimed the Coast for France in 1699. On the other wall, he painted what he called the *Seven Climates*. Occasionally, as he worked, he would look down from his scaffolding and see his seven-year-old daughter Leif taking ballet classes. She remembers feeling "self-conscious," and being teased by the other girls: "He look[ed] so strange in his dirty old clothes and his grubby hat." Guy Northrop, the art critic from Memphis, found him at work one day in June 1951 and was granted a look at the work in progress. Annette was hovering about, ready, no doubt, to elaborate on her son's accomplishments. Bob had been at work for more than three months, doing the preliminary drawings between March 10 and April 3. By mid-June, Northrop said, "he had the entire mural fully sketched in with color, and much of the detail work was there. But he was hesitant to predict when he [would] be through. Several months, maybe a couple of years." It was typical of him, Northrop said, "that when his paints ran low recently, he should mount his bicycle at daybreak and pedal sixteen miles west to Gulfport to purchase new supplies. Employees of the paint store found him waiting at the door when they opened. When they had helped him lash his heavy load to the bicycle they watched him pedal away, back the long sixteen miles. Although there are cars and trucks in the family, he does not drive, nor does he ask others to run his errands. When I called on him, Anderson was high on a scaffold, painting a flight of pelicans. My wife and I were introduced to him by his mother, who then left. Alone with us, the artist climbed down from his roost, wiped his hand on paint-smeared brown pants, and greeted us."

Proudly, though sometimes with tongue in cheek, Bob led his visitor through the seven climates. First, the moon, which he said was meant to have the "lightness of a Christmas card." Then Mercury, envisioned as a baby tree, with a coon and night herons. Venus, conjured up from Walt Whitman's poem "The Dalliance of the Eagles." Mars. "Not too terrible," he said, "not a God of war, but identified with Spring and the mating season." Jupiter was a whirlwind and Saturn—the god whom Goya had depicted eating his children—took the form of a burly bear climbing a fat tree trunk and devouring honey. And, finally, a "questionable God" called Herschel, whom he came across in his reading and saw as an alligator—"a not too ominous, almost comical creature," Northrop commented. "As best he could explain this inspiration, it came from a time when he almost stumbled across an alligator while wading in a bayou, paused quietly to let it decide whether he was friend or foe, and breathed a sigh of relief when it called him friend and slithered away."

Not everyone in Ocean Springs admired the mural. He had wanted to involve as many people as possible in its creation, even children, but no one, Sissy said, wanted their children to work with the "mad artist." The Community Center had been built to promote "healthful, wholesome supervised recreation" for the young people of Ocean Springs, and after the murals were done, some wanted his work painted over, an attitude that persisted into the 1960s. Diane Stevenson, who was a teenager back then, recalls that "every time we decorated the center for a dance or for a ball, I remember hearing from a certain Methodist lady—'matron' is a title that would suit her—that we would be better off painting over those pictures so they didn't interfere with the crepe paper and pasteboard decorations of our theme. She had a point. There was a clash, and it took mental effort not to see Bob's raccoons and bears, his suns and

moons peeking mischievously around and through. . . . They did interfere. They did intrude, almost as if they had a mind to." Having spent almost a year on his labor of love, and overhearing some of those
comments, Bob came to a rueful conclusion about the relation between
the artist and society:

*The artist lives between assistance and opposition and is first overwhelmed
by one and then both together—then is reduced to the ranks and is told that
the gods help those who help themselves. So that he usually ends up living almost entirely on stolen fruit.*

During the time he was living at the Cottage and making his trips to
Horn Island, Peter and Pat would sometimes pass him in his "rotten
boat," on his way back to Ocean Springs, as they made their way out into
the Sound. He would courteously doff his hat, glad to see them, but
"spurn the offer of a tow." They worried about him especially during
hurricane season. In an old filing cabinet at Shearwater is a mimeo-
graphed advisory bulletin from the Miami Weather Bureau warning of
the approach of Hurricane Carla, on September 7, 1961, a category-four
storm that took fifty lives. At the top of the page, someone from the
Biloxi Coast Guard Station has written: "For Walter I. Anderson. Your
brother [Peter] suggested you return home immediately due to the hurricane." No doubt he ignored that notice and stayed on Horn Island, as
he did a few years later, when he lashed himself to a tree during Hurricane Betsy, eager to experience the storm in all its fury. During Betsy, it
was Annette who remembered him, called the Coast Guard, and asked
them to warn him to come home. Sissy doubted they would succeed.
She could picture him in some leafy refuge, or under his boat, laughing
at the cutter tossed about by Betsy. He *was* relishing the storm: "Never
has there been a hurricane more respectable, provided with all the por-
tents, predictions, omens, etc. etc. The awful sunrise—no one could fail
to take a warning from it—the hovering black spirit bird (man o' war)—
only one—*(comme il faut)*."

As for the Coast Guard cutter, it took him completely by surprise. He stared at it from under his careened boat, where he had made a fire to keep himself warm: "A large coast guard boat appeared!—going to and fro in front of my camp—large boat, but there were large seas lifting her up and down; she finally went off, her running lights showing in the water."

In the early 1950s, when Bob was painting the Community Center murals and rowing every few weeks out to the island, his brother's old sloop, the *Gypsy*, became unfit for rough weather and Peter designed and built a larger boat, with a huge inboard motor. The *Patricia* was twenty-six feet long, eight feet wide, half a ton in weight. Pat, who came to think of it as "the source of most of our greatest pleasures in life," recorded its construction. Peter cut heart pine from the Shearwater woods, and brought cypress from a mill where he and Pat combed through piles and piles of lumber for useful boards. He made a shed in the little clearing at the edge of the water—the clearing where Jimmy's house stands today—and for five months, whenever he could steal time from the Pottery, worked there, not far from the kiln house and its weathered brick chimney. He worked at night by the light of a gas lamp and by day in the fragrant shade of "bay trees, sassafras, huckleberry, water oak, and tall, singing pines." Pat marveled, as ever, over the grace and skill of her husband, and wished he would let her help. She was allowed, she said, to grease a few of the three-inch brass screws. "When a tool is misplaced I am allowed to come and find it, [and] I have held a rib or two in place to the best of my ability."

> Oh, Peter knows this and Peter knows that,
> and what is there left for dear old Pat?

When it was finished, some admiring person asked to see the plans. "In my head," he answered, as he did when they asked him about his glazes. He wanted a family boat for fishing and picnicking trips to the islands and for weeklong vacations with or without the children. Sometimes, on Sunday, the whole family would take off for the island. Leif remembers the joy of sitting on the bow, "high above the water, meeting wind and waves head on."

Spray wets your face and legs . . . and hair streams everywhere, as though it knows what freedom is: a dance upon the wind. Peter trawls on our way out, so he has bait when it is time to fish. We get to help when he has spread the net upon the deck and it is full of treasures from the gulf. We have to sort, because he only wants the shrimp and squid. But it is wonderful to see what has been caught . . . to pluck the tiny crabs, pale green, translucent nearly in the sunlight, and toss them overboard, their tiny legs aflutter . . . swimming even before they hit the sea. Then, there are baby flounders, flat and iridescent . . . and blowfish, puffed with air. The oyster fish is strange and almost ugly, like a monster you don't want to touch. We work pretty hard and then we wash our hands in seawater, so we can have a snack. My aunt Pat hands us crackers, spread with cheese and peanut butter, or a sandwich if we're really hungry . . . grapes and apples, too, and opens bottles of Orange Crush. Pretty soon, we see Horn Island in the distance, and we watch the long flat blur become white beach and individual pine trees as it seems to welcome us from our long voyage. Peter throws the anchor over, and rows us in the dinghy to the shore. Pat always wears a dress and she is funny, the way she jumps right overboard, her dress hiked up, and pulls the dinghy right up on the sand.

Often, Michael remembers, those trips would take place on Sunday, after his mother had come home from church. After trawling for bait, his father would head the *Patricia* toward the Dog Keys, anchor, and fish the grass patches for mackerel and blues. And, after that, the far side of Horn Island, the Gulf side, with its heavier surf and shrimp boats riding at anchor, where the water was deeper, and the family could enjoy the beach. Peter would hunger for a cigarette and remember the *Knotty Banana,* the brightly colored little double-ended rowboat he built from knotty pine and sometimes towed behind the *Patricia*.

"Michael! Get in that boat and row out to one of those shrimpers . . ."

"There was no coming back empty-handed," Michael remembers. "I would row out and scale the sides of those shrimp boats until someone produced a cigarette. That's how hard it must have been for my father to give up smoking."

Once each summer the family would cruise for eight or nine hours down the coast of the Sound, past Oldfields and Gautier, to a secluded spot on a bluff over the West Pascagoula river. There they camped in a different world, Pat wrote, a "three-hundred foot wide river and en-croaching, forested banks, a free, wild world with few humans to be seen. Occasional boats, flat river skiffs, with silent, patient perch fisher-men. No roads come to the river's edge, no paths are seen." They would swim and fish there and watch birds and explore the river in the skiff. It was "a sort of bird paradise," Pat told a friend one year, with swallow-tailed kites and hawks and prothonotary warblers that "flashed across the river from every tree and bush." She kept journals of those trips and lists of the birds they had seen. Like her sister and mother-in-law, she wrote short stories, essays, and poems whenever she could find time. She wrote a charming letter to her grandchildren about family history; children's stories; prayers; anything that came to her during those trips on the *Patricia,* or as she sat in the truck on her excursions with Peter. She made lists of magazines to which she could send her work. To *Reader's Digest* she submitted a sketch—never published—of "The Most Unforgettable Character I've Known": her husband. She began it one day while she watched him at work in the bee yard in Vancleave. The bees were "bringing in their late evening loads of nectar," and the place smelled de-liciously of raw nectar and pine straw smoke. To the *Gypsy's* old mast, he had attached a boom and a sort of three-pronged claw to lower the bee-hives safely from the trees to the ground. He handed her a bit of comb dripping with almost crystal-clear honey. "That's the stuff. Pure gall-berry!" During the twenty-eight years of their marriage, there had been moments of almost unbearable pain, and sometimes she wondered how he could seem so remote. But she had never ceased to marvel at his "calm assuredness" as master potter, as apiarist, as gardener, and as boat-builder. One Christmas, he had built a couple of tippy little pirogues for his god-children, and he found time to help Johnny build or fix up a boat or two: much more difficult, Johnny reflected years later, than building one himself. As always, he and Pat struggled to keep the Pottery going. Peter's mastery of the kiln, which he had to rebuild "at fairly frequent intervals," was grounds for admiration. She "could write pages on this kiln, no easily fired electric kiln with a pyrometer, but a real king of a kiln to be loaded with heavy saggers and babied and loved into turning out the most beautiful ware, a kiln with a different temperature at each level and a different glaze for each temperature. It is so well trained on fuel oil that Peter won't change it to gas." In all he did, he had "an eye for form," she wrote, "and his ware was a joy to the beholder."

He seemed tireless in everything he did. Rather than take the *Patricia* to a boatyard in Biloxi, he used to haul her out of the water on ways he had built for himself: an ingenious system with a winch and a track running down into the water. He was a fine gardener and expert orange-tree grafter and he took "personal and loving care of the oyster bed" in front of the house. "He brings in shrimp, crabs, and fish before breakfast. If it is dewberry or blackberry time he brings in a gallon or so of them. He likes to get up at four a.m. In the evening he often makes smaller things such as oars or a tackle box or a few new bee supers. . . . He has made an incredibly careful study of the weather. The clouds, the sunset and the sunrise tell him unendingly fascinating weather news. He speaks the language of the barometer. He and it know exactly the weather that's coming."

Mac, too, had been busy. When his daughters, Sara Margaret (Marty) and Adele Elizabeth, were born (1947 and 1951), he added two bedrooms and a screened porch to the rammed-earth house, cutting a new door through the mud with nothing more than a crosscut saw. He enlivened doors and cabinets with his own oil paintings. With two children to support, he needed a steadier, larger income than Shearwater could provide. Once again, he took a job elsewhere; this time—beginning in 1952—at Ferson Optics in Ocean Springs, where he would work for the next twenty years. At first, his job was to "correct" prisms for gunsights and tanks, flattening them, to within a millionth of an inch. Annette was "shocked indeed" when he told her he intended to take a job, five days a week, away from the Pottery, but supposed it was for the best. As before, when he worked at the shipyards, he continued to sketch, paint, and carve in wood and clay. One day, a family in town—the Leavells—asked him to decorate their house. He painted a rooster on a cabinet, a swamp magnolia on the door of a clothes closet, and a New Orleans scene in the kitchen. Soon he was supplementing his income at the optical plant with a series of public murals. In Pascagoula, the American Legion asked him for a mural of the Legend of the Singing River: it was to adorn the walls of the hospital in Pascagoula. Everyone on the Coast knew the story. Long ago, a young Pascagoula Indian had fallen in love with a maiden from a warring tribe—the Biloxi—who was already betrothed to a Biloxi chieftain. The outraged chieftain attacked the Pascagoula, and both the star-crossed lovers and the entire Pascagoula tribe walked calmly into the river and perished. Ever since, the river had "sung" mysteriously. On quiet summer evenings, there was a musical humming, like a swarm of bees in flight. To Mac, the story seemed too lugubrious. Unable to imagine a hospital waiting room adorned with a tale of collective suicide, he painted a panoramic vision, in soft blues, browns, and greens, of the flora and fauna of the river. He was paid $1,000 and, to his delight, other commissions followed: one on sheets of asbestos around the doors and windows of a fishing camp at Graveline; a wall with a shrimp boat and oyster tongers at the Bayou Inn; a three-paneled screen, of Masonite, of fishing scenes for a restaurant on Fort Bayou; black workers in a cotton field in a house used by the Ocean Springs Garden Club; pine trees and a star—for the cost of the materials—at the Baptist Church on Holcomb Boulevard, not far from Shearwater. In middle age, Mac had come fully into his own as a painter. Drawing on the life around them, all three of Annette's children had created walls of light.

"GOODBYE, OLD LADY"

Shearwater, early 1960s. Annette McConnell Anderson is over ninety years old, with ten grandchildren and nine great-grandchildren. Her sight is so poor that she can no longer read, no longer write her 750 words a day. In one of her last journal entries—1958—her graceful hand-writing has broken down and jags across the page. She can barely see the words. In the kitchen at the Barn, where she sits minding the children, she has closed the door and stopped up her ears with cotton, so as not to hear the "infernal noise" of the TV in the next room. One of her grand-children is watching a Western. She feels contempt for the "dreadful story," but guilty for not finding her grandchild something better to do. If only she could see better, get outside, do some work in the yard. She writes about herself in the past tense, as though she were already gone, or writing about one of her ancestors.

Perhaps living or working out of doors was the answer. Something happened to you when you stayed out of doors. The clouds, the sound of the wind in the trees, the little crowded plants that needed separating, all were sweet and friendly. There was an incredible amount of work to be done. . . . I cannot see what I have written so I start again. Everywhere plants were eagerly trying to find ground to grow in. The little ivy plant at the door could not be stopped. It was crowding under the house and trying to climb up the concrete step on the inside. . . . In living out of doors I shall be so happy with all the clouds and little growing things that I shall develop a new [spirit].

She would have done more had it not been for her cataracts. She had been cross-eyed as a girl, and her father arranged for an operation. The family doctor came to her house and they held her, as he worked, without anesthesia, to the dining room table. She often told that story to her grandchildren, who were sometimes bored by her anecdotes. But how could anyone expect her to undergo another operation? Once in a while, she managed to write out a few lines of poetry. Or was it prose? It didn't matter. Long ago, she had found a voice unmistakably her own. In 1960, on her ninety-third birthday, the family put together a little pamphlet of her poems, *Possums and Other Verse,* adorned the cover with one of her designs—a possum and some grape leaves and graceful tendrils—and had it printed in Gulfport. Unhappy with her work, she carried a stack of the little books into the backyard and burned them on top of an anthill.

Poor eyesight had made her give up driving. Well into her eighties, she was still "caravanning" around in the family truck. There were things to be done, people to help. Mary remembers her "strong sense of social obligation":

It was her duty to entertain the Misses Patterson, two unmarried sisters in their late 70s who lived on the corner of Calhoun and Washington. Driving the Pottery's Ford truck in her inimitable style, she'd arrive at their house at 11:30 on the appointed day. Two straight-back chairs placed side by side in the back of the truck provided strange thrones but good views for the sisters' exciting ride across the Biloxi bridge for lunch at the French Café.

Mère's driving was as idiosyncratic as her style. She preferred to drive slowly down the middle of the street, so she rarely used the upper gears or found any use for the clutch. An uncertain lurch accompanied by grinding groans characterized her forward progress. She seemed unaware of the presence or purpose of the rearview mirror. When I rode with her, I prayed there would be no reason to back up, but Mère sometimes did things without reason. Once, after helping her deliver flowers to the cemetery, I shared her terrifying backward drive down the steep slope into the Fort Bayou marsh. "They've provided no place to turn around," she complained indignantly to the man who brought the wrecker. Nodding wordlessly with the tolerance Ocean Springs accords its eccentrics, he never mentioned that the Evergreen Cemetery Road was, is, and ever has been, one way.

Ocean Springs accepted Mère's distinctive style and tolerated her driving, though many were relieved when, at the end of her 90th year, her family took away her keys to the truck.

She went to the showroom less often now, but the Pottery seemed to be humming along without her, with Peter working harder than ever. Mac was still doing his painstaking work at Ferson Optics, but a local man named Welber (Web) Beaugez—from the family of carpenters who had built much of Shearwater—helped Peter load the kiln, mix slip, cast, prepare grog body, and care for the *Patricia,* and accompanied him on his trips to Lucedale to dig clay. Peter's son Jimmy worked after school, sharing those chores, trimming greenware, raking the yard, doing odd jobs: "whatever was needed." He started full-time at the Pottery in 1966. Pat carried on as business manager, fending off requests for matching pieces, politely reminding the customers—as her father-in-law had done before her—that everything produced was one of a kind.

Shearwater is more than hopeless about orders, but I have hopes of yours coming out of the series of which Peter is at present glazing the first kiln. I know the [football] players were cast and the eggcups thrown, but the matter of controlling the potter as he glazes is beyond a mere humble wife.

To the entire community, Pat had become a symbol of Shearwater. She liked talking to visitors who showed interest in her husband's work, those who wandered into the workshop and marveled at what she called the "miracle of form," the "joy of watching a pot being created." He would stand, she said, "slightly bent, a look of pleasant concentration on his finely chiseled features." After thirty years of marriage, she still felt "deeply stirred," as though she were "an onlooker at the gift of creation." Each opening of the kiln brought the joy and surprise of Christmas. There was always something unexpected and unplanned, a gift of the fire that the family called a "treat." She had never heard him praise his own work. "Didn't that turn out well?" was his usual comment, when he pulled something beautiful from the kiln and showed it to Pat. She enjoyed finding names for the glazes he had created: Blue Rain, Desert Sage, Fall Green, Gray Cloud, Wisteria. . . . In her Bible, she found the words: "Oh Lord, thou art our father, we are the clay and thou our potter, and we are all the work of thy hand."

Diane Stevenson, who worked in the showroom after school, remembers the special atmosphere of Shearwater in the sixties. She was a high-school student, living across the road from the Pottery in a modern brick house, and whenever she went to work she felt she was "entering a magic forest, a different world, a world so different the quality of the light changed, the level of heat and humidity changed, the sounds you heard changed (all those birds.)"

It wasn't just the land that was old, filled to brimming with wild creatures, water moccasins, alligators, pileated woodpeckers, and tame creatures too, cats and dogs, with any number of legs and sway backs and other interesting disabilities, with personalities appealing and otherwise, but the buildings, too, were old and seemed even older than they actually were. Everything had weathered to the silver of pecan trees. Houses, worksheds, the showroom: all looked as if they were on a retreat back to their original, natural shapes, and the trees and bushes around them aided and abetted them. If windows were left open, or doors, all the green things would creep in, and then the green of leaves and the grey of wood would become indistinguishable: you saw that green was grey and grey was green. . . . I think it was only later, after looking more intently at Peter's pots and Bob's water colors and Mac's oil paintings that I realized the compounded glory of colors. Even so, an inchoate sense of that glory was inevitable simply walking there, across the street from my house, where the Andersons lived and where they worked. One walked into a world of color and, especially, of light. It lay speckled at your feet, shaped by all the things it was filtering through. And it sat on shelves and in boxes, in pots and on paper, so luminous the pots and papers looked as if they were their own sources of light and colors.

The Andersons knew all the names for things, not just a giant woodpecker but a pileated woodpecker, not just a broad-leafed magnolia but an umbrella magnolia, and their naming was not just a list, an inventory, but an invocation. A litany. Something magical. The mere giving of a precise name to things in nature would call up that nature. I'm sure this is a mystification, but it is a powerful one, the feeling that a name grants something its true nature, and one with powerful consequences. It makes nature into you, and you into nature. The name becomes an act of communion. Everything around me was transformed. Everything was clearer and brighter, more distinct, and more accessible. The wall of existence wasn't impermeable. I could be invited in. Astonishing that adults held this key. The visual impact of my early childhood was given back to me in high school by these wonderful Andersons who were artists. The peculiar, vivid brightness of childhood memory was resurrected as the ordinary brightness of an ordinary day—if I wanted, if I wanted to look with eyes that looked at ordinary things in an extraordinary way. . . . The Pottery itself felt elsewhere, not so much a real place as a place of the imagination made real.

A "place of the imagination made real." Annette would surely have approved. This was what she had wanted, decades earlier, when she bought Fairhaven and schooled her children in the "ways of artistic fitness." The family now made its living from art, and had turned pottery and painting, sculpture and writing, into a way of life. Sissy remembers her mother-in-law's energy. On her good days, she would do all manner of things. "Sometimes we would come home," Sissy remembered, "and she was in the middle of making a design of some kind on a sheet of paper. And maybe the next day we would come home and she would be doing that design on a piece of linoleum." And then, the next day, she was carving it, and the next, she would be printing it on a big piece of wallpaper. Soon "there'd be a frieze around the whole of the living room at the Barn." Annette felt young, able to go on, with or without the truck keys. When Peter reminded his mother of her age, six weeks before her death, on her ninety-sixth birthday, she answered, "Don't be silly. I'm only 76." Toward the end, Pat wrote, her prodigious memory began to fail. "She forgot the thing that had happened one moment before. She remembered the things that happened before she was twenty." Some days, she waited for Walter to come home, but "he was not much in her consciousness. She remembered her daughters-in-law, but forgot most of the grandchildren and all of their children. She loved her father and thought of what he said and did, and adored her mother and loved her sister Dellie, and often asked when Jimmy, her brother, would be home. Sometimes she went to her piano and played, and at others she lay completely at rest, her eyes closed."

A little after her ninety-sixth birthday, after weeks of faintness and insomnia, she was hospitalized and went into a coma. In one of her poems, she had imagined the moment of death: it would be like getting up early in the morning, to catch the early train into the city.

> I waked at twelve, at two, at four,
> Then smothered the alarm between the sheets, at five,
> And wondered why I had agreed to go—
> To get up in the bitter night—for what?
> It was in bed so heavenly warm and soft,

And every rebel bone cried, Sleep!
Then, praying to forget myself, I flung the covers wide
And stepped out shivering on the freezing floor.
Just so, I think, a soul must shudder forth
From warm, familiar flesh, in death.
And afterwards—the frosty darkness and the Dawn!
The breathless ecstasy of seeing a new world.
Strange forms that might be trees and shade.
The growing light that slowly made dark shapes appear clear
And then, the unbelievable last touch, the Fire
That ran along the fishing boats, the cliff, the vines, the barn.
And in the East, at last, from the transfigured sea,
the shining Sun—so through the little death, to Paradise!

As Sissy sat with Bob in Annette's hospital room, clasping Annette's hand and waiting for the end, she remembered Bob's reaction to the death of his father—a precipitating event in his breakdown and confinement at Phipps—and worried how he would react. He sat in silence, at the foot of the bed, making sketch after sketch of his dying mother. She struggled against death, gasping for air in her oxygen mask, and finally gave "a small sighing smile" and was gone. Sissy gave Bob the hand she had been holding. He let it drop to the bedsheet.

"Goodbye, old lady."

It was the expression his father had used in his letters to Annette, half a century earlier. Sissy was surprised by his calmness and wondered whether his years on Horn Island, his habit of sketching the dead animals that washed up on the beach or died in captivity, had inured him to the sight of death. He stayed for Annette's funeral in Evergreen Cemetery and headed back to the island: it was a little later that he held his house-warming for the animals. Not until eight months later was he able to talk about his mother's death. Sissy remembers a night in August when he came to get her at the Barn.

"Come, come down to the pier. There's a perfect shower of meteorites. I want you to see."

Peter's pier was a swaying collection of long drift planks put together so that they could be easily taken apart and floated to shore and thus saved from storms. He even took my hand to steady me to the platform. We lay down and looked up into the clear, dark sky. Sure enough, the heavens were full of moving lights. There seemed to be no end to them. We lay there. I gasped now and then at a very brilliant streak. . . .

"Souls," he said.

The wind was blowing up the clouds banked on the horizon to the West. It was cold and, before long, the meteorites were hidden from us.

"Mother told me that when I was a little boy," he said, enveloping me with arms, body, legs. "Did you think I didn't care [about her]? In a way I didn't because I felt that it was time. Life, you know, is like light. It is continuous. It is our eyes that seek beginnings and endings. I was trying to find an ending with my pencil, but all I found was that there was no ending."

Pat, too, had stood by Annette's bedside, thinking about the continuity of life. She thought of all that she had never been able to tell her mother-in-law. Annette had nurtured three generations of artists. But it seemed to Pat that there was a sort of love, a "love freely given" that Annette had not known how to show to her family. Ten days later, in the first days of spring, with flowers blooming around her gravestone, Annette seemed closer than she had ever been, "and we to you, with deeper love than we had ever given." God must have received her gladly, she thought, "for you had eyes to see and feel the beauty of the world. A light was in your eye. You used it well."

Bob died just one year later in a hospital in New Orleans, on November 30, 1965, at the age of sixty-two, from complications of an operation for lung cancer. Sissy remembered the funeral at Evergreen Cemetery.

I remember the minister who read the beautiful words and the terrible ones and then we were all standing in the cemetery and the earnest young man ready to consign the dust to dust and the ashes to ashes and the rain was falling quietly on us and on Bob. Suddenly, from down the hill toward the marsh and the silver ribbon of the Bayou came a raucous laugh, again and again. Then our children were laughing too. We looked at each other. We all knew the voice of the little rail, but it seemed perfectly plausible that Bob had entered into a feathered body in order to use its voice for a few minutes, to deny the finality of any grave. As the service ended, the rail flew off down the Bayou, and we said to ourselves, "There he goes!"

A few days later, Pat and Sissy went to the Cottage to clean it. It had been a long time since they had been inside. "The water had ceased to run in his sink and his bathroom," Sissy wrote. "He had been bringing it from a faucet in the yard. The screens were torn and rusted out. The roof and north wall of the bathroom had been crushed by a fallen chinaberry tree. The floors of every room in the house were littered with cigarette butts, empty bottles, and empty beer cans. A dead rat lay behind one shelf of his precious books. Everything was in disorder. Old grocery boxes, overflowing with papers, stood gaping all around. Now we began to realize that the crumbling Cottage was bursting with treasures." One room was locked: the little room that had been added to the south end of the Cottage after Mary's birth when Bob had returned from Phipps. Three decades earlier, when the carpenters were finished, Bob had painted the room himself, and had "made a very professional job of it." It was a sign, she thought back then, of his improvement.

"I don't know why," Sissy said, "but one day, after his death, I decided I had to unlock that door. I got my sister to go in with me. We couldn't find the key so I had to break the lock. My sister was right behind me as we entered the room. The first thing I saw was this huge mound in the middle of the floor and I thought 'Oh my, how am I going to get rid of this mess?' There, piled high to the ceiling, was a mound of debris [Bob] had brought back from the islands. Everything you can think of was in that pile, from old tackle boxes to buoys. Then I heard my sister behind me, breathing hard. I turned to look at her and she was looking over the window. She said, quite loudly, 'Creation at sunrise!' I looked back into the room and then I saw it. A huge mural covering all the walls."

Without a word to anyone, Bob had covered the walls of the little room with an astonishing hymn to light and the beauty of one day on the Coast, beginning on the east wall with a flight of sandhill cranes at dawn, and continuing through noon, sunset, and night. On three sides of the little room, casement windows framed a view of the luxuriant growth outside: pines, magnolias, azaleas, and dogwood trees. In a carved wooden chest were thousands of watercolors from Horn Island. A cardboard box under one of the windows was filled with his papers. Among them was a copy of Psalm 104: "Oh Lord, how manifold are thy works! In wisdom hast thou made them all: the earth is full of thy riches . . . I will sing unto the Lord as long as I live: I will sing praise to my God while I have my being."

TRACES

Along the bluff in front of the house at Oldfields stood a boxwood hedge and a white picket fence that had been there since Pat and Sissy were little girls. The tide had carried the fence and a gate from Horn Island during the 1906 hurricane, months after their parents were married. In an old photograph, one can see the fence surrounding the Horn Island lighthouse. The lightkeeper had been warned of the hurricane's approach, but decided not to leave, and was swept away along with his wife and child and the lighthouse itself.

Oldfields weathered the 1906 storm fairly well, as it did the one three years later and the terrible "blow" of 1916. In fact, it wasn't until 1947 that a hurricane did major damage, felling trees, carving away the bluff, and leaving the west end of the house with nothing beneath it. From the front gallery, Pat could hear the pounding of the surf, nine miles away, on Horn Island.

There were traces of old brick walks in the yard on that side of the house, and part of the yard went, too. That spring, strange flowers sprouted on the beach under the bluff: Johnny-jump-ups, odd-looking petunias, "old-fashioned kinds of little flowers."

Decades earlier, perhaps during the Civil War, someone must have planted a garden. The seeds had stayed over all those years, Sissy said. "There's no other way that all of that could have come up there. They were little flowers you don't see anymore."

As with that garden, as with the blossoming of Oldfield's cutover lands, it is the renewal brought about by hurricanes, and not only the fearful destruction, that has often captured the attention of family members. When Betsy washed over Horn Island, Bob noticed an almost magical change brought about by the Great Leveler. The beach was "beautiful and sad," a "magnificent wide stretch of sand."

Never have I seen more ravishing jewelry than shone in the foam cast up on the beach in thin broken pieces quivering with the slightest breath of air, so that all the colors scintillated with the movement. Half a mile of Sinbad's valley of jewels, with no deadly serpents to guard them, yours for the possession, no one to dispute your ownership, no one to claim prior right, no jealous person to claim more or bigger or better ones.

Shearwater, too, underwent renewal and a change in character. In 1969, when Bob and his mother were already gone, Hurricane Camille blew away the studio Annette had watched him build. Sissy sat with Ellen in candlelight, reading aloud her husband's handwritten account of Betsy a few years before. Michael, who was living at the studio with his family, lost all of his possessions. Smelling a gas leak, he had stepped out the door of the Barn, where he had taken refuge with his family, into seven feet of water ("Use the back one," his wife told him). In the woods, the next day, he found Bob's painted saints, which had been hanging in the studio. At the Pottery, Camille ripped away the back part of the show-room, shattering the windows and carrying pots through the woods, but left most of them unbroken. She scarcely touched Peter's workshop. Pat observed that the "great kiln stack had one brick barely out of line." Salt-water soaked the ground, and the trees suffered from the salinity. Pine borers began feeding on the dead trees and attacked the weaker ones.

After the devastation of Camille, the family noticed a change in Pat. She seemed shaken and weary, as were many people of her generation along the Coast, who felt betrayed by nature. "The enormous force of that storm shook us all, especially the oldest of us," her niece Mary said. "I don't think she ever regained her balance. She was different after that." As Pat drove with Peter down the ruined shore to visit a friend in Pass Christian, she noticed a strange new quality to the light, an unwelcome glare. She felt something she could barely describe: "horror and a strange, angry, questioning hurt, a physical sickness at the destruction, the rubble-strewn land, the beaches piled high with washed out things, bits of houses, chairs, couches, cabinets, stoves, toilets and televisions. . . . Here and there, people sorting, searching, hopeless." The days and weeks after the storm "seemed to go by timelessly, day and night blending into a sort of dream."

At first the strange silence—deadness—no bird songs or chirps, no calling squirrels—not even the ever-present summer insect undertone. Really a vacuum, and there were the tide lines everywhere, and in them, what? Here and there a dead bird, a thrasher, a jay, a few drowned squirrels. Then the heat came, a mighty, pressing humidity. Working, you streamed perspiration; sitting, it trick-led down your back and dripped from neck, forehead . . . Pete and Jimmy took to the shorts they had never worn before. All along the Coast people searched through ruins and tidedrifts. Some for things, some for loved ones lost in the chaos of that awful night. The things found were so sad, so broken, torn or rotten, and the bodies looked for so long in the finding, or found not at all.

Months later, she began noticing signs of life: the hum of insects, the singing and scolding of birds. Wisteria and magnolias burst defiantly into bloom. But she felt tired; something had gone out of her. Two years later, she was diagnosed with cancer. For decades, she had been the heart and soul of Shearwater, her kind, smiling face glowing with pride in its accomplishments. When she died in 1973, the family knew it would never be the same. She had been the family caregiver, and even as she lay dying, she worried about Peter and prodded her children to take care of her beloved Sissy. Peter was crushed by her death. One of the children was shocked to find him alone, sitting on the floorboards of the gallery, leaning against a post, looking out over the Sound. When another storm came up and the tides were unusually high, he pulled the *Patricia* out of the water, and never took her out again.

Bob's son Johnny had been away from Shearwater for a long time, first at the University of Mississippi and then in the graduate program in psychology at the University of Miami. When he returned, he noticed a change in the woods. Many of the first-growth pine trees Camille had harmed were dying or dead. When Hurricane Frederic roared through in 1979, spawning a series of tornadoes, many more pine trees succumbed.

"It was an atypical storm," Johnny remembers. "It came around in a curve and hit the trees from the north and came out onto the water. For years you could see the path that it took, like a lawn mower cutting trees. Trees on the coastal plain, near the water were especially hard hit. They tend to grow in ways that receive stress from the prevailing winds from the south. And this storm came from the other side. And the character of Shearwater changed.

"There *used* to be much more shade. The woods actually had a canopy, and there was less undergrowth. You would see fewer shrubs. It was wonderful. It was a kind of cathedral, this canopy, and the distances and the light were marvelous. But when I returned here after being away for a long time, I began to see the verdure and the abundance that were springing up without that canopy, and at the same time, I could see the next generation, and I could see the parallels. The young people were so full of energy, like a rebirth of the place. It just struck me. I was sad at first. It was no longer the place I remembered. And then suddenly I realized that there was all this fecundity of new growth, and that made me feel a little bit better."

He was thinking fondly of nephews, nieces, and cousins. When his mother died, Jimmy had begun to work in earnest at the Pottery. He had started there when he was old enough to help out. Peter gave him "lots of encouragement to throw," he said, but didn't want him to feel "forced." By 1980, he was throwing enough pieces to mark them with a "JA" because, he said, he didn't want people to confuse his work with that of the *"real* potter."

The seventies and early eighties were a time of homecoming, the new beginning referred to by Johnny. Mac's daughter Adele, who had studied design at the University of Southern Mississippi, came back to the Annex, where she had worked as a child, to redo some of the old molds. As a girl, she had sat on the porch at the Barn, taking art lessons from Annette, and Mac and Sara had scraped together the money for private instruction for her and her sister Margaret. At the Annex, she worked on the molds, painted figurines, and used stencils, as others had, to reproduce her Uncle Bob's old pieces. Soon the stencils seemed to "get in the way," and she began to do the pieces freehand, hoping to capture the free lines and the flow of Bob's work. It wasn't long before she started doing her own decoration, carving original pieces and painting in slip. Mac retired in 1973 from Ferson Optics and returned, once again, to the Pottery, working beside his daughter. Mostly, he stayed at home, decorating vases, and watching Sara print his designs on fabrics and on paper. He began to devote more time to painting, in his own unassuming way. "Do you think it's worth framing?" he would ask after he finished a piece. Marjorie returned to Ocean Springs in 1977 after twenty-four years, and, in 1981—the year Ellen died—she replaced Margaret as business manager. Michael, too, returned in 1979 from a period of working in town, and he and Adele revived production at the Annex. Very little castware had been done during the sixties, but now an electric kiln replaced the big kerosene-fired muffle kiln installed almost half a century earlier by Bob and Mac. In 1981, Patricia returned to her father's Pottery and, over the next few years, did her first work as a decorator. Sissy marveled over her ability to "take hold and teach herself her own techniques"; she seemed "extraordinary." Billy's wife, Carolyn, began reproducing Bob's old block prints. Newspaper articles praised "the family legacy" of three generations working side by side.

It seemed to Marjorie that in the years she had been away—during the sixties and seventies—the whole country had gotten more interested in handcrafted work. In 1966, Peter had begun offering a pottery workshop to a little group of students. One of them, Tommy Wixon, remembers his first glimpse of Peter, darting in and out of the showroom, arranging flowers. "He was dressed as though he worked there for the family, like a handyman," he said.

His glasses were missing a temple piece and were tied on with string. I noticed that he appeared to have only one tooth, off-center on the bottom. Margaret told me a story about that. One day she finally had him talked into going to the dentist and having the last tooth pulled and dentures made. She said he was quiet all the way to the office. They went in and signed in and sat down. She went to the bathroom and when she came back he was gone. She drove slowly home, looking for him, but couldn't find him. When she went to his house he was not there; he is back at the pottery working. She asked why he had left. He said that he had got to thinking. If he had that tooth pulled, what would he use to hold his cast net with? As far as I know, he never got dentures.

Shearwater's fiftieth anniversary—1978—brought a spate of publicity. The mayor of Ocean Springs declared November 3 "Peter Anderson Day," and a journalist guessed that, at age seventy-seven, Peter Anderson was the country's oldest working master potter. Peter had begun to enjoy what he called "the company"—the visitors who came to watch him work—and there were more than ever now. A TV crew from WLOX, Biloxi, did a half-hour program on Shearwater, and Nancy Sweezy, director of Jugtown Pottery, came down to interview Peter, Jimmy, and Sissy. There is a chapter on Shearwater in Sweezy's excellent book on southern potteries, *Raised in Clay*. Tom Jackson, a photographer and writer who accompanied her, captured Peter in words and images. He seemed, Jackson wrote in 1983, "the gentle patriarch of Shearwater . . . a small, slender man of lines and angles who dresses comfortably in loose plaid flannel and dark corduroy and in tennis shoes. With dignified carriage and erect posture, he carries his eighty years lightly. His short, dark hair and his trimmed, full mustache are salted with gray, and his eyes are bright and lively. He has a slightly impish look, as though he can barely contain some delightful and amusing secret. His hands are knobby and large, with strong, thick fingers and short, immaculately clean nails. An experimenter and an innovator, he has a curious mind which seems never to have lost its childhood sense of wonder. He often chuckles as he talks."

Both Jackson and Sweezy marveled at his liveliness. She remembered him vividly, decades later: "He was so sprightly and energetic when I saw him, swinging his mallet to de-air the clay and vaulting up on a shelf above table height to reach something he wanted to show me." He was like "a little blue flame," someone said, remembering him at his potter's wheel. Few outside the family knew that he was fatally ill, diagnosed months earlier with Lou Gehrig's disease (amyotrophic lateral sclerosis) and leukemia. Marjorie remembers that, when he heard the diagnosis, he simply "went on about his business, without showing any particular interest." In the fall of 1983, when his wrists began to hurt and he began to lose weight, he joked about "the passing afflictions of old age." On weekends or Wednesday afternoons, he went to the woods—as he used to do with Pat—to gather fat pine for the stoves and fireplaces, or drove to Vancleave with his springer spaniel to pick flowers for the showroom. He fished with Jimmy or mulleted off the end of his pier. When he could no longer work at the wheel, he sat in the yard or on the beach or in the workshop and watched his son.

Into the following year, at eight each morning, Peter rode his bike down the path to the workshop. By spring 1984, when he could no longer manage by himself, Marjorie, her husband, Pete, and one of their children, Scott, moved into the Front House. In the midst of a crisis in their own family, they found the strength to care for him. He had neglected the place since Pat's death, and they worked hard to get it in shape. "Looks like a real home," she remembers him saying. As she read to him one day and took her turn as caretaker, Leif looked at her uncle's gnarled right hand and felt "her heart contract, acutely sorry, amazed that God should smite the potter's hand, this instrument through which so much beauty found expression." Sissy wondered how such an independent person as he could show such "style and humor" as he sank into total dependence on others. To the end, he lived in the present, although Michael never forgot his admonition: "Remember your Uncle Walter and all he did for this place." In October, when he was no longer able to use his hands and could barely get out of bed, Jimmy and Marjorie drove him to a treatment center in Houston, where doctors gave him a blood transfusion, and confirmed both ALS and leukemia. "Take me home," he ordered, as soon as they got there, but they persuaded him to stay. Peter had thought that the examination there might contribute, in a small way, to research on ALS, and another worry had arisen in connection with Jimmy and those who worked with him. Had the materials used at Shearwater contributed in some way to Peter's illness? Doctors said that they had not. At the Pottery, a few weeks later, Jimmy had a firing, and Sissy saw an empty showroom glowing once again with beautiful glazes.

It is almost exclusively Jimmy, and it is very exciting to see how wonderful he is. You see, the sold-out state was good in a way. Now there is so little that belongs to Peter or to the old joint days [when they were working together] that one can see, at last, the development of the new generation. His mother would be so proud that she would be helped in her acceptance of Peter's disability. He is questioning at the moment, and almost unable to communicate vocally. The wretched disease has ruined the muscles which were such a marvelous part of him.

He died in the hospital on December 20. Sissy remembered that two days later, his eighty-third birthday, "he was brought home for visitation. . . . His face was very beautiful. I thought of him leaning above those divine shapes and his countenance taking on their beauty as the years of his potting passed." A few days later, she walked out to Shearwater Drive—once East Beach Road—to get the paper. "Out at the workshop, Peter's old green truck (Pat's too) has been pushed in by the kiln house. The whole thing makes a picture that brings tears to my eyes."

By the spring of 1986, the azalea bushes that Peter and Bob had planted half a century earlier were as high as trees. As she looked at them, Sissy loved them for their beauty and as a symbol of the Andersons' devotion. She remembered the day the two brothers had brought them from Vancleave: the "balled roots and the careful hole, the loosened earth, the cushion of leaves, the hands setting the little plant like a bright jewel in a small pool of water." She had brought water in a pail, and a sackful of dead leaves, and watched as they worked, hoping to please their mother's artistic eye.

Late in her life, until her death of cancer in August 1991 at the age of eighty-two, Sissy could feel the tug of past and present. It was an easy, pleasurable sort of give-and-take, and the two came together in her writing. The anguish of her early journals had given way to delight in the beauty of Shearwater and the unfathomable richness of human life. To her daughter Leif she wrote, "I seem to be living very hard, simply enjoying the incredible world. Perhaps it is like the rush of goldenrod on the land, hastening to outwit the cold."

She was tempted to write elegy. She could sit in the Barn and listen to the "innumerable large and small, squeaking and scuffling creatures" who dwelt within the safety of its walls. They brought the place alive.

[The Barn] lives, too, because of something else, some spirit thing, some lingering presence of those who have lived here, leaving in the spaces of its air the deep print of their being. . . . So it is that the Barn and I can conjure at will people and events out of our mutual past. At a given hour of the evening, when the slanting sun rays full of dust motes fall across the wall by the old chimney, Mère in her white seersucker, sleeveless dress and little coat sits in the old green chair with the sagging springs and listens to the radio. I can even hear the announcer's voice. Time itself has rolled back. It is 1950 again, but Mère is still in a world of Shavian Socialism and is planning to vote for Norman Thomas in the next election.

Hanging over the Barn, where almost the entire family had lived at one time or another, uprooted by Hurricane Elena (1985), was the sweet gum tree, one of whose "falling stars" had alighted on her head as she joked with Bob about the Methodist minister. Elena wrought terrible destruction, felling the last of the chinaberry trees where she and Bob had watched the tipsy robins. "But remember," Billy told his mother, "you can't tell what wonderful treasure will come up in the open space." Elena's windfall brought the fragrance of "broken stumps and macerated leaves," and much beauty to the eye. "In one little area, behind the Cottage, the blown-off leaves are like nests, and contain all manner of seeds. Hickory nuts, persimmons, chinaberries . . . acorns, magnolia pods spilling their red fruit, sweet-gums, dogwoods, clusters from smilax, brier—all with such a fresh, dewy look."

Like Mère, Sissy thought often about time, and worried about boring people with her memories. In her Book of Devotion, she read the words Mère had surely read decades earlier: "Do not look back. If you spend your life in the past, you will have no future." Too glib, she thought. Without the past, no future is worth living. How it enriched the present! It was *part* of the present. It was "good to think of good people and good times and to ache with the absences." The past returned to her in full force, a couple of times, through discoveries. In the kiln house at the Annex, while installing a new, larger electric kiln, someone found trunks and boxes from Oldfields, filled with Bob's paintings. One of them, done on a piece of wallpaper over twenty feet long, was of Noah and the Ark, and there was a piece of one of the puppets from the attic. Someone bought the old post office at Gautier and, while cleaning out the attic, found some undelivered mail, to Sissy's father and Bob and her. She broke into tears when she thought of the time they had spent together at Old-fields, which had been sold, years earlier, and lay surrounded by a housing subdivision. But the past wasn't something one had to excavate. She could see it every day in the faces of her grandchildren, and in the children of her nephews and nieces. She loved the way it left its impression upon the present, carving its features not only in the faces of her family, but in all of nature. There were "traces" everywhere, traces left by other lives. No matter that life was fleeting. Something always remained.

I love to pull the branch that holds
last spring's nest. To see the rounded cup,
soft curls of rootlets that retain
the curve of the soft breast. The rim
marked with the wing's tip and the tail
that peeked above the stiff twigs.

At night in the light's brightness, I rejoice
to see the flounder's bed where he lay waiting.
The fan of his tail marked in ripples. Every scale,
even the gill-patch and the bright round eye,

the fin's pulse and the ridgy jaw
revealed in sand to me.

She lived time more deeply, more perceptively than others. It was a cycle of joy and sorrow. There were "special days" in her life: anniversaries and birthdays, the wedding dates and death dates of ancestors. There were many of those days, so strong in her memory that the present resonated with them. Beyond them, deeper into the past, was what she liked to call "ancestral memory." A lunar eclipse she watched with Leif made her "hear things far back in time," beyond the reach of consciousness.

Awake in the whiteness of light,
in the deep, warm night
we watch and wait.
She too is waiting, for the time is right.
"Earth lover, I am young. I yield me."
The shadow presses.
"Cover me, as a covered bird, cover."
How slow, how tender moves this lover.
We move as the moon moves
that we may not miss this "covering."
I hear, far back in time, a beat.
A hard and horny hand taps on a hollow log.
Taps joy for the world to hear, not fear.
An Indian living on our Coast
in wood and time has understood.
As the deep dark descends
upon a bank, he dallies with his love.
And in her ear he speaks of lovely things.
"I have seen the cock-quail
thus approach his hen."
"As slow as this?"

"Perhaps not. But she's willing
and he covers her. And then,
you won't believe it, but it's true,
the nest is like a basket in the grass.
Shaped by her breast, it holds the clutch of eggs.
And when they hatch, the birdlings,
hidden in grass in the nest,
the covey is like a scattering of stars
when the cold comes.
That's how I knew:
I marked the small moons,
scattered in the sky."
Almost as tender, in the grass
they lie.
In the far sky, a fuzzy line of light
marks the Earth's slow passage
from the moon.
Only a shadow?
Shadow, then, is real.
I hold my daughter's hand.
Oh sheltering daughter,
walk me to my bed.
You, made from air and earth,
did you, too, sense
an act of love in this still night?
A future birth?

Her letter crossed in the mail with one from Leif. Her daughter *had*
remembered. In New York, she was crossing Broadway with a poet
friend, who asked her if she had seen the eclipse.

Yes I remember the moon
the night

my mother speaking of magic—
She sat beside me
summoning ancient ritual
of mother and daughter waiting on the moon—
Time and waiting had already veiled
my mother's eyes—
Yet she revealed
the darkening moon
with mystery
awareness of the silent and unseen—
The insects were quiet
as I watched her face
and slowly slowly slowly
the shadow was cast—
Mama's face
had attained a coppery glow
from the summer sun. . . .

It was not enough to think about the past, it had to be created—"re-alized," Bob might have said—through writing. All her life, Sissy had longed to write, but had felt overwhelmed by family problems, money worries, and the long, exhausting years of teaching. Now, in the final years of her life, there was time for it. There had been moments, when Bob was away at Phipps or living uneasily at Shearwater, when both past and present had seemed unbearable. But that cloud had lifted, and she could help others—Leif, for example—by having gone through it.

Leif, my darling!

I am so happy. I go on my way rejoicing. What beautiful things are always happening and if there are quiet times when we feel a depression, almost an agony, perhaps they are as necessary as the seed's time in the earth: the airless, dark for a creature of light, and the bursting into two parts. It does seem like the labor of the creative spirit. . . .

Months after Bob's death, Sissy had begun a memoir of their life together, writing in bed at night, jotting down all she could remember.
When she retired as a schoolteacher in 1969, a friend had taught her to
type, and by the fall of 1984, that draft had grown into an enormous
manuscript. Eighteen hundred pages, she told people. Family and friends
encouraged her, and a gifted editor and writer, Patti Carr Black, helped
her trim her work, "telescoping" paragraphs and entire chapters, and
polishing it into a poignant memoir, *Approaching the Magic Hour,* the story
of her relationship with Bob, which stunned some members of the family with its courage and intimacy. In it, she looked back without regret
on the tumultuous years she had spent with him. But even after that, in
the final years of her life, she went on writing and rewriting present and
past. Women *ought* to do so, she thought. How "strangely wonderful"
they were in their role as storytellers. "Most families base their sometimes
hard-to-find family knowledge on the tales told by a distant grandmother
or aunt." Pat, too, had felt that need to record the past, and had made a
beginning, but had been taken away before her time. She had told herself in one of the journals, a little before her death: "The resolution to
write a bit more . . . You'd better get on the ball, because there's not
much left, not many years, and so many precious hours and minutes and
seconds gone into limbo. . . . The subconscious is filled with so much
beauty and joy and sorrow that simply dissolves." There were moments
of "transcendent joy" she wanted to capture, "moments when someone
or something suddenly fills me with an inexpressible gladness."

Before Sissy died, she wanted to gather that knowledge—from her
own memory, from letters and papers—and pass it on to her family and
her sister's. Her grandson Vanja—Leif's son—remembers how she would
"cross her hands on her lap, gaze up at the ceiling or out of the window,
and ease into a story of days long gone by." She "told"—as Pat would
have wanted her to—in the interviews with Joan Gilley, in essays and letters and in a book, still unpublished, for her grandchildren about her
childhood at Oldfields. When, in her daily journaling, she drifted into
past events, she scolded herself: "what about right *here,* right *now?* Aren't

you supposed to be writing a journal? A journal should tell about present time, present space, and about its effect on you and yours."

The present, too, had to be realized. She reveled in the ordinary sights and sounds of Shearwater: the flow of conversation, family meals, excursions to Horn Island, the joy of growing things, her showroom duty once a week, the sayings and doings of the young people who surrounded her and called her "Gran." The swimming pool beside her little house provided special amusement. She shared it with all sorts of creatures, and, with failing eyesight, paused to look at them. One day she noticed "two large, dark crickets taking precarious rides on two colored dogwood leaves. You could almost feel the tenseness of their bodies and see the slight tilt with which they attempted to steer for some desired haven." What creatures she skimmed from that pool before doing her daily laps: "Hundreds of crickets this year, centipedes, millipedes, locusts, dragonflies, moths, bats, rats, snakes, toads, frogs, turtles, lizards. Usually it's a rescue but sometimes a burial."

In the eighties, she watched Jimmy come into his own as a potter. As she helped Marjorie tag his pieces, she delighted in the "depths and variations" of his glazes. He had become, she wrote, "every bit as good as his father." She liked to watch people pick up his pieces; there was often "the little shiver of pleasure" at the presence of beauty. She took groups of visitors through Bob's old Cottage, where they gazed at the murals in the little room, the collection of shells from Horn Island, the furniture and rugs that he had made. She sat there for hours, alone, as did Bob's children, before the little room was lifted onto a flatbed truck and carefully transported to the newly built Walter Anderson Museum of Art. She had worried about visitors destroying the Cottage's special atmosphere, "breaking up the intensity of creative spirit" that had lived there. But people wanted to know "what makes an artist tick"; they wanted "to see and feel the appurtenances of his life." And they had such strong emotional reactions to his work, "as if they were finding a hidden part of themselves suddenly released." He belonged now to others, outside the family. In different ways, she, too, drew closer to him. One summer, she returned to Horn Island. Redwing blackbirds came to meet her, as though remembering the rice Bob cooked for them at his housewarmings, and she wished she had brought his sooty old double boiler. Beauty was everywhere in her family—in Jimmy's forms and glazes; in Mac's oil paintings and prints; in Patricia's poems and plates and bowls; in Mary's writing; in the dancing of Leif; in the painting of Mary's son Christopher Stebly and the acting of her daughter Amelia; in the artistry of Billy as he planted his camellias and azaleas; and in the exquisite printing and coloring of his wife, Carolyn. As she swam her laps or lashed her exercise bike into a fury, she felt "bursting with luck." How had so many talented people come together? Much of it, no doubt, could be traced to Annette. Her enthusiasms, Mary wrote recently, "colored the lives of her sons, her grandchildren, her great grandchildren, and even the latest generation, whose paint-stained fingers enliven our pale rugs and beige slipcovers with jolting streaks of 'gold-vermillion.' " Art had become an ordinary part of family existence. It had sprung up everywhere in forms that could help "heal the world's sorrow." Sissy felt an "extraordinary love for the Art-Expression all around" her, not only within the family but elsewhere in Mississippi, so often stigmatized. "We are people-lovers here in this backward state, where oppression and fear have not been able to still our voices."

Like Annette, Sissy wrote a little poem about her death; offering consolation to one of her children:

> And you will find, my darling,
> That the road
> From consciousness to consciousness
> Is not the long dark passage
> We were taught to fear
> But that love lights it
> Like a star confined
> And all our joys and hopes
> May follow there

And in our memories,
If we are left behind,
There is no barrier to daily converse.
There is no absence of the one we love.

She thought of the Glory Road that Peter had made, and remembered those who had gone down it, stooping to touch this or that bit of brightly colored pottery. "Perhaps a life can be like that, full of shattered beauty that still evokes a reaction, that promises more and more, that lifts us up and gives an easier passage to bliss."

List of Illustrations

List of Illustrations

TENDER MIRACLES *Cat Study,* by Annette McConnell Anderson

FORTUNE'S FAVORITE CHILD Horn Island drawing by Walter Inglis Anderson

"GOODBYE, OLD LADY" *Rain and Sea,* by Walter Inglis Anderson

TRACES *Plants,* by Walter Inglis Anderson

Guide to Color Photo Insert

(Photos by María Estrella Iglesias)

1. Left to right: Teapot thrown and glazed by Peter; plate thrown by Jim and decorated by Patricia; low vase thrown by Jim, decorated by Patricia; tall vase thrown and glazed by Peter; vase thrown and glazed by Peter. Collection of Shearwater Pottery.
2. Pieces thrown and glazed by Peter, with vase (head of girl) thrown by Jim and decorated by Patricia. Collection of Shearwater Pottery and Shearwater showroom.
3. Cast #30 pitcher, decorated by Mac and glazed by Peter. Shearwater Pottery Collection.
4. Vase thrown and decorated by Peter. Shearwater Pottery Collection.
5. Bowl thrown by Peter, decorated by Adele. Collection of Sara Anderson.
6. Left to right: Jug thrown by Jim and decorated by Patricia; blue two-handled vase thrown by Jim and glazed by Peter; cast small bird vase decorated by Patricia; vase of man and sheep decorated by Bob; large green vase decorated by Jim; small cast vase (Peter Anderson shape) decorated by Patricia; aqua vase thrown and decorated by Annette; small cast vase with beheaded woman decorated by Patricia; blue drip vase, thrown by Jim and glazed by Peter. Shearwater Pottery Collection.
7. Bowl thrown by Peter with sgraffito decoration by Bob. Walter Anderson Museum of Art.
8. Bowl thrown by Peter with sgraffito decoration by Bob. Walter Anderson Museum of Art.
9. Bowl thrown by Peter and decorated with ducks by Bob. Private collection.
10. Vase of beheaded woman thrown by Jim and decorated by Patricia; two green vases thrown and glazed by Jim; Cast figures designed by Bob and Mac. Private collection.
11. Figure of Rima designed by Bob. Shearwater showroom.
12. Bowl thrown by Peter, decorated by Mac. Sara Anderson Collection.
13. Bowl (pine-tree motif) thrown by Peter and decorated by Mac. Sara Anderson Collection.

14. Vases thrown by Peter and Jim (coots vase) and decorated by Mac. Molded fish designed by Mac. Oil painting on board by Mac.
15. Thrown by Peter, decorated by Mac. To the left, carved fish vase selected for Robineau exhibit, 1936.
16. Vase thrown by Peter and decorated by Mac with oyster-tonger. Sara Anderson Collection.
17. Thrown by Peter, decorated by Mac. New Orleans dock workers. Sara Anderson Collection.
18. Painting of Bob on Horn Island by Mac. Sara Anderson Collection.
19. Floral vase thrown by Jim, decorated by Patricia. Private collection.
20. Vase thrown by Jim, decorated by Patricia. Private collection. Photo by Trent Boysen.
21. Bowl thrown by Jim and decorated by Patricia. Private collection.
22. Maternity vase thrown by Jim and decorated by Patricia. Private collection.
23. Teapot, plate, and vase thrown by Jim and decorated by Christopher Stebly. Joan Gilley collection.
24. Oil on canvas by Christopher Stebly, 1997. Private collection.
25. Plate decorated by Christopher Stebly. Private collection.

Bibliography

Abbreviations

AGA   Agnes Grinstead Anderson

AGA/Gilley interviews   Agnes Grinstead Anderson, interviews with Joan
           Gilley, Spring and Summer, 1990

AMcCA   Annette McConnell Anderson

GWA   George Walter Anderson

HIL   *The Horn Island Logs of Walter Inglis Anderson*

JXCOT   *Jackson County Times,* Ocean Springs

JMcCA   James McConnell Anderson

Magic Hour   Agnes Grinstead Anderson, *Approaching the Magic
           Hour. Memories of Walter Anderson*

Magic Hour ms.   Unedited manuscript of *Approaching the Magic
           Hour* (rough draft)

McConnell Papers   Papers of James McConnell, Tulane University
           Archives, Special Collections

Meyer Papers   Papers of Adolf Meyer (restricted), Alan Chesney
           Medical Archives, Johns Hopkins University

PA   Peter Anderson

PGA   Patricia Grinstead Anderson

| WIA/Phipps, PA/Phipps | Medical records of PA and WIA, in Medical Records, Johns Hopkins University Hospital |
| Phipps Clinic cards | Summaries of case histories of PA and WIA. See Joseph Stephens, below |

Works Cited

Anderson, Agnes Grinstead. *Approaching the Magic Hour. Memories of Walter Anderson.* Edited by Patti Carr Black. Jackson and London: University Press of Mississippi, 1995.

———."Hellmuth-Grinstead Family," in Rogers, *The History of Jackson County,* 234–35.

Anderson, Annette McConnell. *Possums and Other Verse.* Gulfport. Privately printed, s.a.

Anderson, Mary. "A Personal View of Annette McConnell Anderson, December 16, 1867–January 25, 1964." *Motif* (Walter Anderson Museum of Art), Summer 1994.

———."The Birds of Walter Anderson," in WIA, *Birds.*

———."Introduction," in Walter I. Anderson, *A Symphony of Animals.*

———.*The Voluptuous Return. Still Life by Walter Anderson,* in press.

Anderson, Patricia Grinstead. "Shearwater Potteries." Unidentified clipping, April–May 1951, Shearwater archives.

Anderson, Walter Inglis. *Birds.* Jackson and London: University Press of Mississippi, 1990.

———.*The Horn Island Logs of Walter Inglis Anderson.* Edited by Redding S. Sugg, Jr. Rev. ed. Jackson: University Press of Mississippi, 1985.

———.*A Symphony of Animals.* Jackson: University Press of Mississippi, 1996.

———.*Walls of Light.* See Anne R. King.

———.*Walter Anderson's Illustrations of Epic and Voyage.* Edited and with an introduction by Redding S. Sugg, Jr. Carbondale and Edwardsville: Southern Illinois University Press; London and Amsterdam: Feffer & Simmons, 1980.

Andrus, Olive P. "Isidore Newman School and the Manual Training Movement." M.A. thesis, Tulane University, 1938.

Anonymous. *Lewis the Pecan Man.* Pascagoula, MS. Privately printed, 1917.

Ashley, Marjorie. Articles on JMcCA, WIA, and "Shearwater Pottery and the Andersons," in Betty C. Rogers, ed., *The History of Jackson County,* 110, 65–66.

Backes, Clarus. "Artist in the Eye of a Hurricane." *Chicago Tribune Magazine,* August 17, 1969, 26–31.

Black, Patti Carr. *Art in Mississippi: 1720–1980.* Jackson, MS: University Press of

Mississippi in association with the Mississippi Historical Society and the Mississippi Department of Archives and History, 1998.

Burton, Marda Kaiser. "Portraitist of Nature." *Horizon,* March 1982, 44–48.

Canis, Wayne F., William J. Neal, Orrin H. Pilkey, Jr., and Orrin H. Pilkey, Sr. *Living with the Alabama Shore.* Durham, NC: Duke University Press, 1985.

Carey, Rita Katherine. "Samuel Jarvis Peters." *Louisiana Historical Quarterly* 30:2 (April 1947), 439–80.

Carney, Margaret. *Charles Fergus Binns. The Father of American Studio Ceramics.* New York: Hudson Hills Press, 1999.

Chadbourne, Thomas L. *The Autobiography of Thomas L. Chadbourne.* Edited by Charles C. Goetsch and Margaret L. Shivers. New York: Oceana Publications, 1985.

Clark, Garth, Robert A. Ellison, and Eugene Hecht, *The Mad Potter of Biloxi: The Art and Life of George E. Ohr.* New York: Abbeville, 1989.

Crowfoot, *This Dreamer. Life of Isaac Hellmuth, Second Bishop of Huron.* Vancouver: Copp Clark Publishing, 1963.

Curtis, Edward deF. "Ceramic Art and the Ceramic Artist." *Bulletin of the American Ceramic Society* 5:1 (January 1926), 42–44.

———."Editorial. The Art Division, 1928." *Bulletin of the American Ceramic Society* 7:3 (March 1928), 45–49.

———."Editorial. Coöperation Between Artists and Manufacturers." *Bulletin of the American Ceramic Society* 7:6 (June 1928), 163–65.

———."Industrial Potter Craftsmen." *Bulletin of the American Ceramic Society* 5:3 (March 1926), 177–79.

———."The Small Shop." *Bulletin of the American Ceramic Society* 6:1 (January 1927), 17–21.

Dyer, Charles L. *Along the Gulf. An Entertaining Story of an Outing Among the Beautiful Resorts on the Mississippi Sound.* Published by the Louisville & Nashville Railroad, 1895; reprinted by the Pass Christian Historical Society, 1991.

Gilbert, Bill. "Stalking the Blue Bear: The Fine Art of Walter Anderson," *Smithsonian* 25:7 (October 1994), 108–18.

Goings, Kenneth W. *Mammy and Uncle Mose: Black Collectibles and American Stereotyping (Blacks in the Diaspora).* Bloomington: Indiana University Press, 1994.

Hall, Doris and Burdell. "Shearwater Pottery, A Bastion of Original Design." *Journal of the American Art Pottery Association* 5:3 (May–June 1990), 1, 4–5.

———."Shearwater: Southern Pottery of Sheer Beauty." *American Clay Exchange* 6:9 (June 15, 1986), 7, 8, 12; "A Shearwater Experience," 6:11 (July 1986), 3–4; "George Walter and Annette McConnell Anderson's Legacy," 6:15 (September 30, 1986), 9–11; "Shearwater's Figurines," 6:16 (October 15, 1986), 3–5.

Bibliography

Kaufman, George S., and Marc Connelly. *Beggar on Horseback. A Play in Two Parts.* New York: Horace Liveright, 1924.

King, Anne R. *Walls of Light: The Murals of Walter Anderson.* Jackson and London: University Press of Mississippi, 1999.

Lytal, Bill (producer). *Shearwater Pottery* (video, 27 min.). Clinton, MS: Mississippi College, 1978.

Mahé, John A., II, and Rosanne McCaffrey, eds. *Encyclopaedia of New Orleans Artists 1717–1918.* New Orleans: Historic New Orleans Collection, 1987.

McConnell, James. *The Ethic Elements in the Character and Laws of Nations.* Oration of 1855 delivered to the Alumni Association of the Law Department of the University of Louisiana. New Orleans, 1855.

Owen, Nancy Elizabeth. *Women, Culture and Commerce: Rookwood Pottery, 1800–1913.* Ph.D. dissertation, Northwestern University, June 1997.

Pickard, Mary Anderson. See Mary Anderson.

Poesch, Jesse. *Newcomb Pottery, An Enterprise for Southern Women, 1895–1940.* Exton, PA: Schiffer Publishing, 1984.

Rogers, Betty C., ed. *The History of Jackson County, Mississippi.* Pascagoula, MS: Jackson County Genealogical Society, 1989.

———."Lewis Sha-Oldfields," in *The History of Jackson County, Mississippi.* Pascagoula, MS: Jackson County Genealogical Society, 1989.

Rubin, Cynthia Elyce. "Natural Forms: The Horn Island Logs and Watercolors of Walter Inglis Anderson (1903–1965)." Ph.D. dissertation, School of Education, New York University, 1995.

———."Walter Inglis Anderson." *Country Folk Art,* December 1995, 91–92.

Rudloe, Jack. "The Nature of a Painter." *Natural History,* February 1990, 62–68.

Spencer, Elizabeth. *On the Gulf.* Jackson and London: University Press of Mississippi, 1991.

Stephens, Joseph H., M.D., Pascal Richard, M.D., and Paul R. McHugh, M.D. "Long-Term Follow-up of Patients Hospitalized for Schizophrenia, 1913 to 1940." *Journal of Nervous and Mental Disease* 185:12 (December 1997), 715–21.

Sugg, Redding S. *A Painter's Psalm. The Mural from Walter Anderson's Cottage.* Rev. ed. Jackson and London: University Press of Mississippi, 1992.

Sullivan, Louis. *The Autobiography of an Idea.* New York: Dover Publications, 1956.

Sullivan, Charles L. *Hurricanes of the Mississippi Gulf Coast.* Biloxi: Gulf Publishing, s.a.

Sweezy, Nancy. *Raised in Clay. The Southern Pottery Tradition.* Washington, D.C.: Smithsonian Institution Press, 1984.

Notes

The Magic Union

17 **"The pottery was Peter's place":** Diane Stevenson, "Shearwater Pottery," unpublished manuscript.

22 **"The house that I share now":** Michael P. Anderson, unpublished essay.

29 **"how art entered":** William Morris, quoted by Herbert Read, *Art and Industry: The Principles of Industrial Design* (New York: Harcourt, Brace, 1935), 30.

30 **"Real artists":** letter of AMcCA to WIA, San Diego, November 1933.

31 **"I wish I *could*":** George Walter Anderson, "Shearwater Pottery," January 22, 1930.

35 **"apostles of individuality":** Garth Clark, Robert A. Ellison, and Eugene Hecht, *The Mad Potter of Biloxi,* p. 123.

Blueprints

Annette's unpublished journal of the boys' "sayings and doings," upon which I have drawn for details of home life at 553 Broadway, begins in 1901 and ends around 1916.

39 **John Ruskin, William Morris:** Owen, 114, 119.

309

39 **"For all her enlightenment":** Mary Anderson, "A Personal View," n.p.

39 **"the vision necessary to apply it":** Rough draft of letter from GWA to Quentin Reynolds, March 3, 1936.

42 **"If you want to draw a bird":** Mary Anderson, "The Birds of Walter Anderson," x.

42 **Annette at Newcomb:** On the college, see Jesse Poesch's excellent monograph. On AMcCA's record there, communication between author, Shama Farooq, and Susan Tucker (Curator of Books and Records, Newcomb College Center for Research on Women).

42 **James McConnell:** On AMcCA's father, see "Jas. McConnell, Leader at Bar, Dead at 85 Years," in the New Orleans *Times-Picayune,* 1914 (undated clipping in McConnell Papers) and item 156–1–6 in the same archive. He was born in 1829 to Alexander McConnell (d. 1832), chief surgeon of the Charity Hospital, New Orleans, and to Margaret Nelson (b. Washington, Mississippi, 1803). Alexander McConnell "was a friend of James Bowie, of Alamo fame, and while surgeon of the Charity Hospital in the twenties he was invited and urged by Bowie to join his expedition to Texas in the same capacity." (Will Branan, "The Dean of Chess Players," unidentified clipping, probably from the *Times-Picayune,* in McConnell Papers.)

43 **Woodward on art in the South:** Ellsworth Woodward to Lura Beam, ca. 1925, *Woodward Papers,* Tulane University Library, Special Collections.

43 **Christmas cards:** E. Woodward, "Art Taught as a Means of Expression," ms. 10–2–11, *Woodward Papers.*

44 **"truth made visible," "art is not a commodity":** E. Woodward, address to Southern States Art League, 1933, and "Everyday Art," unpublished manuscript, *Woodward Papers.*

44 **Annette's studies in North:** There is a collection of her father's letters, with frequent mention of Annette, in McConnell Papers.

44 **William Merritt Chase:** *Magic Hour* ms., where Sissy refers to "Chillecott Hills." James McConnell Anderson reports that his mother studied with Chase. Letter to Mr. McDavid, undated, JMcCA archives.

45 **Annette's painting:** AMcCA file of newspaper and magazine clippings in the Historic New Orleans Collection, consulted courtesy of Pamela Arceneaux. Some of the paintings are preserved at Shearwater and at the Walter Anderson Museum of Art. For a bibliography, see Mahé and McCaffrey, 7–8.

46 **Samuel Jarvis Peters:** See the fine biography by Carey; AMcCA's unpublished essay "Bouligny"; and "Father of New Orleans Public Schools," New Orleans *Times-Democrat,* July 7, 1912.

46   **James McConnell as educator:** An undated document in the McConnell
      Papers, entitled "Hon. James McConnell," notes that "Before the war he was
      a director in the Public Schools of New Orleans, and that it was doubtless
      owing to his labors in behalf of public education that he was named by Mr.
      Paul Tulane one of the two vice presidents of the Board of Administrators of
      the Tulane Educational Fund."

46   **"confused scene":** James McConnell, *Ethic Elements,* 5–6.

46   **In his will:** "Jas. McConnell's Will Probated by Judge Monroe," New Or-
      leans *Times-Picayune,* November 1914; undated clipping in McConnell Papers.

46   **greatest ambition:** James McConnell to James McConnell, Jr., April 18,
      1907.

47   **Finney's School:** *Magic Hour* ms. and AGA/Gilley interview, July 17, 1990.

47   **Mac's art lessons and tile:** GWA to AMcCA, March 27, 1917. On
      Urquhart (1865–1929), who probably studied at Newcomb with Annette, see
      Poesch, 105.

47   **"carpenter's workshop" and pigeon house:** GWA to AMcCA, August 1
      and 2, 1911, and September 13, 1912.

47   **St. John's School, Manlius, New York:** Founded by an Episcopalian bishop
      in 1869, Manlius became a military school in 1880 (it is now coeducational
      and known as Manlius Pebble Hill School). During Peter and Bob's days
      there, about 120 boarders lodged in double rooms, under the supervision of
      William Verbeck, a former missionary to Japan, and his son Guido. AGA
      speaks of Bob's life at Manlius in AGA/Gilley interview, July 17, 1990.

47   **"whole proposition" and boys at Manlius:** GWA to AMcCA, July 5,
      1915; March 28, 1917; and June 22, 1915.

48   **"other two birds have flown":** GWA to JMcCA, June 25, 1915. Mac has
      accompanied Annette to Manlius with Peter and Bob. GWA adds: "The kit-
      ten is well, the cat is well, also the rabbits and the pigeons. . . . What is this I
      hear about your putting a robin's nest—no, a robin's egg—in your mouth?
      Don't you know that that is no place for eggs?"

48   **harden him up:** A letter from the director of Camp Moosilauke (Pike, New
      Hampshire), July 20, 1916, reports that Mac's "timidity has entirely disap-
      peared," and that he has "already learned to swim a little."

48   **sheet . . . slit in middle:** *Magic Hour* ms.

49   **"I know what [discipline] is":** WIA to AGA, undated, ca. November
      1930.

49   **WIA letters from Manlius:** WIA to parents, undated, and to JMcCA, Au-
      gust 12, 1915 (archives of Sara Lemon Anderson).

49   **"awareness of nature":** Mary Anderson, "The Birds of Walter Anderson," xi.

49   **Weekend trips with father:** *Magic Hour* ms.

49   **"Anderson Incorporated" letter:** GWA to AMcCA, February 25, 1921.

Midlife Journey

53   **GWA's letters to AMcCA:** I have quoted from letters of June 15 and 22, 1915; August 8, 1908; and March 21, 1917 (on the wisteria and irises).

54   **business had been thriving:** For example, in July 1915, at the close of the fiscal year, GWA earned $74,200 as his share of profits in G. B. Fox, Exporter, Grain and Cotton Seed Products (letter of GWA to AMcCA, July 9, 1915). On July 12, he reports that, after depositing his yearly bonuses, he has a "respectable" $69,000 in savings.

54   **about $825,000:** Here and elsewhere, I have relied on the American Institute of Economic Research Cost-of-Living Calculator.

54   **rent a house in Biloxi:** A reporter who visited Shearwater in 1929 remarked that "Mr. Anderson loves to tell how he 'got' [Fairhaven] . . . One summer day the wife was sent to Biloxi, to rent a house for the summer. When Mrs. Anderson returned to New Orleans that night she was asked with what success did she meet in leasing a place, and very calmly informed the husband she had bought a place that day at Ocean Springs. Good for the wife!" *JXCOT,* September 28, 1929. See also *JXCOT,* June 1, 1918, June 8 ("consummation" of sale) and June 15, 1918, "Real Estate Transfers" (sale of property from Mary Hamlin Ashman and G. H. Ashman to AMcCA): "Dr. and Mrs. Ashman have sold their beach property, known as the De Pass place, to Mrs. Walter Anderson of New Orleans who, with Mr. Anderson, have taken possession of the place and expect to make Ocean Springs their home during the summer season, at least."

54   **Mary on AMcCA:** Mary Anderson, "A Personal View."

55   **"Must a woman" and John Milton:** "Mrs. Ewing's Questions," AMcCA Papers, archives of the family of Walter Anderson, undated.

55   **"white sails":** Anonymous, *Along the Gulf.*

55   **Annette's poem:** "The Winds from the Islands (After a day in the city. Midsummer)," *Possums and Other Verse.*

56   **McConnell house:** Anonymous, "Bay Saint Louis: Some Small Scraps of Its History," in *Along the Gulf.*

57   **Blanc house:** AMcCA, undated unpublished essay, "The Childhood of Delphine Blanc."

57   **"birds from the Islands":** AMcCA, Journals.

57   **"women who had lost everything":** from an unpublished essay by AMcCA, "On Collecting."

58   **Vicksburg:** There he commanded "three pieces of light artillery" and was attached to the brigade of Alfred Cumming. McConnell Papers, 156–1–9.

58   **Delphine Angelique Blanc:** AGA Journals, 1986. AGA heard the story often from AMcCA.

58   **died of yellow fever:** AMcCA, undated, unpublished essay, "My Life."

58   **"Battle Hymn of the Republic":** Mary Anderson, "A Personal View."

58   **Ocean Springs:** Ocean Springs history has been meticulously described and documented each week since 1993 by Ray L. Bellande in his column "Sous les Chenes," in the Ocean Springs *Times-Register.* See also: Charles E. Schmidt, *Ocean Springs French Beachhead* (Pascagoula, MS: Lewis Printing Services, 1992); Regina Hines Ellison, *Ocean Springs,* 1892 (same publisher, 1979 and 1991); Jay Higginbotham, *Fort Maurepas, Birth of Louisiana* (Mobile: Colonial Books, 1968, revised 1971, and republished 1998); Thomas E. Dabney, *Ocean Springs: The Land Where Dreams Come True* (originally published ca. 1915. Reprinted by Lewis Printing Services, 1974); Betty C. Rogers, ed., *The History of Jackson County, Mississippi;* Ray L. Bellande, *Ocean Springs Hotels and Tourist Homes* (Ocean Springs, 1994); and Elizabeth L. Roberts and J. K. Lemon, with text by Ray L. Bellande, *Ocean Springs: The Way We Were 1900–1950* (Ocean Springs: Ocean Springs Rotary Club, 1996); and Ray L. Bellande, *Cemeteries Near Ocean Springs–Jackson County, Mississippi* (Ocean Springs: privately printed, 1992).

58   **Louis Sullivan:** *The Autobiography of an Idea,* 256.

59   **Russell:** On the pecan in Ocean Springs, see the catalogue/advertising pamphlet *Lewis the Pecan Man;* for Russell, p. 8.

59   **built in the 1840s:** On the history of the property, Ray L. Bellande, "Pre-Shearwater Pottery History (1837–1918)," *Ocean Springs Record,* January 19 (p. 18) and January 26 (p. 16), 1995.

59–60   **no factories:** A visitor to Ocean Springs in 1919 observed that the town "needs no mills or factories. They would bring in one class of people, and drive out another." "Ocean Springs Visitor Gives His Impressions of Town and People," *JXCOT,* September 27, 1919.

Art and Industry

63   **WIA nearly drowns:** See "Boy Believed Dead . . . ," *New Orleans States,* August 26, 1920, p. 1; "Tide Sweeps Boy . . ."; and "Grips Lake Light 24

Hours, Boy Is Saved"; all three clippings—the last two unidentified—are in the WIA Papers.

63   **Curriculum at Isidore Newman:** Courses offered included gardening, drawing, sheet-metal work, wood-turning, joinery, cabinet-making, furniture construction, English, and math. "The pottery department was particularly successful. Everything was made, from the daintiest little cup and saucer to the largest jardiniere. There were pitchers, vases, urns and teapots, inkwells and trays. The designs were made by the children. Much of the work was related to the study of Grecian art." Andrus, 142. During the years Peter and Bob studied at Isidore Newman, there were from twenty-three to thirty-nine students in the senior class.

64   **"Please try to get me a job":** WIA to AMcCA, Highlands, N.C., June 25, 1919.

64   **wooden chest:** Mary Anderson, "Introduction," in WIA, *A Symphony of Animals,* ix.

64   **WIA at Parsons:** I have drawn on his letters to AMcCA of September 25, October 8, and October 15, 1922; January 25, February 7, February 27, March 10, April 24, May 1, and December 13, 1923; and on Alice Perkins to AMcCA, October 22, 1922; GWA to WIA, March 23, 1923.

65   **"alone in the great city":** WIA to JMcCA, December 24, 1922.

65   **JMcCA on Baylorites:** JMcCA to AMcCA, undated, probably November 1922.

65   **Independents:** On the Independents show, see *International Studio,* March 1923. WIA might also have seen Best Maugard's work in Juan José Tablada, "Mexican Painting of Today," *International Studio,* January 1923, 267–77. AMcCA subscribed to the magazine, and sometimes sent it to her son.

66   **drawings and watercolors of birds:** It was at Parsons that he designed one of his first bird plates. See Rubin, "Natural Forms," 47.

66   **Cave paintings impressed WIA:** interview with AGA in Rubin, "Natural Forms," 63.

66   **Gurdjieff:** Rubin, "Natural Forms," 59–62.

66   **PA aversion to office work:** GWA to the potter Leon Volkmar, March 21, 1927 (Peter's father is trying to get him an apprenticeship with Volkmar). "[Peter] has worked as I have never seen any man work, though I have seen many: dug his own clay, dried it and handled it, etc., and turned it into pottery, of which he exhibited some pieces at Detroit last month. He used a Hauk burner and direct flame. He has had endless failures in firing, etc., and few successes, and is still as determined to succeed as ever. He has worked entirely by himself. He has practically let everything else go that a boy looks for

in the way of amusement. . . . For instance, when he fires his kiln, he does not leave it except for meals, for 25 or 26 hours on end. His shortest firing has been over 15 hours. Time after time, 50 to 75% of the contents of a kiln would be what he calls seconds or total failures. This was at first, and he is now doing much better, but he is very dissatisfied with the quality of his very best pieces, and did not want to send anything to Detroit, but Miss Sheerer wanted him to do it and to go himself. He would not leave the pottery."

67   **George Ohr's kickwheel:** See "Pottery Exhibition," Biloxi *Daily Herald,* August 6, 1929, p. 2 (clipping courtesy of Ray L. Bellande): "The old foot power wheel of George Ohr is in the shop, but has been replaced by a modern electric one." Also, GWA history of Shearwater, prepared in October 1931 for W. & J. Sloane Co., New York: "One of the potter's wheels was formally used by Mr. Ohr, of the Biloxi Pottery. It was with this wheel that the Shearwater Pottery made its start. Since then, a modern power wheel has been added." A 1947 article in *Grit,* by a writer who had interviewed Annette at Shearwater, reports that "It all began at an auction sale. Mrs. Walter Anderson . . . was the highest bidder for a potter's wheel. A graduate of Newcomb Art School, in New Orleans, she was inspired by the late Adolf [sic] Meyer, famed New Orleans potter, to 'throw' pottery. . . . She also taught her three sons the art." "Family Pottery Factory," *Grit,* July 27, 1947. On Ohr, see the excellent book by Clark, Ellison, and Hecht.

68   **Lesson from Meyer:** Lytal film. On Meyer, see Poesche, throughout, and Ray L. Bellande, "Joseph Fortune Meyer (1848–1931), *Mississippi Coast Historical and Genealogical Society* 31:1 (March 1995), 17–23, with bibliography, and "Joseph Fortune Meyer (1848–1931)," Ocean Springs *Record,* September 14, 1995, 20.

68   **groundhog kiln:** Nancy Sweezy, interview with PA and James Anderson, November 15, 1982, and Marjorie Anderson Ashley, notes to Nancy Sweezy letter of July 12, 1983 (archive of Nancy Sweezy), and history of Shearwater Pottery prepared by GWA, probably in Fall 1931 for W. & J. Sloane Co., New York: "The work began in 1924, in a small hillside kiln built by Anderson, according to book, fired with pine knots. This proved a dismal failure."

68   **"We are in trouble":** GWA to Mary Sheerer, November 16, 1925, and Sheerer's reply of November 17, 1925, in which she explains: "I commenced my work here by getting sample collections of *Majolica Colored Glazes* and of underglaze colors. . . . The Newcomb standard glaze, colorless, was bought ready-made for a long time from dealers. More expensive but more practical until you have some equipment. It would do you little good to use the glazes we make, unless we could continue to supply you, which we couldn't do."

68 **Tchoutacabouffa River:** Pronounced "Shoot-a-ca-buff." See Ray L. Bellande, "Holley's Bluff, Where George E. Ohr Dug Clay," *Mississippi Coast
Historical and Genealogical Society* 31:1 (March 1995), 10–16.

68 **Walter wrote to the company:** GWA to John Sent and Sons, November
30, 1925.

69 **"Chemists" write for instructions:** GWA to L. Reusche and Co., November 30, 1925: "I do not know exactly how much to order, but would like
enough to experiment on some forty or fifty vases, pots, etc., none over eight
inches high. . . ." Reply of December 4, 1925. Correspondence with many of
Shearwater's suppliers is preserved in the Pottery archives.

69 **Placing of wares in kiln:** PA's son James explained to Nancy Sweezy in
November 1982: "It's stoneware at around cone 6, but most of our ware is
earthenware. Our kiln ranges from about 01 at the bottom—01 to 1—up to
probably about 7 at the hottest point at the top and the middle, in the same
firing."

69 **"main test":** PA comments, Lytal film.

70 **"The designers who work up through the industry":** Curtis, "Editorial.
Coöperation," 164.

70 **"jar himself loose from . . . colloidal chemistry":** Curtis, "Ceramic
Art," 43.

71 **potter "must have his art training":** Curtis, "Industrial Potter Craftsmen,"
177.

71 **Curtis on education:** See, for example, his letters to Charles F. Binns, in
the Papers of Charles F. Binns, Archives of American Art, Smithsonian Institution, microfilm reels 3606–3611, in particular his letter of December 15,
1925: "[I] have made up my mind to do all I can to raise the present condition of craftsman potters from a 'studio' proposition to one of real dignity in
which they can follow the work [?] they enjoy and at the same time earn a
living. The big hitch seems to be in the cost of the shop and the lack of
training in shop methods, and the fact that the potters don't make things that
will sell, and these are the points I'm going after." Also his "Editorial, The
Art Division, 1928," *Bulletin of the American Ceramic Society* 7:3 (March
1928), 45–49.

71 **"in ceramics . . . Art for Art's Sake":** Curtis, "Ceramic Art," 42: The
"question of 'making it pay' is almost an integral part of the work. Ceramic
art does not lend itself to 'art for art's sake.' The artist's tools are expensive to
operate and to attain perfection he must be using them."

71 **Curtis letter, "I'm so glad . . .":** Curtis to GWA, December 8 and 20,
1925.

71 **boardinghouse:** The boardinghouse, at 206 Bloomingdale Avenue, has been obliterated by condominiums. The Conestoga Pottery, at Lancaster Avenue and Sugartown Avenue, has disappeared.

71 **"Mystery Man":** Frank Baisden to Lewis I. Sharp, Jr., The Henry Phipps Psychiatric Clinic, May 6, 1937 (WIA/Phipps): "At the Academy Walter was often called 'the mystery-man' in fun, because of his extremely taciturn nature. This seems to be a characteristic of the family. I was struck, upon my last visit to Ocean Springs [December 1936], by the fact that this taciturnity had not mitigated in the slightest."

72 **Correspondence between PA and parents:** AMcCA to PA, January 19 and 28, February 3, March 12, 1926; GWA to PA, February 6 and 17, March 2 and 11, 1926.

73 **Mrs. French:** probably Myrtle M. French (1886–1973), a graduate of Alfred and a teacher in the Alfred Summer School.

74 **PA plans to set up his own shop:** See Curtis, "The Small Shop," 17–21.

77 **He left here:** WIA to GWA and AMcCA, undated.

Growing Weather

78 **"Here, we learn":** "Ocean Springs to be Art Center of Coast," *JXCOT,* April 24, 1926, 1.

79 **Arts Colony at Fairhaven:** Quotation from "Art Colony Established at Ocean Springs," *JXCOT,* May 29, 1926, 3; and from an unidentified clipping with several photographs (from the Sunday *Times-Picayune?*) in the Shearwater archives: "Not All Work at Gulf Coast's New Art Colony." For additional information, see "Art Colony Has Interesting Exhibit," *JXCOT,* August 7, 1926, 4, and Historic New Orleans Collection, Williams Research Center, Arts and Crafts Club Scrapbook 2 (1926–1930), Mss. 247, folder 441.

81 **"sort of poetry":** "The Shearwater Legacy," *Mississippi. A View of the Magnolia State,* May/June 1984, 19.

81 **Beach clay:** PA, interview with Nancy Sweezy, November 15, 1982. By Spring 1928, he had ceased using it. GWA to C. Laybies, May 11, 1928: "The brown piece presents difficulties. That particular brown was produced by using our beach clay, which is saturated with salt, with a colorless glaze, and we have given up using it owing to the presence of the salt."

82 **account of sales:** GWA, "Profit & Loss A/C (1926/1927)," June 30, 1927; GWA to the Bradstreet Co., Mobile, June 23, 1928; and GWA to R. G. Dun and Company, Mobile, July 1, 1929. In 1929, GWA and Annette had "advanced about $10,000 for buildings, equipment, etc.," and had "a stock of un-

sold pottery and pottery in course of manufacture worth $3,000 to $4,000 at a guess, with orders in course of execution of about $700 gross."

82 **"I am afraid Annette thinks":** GWA to Ellsworth Woodward, November 9, 1927. See also GWA to Woodward, October 26, 1927, comparing Shearwater's methods of bookkeeping with those of Newcomb.

83 **Atmosphere at Alfred:** AMcCA to PA, March 4, 1926.

83 **PA at Alfred:** "Record of Peter Anderson," Alfred University Summer School, July 5, 1927 (Alfred University Registrar), Art Librarian, shows that he enrolled in "Design and Pottery Production" (a beginners' course) and received a B.

83 **"The qualifications of a craftsman":** Carney, 13.

83 **"A piece of pottery . . . essentially a vessel":** Remarks by Charles F. Binns in "Introduction," program for "Exhibition of Contemporary American Ceramics, W. & J. Sloane," November 2 to 30, 1931.

83 **Letters with news of pottery:** GWA to PA, July 15, 1927; AMcCA to PA, July 18, 25, and 27, 1927, and letter from Brattleboro, Vermont, August 10, 1927.

84 **Exhibition Hall and Shearwater opening:** GWA to Charles Graham, November 20, 1927; and "Many Visit Shearwater Pottery at Opening," *JXCOT,* January 21, 1928, and follow-up article in the same newspaper, January 21, 1928; and GWA to C. Labouisse, February 2, 1928.

85 **"It is so lovely down here":** GWA to R. C. Jordan, General Agent, Export Grain, Illinois Central Railroad, February 8, 1928. Jordan, who had worked closely with GWA in the grain business, envies his freedom "from many of the problems and cares incidental to the merchandising of Grain: no question concerning the keeping qualities of your pottery, or whether it will meet the requirements of Federal Standards for #2 Mixed, #2 Yellow Corn, or #2 Hard Wheat." Letter of February 4, 1928. GWA persuaded Jordan to run an article in the railroad's magazine, reprinted in *JXCOT,* August 11, 1928, 1: "Shearwater Pottery is Coast Showplace."

85 **Change in local landscape:** On coastal development, see "New Bridges Have Opened Way to Coast," *JXCOT,* August 3, 1929, 1; "Ocean Springs on the Mississippi Gulf Coast," *JXCOT,* September 28, 1929 (on the seawall); "Millions Entering Coast Development," *JXCOT,* August 11, 1928, 1; and "The Coast Makes Wonderful Progress in Past Two Years," *JXCOT,* January 21, 1927, 1.

86 **"The men who come . . . regulation art shop":** GWA to R. C. Jordan, February 2, 1928. He adds: "My wife's idea is eventually to make our place a sort of Art centre. . . . There is so much art in the family that I want

the pottery to be self-supporting; hence my desire to make the place known."

86 **"Biloxi lighthouse"**: "I would like to make Shearwater Pottery as well known as the lighthouse at Biloxi. I am sure it is equally interesting." GWA to George P. Money, Editor, Biloxi *Daily Herald,* August 9, 1928.

86 **"At first I thought"**: GWA to R. C. Jordan, February 2, 1928.

86 **"like one big city"**: "Millions Entering Coast Development," *JXCOT,* August 11, 1928, 1.

87 **Lorimer:** "Editor of Noted Weekly Visits Coast," *JXCOT,* February 26, 1927, 1, and "Native Foliage and Trees on Coast," *JXCOT,* March 5, 1927, 1. On Pascagoula's epithet, see *Lewis the Pecan Man.*

87 **"It is a place for poets"**: "Ocean Springs on the Mississippi Gulf Coast," *JXCOT,* September 28, 1929.

87 **150 to 200 pieces per month:** GWA to Fannie W. Volck, May 2, 1928.

88 **WIA knights and AMcCA letters:** AMcCA to WIA, November 30, May 22, and 30, 1928.

88 **Labouisse:** I have quoted from Labouisse to GWA, October 7, 1927, and February 29, 1928; Labouisse to WIA, December 28, 1927; and Labouisse to PA, October 25, 1927. In her letter to Bob, she adds, "I think the angels are charming, and really like the crudity of your carving, as it is in the proper spirit."

90 **"We want to try"**: WIA to Catherine Labouisse, May 14, 1928.

90 **"Peter's modesty"**: GWA to Martha T. Gasque Westfeldt, July 2, 1928, in reply to her letter and enclosure of a few days earlier. On the commissioner of agriculture, GWA to J. C. Holton, October 19, 1928.

91 **"you would have produced"**: WIA to PA, July 21, 1927.

91 **Design of kiln by Cox and Rogers:** E. Woodward to GWA, February 25, 1928; H. W. (Harry) Rogers to GWA, February 25, 1928 (with drawings of PA), May 16, 1928, June 7, 1928, June 27, 1928, and November 12, 1928 (on exhaust fans); GWA to H. W. Rogers, May 17, 1928, May 19, 1928 (on the installation of a filter press), July 2, 1928, November 8, 1928, and November 17, 1928. GWA to Laclede-Christy Clay Products, February 11 and July 30, 1928. GWA to Interstate Electric Co., November 8, 17, and 25, 1928, and reply of November 13, 1928. GWA to National Blow Pipe and Manufacturing, November 17, 1928, with sketch by PA and reply of November 20, 1928.

91 **Paul E. Cox:** Letter to GWA offering to design the kiln and provide details on "sagger sizes, directions for making saggers, setting the kiln, burning the kiln, and many other things." Cox was director of the Department of Ce-

ramic Engineering at Iowa State College. See Poesch, 94–95, and Susan Russo, "Paul E. Cox," in Carney, 219–20. In an autobiographical note, JMcCA writes that—in 1931?—"Cox . . . came down and worked with Peter experimenting with glazes. He gave the Annex a clear glaze and introduced us to silicate of soda which cut down the amount of water used to prepare slip. It was possible to use the same mold twice in one day, if so desired. Very useful for mass production."

91   **"There was a retired bricklayer"**: PA interview with Nancy Sweezy, November 15, 1982. Measurements of the kiln are taken from the same interview, and from Sweezy, *Raised in Clay,* 255. It is a circular, steel-encased downdraft kiln whose interior measures six feet, nine inches in diameter, and six feet, ten inches from the bottom of fire well to the top of the dome. It has a sprung-arch doorway, which must be bricked up at each firing and taken down, ten to twelve hours later, when the kiln is unloaded. There are three burners in the brick fireboxes below the kiln with an impeller-type air blower. Number two diesel fuel is used, and gases and exhaust from the kiln run underground through a brick flue and rise into the outside air through a brick chimney.

92   **First firing of kiln:** GWA to R. Oliver, December 11, 1928, and to Catherine Labouisse, December 15, 1928.

92   **"cubistical blue cat"**: GWA to W. T. West, October 27, 1928, and to Virginia R. Eskrige, October 5 and 14, 1928.

92   **"Glory Road"**: *Magic Hour* ms.

93   **"making and breaking pottery"**: GWA, undated essay, "Shearwater Pottery," published by Marjorie Ashley in Rogers, 66.

Love and Glazes

I have quoted from the following in the correspondence between PA and PGA (which Marjorie Anderson Ashley kindly allowed me to copy): PA to PGA, September 20 and 24, 1929; October 1, 11, 21, and 23, 1929; November 4, 6, 8, 20, and 26, 1929; December 2, 5, 10, 11, 13, 20, 22, and 29, 1929; January 8, 15, 17, and 30, 1930; February 3, 5, 6, 15, 19, 20, and 21, 1930. Also PGA to PA, September 23, 1929; October 17, 18, and 22, 1929; November 15 and 22, 1929; undated, November 1929.

94   **"potbound"**: GWA to Edward A. Morgan, June 1, 1929.

95   **"You don't want to go there"**: Conversation with Patricia Findeisen. PGA gave a somewhat different account to Clarus Backes in 1969: "The first time mother and I came to Ocean Springs and saw the Shearwater Pottery

sign, everybody told us, 'Those people are nuts in there: don't go in there.' They were different from anything Ocean Springs had ever known—all artists." Backes, 29.

95   **"[He] walked toward me down a quiet road":** PGA, Journals, undated.

96   **"that I had had the habit . . . soul and heart to people":** PGA, Journals, undated.

96   **"You had with you . . . something very important to work for":** GWA to Marjorie Grinstead, July 17, 1929.

96   **"engaged to marry one of the nicest girls":** GWA to E. A. Morgan, July 17, 1929.

96   **"That'll be my present":** PGA, Journals, undated.

96   **"Peter's latest idea":** GWA to E. A. Morgan, July 17, 1929.

97   **An exhibition was planned:** "Shearwater Pottery Showroom Open Week of 12th to 17th," *JXCOT,* August 10, 1929, and correspondence of GWA on the exhibition.

97   **"This Pottery is a local enterprise":** GWA to PGA, August 6, 1929, addressed humorously to "Miss Patricia Grinstead, Editor, Pottery Notes, *The Oldfield Times,* Gautier."

97   **"deeply impressed":** William Wade Grinstead to GWA, July 26, 1929.

97   **"to make better and better individual pieces":** GWA to W. W. Grinstead, July 25, 1929, and GWA to PGA, January 31, 1930.

99   **"How should a father–in–law":** GWA to PGA, September 23, 1929.

100   **Annette wrote, too:** AMcCA to PGA, February 24, 1930.

100   **"And now you have come . . . Dear old Peter":** Letters of Adele (Daisy) Anderson to PGA, October 21, 1929, and February 18, 1930.

101   **Ellen Wassall:** On the drowning of J. W. Wassall, which occurred when Ellen (1896–1981) was thirteen or fourteen, see Chicago *Daily Tribune,* September 20, 1909, 1; on Thomas Chadbourne, his *Autobiography;* on the battle for custody, "Wassall Girl, Fate's Victim, Awaits Arrival of Mother," Chicago *Daily Tribune,* September 23, 2; "Wassall Girl Fights Mother," Chicago *Daily Tribune,* September 24, 1909, 3; and the letters of William and Marjorie Grinstead from Oldfields in September 1909 (archives of Marjorie Anderson Ashley).

103   **"help–wanted" ad:** GWA to PGA, November 21, 1929.

106   **silver blue and bronze:** Silver blue was developed "to take the place of turquoise blue," which had "a strong tendency to run when fired. [Bronze] is the newest glaze and is, we find, very satisfactory. In many pieces it has a bright bronzed appearance that is striking." GWA to C. Labouisse, April 27, 1929. Silver luster "lights up at night by electrics. Would make a wonderful glaze for lampbases." GWA to H. Lincoln, May 23, 1929.

107   **Front House:** In 1929, the Front House was only feet from the water. A decade later, Annette donated part of her waterfront acreage to the town, which dredged it to create Ocean Springs's "inner harbor." In return, she received the dredge spoils, which added two hundred feet to the Shearwater frontage.

107   **"The rooms are very well proportioned":** Adele (Daisy) Anderson to PGA, February 18, 1930.

110   **Soda spar from North Carolina:** Spruce Pine, North Carolina.

111   **"Can't you know, beloved Peter":** PGA to PA, November 17, 1929.

Mud and Paint

From the correspondence of WIA and AGA (Papers of Walter Anderson), I have quoted from the following letters: WIA to AGA: August 19, 20, and undated letter from August 1930; September 1, 5, 10, 11, 17, and undated letter from September 1930; October 15, 19, 22, 27, 29, and 31, 1930; November 2, 3, 6, 8, 11, 17, 19, 21, and 30, 1930; February 4, 1932. Also, AGA to WIA, August 19, November 3, and December 2, 1930; October 6, 11, 14, and 16, 1931.

114   **"Dear Bob: You must know":** AGA to WIA, August 19, 1930, "3:40 p.m. [on the train] Just out of Brewton [Alabama]."

115   **AGA on romance and dating:** *Magic Hour,* 3–4, and *Magic Hour* ms.

115   **"no one to compare with *any* Anderson":** PGA to PA, late October, 1929.

115   **"I have always been a great believer":** WIA to AGA, September 1930.

125   **Hearn on Saint Malo:** "St. Malo Story," *Harper's Weekly,* March 31, 1883.

126   **Sissy on Indians and buckeyes:** AGA/Gilley interview, May 8, 1990.

126   **WIA's driving:** *Magic Hour,* 11.

126   **Annette's poem on Graveline:** *Possums and Other Verse,* n.p.

129   **Peter's domestic happiness:** PGA to PA, undated letter, 1931.

129   **"considerable force and scorn":** *Magic Hour,* 5.

130   **"dug fossil oysters out of a sandstone cliff":** AGA to WIA, October 27, 1931.

130   **"my parents' stock solution":** *Magic Hour* ms.; cf. *Magic Hour,* 9.

Making Widgets

Quotations from the WIA-AGA correspondence are from the following letters. WIA to AGA: October 10, 16, 17, 23, 25, and 30, 1931; November 2, 3, 14, 19, and 27, 1931; December 17, 24, and 31, 1931; undated letters, November and December, 1931; January 11, 13, 14, 21, 24, 26, and 28, 1932; February 7, 14, 16, 18,

20, and 25, 1932. Also, AGA to WIA: November 2 and 7, 1931; and undated letter, Sewickley, 1931.

131 **family meeting:** PA to PGA, October 11, 1929.

132 **most perfect world:** PA to PGA, October 1, 1929.

132 **eggcups:** PA to PGA, October 27, 1929.

132 **"couchant cats . . . artistic bean pots":** GWA to Esther Cooley, March 18, 1929.

132 **Shipments to Marshall Field and Carson Pirie Scott:** GWA to J. C. Akeley, August 27, 1929, and September 2, 1929; J. C. Akeley to GWA, Evanston, August 23 and 28, 1929; GWA to Carson Pirie Scott, August 27, 1929; GWA to Marshall Field, August 27, 1929.

133 **JMcCA production:** Several ledgers showing inventories, contents of kiln firings, and "accounts owable" to the three brothers for 1928 through the 1930s are in the Shearwater archives.

133 **Pots came back:** "We regret to inform you that we are not interested in articles of this character just at present. It is quite true that these have an individuality, but we have so many things in our department that in a manner resemble them . . ." Marshall Field & Co. to GWA, Chicago, September 6, 1929.

133 **"As an ex-European Grain Exporter":** GWA to Carson Pirie Scott & Co., September 19, 1929.

133 **"when our pottery has reached . . . development":** GWA to Marshall Field & Co., September 19, 1929.

134 **"not the people we want to sell to":** PA to AGA, January 20, 1930.

134 **"direct from heaven":** E. deF. Curtis, "Ceramic Art and the Ceramic Artist," 44.

134 **blistering, and bubbling . . . identical pieces:** Letter to GWA, September 11, 1929, of R. A. Brede, Brede & Schroeter, Decorators and Furnishers; reply of September 16; and GWA to the Flint and Horner Co., New York, September 16, 1929.

134 **Lincoln Chair Company order:** GWA to H. Lincoln, President, June 5, 1929.

135 **"[Item numbers] 1906 and 1936":** GWA to the J. M. Strassel Company, Louisville, October 9, 1929.

135 **"What I really want":** GWA to J. C. Akeley, July 14, 1929.

136 **"in steady demand all through the bad business":** GWA to W. & J. Sloane Co., New York, September 24, 1931.

136 **Unemployed pottery workers, 1932:** Ross C. Purdy, "Report," *Bulletin of the American Ceramic Society* 12:3 (March 1933), 59.

136   On the history of American art pottery see: Paul Evans, *Art Pottery of the United States. An Encyclopedia of Producers and their Marks . . . ,* 2nd ed. (New York: Feingold and Lewis, 1987); Ralph and Terry Kovel, *American Art Pottery: The Collector's Guide to Makers, Marks, and Factory Histories* (New York: Crown, 1993); David Rago, *American Art Pottery* (New York: Knickerbocker Press, 1997); Paul Royka, *Fireworks: New England Art Pottery of the Arts & Crafts Movement* (Atglen, PA: Schiffer Publishing, 1997); Sharon S. Darling, *Teco: Art Pottery of the Prairie School* (Erie, PA: Erie Art Museum, 1989).

136   **"gasping for breath":** "Editorial, Report of General Secretary Ross C. Purdy," *Bulletin of the American Ceramic Society* 12:3 (March 1933), 60.

136   **"We shall never see the day again":** Eckardt V. Eskesen, "Editorials. Presidential Address . . . ," *Bulletin of the American Ceramic Society* 11:4 (April 1932), 77.

136   AGA reminisces about the Depression in AGA/Gilley interview, June 7, 1990.

137   **WIA and JMcCA "have gone in together":** PA to PGA, January 15, 1930.

137   **New kiln and showroom:** PA to PGA, January 3 and 27, 1930.

139   **Mr. Aspirin:** *Magic Hour,* 18.

139   **Sears wind-up toys:** See Doris Y. Wilkinson, "The Toy Menagerie: Early Images of Blacks in Toys, Games and Dolls," in *Images of Blacks in American Culture. A Reference Guide to Information Sources,* ed. Jessie Carney Smith (New York: Greenwood Press, 1988), 280.

140   **"Her head was neatly bandanned":** PGA, "The Unforgettable Character in My Life," undated, probably written for *Reader's Digest,* a description of Isabel Davis, "born a slave in about 1850," and her husband, John, who served the Grinsteads at Oldfields. There is another description in PGA, "To My Grandchildren," unpublished essay. See also AGA's description of the midwife who delivered PGA in AGA/Gilley interview, May 9, 1990.

142   *New York Times, Christian Science Monitor:* "Realism and Fantasy in Pottery Today," *New York Times,* November 1, 1941, 14; Carl Greenleaf Beede, "Pottery of Today in America," *Christian Science Monitor,* November 21, 1931. See also "Contemporary American Ceramics," *American Magazine of Art* 23:5 (November 31), 432–33; "The Work of Contemporary American Artists," *Arts and Decoration,* November 1931, 30.

145   **Kaufman and Connelly:** *Beggar on Horseback,* 132–33.

146   **"brilliant blue, copper-splashed glaze":** At least one reviewer liked them better that way. "Some of the Negro figurines are superb. . . . The strong features, heavy grace, and feeling of dormant, savage life are even more pro-

nounced in this set done in brilliant blue, copper-splashed glaze, than in the ivory and colored figures. The colors add a gaiety and humor that obscure the force of the pieces, while the brilliant, deep glaze emphasizes their strength." "Andersons' Ceramic Exhibition on Display at Museum Here," Richmond *Times-Dispatch,* December 5, 1937.

146 **"Peter liked plain pottery":** AGA/Gilley interview, May 29, 1990.

149 **AGA memories of wedding day:** AGA, *Journals,* April 26, 1986.

Moths and Bees

151 **Methodist minister and watered shoot:** AGA, *Magic Hour* ms., 73–74.

154 **"He looked for everything" and story of Peter's bees:** PGA, "Bee Fever," unpublished manuscript.

154 **Story of moth-baiting:** AGA, *Magic Hour* ms.

156 **Florida trip:** AGA, *Magic Hour* ms. and WIA to AMcCA, undated ("Dear Mother: We are back as you have probably heard . . .").

156 **"float down the Mississippi . . . unmentionable camera":** AGA to WIA, January 2, 1932, and WIA to AGA, undated, December 1931.

156 **Canoe trip down Mississippi:** There is a journal of the trip, kept by AGA, covering May 25 to June 7. See also *Magic Hour,* 34–41, and AGA, Journals, July 22, 1988.

157 **quiet times . . . in the Cottage:** AGA/Gilley interview, June 7, 1990, on the early years of their marriage; *Magic Hour,* 14–20; and *Magic Hour* ms.

157 **"Looking out the back door":** *Magic Hour* ms.

159 **Murals in Ocean Springs Public School:** See *Magic Hour,* 19; AGA/Gilley interview, June 7, 1990; King, *Walls of Light,* 29–40; "Anderson Tiles, School Murals Attract Visitors," Mobile *Times,* Mobile, Alabama, July 7, 1934; Ruth Dyrud, "An Appreciation of the Tiles in the Local High School Auditorium, *JXCOT,* June 9, 1934; "Local Artists Highly Praised by Officials," *JXCOT,* June 9, 1934; letter of Melchor Rosenberg to AGA or AMcCA, July 8, 1934, complaining that an ugly curtain had been hung beside the murals.

160 **Jackson Post Office mural:** Letter of Lucile N. Henderson, Mississippi Baptist Hospital, Jackson, to Olin Dows, Chief, Treasury Relief Art Project, September 15, 1935, Archives of American Art. Henderson's favorite, at the time, was obviously Marie Hull: "Undoubtedly the most outstanding artist in all types of painting in the state. She has won many prizes of great value, and is represented in most of the larger museums in the U.S. She did not compete in the Mural contest because her husband was the architect and was on the committee to select the winning design for the Post Office. I can recommend

her most highly. You have only to look at the other Government work which she did under the project which was directed by Mr. Ellsworth Woodward, of New Orleans." In *Art in Mississippi* (pp. 189–90), Patti Carr Black chronicles WIA's efforts in 1938 to win the commission. WIA submitted "five different versions" of a design, but, the mural was entrusted to a Russian artist, Simnka Simkhovitch, of Connecticut, who had never visited the state.

161 **"There was only so much time . . . no good at all":** *Magic Hour* ms.

161 **Painting seemed out of the question:** AGA/Gilley interview on mental illness, 1990.

161 **"It was a terrific step that I took":** AGA/Gilley interview, June 7, 1990.

162 **AGA begins epic poem:** *Magic Hour* ms.

162 **little theater group:** AGA/Gilley interview, June 7, 1990; and *JXCOT,* October 20 and November 10, 1934. The group was called the Little Theatre Guild.

162 **Bob's desire to have Sissy depend on him:** WIA to AGA, March 17, 1932: "You must know how much I want to give [my protection] to you. It's curious how much I want you to be dependent on me. The truth is, I suppose, that I want to own you, have absolute possession of you. That sounds alarming, doesn't it?"

162 **"get something from me without having to put it in first":** AGA *Journals,* June 7, 1938.

163 **"creative act was the giving of oneself":** *Magic Hour,* 40.

163 **"never really forgave him":** *Magic Hour,* 52.

163 **WIA's observation of pelicans:** *Magic Hour,* 21–22.

163 **"There comes a time":** From an undated essay, WIA Papers; probably 1950s.

163 **Importance of pelicans to WIA:** Mary Anderson, "The Birds of Walter Anderson," xvi.

164 **No danger in WIA's work:** *Magic Hour* ms.

164 **" . . . little flare-ups, small explosions":** *Magic Hour,* 41.

164 **Bob breaks phonograph records:** *Magic Hour,* 41–45.

164 **"It was not just the fact that he was [Annette's] favorite":** *Magic Hour* ms.

"Trembling, On the Edge of Light . . ."

166 **Iris-hunting trip:** *Magic Hour,* 50–54.

167 **Walter's "book" on putting:** Several versions of the manuscript, one with the title "Diary of a Dub," are among his papers in the Shearwater archives.

See also his letters of May 18, 1935, and March 3, 1936, to the writer Quentin Reynolds, whom he tries to interest in the book, which "would cater to a very large reading public." Plans for publication and appointment of a literary executor were recounted by a "friend of the family" to WIA's doctors at Phipps. WIA/Phipps.

167   **WIA's reaction to father's death:** *Magic Hour,* 54–55; *Magic Hour* ms.

167   **Behavior during breakdown:** Alexander H. Leighton to Adolf Meyer, Baltimore, November 10, 1937, Meyer Papers. AGA to Adolf Meyer, April 2, 1937, WIA/Phipps. The "passing car" incident may be the one AGA describes in *Magic Hour,* 56–58.

168   **"homosexual" experience:** *Magic Hour* ms. WIA told his doctors that he suffered from three months of depression after this incident (Phipps Clinic card). He heard Orage in Trenton on January 21, 1927, and a few days later in New York (WIA to AMcCA, January 24, 1927).

168   **Edwards A. Park:** Park gave WIA *Chapman's Color Key to North American Birds* (Mary Anderson Pickard, "The Birds of Walter Anderson", xi; cf. Rubin, 82, "Natural Forms," and *Magic Hour* ms.

169   **"growing shadow of the psyche":** Henry Mead to Adolf Meyer, November 13, 1936, Meyer Papers.

169   **Lidz on Meyer:** Theodore Lidz, M.D., "Adolf Meyer and the Development of American Psychiatry," *American Journal of Psychiatry* 123:3 (September 1966), 320–32.

169   **"exceedingly interesting":** Adolf Meyer to Harry M. Murdock, the Sheppard and Enoch Pratt Hospital, May 27, 1939, Meyer Papers.

169   **Meyer's diagnosis.** WIA's son, John G. Anderson, writes that his father's "prolific artistic output and the age at which he first experienced serious mental problems mitigate strongly against a diagnosis of classical schizophrenia. These elements among others strongly indicate a probable bipolar disorder (manic-depressive illness), with occasional schizophrenaform episodes." On manic-depressive disorder in artists and writers, see Kay Redfield Jamison, *Touched With Fire: Manic Depressive Illness and the Artistic Temperament* (New York: Free Press, 1996).

170   **"stop the workings of his mind":** AGA, Journals, April 16, 1987.

170   **"Sweet as the morn . . .":** AGA, Journals, December 5, 1937, three days before Mary's birth.

171   **"I felt as if my whole self":** *Magic Hour* ms.

171   **"little dream of beauty":** AGA, Journals, December 10, 1937.

171   **"It's been a sort of interlude":** AGA, Journals, December 1937 (date illegible) and January 9, 1938.

172   **Metrazol treatments:** See: Max Fink, M.D., "Meduna and the Origins of Convulsive Therapy," *American Journal of Psychiatry* 141:9 (September 1984), 1034–1041; L. de Meduna, "New Methods of Medical Treatment of Schizophrenia," *Archives of Neurology and Psychiatry,* vol. 54 (1938), 361–63; L. von Meduna, "The Significance of the Convulsive Reaction During the Insulin and the Cardiazol Therapy of Schizophrenia," *Journal of Nervous and Mental Disease* 87:2 (February 1938), 133–77; Meduna, "General Discussion of the Cardiazol Therapy," *American Journal of Psychiatry* 94: supplement (May 1938), 40–50; Hans H. Reese et al., "The Effect of Induced Metrazol Convulsions on Schizophrenic Patients," *Journal of Nervous and Mental Disease* 87:3 (May 1938), 571–83. Estimates of percentage of patients treated with Metrazol who "recovered or markedly improved" ranged from 32 to 70 percent between 1938 and 1944; Garfield Tommey, "Therapeutic Fashions in Psychiatry," *American Journal of Psychiatry* 124:6 (December 1967), 99.

172   **"You can throw anybody":** Meyer comment in "Monday clinic, May 23, 1938," WIA/Phipps.

172   **"Since the attack begins" and "[Schizophrenia] represents":** Meduna, "Discussion of the Cardiazol Therapy," 46, 50. For a more detailed account of the convulsions, see Reese et al., 572.

173   **"an explosive which makes a breach":** F. Humbert and A. Friedemann, "Critique and Indications of Treatments in Schizophrenia," *American Journal of Psychiatry* 94 (May 1938), 183.

173   **"They want to use," "wept like an idiot," "with the best possible spirit," "just as energetic":** AGA, Journals, December 21 and 29, 1937, January 4, 1938, February 2, 1938.

174   **Ellen in love:** *Magic Hour* ms. Mead and his first wife were divorced on June 29, 1939, and he married Ellen less than a week later in New York (Henry C. A. Mead to Meyer, July 6, 1939, Meyer Papers).

174   **Story of Delphine M. McConnell ("Dellie"):** Clinical summary, including diagnosis ("morbid sexual tendency") and symptoms ("laughed and cried without reason"), provided to Phipps by AMcCA and by Friends Hospital in 1937 or 1938 (WIA/Phipps); AMcCA, "Family History," manuscript, January 25, 1954; "Copy of Dr. J[ohn] B. Elliott Opinion" (copy of a letter of May 28, 1891 to James McConnell, McConnell Papers, 156–2–9); unsigned contract between James McConnell and Friends' Asylum for the Insane, 1903, in the same archive; AMcCA to Richard McConnell, May 3, s.a., McConnell Papers (on rumors about Annette's mother); and AGA, Journals, undated (April 1986?), where AGA gives a different version of the story, alleging that Judge McConnell confined Dellie to her room for several months. For a ficti-

tious account (based on conversations with Sissy), see "Marie Tells How Her Sister Was Put Away," in Kathryn Kendall, *Woman Talk,* New Orleans, privately printed, 1976, with illustrations by Leif Anderson and Patricia Findeisen. Sissy remarks that Dellie had "a very large growth on her neck. She had a set of steel knitting needles with which she knitted socks, and developed the habit of sticking them into the growth, puncturing it to make it go down like a balloon" *(Magic Hour* ms.).

176 **"He is improving rapidly":** James McConnell to his son, East Gloucester, Massachusetts, September 6, 1898, McConnell Papers, 156–3–5.

177 **Walter's mother, heredity:** *Magic Hour* ms., 98–99. Walter's mother was Adele Briggs, born in New Orleans.

177 **"crusade against injustice":** Remarks by Annette reported by Pat to Dr. Maurice Aubrey Partridge in PA/Phipps, "Past History," undated, 1938.

177 **"She was living in Bay St. Louis":** AGA, Journals, undated (April 1986?).

177 **burial markers:** Letter of Mary Anderson Pickard to authors, November 1999.

178 **"Each night, when I come up," "almost pretend that," "depressive panic," "count with joy the blessings," "The present can be":** AGA, Journals, April 26, 1938, March 27, 1938, March 13, 1938, June 26, 1938, and WIA/Phipps, "Monday Clinic," May 23, 1938.

178 **Sissy's interest in forms and glazes:** AGA, Journals, January 20, 21, and June 17, 1938.

179 *Christian Science Monitor:* "Southern Art Shaped by the Hand of the Potter," August 4, 1937.

179 **"Somehow I couldn't," "simple, sturdy tea and beverage sets," exhibitions:** see "Roadside Sign Inspires Colt to Arrange Pottery Exhibit," Richmond *Times-Dispatch,* September 4, 1937, and "Anderson Pottery on Display in New York Gallery," *JXCOT,* November 9, 1940, 3.

179 **"pretty poor," "There is no money":** AGA, Journals, January 17, 22, 1938.

180 **"farther and farther away," "wonderful old Pat," "I feel lonely," "like an old road":** AGA, Journals, April 15 and February 17, January 26, March 10, 1938.

180 **"Love me, and lift me up," "Here I sit":** AGA, Journals, April 1, 1938, and May 15, 1938.

181 **"Why can't I just enjoy," "placid like a cow," "Something is sort of hibernating":** AGA, Journals, March 6, February 11, February 8, 1938.

181 **"sales appeal . . . a bit too elaborate":** James Matchal (?), Design Publishing Company to JMcCA, Columbus, Ohio, October 7, 1937.

4

Notes

4

182 **Mac's rammed-earth house:** From an autobiographical essay, in his own hand, undated, archives of Sara L. Anderson. See also Virginia T. Lee, "The Column," August 7 and September 11, 1937, 4.

183 **Article on rammed-earth house:** Jacqueline Anderson, "Gumption Story #6: This $1,020 Home Took 'Git Up and Go,'" *American Home,* May 1941, 42–43.

183 **box of hankies, cradle, handbag, hooked rugs:** AGA, Journals, April 12, 1938; March 13, July 6, and 27, 1938.

184 **"It mentioned the various pieces," "I'm also glad to learn":** WIA to AGA, March 30 and April 7, 1938. The gallery he refers to was the Walters Art Gallery.

184 **"and he sang in a quartet," "straightening itself out":** AGA, Journals, August 7, 1938.

184 **"She was Russian":** *Magic Hour* ms.

185 **"I love you":** AGA, Journals, August 19, 1938.

185 **"a desire to spend," "I am the wand, the willow wand":** AGA, Journals, July 30, 1938.

Homecoming

186 **He spoke with great ease:** Notation by Meyer, September 30, 1938, Meyer Papers.

186–87 **Bob's train ride home and Peter's reaction:** AMcCA to Meyer, September 28, 1938, Meyer Papers and PA/Phipps, report by M. Partridge, undated.

187 **"Yellow butterflies," "Blank pages," "It's funny how the world":** AGA, Journals, October 6 and 4, 1938.

188 **"We have been home two weeks":** AGA to Meyer, October 17, 1938, Meyer Papers.

190 **"I fully understand the real difficulty":** Meyer to AGA, October 22, 1938, Meyer Papers.

191 **"Your confirmation of my own feeling":** AGA to Meyer, November 21, 1938, Meyer Papers.

193 **"with all continuity severed," new phase:** AGA, Journals, November 1, 1938.

193 **Peter's extramarital affair, guilt and paranoia:** Phipps Clinic card.

193 **"Peter is down in the depths," "Yes, it has happened":** AGA, Journals, November 23 and 27, 1938.

194 **"a little jealous," "as full of courage":** AGA, Journals, December 11, 1938, January 2, 1939.

194 **"The room I have":** PA to AMcCA, December 8, 1938, PA/Phipps.

195 **"We all miss you terribly":** AGA to PA, January 9, 1939, PA/Phipps. On Henry, see also AMcCA to PA, January 20, 1929, PA/Phipps.

195 **Henry Weyerstall** (1913–1987) had been living in Ocean Springs since 1929, according to Ray L. Bellande. After leaving Shearwater, he purchased a wheel and began throwing his own pieces (letter to C. Maurer, February 2, 2000).

195 **"considerable impulsiveness":** Meyer to AGA, January 28, 1939, Meyer Papers.

196 **PA's fear of punishment:** PA, Phipps Clinic card.

196 **"I can't look about the place":** PGA to Lidz, PA/Phipps.

198 **"I'm going to heaven," "Don't worry":** PGA to M. Partridge, January 12, 1939.

198 **WIA's Christmas gifts:** AGA to Meyer, January 24, 1939, December 24, 1938.

198 **Shearwater poster:** AGA's copy of the poster is preserved in the Meyer papers. See also AGA, Journals, January 24, 1939.

199 **"There is no doubt":** Meyer to AGA, January 28, 1939. Despite family problems, Shearwater held an open house for the pageant. See "Ocean Springs Welcomes Pageant Visitors," *JXCOT,* March 30, 1940, 1.

199 **WIA's strange behavior, "He came in in about ten minutes," "I do not know how much longer":** AGA to Meyer, February 5, 1939.

200 **"Jackie has gone back":** AGA, Journals, March 26, 1939.

200 **Opinion of Andersons in Ocean Springs:** Report of Henry Mead, May 23, 1938, WIA/Phipps. His informant was Ellen Wassall; and summary of Dr. Partridge, PA/Phipps, undated.

201 **"You should have seen your great grandmother":** PGA, "To My Grandchildren," unpublished manuscript.

201 **ranch:** Elkhorn Ranch (Ennis, Montana) to AGA, November 29, 1939, and Spring Lake Ranch (Cuttingsville, Vermont) to AGA, November 27, 1939.

201 **"present obsessive behavior":** Meyer to AGA, February 11, 1939.

201– **"One day . . . carved cedar bird," "clinic for poor wives":** AGA to
202 Meyer, February 14, 1939.

202 **"definitely not normal":** PGA to M. Partridge, January 12, 1939.

202– **WIA's admission to Whitfield, "Which of you is God?," "very beauti-**
203 **ful place," "stack of drawings":** AGA and PGA to Meyer, February 27, 1939.

204– **AGA on babies and child-rearing, WIA on having children, Pat's**
205 **comment:** AGA, Journals, March 6, March 13, May 7, 1939; *Magic Hour,* 13, 17; PA/Phipps.

205 **"I should have lived one hundred years ago":** AGA, Journals, January 18, 1939.

205 **Pat's love for PA:** PGA to M. Partridge, February 17 and March 29, 1939, PA/Phipps.

206 **"You can tie me up":** AMcCA to Adolf Meyer, May 18, 1939, Meyer Papers.

206 **"almost ready to go out":** AMcCA to Adolf Meyer, May 1, 1939, Meyer Papers.

206 **WIA activities at Sheppard Pratt:** AMcCA to Meyer, May 10, 1939, Meyer Papers, and abstract of Sheppard Pratt records on WIA, sent to Henry M. Fox, at Phipps, on June 16, 1939.

207 **"From something [your son Peter]":** Meyer to AMcCA, May 16, 1939, Meyer Papers.

207 **"About Peter, it is incredible" and WIA drawings:** AMcCA to Meyer, May 18 and June 19, 1939, Meyer Papers.

207 **WIA escape from Sheppard Pratt:** Date deduced from PA/Phipps and WIA/Phipps. For AGA's version of the escape, *Magic Hour,* 68.

208 **"It is evident":** Notation in PA/Phipps, August 8, 1939.

208 **PA's return to Shearwater:** PGA to Theodore Lidz, August 20, 22, September 4, 22, 1939; PGA to Meyer, September 1, 1939, PA/Phipps.

210 **WIA arrival in Ocean Springs and return to Whitfield:** AGA, Journals, October 7, 1939; PGA to Lidz, October 1939, PA/Phipps.

210 **"prowled the grounds":** PGA to Lidz, October 7, 1939.

210 **"His greatest luck":** PGA to Meyer, November 21, 1939, Meyer Papers.

211 **WIA escapes from Whitfield and AGA's visit:** AGA, Journals, December 10, 14, 1939, February 8, 1940; PGA to Lidz, December, 1939.

211 **"different person," "renewed person," WIA activities at Shearwater:** AGA, Journals, February 27, 1940, April 24, 1940, and PGA to Lidz, May 7, 1940.

212 **WIA and Marjorie:** PGA to Theodore Lidz, July 22, 1940, PA/Phipps.

213 **AGA considers divorce:** AGA, Journals, June 29, 1940. Sissy explained to Joan Gilley in one of her 1990 interviews ("Mental Illness"): "At that time . . . you couldn't get a divorce in this state based on a partner's mental illness. It was impossible. . . . I went to a lawyer. He said no, no. Actually, I didn't really want one."

213 **AGA trip to Winnetka:** *Magic Hour,* 76, and PGA to Lidz, July 22, 1940: "Sissy has at last gone away worn out after six months with Bob. . . . He stays pretty much the same: working hard, doing wonderful things and being just as 'crazy' as is possible."

213 **"We've always, even in the best days":** AGA to WIA, undated.

214 **"tenderness," "consideration," stay with Dusti Bonge, and plans for Oldfields:** AGA, Journals, October 29, November 5, 30, December 15, 1940.

Oldfields

215 **Trip to Oldfields:** AGA, Journals, January 26 and 27, 1941. In *Magic Hour,* 83, Sissy writes: "The Oldfields years, as I think of them now, stretched from 1940 to 1948."

216 **"feeling of continuity," sense of past:** AGA/Gilley interview, June 7, 1990.

216 On Marjorie Hellmuth's boardinghouse in Ocean Springs and on her first marriage, see Ray L. Bellande, "Parker Earle (1831–1917)," in three parts, Ocean Springs *Register,* October 14, 21, 28, 1993, pp. 17, 17, and 22, respectively.

216 **"woods and orchards":** Mary Anderson Pickard, unpublished essay on Oldfields.

216 **"as satisfactory an income":** William Wade Grinstead, autobiographical account in *Harvard Class of 1887. Fiftieth Anniversary Report.* Cambridge, 1937, 194–95.

217 **Billie Grinstead nostalgia for Coast:** Letter to PGA, April 27, 1930.

217 **Mead reports on WIA:** Henry C. A. Mead to Paul Lenkau, April 21, 1941, WIA/Phipps.

218 **impression that Bob "was a new creature":** *Magic Hour,* 90.

218 **"I had never seen the sea":** Mary Anderson, "Introduction" to *A Symphony of Animals,* xv.

218 **"the alienated must seek forever":** *Magic Hour,* 84.

218 **Rediscovery of Fairy Land:** AGA, Journals, July 16, 1985.

219 **WIA illustrations and translation:** See Sugg, ed., *Walter Anderson's Illustrations.* The history of art was an early volume of Josep Pijoan's *Summa Artis: Historia general del arte,* 1931 ff. He had begun working on it in September 1940, when Sissy was in Winnetka. "I translated . . . with difficulty; most of it was about the pyramids and there were a good many technical terms such as crowbars, machinery, teodolytes, etc. The Wells dictionary helped me a lot."

219 **block prints:** *Magic Hour,* 116–17. Sissy dates them in 1945. On WIA's artwork at Oldfields, *Magic Hour,* 87–88.

219 **"We rather revel in candles":** AGA, Journals, October 3, 1944.

219 **AGA stories for children:** Letter of Mary Anderson Pickard to authors, November 1999.

221 **Nervous breakdown of William W. Grinstead:** WIA/Phipps Clinic card: "[19]29: blamed self for nervous brk of prospective fa-law."

221   **"had reached a time in his life":** AGA, *Magic Hour* ms.

221   **"Family Circle":** Unpublished short story, © Mary Anderson Pickard.

230   **Puppet plays, tepee:** An undated entry for June 1943 in AGA, Journals— "Bob is rigging up a puppet theater in the attic"—is followed by an undated outline by Sissy of a puppet play ("The sun rises on one of the murky days of first creation . . ."). "The cast of characters includes a creeper on a damp tree trunk, a frog, a falling leaf-moth, a fern frond, and a lizard." See also AGA, *Magic Hour,* 85–86, 103.

231   **WIA takes Leif swimming:** AGA to Leif Anderson, May 19, 1974.

231   **Sale of timber:** AGA, Journals, January 29, 1941.

231   **"My father recorded":** Mary Anderson, unpublished.

232   **figurines done around 1941 or 1942:** On December 21, 1941, *The Dixie Gulf Coast Guide* reports that at Shearwater "a set of figurines portraying life along the Gulf is now in preparation. There will be trawlers, oystermen, shrimpers, all with their proper gear. An exhibition is to be held in the Spring. Visitors are delighted at a plantation group of figurines, including a green china cabin, the top or roof of which comes off, and a chinaberry tree. The last two items were made as props but there has been a call for duplicates. Two brand new Jean Lafitte pirates, very bad and bold, had just come from the kiln, not yet seen by the public."

232   **one of the world's worst mold-makers:** Backes, "Artist in the Eye of a Hurricane," 30.

233   **"I spent the day painting little figures":** WIA, undated unpublished manuscript, WIA Papers.

233   **Building and firing of kiln:** AGA, Journals, February 6–12, probably 1942.

234   **"I do not know just how terrible":** AGA, *Magic Hour* ms.

234   **garden:** AGA, Journals, May 18, 1943.

236   **"bearing horrible burdens," "Why are you so cross?":** *Magic Hour,* 107.

236   **Sissy's writing and daily activities:** AGA, Journals, May 25, 1943, January 29, 1944, October 2, 1944.

236   **I'm not coming back, ever!":** AGA, *Magic Hour,* 118. Until Sissy moved out, Bob lived in Ocean Springs but continued to visit her.

236   **"The puppets hung wearily":** AGA, *Magic Hour* ms.

Tender Miracles

This chapter is based principally on the journals of AMcCA, a series of copybooks and loose pages, kept unsystematically and often undated. Annette sometimes used any copybook she found at hand, and some contain nonsequential entries from as many as three different years. In many cases, I have had to guess at the year from the contents. There are journals and fragments from 1943–1947, 1949–1951, and 1953–1959. In the notes that follow, I have documented separately only the fragments whose date seems especially important.

238 **"to grow into the person"**: AMcCA, Journals, June 28, 1946.

239 **"I always take the other side"**: Manuscript poem, AMcCA.

240 **"the lesson I should have learned"**: "Good Taste," unfinished essay, undated. Perhaps around 1957. On gifts given her during her childhood, see the many drafts of "On Collecting."

240 **Disagreements between PGA and AMcCA:** AGA/Gilley interview, May 29, 1990.

240 **Differences over pricing:** PGA, fragment of a letter, probably July 1940, for WIA had just done "some beautiful black and white decorated pots."

241 **Prayer:** AMcCA, manuscript fragment, perhaps April 1951, beginning "The most interesting subject in the world, I think, is prayer. . . ."

242 **"Last night Billy and then Mary"**: AMcCA, Journals, July 17, 1947.

242 **"Sometimes my grandmother"**: Leif Anderson, *Lifedance,* unpublished memoirs.

243 **WIA's teaching in Gulfport, Brownie Scouts:** AMcCA, Journals, June 5 and 11 and July 3, 1947.

243 **"Last night went down to Bob's"**: AMcCA, Journals, January 25, 1950.

244 **PA's desire to experiment:** AMcCA, Journals, undated, perhaps Fall 1955.

244 **"straightener"**: A "straightener," Mac explained, is the worker who uses heat and water to straighten plates that buckle when they are welded. Jeanne Lebow, "In Praise of James McConnell 'Mac' Anderson," Ocean Springs *Register,* April 9, 1998.

245 **Juan José Calandria:** There are a number of clippings about this little-known painter in the Historic New Orleans Collection scrapbooks on the Arts and Crafts Club.

245 **"Always she is pleasant"**: AMcCA, Journals, undated entry. 1942?

246 **JMcCA marriage to Sara Lemon:** "Anderson-Lemon," *JXCOT,* April 13, 1946, 4; clipping courtesy of Ray L. Bellande.

246 **JMcCA's activities at Annex:** JMcCA, autobiographical account.

246 **Shearwater expansion:** *JXCOT,* September 24, October 1, 3, November 19, December 3, 10, 24, 1948; January 28, 1949. I am indebted to Ray L. Bellande for sending me these articles.

247 **"a sort of magnet," "wonderful smile"**: AGA, Journals, undated, 1980s.

247 **"I was twenty-four years old"**: Pete Seeger to C. Maurer, April 7, 1999. Annette's journal entry on Seeger appears to be from June 1943.

248 **"a great appetite for ideas"**: AMcCA, Journals, February 1, 1946.

248 **"Mère preferred the goats"**: Mary Anderson, "A Personal View."

248 **"On Sunday I was alone with the Showroom"**: AMcCA, Journals, April 17, 1946.

249 **"Yesterday a young couple"**: AMcCA, Journals, June 12, 1946.

249 **"long summer mornings"**: Mary Anderson, "A Personal View."

250 **"This morning after precautions"**: AMcCA, Journals, August 24, 1947? and undated manuscript fragment (on frog).

251 **Memories of Bouligny:** There is a typed manuscript, "Bouligny," in AMcCA's papers and many autograph notes and drafts, variously titled: "750 Words," "750 Words a day, My Mother," "Bouligny," etc. These were probably written ca. 1955.

251 **Poem: "My mind is just a path":** "Me. In a Mood Periodic in the Country," *Possums and Other Verse.*

Fortune's Favorite Child

255 **Ceramics in Metropolitan Museum:** WIA, undated log from a trip to New York.

255 **WIA comments on water and nullahs:** Undated logbooks. See also *Magic Hour,* 94–95.

256 **Trip to China:** *Magic Hour,* 132–35.

256 **"I hope that you will be able":** WIA to UNA Johnson, December 27, 1948, in Rubin, "Natural Forms," 136 (who provides an excellent history of the exhibition), and "Printed Scroll Exhibit of Fairy Tales Shown," Ridgewood *Times,* May 27, 1949.

256 **"A genius is amongst us":** "Commercial Appeal Praises Work of Local Artist," *Gulf Coast Times,* September 22, 1950; reprint of original article in the Memphis *Commercial Appeal,* September 17, 1950.

257 **"Walter Anderson couldn't find half of the blocks":** Dorothea Ward to Lura Beam, November 8, 1950, in Rubin, "Natural Forms," 148–49.

257 **"infinitely seductive" woman:** AGA, Journals, undated, 1986.

257 **umbrella for a sail:** A friend recalls that from Oldfields, WIA would sometimes "hop into his leaky little banana boat, hoist an umbrella for a sail and catch a fair wind all the way to Ocean Springs." Mary Brister, "Walter Anderson and Family: A Group of Rare Individuals," *Clarion-Ledger Jackson Daily News,* Jackson, July 30, 1967, D2, quoted in Rubin, "Natural Forms," 96.

257 **"at least five methods of propulsion":** HIL, July 1959, 137.

257 **"he wished to approach nature":** Redding Sugg in *HIL,* 20.

257   **"The band of his old felt hat"**: Mary Anderson, *The Voluptuous Return,* 143.

258   **man "can smell and touch and hear"**: *HIL.*

258   **"A bleak dawn"**: *HIL,* 163.

258   **"no longer a spectator"**: Sugg in *HIL,* 173.

259   **"I saw a wonderful thick flock"**: *HIL,* 135.

259   **"observed and appreciated"**: Rubin, "Natural Forms," 127, quotes from a note by WIA: "To regard nature not as something striving to improve or to become but as something which has become and needs only to be observed and appreciated."

259   **"I looked up into a dead pine," "a single image," "an incidental thing," Nature loves surprise, "Man begins by saying"**: *HIL,* 139; Mary Anderson, *The Voluptuous Return; HIL,* 143, 126, 82.

260   **"Why do I write this?"**: *HIL,* 156.

261   **Leif on the "islander within"**: Leif Anderson, unpublished memoirs. Cf. AGA/Gilley interview, May 31, 1990: "He took her [Leif] over. He had never been present before when a baby was born and when it was tiny. . . . She spent her whole first two or three years with him. He taught her to dance. . . . That was his baby. Everybody knew it. Everybody could see it."

261   **"world of man," "sordid thing"**: *HIL,* 145, 151.

262   **WIA's "housewarming"**: *HIL,* 187.

262   **"He tried. He really tried"**: Backes, 30.

263   **Comments of John Anderson and quote from WIA ("All movement . . .")**: Interview, October 1997.

264   **Northrop visit to mural**: Guy Northrop, Jr., "Town Gets Big Mural for $1 From Gifted Anderson Brush," Memphis *Commercial Appeal,* June 24, 1951, V 10. On the murals, see also King, *Walls of Light,* and *Magic Hour,* 136. Sissy told her son Johnny that she thought Bob was speaking "largely tongue-in-cheek" (conversation with John Anderson, September 1999).

265   **"healthful, wholesome"**: King, 51.

265   **"every time we decorated"**: Diane Stevenson, unpublished manuscript.

266   **"The artist lives"**: Burton, 43.

266   **"spurn the offer"**: PGA, untitled poem, 1958: "Bob came in today./Peter saw him coming in his rotten boat./He rowed and rowed./He spurned our offer of a tow."

266   **"Never has there been a hurricane," "A large coast guard boat"**: *HIL,* 231.

267   **Building of *Patricia***: PGA, undated journal entries.

268   **"Spray wets your face"**: Leif Anderson, *Lifedance,* unpublished memoirs.

269   **PGA description of river trips:** PGA to "Jean," June 18, 1957.

269   **PGA description of PA:** PGA, "My Most Unforgettable Character," unpublished ms.

271   **Mac's murals:** JMcCA, autobiographical manuscript. Also, "River Scene Preserved in Hospital Renovation," *Mississippi Press,* June 6, 1979, 5A. The hospital mural was restored in 1999 in a campaign organized in Ocean Springs by Ray L. Bellande and Tommy Wixon. It now hangs in the Jackson County Courts building. See "Art Restored," *Sun Herald,* Jackson County Section, 1, June 19, 1999.

"Goodbye, Old Lady"

273–   **Grandchildren and television; "Perhaps living or working out of**
74   **doors":** AMcCA, Journals, undated, probably 1955.

274   *Possums:* She may have first thought of publishing it in the summer of 1945. A letter from Thomas Sandon (?), of the Pascagoula *Chronicle-Star,* August 27, 1945, congratulates her on having captured the atmosphere of the Coast, and adds that he liked best "the images of the islands, the surf and birds, and the feeling of leaving New Orleans on a summer day."

274   **AMcCA's driving:** Ruth Redmann, "Mère Anderson, Grandeur of Old," in *Daily Biloxi Times-News,* February 3, 1964.

275   **"It was her duty":** Mary Anderson, "A Personal View."

276   **"Shearwater is more than hopeless":** PGA to Mrs. Frank W. Homan, November 10, 1955.

276   **Pat's comments on Peter at work:** PGA, essay, untitled and unpublished, "Today I stood and watched the potter at his wheel . . ."

276   **"It wasn't just the land that was old":** Diane Stevenson, unpublished manuscript.

278   **"Sometimes we would come home":** AGA/Gilley interview.

278   **"She forgot the thing":** Paraphrase of an undated poem by PGA, "A.McC.A., 1867–1964."

278   **"I waked at twelve, at two, at four":** "Catching the 6:20 Train," AMcCA, *Possums and Other Verse.*

279   **Bob's reaction to his mother's death:** *Magic Hour,* 144.

280   **"Come, come down to the pier":** *Magic Hour* ms.

280   **PGA reaction to death of AMcCA:** PGA, undated note.

281   **"I remember the minister who read":** AGA, Journals, undated.

281   **"The water had ceased to run":** AGA, manuscript fragment, prepared perhaps for the Walter Anderson Museum of Art. Cf. *Magic Hour,* 173.

281 **"I don't know why":** Pat McArthur, "The Memory and the Art Still Live," Mobile *Press,* undated clipping, Pascagoula Library Genealogy Collection.

282 **Cottage mural:** See Sugg, *A Painter's Psalm.*

Traces

283 **Horn Island lightkeeper:** The body of the lightkeeper was found seven miles away. See "Body of Charles Johnson Recovered," Pascagoula *Chronicle,* October 6, 1906.

284 **Strange flowers in yard:** AGA, interview with Betty Rodgers, August 1985, Pascagoula Public Library, G/MS OH O Oral.

284 **"Never have I seen more ravishing jewelry":** *HIL,* 232.

284 **Hurricane Camille:** PGA, "Camille Devastation, August 17, 1969," unpublished manuscript.

285 **"At first the strange silence":** PGA, "Camille Devastation."

287 **the *"real* potter":** Interview with James Anderson, October 2, 1997.

287 **seventies and early eighties:** See Nedra Harvey, "Fifty Years of Imaginative Pottery," *Down South,* 28:4 (July–August 1978), 3.

288 **AGA on *Patricia:*** AGA, Journals, March 1987.

288 **His glasses were missing a temple piece:** Tommy Wixon to C. Maurer, June 7, 1999.

289 **"the gentle patriarch":** Tom Jackson, "Shearwater Pottery," unpublished manuscript; courtesy of Nancy Sweezy.

289 **"He was so sprightly and energetic":** Nancy Sweezy to C. Maurer, October 3, 1997.

289 **Peter's final illness:** Interview with Marjorie Anderson Ashley, Summer 1999.

290 **"her heart contract":** Leif Anderson, *Lifedance,* unpublished memoirs.

291 **"It is almost exclusively Jimmy":** AGA, Journals, November 12, 1984.

291 **"he was brought home for visitation":** AGA, Journals, December 22, 1984.

291 **"balled roots and the careful hole":** From a poem in AGA, Journals, March 1988.

292 **"I seem to be living very hard":** AGA to Leif Anderson, October 16, 1982.

292 **"[The Barn] lives, too, because of something else":** AGA, undated, untitled typescript page.

292 **"But remember":** AGA, Journals, 1986?

292 **"In one little area, behind the Cottage":** AGA, Journals, September 2, 1985.

293   **"Do not look back":** AGA, Journals, August 21, 1988.

293   **"good to think of good people":** AGA, Journals, December 31, 1987.

293   **Discovery of Oldfields trunk:** "Trunk of Anderson Paintings Discovered," Ocean Springs *Record,* October 1, 1987, 1, and "Paintings Discovered in Box," New Orleans *Times-Picayune,* September 28, 1987.

293   **Installation of electric kiln:** Marjorie Ashley writes: "Mac's muffle kiln was never a very good kiln and in the late sixties we had very little underglaze ware coming from the Annex. In the seventies Margaret [Anderson] purchased a small used electric kiln which, with Michael and Adele's help, brought the Annex production back to life. That kiln died and at Michael's request in 1987 we purchased the large electric kiln that Jimmy is presently using. It proved too large for the Annex output, so a new small electric kiln was purchased for the Annex. Jim uses the large electric kiln for now and it will be his decision when and if he uses the large diesel kiln again." (Letter to the authors, November 11, 1998.)

294   **Eclipse poems by AGA, Leif Anderson:** 1982, papers of Leif Anderson.

296   **"Leif, my darling!":** AGA to Leif Anderson, November 1, 1982?

297   **women "strangely wonderful" as storytellers:** AGA, Journals, August 21, 1988.

297   **"The resolution to write":** PGA, Journals, August 28, 1971.

297   **"cross her hands on her lap":** Ivan Philipoff, "Personal Essay," March 4, 1993.

298   **"every bit as good as his father":** AGA, Journals, October 13, 1986?

299   **"colored the lives":** Mary Anderson, "Apologia," privately published, 1998.

299   **"And you will find, my darling":** AGA, unpublished poem.

Shearwater Marks and Dates*

On January 14, 1930, Peter Anderson drew a Shearwater mark for his fiancée and wrote: "We have a new stamp to put *Shearwater* on the bottoms of pots with. Smaller and circular like this though not quite, fortunately. The nice thing about it is that the letters are sharp edged and will bite into the clay with much greater ease than the old one, which was so blunt the pressure required sometimes cracked the bottom of the pot. Do you find all of this *horribly* interesting, beloved?"

Because such documentation is rare, it is difficult to date early Shearwater pieces with any precision. On August 3, 1928, after the Pottery had been open to the public for eight months, its methodical secretary-treasurer, Peter's father, George Walter Anderson, began a system for identifying pieces inspired by the one in use at Newcomb College. Warm from the kiln, each piece was given a stock number, affixed to the bottom of the pot on a paper label bordered in red. When the label survives, the date of the pot can often be deduced from records in the Shearwater

*Based on information provided by Marjorie Anderson Ashley.

archives. For example, a firing on April 10, 1929, produced pots numbered from #0152 (a fish bookend in bronze) through #0176 (a blue platter). The system appears to have been discontinued after Walter's death. Over the years, commonly produced shapes were sometimes assigned numbers: for example, an invoice mentions the "#40 vase with handles at $1.50, and #150, just a bit smaller than #40, with handles at $1.25, both of these being approximately 5 inches in height."

Forms, colors, functions, and prices (the latter still visible in pencil on the bottom of some pieces) provide another way to date Shearwater pots. Correspondence in the Shearwater archives provides pertinent information. We know, for example, that in January 1930, "flower pots, made by the jigger process and decorated with slip or relief" were still an "ambition" for Peter, but that they were produced in quantity in the 1930s. Casseroles, honeypots, ashtrays, etc., were produced at particular periods, and old letters and invoices show, for example, that glazes that Pat named "Grey Cloud" or "Blue Rain"—the latter a "dark cobalt, mixed with a little greyish or brownish"—were in use in 1957; that Copper Red was a "new and expensive" glaze at Shearwater in December 1937 (see p. 178 above); that in 1929 Peter developed a lavender-over-blue glaze with the "color of the pristine plum" (p. 107); or that glazes that required tin oxide—e.g. Shearwater's "Turquoise"—were scarcer during the war years (p. 235). Lavender was discontinued in 1940.

Marjorie Ashley Anderson, business manager of the Pottery, notes that the color of the clay is sometimes a help in dating the pieces: "a red clay was sometimes used for a brief time in the early thirties; a grayish white clay in the late thirties to early forties; and Peter, after much searching, found a very suitable buff-bodied clay circa 1940 not so far away. The clay is still being used today."

Since 1988, all Shearwater pieces have been stamped, dated, and initialed (when appropriate). There is no complete record of the marks used before then. The dime-sized stamp referred to by Peter in his letter appears on many pots thrown during the early thirties, but at times, for example in 1931, Peter appears to have signed and dated his pieces. The initials

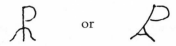

and the handwritten year (for example, '31) sometimes appears beside a round, dime-sized Shearwater mark.

A rectangular mark appears on many pieces—particularly cast ones:

SHEARWATER

The early dime-sized mark was replaced at an unknown date with a larger one about the size of a quarter:

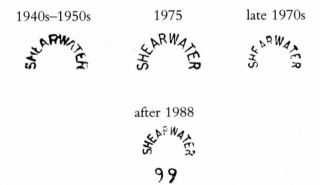

The incised, handwritten mark $\mathcal{S}$ was used for ware with smaller bottoms; for example, the forty-six black figurines designed by Bob and Mac, or the approximately twenty-six pirate figurines designed by Bob, all of which were made from a white ball clay from Kentucky. This handwritten mark was also used when the cylindrical stamp, normally kept on a shelf by the potter's wheel, was misplaced or lay out of reach. Today, all ware that missed being stamped or marked at the workshop or at the Annex (where the underglaze castware and decorated work is done) is stamped in the showroom with a rubber Shearwater stamp in indelible black ink.

Pots thrown by Peter and decorated in a carved design by Walter (Bob) or James McConnell (Mac) Anderson and finished with glazes developed by Peter had only the Shearwater stamp. Walter Inglis Anderson (known in the family as Bob) did not sign or date any of his work, nor did Mac in Shearwater's early years. Mac's earliest-known signed and dated decorated pot is from 1945 and is signed:

Later, he replaced this with

J M^{c}CA

Mac's wife, Sara, put his block print designs on material from around 1950 to 1997, and continues to print them on paper. Block prints by Bob began selling in the showroom around 1945.

Peter's son James Anderson, who joined his father in 1966, began selling his wares in the showroom in the late 1960s. Around 1978, to distinguish his work from Peter's, he began signing his work with his initials:

For Shearwater Pottery's fiftieth anniversary, pots were marked with the half-circle Shearwater mark, accompanied by the handwritten 1928–78.

Mac's daughter Adele Anderson Lawton, who decorated at Shearwater Pottery from about 1973 to 1986, signed her pieces in two ways:

Patricia Findeisen, who is Shearwater's principal decorator, did not sign or date her earliest pieces, but now signs:

Christopher Inglis Stebly, a grandson of Walter Inglis Anderson, began decorating Shearwater jiggered plates and pots thrown by James Anderson around 1990. Not all of his pieces, however, have been thrown or jiggered at Shearwater. All are marked with his initials:

Peter Michael Anderson (Michael) did a small amount of decorating around 1985. He has also done some underglazed castware, and some hand-built bird feeders and bird baths. He signed his decorated pieces:

Francis A. Ford (b. 1916), who worked for Newcomb Pottery from 1933 to 1948, worked for Peter Anderson at times during the late thirties and forties, and threw on the wheel. His pieces, glazed in Shearwa-

ter glazes, are sometimes marked with an "F" inside the circular Shearwater mark.

At the turn of the century, in winter 2000, Peter Wade Anderson,
James Anderson's son, seemed likely to succeed his father someday as
master potter at Shearwater. He was throwing pieces on the wheel and
signing them:

Index

Anderson, Billy, 230, 242, 292, 299
  in story by his sister, 224–30
Anderson, Bob. *See* Anderson, Walter
  Inglis
Anderson, Carolyn, 288, 299
Anderson, Daisy, 100–101, 175, 193
Anderson, George Walter (Walter):
  and Bob's sailing mishap, 63
  character, 49, 50
  correspondence: with Annette,
    50–51, 53–54; with Bob, 48–49;
    with Pat, 99–100, 103; with
    Peter, 72–76
  finances, 54, 167
  interests, 68; ceramics, 68, 69; golf,
    153, 167; sailing, 49, 67
  life: youth, 39, 175–76; early mar-
    ried life, 39; illness and death, 167
  nervous breakdown, 176
  relationships: with Annette, 52–53;
    with mother, 176
  and Shearwater Pottery, 75–76, 81,
    94, 106, 107; as business manager,
    82, 89–92, 97, 132–36
  thoughts and feelings: alcohol, 76;
    business of art, 72; commercial-
    ization of the pottery, 31, 82;
    Peter's character, 96; sons' school-
    ing, 47, 48, 64
Anderson, James (Jim, Jimmy) (son of
  Peter and Pat), 4, 10, 14, 18–22,
  30, 242, 290
  pottery work, 21, 34–35, 275, 287,
    290–91, 298, 299
Anderson, James McConnell (Mac), 7,
  29–31, 88, 107, 109, 125
  art studies, 245
  and brothers' breakdowns, 194, 200
  character, 29–30, 213

health, 48, 88
house, 29–30, 153, 181–83, 271
life: birth, 39; childhood, 39–42, 47,
  48, 49–50, 57, 140; education,
  47, 48, 64, 65, 82, 87–88; marries
  Jackie, 182; Jackie leaves him,
  200, 245; move to New Orleans,
  244–45; marries Sara and returns
  to Shearwater, 245–46, 270–72;
  death, 31
pottery work, 30–31, 82, 84, 133,
  143–44, 158–59, 178, 200; after
  marrying Sara, 246, 287; figurines, 131–32, 137, 141–47, 181,
  246
thoughts: on Annette's preference
  for his brothers, 30; on his talent,
  159
work: artwork and fabrics, 29–30,
  181, 271–72, 287–88, 299; jobs
  away from Shearwater, 244–45,
  271. *See also* pottery work *above*
Anderson, John (Johnny), 24–26, 236,
  241, 262–63, 270, 286–87
Anderson, Leif, 27–28, 35, 231, 290,
  292, 294, 299
  on her childhood, 242–43, 261,
  268
  poetry, 295–96
Anderson, Mac. *See* Anderson, James
  McConnell
Anderson, Margaret (wife of Jimmy),
  14, 288
Anderson, Mary. *See* Pickard, Mary
  Anderson
Anderson, Michael. *See* Anderson,
  Peter Michael
Anderson, Patricia (daughter of Peter
  and Pat). *See* Findeisen, Patricia

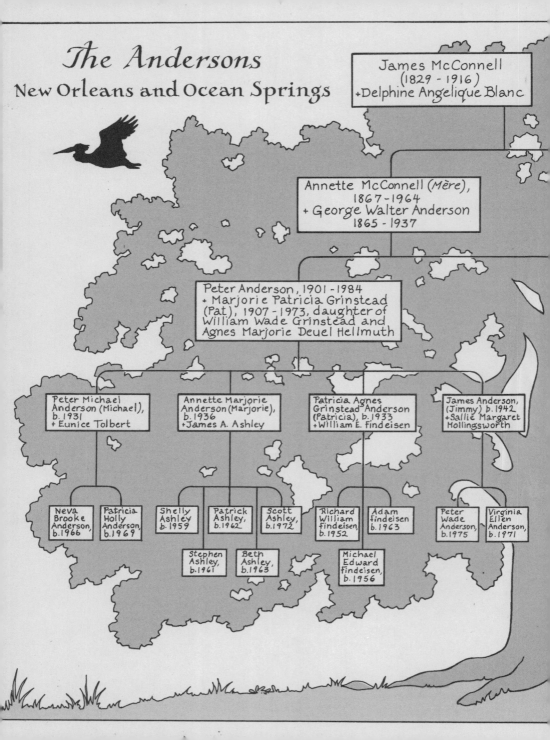

The Andersons
New Orleans and Ocean Springs

James McConnell
(1829 – 1916)
+ Delphine Angelique Blanc

Annette McConnell (*Mère*),
1867 – 1964
+ George Walter Anderson
1865 – 1937

Peter Anderson, 1901 – 1984
+ Marjorie Patricia Grinstead
(Pat), 1907 – 1973, daughter of
William Wade Grinstead and
Agnes Marjorie Deuel Hellmuth

Peter Michael
Anderson (Michael),
b. 1931
+ Eunice Tolbert

Annette Marjorie
Anderson (Marjorie),
b. 1936
+ James A. Ashley

Patricia Agnes
Grinstead Anderson
(Patricia), b. 1933
+ William E. Findeisen

James Anderson,
(Jimmy) b. 1942
+ Sallie Margaret
Hollingsworth

Neva
Brooke
Anderson,
b. 1966

Patricia
Holly
Anderson,
b. 1969

Shelly
Ashley,
b. 1959

Patrick
Ashley,
b. 1962

Scott
Ashley,
b. 1972

Richard
William
Findeisen,
b. 1952

Adam
Findeisen,
b. 1963

Peter
Wade
Anderson,
b. 1975

Virginia
Ellen
Anderson,
b. 1971

Stephen
Ashley,
b. 1961

Beth
Ashley,
b. 1963

Michael
Edward
Findeisen,
b. 1956